The Politics of Fashion
in Eighteenth-Century America

GENDER AND AMERICAN CULTURE

Coeditors
Thadious M. Davis
Mary Kelley

Editorial Advisory Board
Nancy Cott
Jane Sherron De Hart

John D'Emilio
Farrah Griffin
Amy Kaplan
Linda K. Kerber
Annette Kolodny
Nell Irvin Painter
Janice Radway
Barbara Sicherman

Emerita Board Members
Cathy N. Davidson
Sara Evans
Wendy Martin

A complete list of books published in Gender and American Culture is available at www.uncpress.unc.edu.

The Politics of Fashion
in Eighteenth-Century America

KATE HAULMAN

The University of North Carolina Press Chapel Hill

© 2011 The University of North Carolina Press. All rights reserved. Manufactured in the United States of America. Designed by Courtney Leigh Baker and set in Filosofia with Nelly Script display by Rebecca Evans. The paper in this book meets the guidelines for permanence and durability of the Committee on Production Guidelines for Book Longevity of the Council on Library Resources. The University of North Carolina Press has been a member of the Green Press Initiative since 2003.

Library of Congress Cataloging-in-Publication Data

Haulman, Kate.
The politics of fashion in eighteenth-century America / by Kate Haulman.
p. cm.—(Gender and American culture)
Includes bibliographical references and index.
ISBN 978-0-8078-3487-9 (cloth : alk. paper)
1. Politics and culture—United States—History—18th century. 2. Fashion—Political aspects—United States—History—18th century. 3. Clothing and dress—Political aspects—United States—History—18th century. 4. Symbolism in politics—India—History—18th century. 5. Nationalism—United States—History—18th century. 6. United States—Social life and customs—To 1775. I. Title.
E163.H38 2011   306.20973—dc22   2010053995

cloth   15 14 13 12 11   5 4 3 2 1

To Guy

CONTENTS

Acknowledgments ix

INTRODUCTION
That Strange, Ridic'lous Vice 1

ONE
The Many Faces of Fashion in
the Early Eighteenth Century 11

TWO
Fops and Coquettes
Gender, Sexuality, and Status 47

THREE
Country Modes
Cultural Politics and Political Resistance 81

FOUR
New Duties and Old Desires
on the Eve of Revolution 117

FIVE
A Contest of Modes in
Revolutionary Philadelphia 153

SIX
Fashion and Nation 181

EPILOGUE
Political Habits and Citizenship's Corset
The 1790s and Beyond 217

Notes 227   Index 275

ILLUSTRATIONS

Mary Alexander fabric order 12
Mary Alexander fabric order 13
Benjamin Lay 23
Robe à la française 37
"The Review" 55
A page from Solomon Stoddard's pamphlet:
    An Answer to Cases of Conscience Respecting the County 61
"The Five Orders of Periwigs" 63
Portrait of Daniel Parke II 66
"Let Sloth Adornd with Splendid Arts
    Another's Labour Own" 95
Portrait of Isaac Winslow 98
Portrait of Isaac Winslow and his family 99
Portrait of Ann Tyng 101
Portrait of Rebecca Boylston 103
Portrait of John and Elizabeth Cadwalader
    and their daughter Anne 132

"What is this my Son Tom" 136
"Coiffures" 140
 Anna Green Winslow 142
"A New Method of Macarony Making
    as Practiced at Boston" 155
"Bunker's Hill, or America's Head Dress" 158
"Miss Carolina Sullivan, one of the obstinate
    daughters of America" 159
"Oh Heigh Oh, or a View of the Back Settlements" 160
"Dress: The most distinguishing mark of
    a military Genius" 164
"The Wishing Females" 171
 Sketch of a Meschianza belle 173
 Robe à la polonaise 190
 Trade card 215
 Grecian gown 218

ACKNOWLEDGMENTS

There is a line in Shakespeare, "Things won are done; joy's soul lies in the doing." Perhaps that is why I worked on this book for so long, accumulating many debts along the way. It began at Cornell University under the expert direction of Mary Beth Norton. Her support has been unflagging, her guidance essential, and her model combination of historian of early America and of women/gender has always inspired me. I have been incredibly fortunate to call her my adviser, mentor, and now friend. Cornell's history department, from which I received generous funding, also afforded me the privilege of working with Rachel Weil and Margaret Washington, who also taught me much about the practice and the politics of history. The roots of my interest in early American history run deeper and farther south, to Southern Methodist University, where Edward Countryman and the late David J. Weber introduced me to the field and helped launch me into it, always keeping tabs on my trajectory.

Without the material support from a host of generous institutions, and the research assistance of many expert archivists, librarians, and curators, this book would not exist. I am grateful to the American Antiquarian Society for a Legacy Fellowship that funded the project in its infancy and for the assistance of the institution's tremendously knowledgeable and helpful staff, especially Georgia Barnhill, Joanne Chaison, John Hench, Tom Knoles, Marie Lamoureux, Russell Martin, Jackie Penny, Laura Wasowicz, and Bill Young. I also thank The New-York Historical Society and the David Library of the American Revolution, from which I received fellowships, as well as the Library Company of Philadelphia, who awarded me a Society for Eighteenth-Century Studies Fellowship. There, the help of Jim Green, Nicole Joniec, Connie King, Phil Lapsansky, Charlene Peacock, Erika Piola, Nicole Scalessa, and Sarah Weatherwax was invaluable. I was especially fortunate to receive a National Endowment for the Humanities Fellowship for a half year's work in the collections at the retreat-like Winterthur Museum and Library. Curator of Costumes Linda Eaton patiently and expertly instructed me in the wonderful world of fabric. Ann Wagner helped with other fashion-related objects; Rich McKinstry, Laura Parrish, and Jeanne

Solensky assisted with the library's collections; and Kate Cooney covered rare books while running the fellowship program. The project also benefitted from the collections and staff of the Historical Society of Pennsylvania and of the American Philosophical Society, namely Rob Cox, Roy Goodman, and Chuck Greifenstein. For assistance procuring images, I thank Jamison Davis at the Virginia Historical Society; Eleanor Gillers at the NYHS; Ryan Jensen at Art Resource; Jennifer Riley at the Museum of Fine Arts, Boston; and Giema Tsakuginow at the Philadelphia Museum of Art.

Over the years this book, like its author, has seen many locales and institutional homes. But it is the people of those places that shaped the work by enriching my intellectual life while providing moral support. At Tulane University they include Rosanne Adderley, Rachel Devlin, and Natalie Ring. At the University of Alabama in Tuscaloosa, I thank my colleagues in the history department, in particular Lisa Lindquist Dorr, Josh Rothman, and George Williamson. At Ohio State University, members of the lively history department, in particular Leslie Alexander, John Brooke, Alice Conklin, Steve Conn, Saul Cornell, David Cressy, Alan Gallay, Jim Genova, Robin Judd, Margaret Newell, Geoffrey Parker, Randy Roth, Jennifer Siegel, Stephanie Smith, and Judy Wu, created an intellectual and social home. For providing opportunities to circulate my work and for sharing probing questions and constructive comments, I thank members of the Women's Studies Brown-Bag at the University of Alabama, the Early American Seminar at Ohio State University, and the Seminar at Johns Hopkins University.

The book saw its final stages at American University, where all of my wonderful colleagues in the history department helped usher it to completion. In particular, fellow early modernists Andrew Lewis and Phil Stern gave generously of their time and thoughts, while Eileen Findlay and Pam Nadell served as supportive and inspiring mentors. I am especially indebted to our chair Bob Griffith, and to him as well as the rest of the department for authorizing support from the Patrick Clendenen Fund in the form of a two-year named professorship that afforded a reduced teaching load as well as additional research funds. That, and a generous Mellon Grant from the College of Arts and Sciences, made completing this book a pleasure. At AU I have also been fortunate to connect with a vibrant group of junior faculty, exceptional women all, from various disciplines. They read and lent trenchant insights to various parts of the manuscript while providing an encouraging and sometimes raucous female social circle. And so I happily thank my fellow Sohos: Kristin Diwan, Adrea Lawrence, Rachel Sullivan Robinson, Susan Shepler, Brenda Werth, and Elizabeth Anderson Worden.

A few of my exceptional colleagues in the discipline of history are also close friends and committed feminists who have cheered and inspired me: Carla Bittel, Micki McElya, and Jenni Siegel. Rare is it to connect on professional and personal levels, and nothing represents that happy confluence better than my friendship with fellow early Americanist Serena Zabin. She has supported me wholeheartedly in work and in life, and this book bears her influence in so many ways. It is not too much to say that, without Serena, the project may not have gotten off the ground. Other friends who supported both the intellectual and social parts of my life along the way include Matt Abramowitz, John Bagwell, Brian Bishop, Alexis Boylan, Joel Brouwer, Gary Darden, Laura Free, Brooke Geller, Ed Harcourt, William Harris, Merrily Harris, Nancy Kadowitz, David Karr, Cindy Lobel, Ashley Oates, Wendy Rawlings, Greta Rensenbrink, and Laura Schiavo.

Within the field of early American history, many scholars have contributed their insights and expertise to this work. They include Kathy Brown, Seth Cotlar, Paul Erikson, Toby Ditz, Bill Foster, Craig Thompson Friend, Woody Holton, Brooke Hunter, Cindy Lobel, Bob Lockhart, Jane Kamensky, Cathy Kelly, Carl Keyes, Brendan McConville, Renee Sentilles, David Shields, Eric Slauter, Bob St. George, Fredrika Teute, Laurel Thatcher Ulrich, and Karin Wulf. Portions of Chapters 4 and 5 appeared in my article "Fashion and the Culture Wars of Revolutionary Philadelphia," *William and Mary Quarterly*, 3rd ser., 62 (October 2005): 625–62, and I thank the journal for allowing them to be reproduced here.

I was thrilled to place this project with UNC Press, whose books I have long admired, under the practiced editorial hand of Chuck Grench. He doled out good advice about book-writing going years back; in return I have given him fits, which he has borne with equanimity. I thank my eagle-eyed copyeditor Mary Caviness, Tom Franklin for struggling with the images, and Beth Lassiter. I am deeply indebted to the esteemed Linda Kerber and the other unnamed reader for providing such thorough, rigorous, and helpful suggestions on how to strengthen the manuscript. I reserve special thanks for the editors of the Gender and American Culture Series, Thadious Davis and especially Mary Kelley, whose combination of insight and encouragement is unparalleled, and provides a model of how to be.

Although an only child, I have a large family who has loved and supported me as I toiled away on "the book." I thank my parents, Cathy Campbell and Clyde Haulman, for teaching me to enjoy reading and thinking, as well as my grandmother Frances Jones, and my grandfather C. Austin Haulman, who lived long enough to see the dissertation completed and the book begun.

My aunt Beth Campbell-Work loves me like one of her own, and her "boys," including my uncle Mac Work, and my "brothers" Graham, Hamp, and Brut Campbell-Work are like immediate family. Rounding out my circle, I thank Dawn Campbell, Bruce Haulman, Emily Henderson, Jim Reese, Nancy Stander, Fredrika Teute, all of the Pattons, as well as relatives-in-law Martin and Dawn Refvem, Martin and Ellery Smith, and especially Vince and Cynthia Nelson for their support. The most inexpressible thanks go, of course, to Guy Nelson, to whom this book is dedicated. It is as much his as it is mine—he has nurtured it though every stage, from the seed of an idea to full bloom between covers, reading every word and improving my life and work in countless ways all the while. This book represents just one of the many ways in which our lives have long been richly intertwined. It was a wonderful confluence—and not, I think, a cosmic coincidence—that I submitted the manuscript just as Thomas Haulman Nelson entered my life. He and Guy are truly joy's soul to me.

INTRODUCTION

That Strange, Ridic'lous Vice

In his 1705 poem "The Grumbling Hive: or, Knaves Turn'd Honest," philosopher and satirist Bernard Mandeville wrote,

> Their darling, Folly, Fickleness
> in Diet, Furniture, and Dress
> That strange, ridic'lous Vice was made
> the very wheel that turn'd the Trade.

It was a paradox that puzzled many Britons during the eighteenth century: How could fashion be at once a social "folly," a moral "vice" born of envy and appetite, and an economic good, "turning the trade" and contributing to the success of the English nation and British empire? Bernard Mandeville believed that in an imperial, commercial context the relationship between private vices and public benefits was salutary. If Britons were curbed of the impulse to fulfill their own desires, he argued, they would grow weak and dull. "As pride and luxury decrease, so by degrees they leave the Seas," he rhymed, linking self-indulgence with the common good.[1] Without the individual appetites for fashion that stimulated commerce, the nation withered on the proverbial vine, becoming economically moribund and militarily impotent. Yet other British writers openly decried fashion and its followers as feminized, Frenchified threats to social hierarchy and the health of the nation.[2] Although far more sanguine about the effects of fashion, Mandeville himself considered the women who donned style after novel style to be "fickle strumpets."[3] What strengthened political economy might compromise morality.

Over seventy years later, American revolutionary leader Samuel Adams allied himself with critics and moralists when he cautioned that, "should foppery become the ruling taste of the great, the body of the people would be in danger of catching the distemper."[4] In conjuring the fop as part of his warning, damning fashionable men and their susceptible followers alike, Adams drew on a long-standing image of the preening, mincing man of fashion, concerned only with dress and affectations. But whereas foppery had been the object of social ridicule since before the age of Mandeville, by the late eighteenth century it had become an infectious disease threatening the health of the new American republic—vitality that, for Adams, depended on particular performances of masculinity.[5]

Writing from distinct chronological and geographical vantage points, Mandeville and Adams situated fashion and its pursuit in quite different relationships to the state. Mandeville clearly considered fashion bad for society but good for the nation, whereas Adams closely linked the fates of nation and society; one could not succeed if the other failed. Connecting the personal with the social, and the social with the political, Adams worried that the style of the few would corrupt the many, on whose shoulders the fate of the republic rested. Linking gendered performance, social influence, and political order, he illuminated a politics of fashion that—unfortunately, from his perspective—combined all three. This was, perhaps, the unhappy consequence of grounding political legitimacy in "the body of the people"— too many individual, self-serving bodies.

Yet the two men's assessments shared a fair bit as well, chiefly the way in which anxieties about gender and power, expressed through the topic of fashion, infused their musings about state and society. Whether strumpets or fops, certain unsavory figures came under attack when one considered fashion's influence. Although much had changed in the British Atlantic world between 1705 and 1778, concerns about the feminine and feminized form of power that was fashion persisted, adapting to changing social and political circumstances. By the age of the American Revolution, sexualized women of low rank, or "fickle strumpets," seemed far less a threat to the formal body politic than foppish men.

The Politics of Fashion in Eighteenth-Century America began with a deceptively simple question: How was fashion political in eighteenth-century British North America? One possible answer is equally simplistic, calling to mind a world of public, electoral politics marked by explicit sartorial demonstrations of support such as American flag lapel pins. In this view, fashion in dress is a mere reflection of political allegiance, narrowly defined— fixed in one meaning and stripped of all others. Yet by taking cues from Mandeville, Adams, and a host of other eighteenth-century voices, we can see that fashion has a politics that exists apart from, yet intersects with and influences, the realm of what is commonly considered "the political," or relations to the state. In particular, fashion's gender politics figured prominently in many of the eighteenth century's topics of debate, from household governance to political legitimacy.

This book employs an expansive definition of politics to explore fashion as a site of contests over various forms of power during the eighteenth century. Its approach links material and discursive worlds and allows for exploration of broad, transatlantic themes and trends while maintaining a concern for local, colonial social experiences. This book considers fashion both as a concept, a shape-shifting vessel of an idea that people fill up with various meanings depending on time, place, and circumstance, and as changing styles of personal adornment, whether *la mode* or other modes of the day.[6] In this light, fashion serves as a set of symbols that members of a community recognize but do not necessarily regard, evaluate, or act upon in the same manner.[7] Although fashion can include forms of bodily performance such as speech, gestures, and habits such as dipping snuff, fashion in dress is immediately and always on display.[8] And unlike other genteel "graces" that could be purchased through the instruction of a French teacher or dancing master in the eighteenth century,[9] items of fashion in dress were material commodities central to imperial commerce and political economy.

Continually debated in print and displayed on people's bodies, fashion was a screen onto which people projected ideas about issues such as gender relations, social order, and political authority, and a vehicle through which they expressed those ideas during an era in which traditional hierarchies were deeply in flux. Fashion in dress, a form of power and distinction that was conceptually feminized yet pursued by both men and women across ranks, served as a flash point for social, economic, and political conflicts across the eighteenth century that were, fundamentally, about gender roles and relations. Concerns over gendered power shaped the imperial crisis of the 1760s and 1770s and ultimately influenced the relationship between the social and the political in late-eighteenth-century America.

The book focuses on four major port cities of British North America: Boston, New York, Philadelphia, and Charleston. As increasingly dense and diverse commercial entrepôts, these cities became centers of consumption and arenas of display, progressively cosmopolitan and Atlantic in their natures. All were growing in economic scope, social complexity, and cultural sophistication, but each possessed a somewhat distinctive character.[10] Boston, the oldest and initially the largest of the ports, entered the eighteenth century grappling with its Puritan identity and coming to grips with its mercantile character and place in the commercial empire. Its refinement grew in proportion to its wealth in trade.[11] Philadelphia, influenced by a Quaker, largely mercantile, social and political elite who espoused the rejection of *la mode* even as they benefited economically from its sway, became the most populous and cosmopolitan colonial city by 1770 and, like New York, was demographically diverse.[12] New York exhibited characteristics of the commercial mecca it would later become and supplied arenas for fashionable display (in addition to the city streets) from the early part of the century.[13] Periodically, political wrangling and class tensions shook the northern port towns, as commercial and landed elites, and eventually artisans, vied for political as well as cultural dominance.[14] By contrast, Charleston was less plagued by political instability and was home to some of the wealthiest residents of British America, members of South Carolina's planter and merchant elite. Yet as the capital of a slave-society colony that contained a large African American population comprising half of the city's residents, Charleston witnessed its own power struggles.[15] In all four cases, the movement of people and goods underpinned the cities' commercial character. Even as they became increasingly stratified socioeconomically over the course of the century, the towns promised at least the possibility of economic opportunity and social fluidity, as the advertisements for escaped servants and slaves that filled their newspapers testified.

In these see-and-be-seen urban environments, a person's attire spoke volumes, but the content of those messages could vary widely: one woman's newly acquired calico gown was another's cast-off or work dress; one man's full periwig was another's symbol of foppery. The sheer variety of styles in the port cities, as well as the existence of distinct colonial preferences, made fashion in dress an unreliable and confusing social language. In an increasingly commercial, consumer society, elite men and women often relied on high fashion to perform status, but they also attempted to undercut its ability to do so for others. Such disdain served as a way to safeguard social position in sartorially fluid cities and to maintain gender hierarchy in a world in which many women's consumer power was expanding. Even as some pursued the mode, Euro-Americans attempted to control the power of fashion by regulating relations between men and women and vice versa, discursively using fashion to discipline relations that had the power to enforce or compromise other social arrangements. These gendered social struggles ultimately spawned new forms of distinction, sartorial and otherwise, by midcentury. Colonial elites developed a number of strategies that might be considered culturally "middling," including the cultivation of sensibility, the embrace of understatement in adornment, and the rejection of ostentatious display, always positioning themselves as judge and jury in matters of taste.

As the river of imported goods became a flood during the period of the Seven Years' War, agitation for the production and consumption of domestic goods paralleled an emerging discourse of genteel femininity that possessed a decidedly domestic component. Attempting to discipline female and feminized appetites, and with them women's spending power, the new model of femininity encouraged Anglo-American women—of the young, unmarried, and urban variety in particular—to renounce fashion's artifice, shun the gaze, and become modest, frugal, and productive "country" wives. These ideals, as well as gender norms that described men of sense, not of fashion, were deployed during the imperial crisis of the 1760s. Colonial resisters attempted to forge a political movement by making fashion hew to their own agendas, casting social standing and political virtue (or social virtue and political standing) as mutually dependent.

Yet as a political strategy, control of fashion proved elusive; the personal politics of fashion persisted, especially among women and other feminized figures that became a political problem for Whigs. The climate of surveillance created by committees of correspondence and 1774's Continental Association made certain sartorial expressions, and the pro-British sentiments they were thought to represent, politically unwelcome in the port cities. This book demonstrates that sartorial struggles, fueled by hierarchies of gender and status, shaped the contests of the revolutionary era, as particular styles mapped uneasily onto increasingly rigid political categories and yet ultimately came to constitute them. Styles clashed as the period of the American Revolution witnessed competing visions of power, legitimacy, and society. After the Revolutionary War, it appeared that fashion in the European mode had triumphed over republican simplicity, despite a Continental military victory. At issue in the 1780s, as imported goods flooded the port cities, was the question of how Americans could reconcile appetites for imports and the need to appear legitimate on a world stage with the sartorial demands of republican virtue. The politics of fashion infused national debates over the new political and social order and ultimately helped to mark the exclusions of the republican body politic.

THE EARLY MODERN PERIOD saw the elaboration of a fashion system in Europe and its colonies as changes in supply both created and responded to demand for consumer goods. Economically, changes of fashion and appetites for novelty fueled the ongoing cycle of production and consumption that helped spawn a consumer culture.[16] Socially, fashion in dress simultaneously confused and reified expressions of power and position. As sociologist Gilles Lipovetsky writes, "On the one hand it blurred established distinctions and made it possible to confront and confuse social strata. On the other hand, it reintroduced—although in a new way—the timeless logic of signs of power, brilliant symbols of domination and social difference."[17] In the eighteenth century, as today, people used taste and style to distinguish themselves from one another both within and among social groups.[18] Although "to accentuate differences is always the purpose of fashion," such practices were not necessarily attempts at sartorial emulation of higher ranks, nor did London styles wholly dominate the fashion system.[19] Fashion certainly could and did perform an exclusionary function that reified hierarchies of material wealth and political power. Yet a central eighteenth-century preoccupation was that it often failed to reflect those distinctions accurately. Further confusing the social landscape, residents of the port cities embraced many forms of sartorial distinction. But whether *la mode* or other modes, fashion in dress was a primary site for the creation and contestation of social differences and distinctions in an expanding consumer culture.

One form of difference and hierarchy that was particularly fraught and in flux throughout the eighteenth century was gender. As sociologist Joanne Entwistle has observed, "Fashion is obsessed with gender . . . constantly working and reworking the gender binary."[20] Nowhere was this truer than in the eighteenth-century British Atlantic world, where gender difference was acquiring new explanatory rationales as it intersected with other forms of hierarchy, in particular social status. The conceptual feminization of fashion (as well as luxury and consumption) confronted the masculinized spheres of commerce and politics and chafed against expressions of fashionability that were clearly heterosocial and necessary for the performance of social rank. If status could be created or counterfeited, as many feared, and was thus eroding as a divinely ordained or natural form of difference, what about differences of male and female?[21] And if fashion was a feminine and feminized form of power, what did men's reliance on fashion mean for masculine identity as well as for gender relations? *The Politics of Fashion in Eighteenth-Century America* demonstrates that figuring out how to read people socially became deeply implicated in ideas about gender and sexuality, leading to new gendered norms, both sartorial and behavioral, for expressing social status.[22] These served the twin and somewhat contradictory purposes of distinguishing people of sense and taste while disciplining the consumer appetites of others.

The upheavals of the revolutionary era were also a series of culture wars in which views of society intersected with visions of the new nation-state.[23] Cultural forms and practices, in this case fashion, infused political contests and responded to them. The emerging cultural imperatives of midcentury were featured in struggles over governance, as the cultural politics of fashion influenced political crises, conflicts, and culture. The imperial crises and revolutionary contest of the 1760s and 1770s made fashion, laden with gender and status baggage, a site of struggle as consumer goods became politicized. One consequence of a focus on fashion was that the colonial resistance movement placed courtship and connections between the sexes at the center of a political movement, embedding within the issue of home rule questions of who would rule in the home. It attempted to link social influence with certain political ideas and actions but met with mixed success, as older ways of performing status and legitimacy persisted through and beyond the war years. The new American republic and its inhabitants displayed an obsession with appearance, as fashion was featured in debates over political economy and social order. Concerns about culture and society were never far from those about the state and its future, and fashion, due to its symbolic as well as material significance to political economy and social order, was the vehicle that linked the two.

THIS BOOK IS ORGANIZED into three parts that proceed roughly chronologically, moving through the eighteenth century. The first section (Chapters 1 and 2) describes the cultural politics of fashion in the port cities during the first half of the century, exploring the intersection of social status and gender in a colonial context. Clothing was a site for expressing hierarchies of rank and categories of gender, but individual expressions and the sheer variety of styles adopted by increasingly diverse urban populations worked to confuse how social order was supposed to "look." Practices of social and colonial distinction undermined traditional notions of sartorial privilege. Although *la mode* could signal elite masculinity and femininity, fashion could also expose its adherents to criticism for eroding the gender and social boundaries that dress was supposed to maintain. Gender-specific styles came under fire for not being masculine or feminine enough for their wearers, who mimicked the affect and usurped the prerogatives of the opposite sex in ways that signaled not only gender inversion but status confusion. Yet through attracting attention and enhancing desirability, fashion could facilitate the social and romantic connections so critical to securing the privileges of high social status.

Section two (Chapters 3 and 4) connects the cultural norms and sartorial forms that were emerging by the middle of the century to the imperial crisis of the 1760s and 1770s. Fashion, long the crucible of social contests, became a flash point of political authority. Colonists that resisted newly imposed taxes in the wake of the Seven Years' War married a genteel "country" aesthetic to the rhetoric of domestic production, meaning "American," "household," and "by women." By promoting homespun cloth as fashionable while renouncing fashion itself as distasteful and debauched, leaders of the American resistance movement used newspapers to invest the country mode with fresh visual and material signifiers. Drawing on and enhancing existing prescriptions of modesty and frugality, they crafted a set of cultural norms grounded in the visually verifiable rejection of English fashion and the social distinction and romantic success that would theoretically follow from such displays of liberty. Although declaring the popularity of homespun among the people of fashion helped to proclaim the success of the resistance movement, few colonists bought the new American modes in any sustained manner. Homespun, however fine, was not high style, which resurged in the early 1770s, suggesting a backlash to Whig prescriptions of plainness and sacrifice.

The book's third section (Chapters 5 and 6) explores how the politics of fashion infused the revolutionary contest and the struggles of the new American nation in the final quarter of the century, when fashion became a litmus test for political loyalty. As military conflict led to a British occupation of the capital city Philadelphia, high rolls confronted leather aprons, and frontier-style hunting shirts met epaulets in contests for cultural authority that were critical components of revolutionary struggles. By the mid-1780s, imported goods flooded American markets as the confederation stood powerless to enact commercial policy and many continued to look to Europe for *la mode*. Americans balanced traditional expressions of position and authority against new, nationalist prescriptions and proscriptions, and attempted to reconcile them by appearing at once appropriately republican and legitimately powerful to various audiences—local, national, and international. Printed rhetoric in the young United States grew increasingly inflamed, claiming that appetites for fashionable "gewgaws," particularly by women, signaled the republic's downfall. Lambasting fashion helped to persuade readers that the nation's look and its framing document, the Articles of Confederation, needed alteration.

Yet even—or perhaps especially—in a country without a court, fashion's cultural politics continued to influence state politics. The cut and cloth of a man's breeches and the color of one's cockade signaled either anarchy or order, according to Federalists, and populism or elitism, according to Democratic Republicans. By the turn of the nineteenth century, the triumph of masculine sartorial simplicity signaled the political emergence of a cross-class coalition of white men, voters and leaders, legitimated through and yet regardless of fashion. Fueled by ideologies of innate difference, arguments about who deserved and could handle what kinds of power hardened, as particular fashions, or rather the bodies they adorned and made legible, marked the bounds of American citizenship.[24] Fashion would continue to be debated into the nineteenth century and beyond, but as gender-based rationales for political participation replaced those based on masculine rank, the worlds of the social and the political grew increasingly distinct conceptually. Formal politics, at least in theory, became a fashion-free realm of power and legitimacy. The paradox in which fashion was good for a nation's political economy but bad for society was resolved as the United States grew into a country of self-interested consumers and, eventually, producers of changing modes governed by men who were unconstrained by fashion's feminine and enslaving embrace.

The Many Faces of Fashion in the Early Eighteenth Century

When Mary Alexander, a merchant who operated a business with her husband, James, in New York, placed a large order for fabric with her English suppliers in 1726, she included three pages of samples: a sheet filled with ribbon pieces, another displaying fifty-eight mixed fabric swatches, and a third containing thirty strips of calico and chintz. The sheets and their contents remain preserved as beautiful artifacts, bright and textured collages in which the materials have retained their brilliance after nearly three hundred years. A viewer is struck not only by the quantity of fabric Alexander ordered but the variety of colors, patterns, textures and qualities—including black and white crapes, camblets of deep fuchsia and aqua, blue and red striped calicos, and gold and silver laces. Yet whatever the sheets' aesthetic appeal, they served a clear commercial purpose: to communicate to Alexander's suppliers with exacting precision what she desired for her market. They were a visual guidebook of sorts, one in which she sometimes scrawled notes alongside a fabric she wanted in a tone "less blewish" or to have "a wider stripe."[1] The specificity of Alexander's requests suggests the particular demands of her market.

Yet no matter what merchants such as Alexander ordered or received, they promoted the fabrics in the public prints as the latest and most fashionable styles from abroad—one of the many contradictions that characterized the sartorial culture of the port cities.[2] Alongside newspaper advertisements that featured the language of fashion appeared other notices seeking the capture of self-emancipated servants and slaves who had taken or were wearing clothes of the same sorts of fabrics Alexander ordered, or garments "made fashionable." Such descriptions expressed an assumption that people knew what the phrase meant and thus what such a coat or gown looked like—a style that was, on the one hand, exclusive and cosmopolitan and yet, ironically, made its wearer legible as a "lower sort." These linguistic juxtapositions, which helped to create material distinctions, had the power to influence the very meaning of "fashion," which possessed many and var-

Swatches of material attached to sheets, used by Mary Alexander, ca. 1750. The use of swatches and text allowed merchant Mary Alexander to show and tell her supplier in England precisely what she desired in an order for fabrics. Department of Manuscripts, Alexander Papers, negative number 26276b, Collection of The New-York Historical Society.

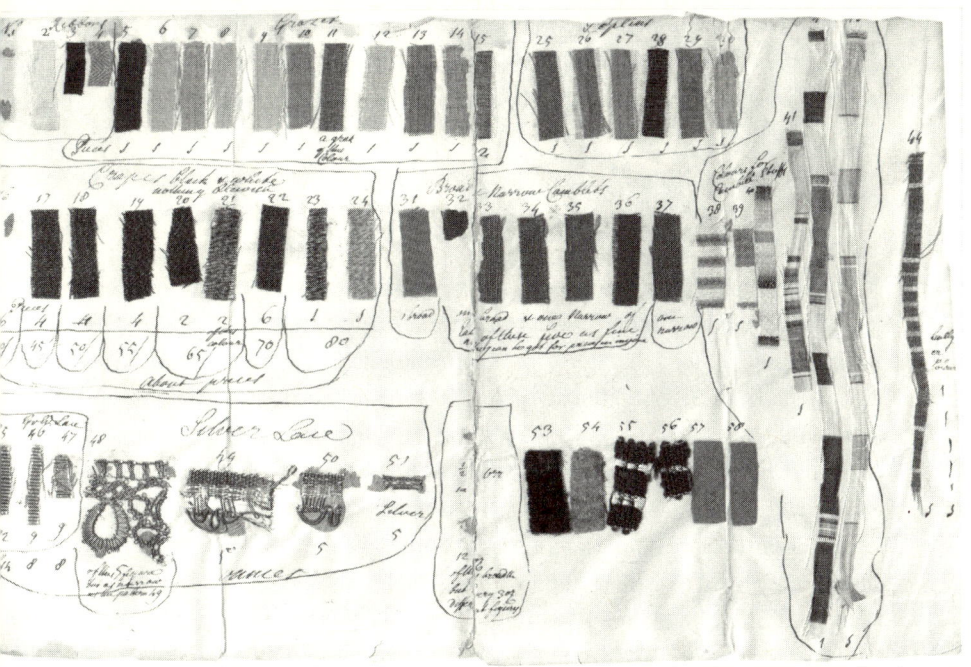

Patterns of eighteenth-century ribbons, grazets, poplins, crapes, broad and narrow camblets, camblet stuffs, gold and silver lace, and various unidentified textiles used by Mary Alexander, ca. 1750. Department of Manuscripts, Alexander Papers, negative number 26276g, Collection of The New-York Historical Society.

ied associations in the port cities, from high status to low rank, and metropolitan affiliation to colonial position. Although fashion in dress was a site for expressing hierarchies of rank, gender, and empire, individual expressions and the variety of styles adopted by an increasingly diverse population could undermine how these forms of order were supposed to "look" in the eighteenth century and compromise easy associations of dress and identity.[3]

Examining the range of sartorial forms that characterized urban colonial settings reveals the various practices of distinction that produced a complicated and often confusing social landscape in the port cities of British North America. Calling an item "fashionable" or "the fashion" suggested both its aristocratic, European credentials and its widespread appeal. Fashion was at once elite and popular, exclusive and accessible. *The* fashion, dictated by Paris and London, might signify the scope and spoils of trade with "exotic" locales, participation in a cosmopolitan world of commerce and culture, and connection to the sphere of the court and the beau monde. But, as the case of the fabric calico suggests, it could also be associated with the colonies. Even as fashion in dress gestured toward a broad geography, it possessed intensely local significance, serving as a means of distinguishing among and within social groups; achieving sartorial distinction within a social circle was as important as distinguishing among ranks.

Although arenas of display such as tea tables and balls, with their imperial associations, segregated a city's population by rank, city streets brought people into regular contact with one another. It was in this "out of doors" setting that fashion, materially and conceptually, could also be associated with socially and geographically mobile bodies of the "lower sorts." Critics bemoaned that people of low rank and little means dressed above their station, but historians should not necessarily follow their lead by regarding such practices as social emulation. Whether the garments were purchased or pilfered, luxe or plain, fashion in dress was about distinguishing oneself sartorially in ways that could result in social confusion; such illegibility was often intentional. Some attempted to dress their way out and up, while others chose to dress down and out. As a material practice and a concept, fashion was protean and shifting, its meanings unstable, contested, and as various as changing styles themselves. It was Atlantic but local; metropolitan and colonial; a would-be establisher of imperial and social hierarchies and their potential obscurer.

Arenas of Display in the Port Cities

The play of fashion in dress would have meant little without an audience. In order to communicate social codes and personal identity, attract attention, and engender desire, attire had to be paraded before other eyes and was often chosen with such reception in mind, even when choices were circumscribed. The visual consumption that fashion at once encouraged and relied upon fueled the engine of material consumption; this was the function of fashion and the distinctions it created. Yet the transmission of certain messages did not ensure their unaltered receipt; the appraising gaze could give and the gaze could take away. Since people often dressed to impress, all the while assessing others' fashion choices, sociable settings were see-and-be-seen arenas of display, acquiring the quality of competition spaces. In some venues that suggested urbane cosmopolitanism, such as around tea tables in private homes or in assembly rooms, elites viewed and competed chiefly with one another. Other arenas, such as churches and the city streets themselves, brought residents of various ranks into one another's visual fields. As the port cities matured economically and culturally, they provided many opportunities for sartorial display and arenas to showcase it, some more exclusive than others.

The Scottish émigré and keen social observer Dr. Alexander Hamilton frequented and recorded the range of venues over the course of his journey from Maryland to Boston and back in 1744. As a gentleman, Hamilton enjoyed entrée into virtually every social space, from modest roadside taverns and inns to wealthy homes and sumptuous assemblies, and everything in between. He used settings and activities as a means of comparing the northern port cities, creating a geographic hierarchy of refinement based on how—and where—residents vetted their sartorial choices and engaged in social intercourse.[4]

The most "private" settings were homes where people dined or took tea. By midcentury, many British Americans drank tea with breakfast among family and socially in the afternoon, and Hamilton visited tea tables in every place he visited. As spaces where groups of social peers gathered, they were semipublic arenas of fashion, especially for the women who oversaw the tea ceremony. Tea drinking evolved into an "elaborate kind of theater" with roles that had to be properly mastered and expensive props that called for correct handling. The hostess or mistress of the house both directed the production and served as its leading lady, making and pouring the tea, while expecting the supporting cast of guests to know their parts, that is, how to consume it. A complicated ritual, taking tea also involved a wealth of objects known as the "equipage"—pots, cups, saucers, spoons, and linens of varying degrees of fineness, as well as the tea table itself—all of which indicated the position of the hostess and her husband. Around the table everyone was on display, but no one more so than the woman who presided over it as director of the show and its star.[5]

With respect to more public or semiprivate venues, Hamilton had high expectations. Disappointed when Philadelphia failed to supply the desired forms of elite sociability, he wrote of the town's apparent "aversion to publick gay diversions" such as balls and concerts. By contrast, he lauded Boston's regular "assemblys of the gayer sort." As scholar David S. Shields has shown, the members-only dancing clubs that sprung up in most British colonial cities were primary arenas of fashionable display and social competition among local elites. Dancing the minuet one couple at a time put a man and woman on display as all eyes fixed on two figures. New York, "one of the most social places on the continent," according to William Smith, boasted balls and "concerts of musick." Just a few years later, the Quaker City would have its own dancing society, the Philadelphia Assembly. But in 1744, lacking such settings, Philadelphians relied on church as a backdrop, Hamilton observed, although he noted this practice of church as tableau in each of the cities. Again, he reserved the highest praise for Boston. There he found the women "in high dress" at meeting and the men "more decent and polite" in their clothing than those in other towns. While balls were accessible only to elites, and therefore provided places to perform social distinction within a circumscribed in-group, church supplied a more socially heterogeneous setting where elites might not only view one another but see others and be seen by them.[6]

Whether in drinking, dancing, or worshiping, the relationship between high rank and high fashion was well established within these fairly insular communities, networks in which everyone likely knew everyone else. Yet their insularity by no means made them safe social spaces. As Hamilton's gossipy observations suggest, a person's fashion choices could be discussed and critiqued. While tea tables were notorious for this sort of chat, which critics denounced as insipid and yet powerfully cutting, maligning the tea table's reputation also served to displace the common practice of sartorial backbiting (often engaged in by Hamilton himself) onto those female-controlled arenas. When getting dressed for any social gathering, particularly those in which your person might be studied at some length, men and women had to consider whether to blend in and avoid censure but also forgo admiration or to step out sartorially and potentially invite both.

Similar calculations influenced appearances made "out of doors," on the city streets. In assessing this most public and heterogeneous arena of display, Hamilton initially considered New York City supreme, approving of its "urban appearance" and its lively "promenade" in which the ladies appeared dressed far better than in Philadelphia, he observed. But New York was ultimately bested again by Boston, where people ventured "rather more abroad than att York." The existence of settings similar to the walks and pleasure gardens of London, and residents willing to take full advantage of them, was a key benchmark of refinement for Hamilton, for whom the promenades almost functioned as movable, outdoor assemblies.[7] But North American cities were not populated by the wealthy alone, and although the ports were still small, "walking" cities in which many of the residents knew one another, they hosted expanding and increasingly diverse populations. People from all walks of life, hailing from places spanning the Atlantic world, jockeyed against one another out of doors, filling the cities' streets, retail establishments, and public markets. These were places where goods could be procured in a number of ways, but they were also settings in which sartorial distinction might be viewed across social groups, taking advantage of a broader audience—indeed, multiple audiences. It was this largest and most diverse of arenas that presented the greatest challenges to securing the relationship between sartorial display and social order.

Dilemmas of Distinction

The port cities of British North America experienced rapid social, economic, and demographic changes in the third and fourth decades of the eighteenth century, a period of peace between the imperial conflicts known as Queen Anne's (1702–13) and King George's (1739–48) Wars. Waves of free and indentured Europeans, and a smaller but still significant number of free and enslaved persons of color, mainly Afro-Caribbeans, enlarged and diversified the populations of Boston, New York, and Philadelphia. Charleston's population, at 50 percent African American, reflected its position as the capital of a colony whose social and economic order rested on chattel slavery, but the city also put the wealth and refinement of its planter ruling class on obvious display. By the 1720s all towns housed weekly newspapers that disseminated information about trade, goods, the courts, and imperial and provincial politics, fostering a colonial culture of print. The cities enjoyed new degrees of prosperity due in part to the spoils of burgeoning trade, yet even as their total wealth increased, economic stratification was shaping their social landscapes.[8]

As the ports grew in size, demographic diversity, and cultural sophistication, residents developed tastes for imported goods, items that could improve a person's style of life materially and socially.[9] Even before the "flood" of consumer goods and the lengthy lists thereof that would come to typify newspaper advertisements of the 1750s,[10] fashion in dress promoted social distinction yet also contributed to social fluidity in urban environments; it could establish order in accordance with early modern ideas of rank as fixed and permanent, but possessed at least the potential to facilitate social as well as geographic mobility. As such, it expressed the tension between group identity and forms of individual expression. Styles of dress signified belonging to a particular social group, whether indentured servants, Quakers, or wealthy planters, but could also set a person apart from his or her peers. At all ranks, individual choices and the practices of personal distinction had the power to disrupt a social hierarchy grounded in, and comprehended through, sartorial order.

Beginning in the early 1730s, stay makers, the artisans who created boned women's undergarments designed to shape and hold the body, were the first advertisers in Philadelphia to place advertisements that used the term "fashion." They attempted to attract female clients who desired stays constructed in the "latest" or "newest" fashion, items that promised to "make crooked bodies appear straight."[11] The advertisements suggest desire for the European ideal of an erect stance, sought by men and women alike in the early eighteenth century.[12] Genteel carriage was no longer the exclusive province of the elite, no longer purely a consequence of lineage or great wealth. Anyone who could employ a stay maker might look "straight," and advertisements suggest appeals to a wider reading public. Their use of the term "fashion" referred to workmanship—the process of construction, or its end result in an article's particular make or shape—but also suggest changing styles. Erect carriage might be purchased through stays, but what underpinned and produced that posture evolved. The ads denote the importance of acquiring the latest and best stays in a period where free women of all ranks wore them or jumps, slightly more flexible garments that gave physical support to women engaged in household tasks. These women likely could not afford to adopt changing styles of stays. Although some colonists desired an erect stance, which characterized the posture of those members of society "in fashion," the stays that helped produce it, hidden as they were from public view, were not immediately recognizable as obvious items of fashion. Still, the right stays literally underlay an overall fashionable appearance, as women of means pressed their bodies into upright submission.

Unlike stays, fabric was an obvious indicator of fashionability for men and women alike,[13] and merchants and retailers promoted it accordingly. Since purveyors of goods were not as specialized in their trades as they would come to be later in the century, they sometimes sold nails and needles alongside silks and satins.[14] But whereas the utilitarian items usually came last in advertisements, sometimes followed by "and other goods too numerous to mention," fabrics appeared first and apparently listed in toto. Although many of the other durables were also fashionable or luxury items such as playing cards, looking glasses, writing paper, and spices, advertisements established a hierarchy of desirability in which fabrics always held the top spot in printed promotions of newly arrived merchandise. In 1736, the first notice of its kind to appear in the *New York Gazette* heralded the arrival of over two dozen styles of cloth, including velvet, lustring, damask, silk, and chintz. A similar advertisement placed in the *Pennsylvania Gazette* the following year promoted camblet, broadcloth, fustian, calico, callimanco, paduasoy, and exotic spoils of trade such as "China . . . and Persian Taffeties."[15] These descriptive references to eastern locales created the idea as well as the visual signifiers of far-flung British commerce, the spoils of which colonists might wear. Colonial merchants were bringing a nascent empire home.[16]

Imported fabric was significant in part due to its utility. All residents of British North America needed cloth for attire, but laws prohibited its manufacture in the colonies. As the production of cloth increased and prices fell, purchasing fabric made more sense than investing time and energy in the creation of homespun, particularly in port cities where imported cloth could be had easily and cheaply. But the prominence of fabrics in advertisements reveals something more: the way in which retailers stimulated demand through cultivating the desire for distinction. They accomplished this by promoting and describing variety. Most advertisements heralded the "assortment" to be sold: linen "of sundry sorts," broadcloths of "all sorts," a "variety" of haberdashery. Adjectives describing color, texture, and quality often followed references to selection. For instance, Charles Willing of Philadelphia listed "white, purple, and printed calicoes" and James Wallace vaunted his "great choice of light and dark ground calicoes and chints of the newest fashioned patterns" and "white, pink, blue, green and cloth coloured English and India damasks." As for texture and quality, which often went hand-in-hand, many ads listed "broad and narrow" (indicating the weave) or "coarse and fine" options for various fabrics, hoping to appeal to a range of pocketbooks but also to indicate selection even within a particular kind of cloth. Finally, fabrics were always described in plural: velvets, taffetas, broadcloths, calicoes, Persians, sarcenets, indicating choice within an already broad array.[17]

In addition to newspaper advertisements, the orders, business strategies, and correspondence of the New York City merchant Mary Alexander establish the importance of fabric as fashion and the role distinction played in demand and therefore in commerce. Alexander was born Mary Spratt, the daughter of a Dutch female trader, in 1693. She married Samuel Prevoost in 1719, and when he died eight years later, she inherited and carried on his mercantile business. Within two years she married another merchant, James Alexander, and their trade steadily increased, with Mary handling the sizable part of the business through which they imported and sold cloth.[18]

Born into the world of commerce, and having spent most of her adult life involved in trade, she developed a keen eye for fashions in fabrics, though perhaps no more so than other powerful merchants in her community. As a savvy businesswoman, Alexander would not have requested what she did not expect to sell. The large order she placed in 1726 illustrates the variety of fabrics and trimmings available in New York as early as the mid-1720s.[19] Throughout the 1730s, Alexander continued to import an array of fabrics in a range of prices, changing her orders in accordance with what she imagined to be the demands of her market. She always strove for variety in her shipments, sensing that customers sought to distinguish themselves from one another. For finer fabrics in particular, she often ordered only a piece or two of fifteen or twenty different patterns to give those with means choice within an array. In her 1726 order she requested nine styles of black and white crapes and broad and narrow weaves of seven different silk camblets "as fine as they can be got."[20] A decade later she ordered twelve pieces of "newest fashion" camblets, "good colours and glossy, all different colours," and ten pieces of "London shalloons . . . 1 black, 1 blue, 1 red, 1 green, 1 olive and 5 pieces of other good cloathe colours."[21] In a later invoice, she specified four pieces of blue rushell, "but every ps a different blue."[22] It was not enough to have a gown or waistcoat made of silk; if one hoped to cut a figure, it had to be of a pattern, color, or texture that few others were wearing.

Although Alexander's fabrics tended toward the high end of the market, indicating that her customers sought individuality within a fairly exclusive range of options, distinction did not always require appearing finer or more fashionable than other people. Counteridentification with "the fashion" served as an equally important sartorial statement in colonial North America. The club of Philadelphia artisans called the Junto, formed in 1726 by Benjamin Franklin, was also known as the Leather Apron club, a reference to the garb of a tradesman.[23] These working men, although more educated and up-and-coming entrepreneurs than artisans, did not (at least openly) aspire to don silks and brocades but instead made their class position into a positive sartorial expression—a fashion statement.

What is more, even colonists of great means sometimes chose to shun the dictates of changes in fashion. At various stops along his 1744 journey, Dr. Alexander Hamilton, being himself extremely fashion conscious, stood perplexed by the appearances of some men reputed to be wealthy gentlemen. Breakfasting in a tavern in Perth Amboy, New Jersey, he observed a man dressed in an "old plaid banyon, pair of thick worsted stockings, a greasy worsted nightcap and no hat." He was then informed by the proprietor, who called the man "originall," that he was a rich property holder, owner of most of the buildings in town. At an inn in New York, a "grave old don . . . a parson and a physitian," wore "mean attire," in Hamilton's estimation, including a discolored wig, worn leather breeches, and a pair of "old greasy gloves." Another in the same company, a Major Spratt who was deep in his cups, "bragged that his coat was thirty years old," and Hamilton "believed him, for every button was as large as an ordinary turnip, the button-holes at least a quarter of a yard long." The major took pride in his superannuated coat, while the don clearly cared not a whit for his appearance, or perhaps cultivated a certain academic or clerical carelessness—a man of the mind and spirit, not the world. Most surprising of all, the don returned for his gloves after getting two miles down the road. When Hamilton expressed shock and even dismay at this oddly parsimonious behavior, the owner of the inn mentioned that he was "worth 5000 pounds sterling and had got it by frugality," to which Hamilton drily replied that the man's cherishing of his gloves was such that "I wondered he was not worth twice as much."[24]

Lest these examples read as rare exceptions to the rule of genteel fashionability among members of the colonial elite in the eighteenth century, consider that others of means and high status also used fashion to reshape gentility in their own mode. Quaker "plainness" presents the most obvious example of stylistic counteridentification practiced by Philadelphia's elite.[25] Charged with cultivating the "inner light," Quakerism instructed its adherents to heed biblical proscriptions of external display. In marked contrast to the pursuit of distinction, "singularity," meaning individuality or distinctiveness, was to be avoided. Yet having garnered wealth and position in Pennsylvania through transatlantic commerce, many members of the Society of Friends possessed both knowledge of and access to the latest trends in fashion, as well as the money to spend on their appearances. As some Friends fared well economically and socially, they dressed accordingly, generating concern within the sect. A testimony from as early as 1695 urged the renunciation of attention-getting buttons, ribbons, wigs, and "strip'd or flower'd stuffs or other useless and superfluous things."[26] The tension between cultivating a rich material life and a rich spiritual one plagued Quakers.

In the eighteenth century, "plainness" became a means of reconciling the apparent contradictions of worldly and spiritual success. To dress "plainly" primarily meant the absence of excessive ornamentation, not coarseness of fabric or ill fit. Indeed, plain was never incompatible with "fine," and Quakers compensated for their lack of effrontery by wearing clothes of high-quality fabrics. Swedish naturalist Peter Kalm observed in 1748 that "the women have no clothing that differs from that of the English ladies . . . and although they censure all adornment I have seen them wear as gaudy shoes as other English women." The men's clothes, by contrast, "differed somewhat" from prevailing styles. But "although they pretend not to have their clothes made after the latest fashion . . . and be dressed as gaily as others, they strangely have their garments made of the finest and costliest materials that can be procured."[27] Thus through plainness, Quakers could signify spiritual purity without sacrificing the pursuit of material wealth and the enjoyment of its comforts.

In addition, plainness cemented a distinctive Quaker identity in a time of challenge and flux, becoming an increasingly important distinguishing characteristic that visually set Friends apart from the world as it connected them to one another. But, paradoxically, the plainness that was undoubtedly "singular" or unusual in terms of the larger world, and designed to be so, could become the very kind of singularity so distrusted within the community—its own form of pride to be guarded against. Revivalist Quakers such as Benjamin Lay attacked Friends' wealth and social practices he regarded as hypocritical from within the ranks, staging elaborate displays of asceticism such as lying in the snow barefooted in front of a meeting. He renounced not only conventional fashionability but also the Quaker plain-but-fine mode. In the single extant image of Lay, he appears clad in coarse, ill-fitting attire, his legs bare except for short black stockings, his gravely concerned expression an indicator that matters far more serious than the cut of his coat occupied him.[28] In his day, Lay was the inverse of gentility and the apotheosis of antifashion fashion.

Sartorial distinction was no less of an issue for those of little means in the port cities, and retail purchase supplied only one means by which fine fabrics and articles of clothing might be acquired. Theft, pawning, and peddling constructed an informal, underground economy of consumer goods that expanded access to them and created "hidden demand."[29] In taverns and small shops, the acquisition of goods took place through barter, making items available to people with little or no cash or credit. In New York City, over half of the larceny cases from 1700 to 1760 dealt with stolen clothing or cloth, items that were easily transported and transferred.[30] In Philadelphia, Dr. Alexander Hamilton found goods to be "extravagantly dear" in 1744, their high retail cost increasing the desirability of certain items, and likely contributing to their presence on the black market.[31] When a host of goods, including clothing, jewelry, and teaspoons went missing, their

Quaker Benjamin Lay (pictured here) deliberately rejected a fashionable appearance. Courtesy The Library Company of Philadelphia.

rightful owner in Bucks County pleaded to the reading public that "if any of the above things are offered to paun for sale, they are desired to be stopt." Another Philadelphia gentleman, Jacob Shoemaker, offered a reward and appealed to tailors to identify and return his great coat "if brought to be altered."[32]

While some theft undoubtedly arose out of simple need for serviceable attire, often the articles taken were costly garments.[33] But perhaps drawing a distinction between things "serviceable" and things fine is somewhat artificial. If status could be performed through attire as one wandered through a town, then luxury or fashionable items might prove more useful for thieves than something merely utilitarian, insofar as they could facilitate social and actual mobility. Elizabeth Fulks clearly believed so. In 1734, she and her husband, John, stole from Marcus Kuhl's store on Market Street in Philadelphia several items of clothing, a parcel of handkerchiefs, and a piece of callimanco. Announcement of the theft in the *Pennsylvania Gazette* featured the length of fabric prominently, listing it first, and describing it as having "narrow stripes of red, green, blue, and two stripes of yellow." The notice claimed that Fulks, a "lusty fat woman much pockfretten of red complexion," had with her a flowered calico gown of lavender and red, a Bengal gown of a light mouse color trimmed with spotted calico, an old striped petticoat, a short brown camblet coat and "a new gown" made of the stolen callimanco, "cuffed and robed with Green persian and tied . . . with a broad green ribband."[34] It remains unclear how Kuhl knew that she had turned his callimanco into a stylish dress—perhaps a local mantua maker alerted him. While Fulks wished to "go fine," he hoped that very fineness, or the juxtaposition of it with her rough face and form, would proclaim her criminal status. In this instance, the distinctiveness of high-quality fabric could become a badge of illegality, inviting surveillance.

By the 1740s, even convicted criminals appeared *à la mode*. Mary Rogers, who used at least three aliases and was sentenced to death for repeated burglary, "walk'd to the gallows with a velvet hood on," the *Pennsylvania Gazette* reported. Not content with a fine cloak alone, she wore "her hair curled (as is the fashion among our prim ladies)," the notice mocked, taking aim both at Rogers for her pride and, more obliquely, at the fashionable women of Boston, suggesting that they shared their high style with a common thief.[35] Imagine Rogers lowering her velvet hood to reveal a fashionably coiffed head as she was about to swing—what a display of pride, a flouting of the power of state and society to brand her and make her appear a criminal. Rogers was pardoned at the last moment but seemed "very little affected" considering the great "alteration in her circumstances," the piece noted. The author seemed to expect some expression of glee or relief, and perhaps questioned the authenticity of the revelation. Had this haughty woman, clad in potentially stolen velvet and ornamented with curls, brokered some arrangement? Or was she just that prideful? Regardless, she again joined the ranks of the free.

Others, such as enslaved women living in Charleston, were decidedly unfree, with little chance of becoming otherwise. Yet the buying and selling of goods in the urban marketplace, as well as access to fine dress and other forms of self-fashioning, allowed them some power and autonomy in a slave society. As "marketeers" who hustled and haggled with white customers, bondswomen in the market were derided as "idle" or "disorderly."[36] Provoking such attacks was the upper hand they sometimes enjoyed in commercial exchanges, likely enhanced by their carriage, demeanor, and dress. As one historian writes, "In South Carolina, bondwomen and urban slaves drew especial fire for dressing above their station," sometimes receiving cast-off clothes as gifts and occasionally purchasing finery themselves.[37] The relative sartorial splendor of slaves was a problem in the eyes of white South Carolinians. The colony's Slave Act of 1735 contained a sumptuary provision, which was reiterated in 1740 in the wake of the Stono Rebellion. It prohibited enslaved African Americans from dressing "above the condition of slaves" and required them to wear clothes made only of specified, coarse fabrics, indicating that the state considered fine clothing part of a general culture of resistance and rebellion in which women played key roles in terms of appearance, as well as behavior.[38] Yet apparently the statute did not curtail the donning of finery, for four years later a jury isolated "negro women in particular" for "apparel quite Gay and beyond their condition."[39]

Women such as the Charleston marketeers, Elizabeth Fulks in Philadelphia, and Mary Rogers of Boston used fashion to perform a social position they did not, according to society, possess. They sought not so much to counterfeit social status or "pass" but rather to mock the social hierarchy and gradations of rank that fine and fashionable dress was supposed to establish. Their attire signaled that they too enjoyed access and could shape their appearances as they wished.

In addition to altering the presentation of one's self and social position, stolen fabric and clothing could alter status by generating income. One "wandering woman" was discovered with four chintz gowns, two petticoats, women's shifts, and aprons and ruffles, plus men's shirts, the last clearly intended to be sold. In 1735 in Connecticut, two "Irish men" broke into Samuel Belden's shop and took

> three pieces and half of chince or fine callico, one of them . . . sprig'd with red, another the ground green, flower'd with red and white; another, spotted with red and dark purple, and the half piece purple and white, spotted with red and the flowers bold; One piece striped lutestring, One Piece of Flowered striped Lutestring, Four Pieces of Camblets, One Piece of Muslin, One piece gray duroy,

> One piece of Diaper, several pieces of ribbon, Men's grey stockings, and women's blue stockings, half a piece of light colour'd East India Sattin.[40]

The supposed perpetrators, John MacNeil and William MacKeel, soon tried to peddle some of their impressive haul. Peddling itself was not illegal in colonial cities, but peddling stolen goods compounded the crime of theft with that of profiting from the misdeed. According to the notice and the network of information that flowed between the port cities, they had last been spotted in the "City of New York, where they have disposed of some of said goods." Someone patronizing MacNeil and MacKeel could end up with a piece of fine calico or East India satin. The notice speculated that the two men were probably in the Jerseys or Pennsylvania, perhaps en route to Maryland. Samuel Belden clearly thought they might try their luck passing through Philadelphia, or else he would not have placed the advertisement in the *Pennsylvania Gazette*, offering ten pounds reward for the capture of the men "with the said stolen goods."[41] Shopkeepers undoubtedly wanted thieves brought to justice but also desired the return of their property, and realized that the port cities were hotbeds both of illicit trade and social confusion.

Often the "property" to be regained *was* the person, who then also took items from the household. Servants breaking their indentures and African Americans fleeing slavery usually took with them attire, either to wear or sell. Most practically and simply, they stole garments in order to clothe themselves. Although items made of coarse "negro cloth" might have served that purpose alone, for African Americans to continue to don those visual markers of enslavement would have been odious in at least two ways: one, reminding him or her of a life of bondage and the specter of returning to it, and two, attracting unwanted attention. Particularly for people attempting to move from southern colonies, slave societies, to cities farther north, plantation attire would have appeared unusual. Rather than coarse garments or work clothes, they tended to take fine, fashionable items.[42]

Given the presence of an underground economy fueled by the exchange of goods, attire might serve as currency, whether used as bribes to secure safe passage from place to place or converted into actual currency through sale.[43] One indication of the impulse to sell or pawn items is the volume of clothing taken—far more than one person could wear, even if desiring a change or two of clothes. Thomas Powel, fleeing from his indenture in North Carolina in 1738, left not only with what he wore but also ruffled holland shirts, checked shirts, and various "other cloaths." His traveling partner, Henry Watkins, had already been arrested once for stealing clothes from Thomas Spicer, Esquire, but had fled that capture, and then "entic'd a negro man . . . to runaway and steal what he could from his master." In addition to a couple of short gowns and petticoats, Alice Dodd took three or four aprons and several caps in 1752, including one "edged with lace." A person on the move sometimes took items belonging to the other gender, garments they would more likely sell than wear. In 1732, a "likely mulatto serving wench" named Sarah stole a "striped satten silk wastcoat" and a "striped callimanco wastcoat and petticoat," but also took a "Negro man's light colour'd Coat with brass buttons."[44] If Sarah did not intend to disguise herself as a man, she likely expected to pawn it, either for money or in exchange for more attire for herself.

If kept and worn rather than sold, the attire of their households could allow people fleeing slavery and servitude to manipulate their appearances in new environs, thereby altering the perception of their social position and, consequently, their status.[45] Several notices describe men wearing "fashionable" coats or clothes "made fashionable." Thomas Powel donned a "fashionable coat with waistcoat sleeves of a dark cinnamon colour," a striped waistcoat and breeches made of holland, a high-quality linen fabric, and he also took holland shirts—enough clothing to maintain a respectable appearance.[46] Mark Woods took his leave wearing a "dark colour'd fashionable Coat," while a servant named Anthony Lea wore a "fine broadcloth second-hand coat fashionably made."[47] That items could be recognized as at once made of fine fabric, used, and fashionable, ornamenting the bodies of those who inhabited society's lowest social echelon, suggests the confusing politics of fashion. What is more, a coat of low-quality fabric could be made—that is, cut, shaped—fashionable, its modish form belying its cheap fabric. The material of a garment was undoubtedly important, but form had a role in fashionability as well, and from a distance, a "high" quality of fit might help disguise low-grade fabric.

Along with, and often alongside retail advertisements, notices seeking the return of "runaway" men and women suggest a widespread visual literacy of fashion, fabric and form, among readers of newspapers as well as the people the advertisements sought to apprehend. People at all ranks had a sense of the potential meanings communicated by attire, although they might not agree on those meanings. Urban dwellers, the notices imply, knew calico from callimanco, and likewise recognized the look of a coat "made fashionable" from one not. Furthermore, they demonstrate that the ability to don fine and fashionable dress was not limited to those with wealth and high social standing. Within a fashion cycle in which styles constantly changed and expressions of sartorial distinction did not map neatly onto rank or wealth, how was one to ascertain the difference between a freed servant and a person on the cutting edge of style? Moreover, who knew with certainty what the latter looked like? Those seeking mobility could use this sartorial confusion to social advantage.

Display in dress might, however, restrict movement by drawing unwanted attention to one's person. In addition to clothing themselves, renouncing unfree status, generating income, and facilitating social and geographic passing, slaves and servants crafted new identities through expressions of personal style. Two historians have called the process of combining high and low modes and its resulting hybrid style bricolage the predecessor of a distinctive African American fashion.[48] Through combining pilfered attire with items of their own, they probably cut distinctive figures. An advertisement in the *American Weekly Mercury* seeking five servant men referred, for example, to the "remarkable clothing" in which they had fled, which included new sea-green cotton waistcoats, leather breeches, and plaid hose. The breeches were the look of the frontier or the farm, whereas the waistcoats represented urbane daywear. One man wore a figured calico waistcoat and another a coat made in the French frock fashion. At least two "negro women" who ran away in Boston wore handkerchiefs around their heads. One named Mimbo, "lately from Jamaica," paired her head scarf with a dark baize gown, blue-and-white striped petticoat with a red one underneath, and a striped callimanco jacket.[49] The look was equal parts Afro-Caribbean and English.

Such attire stood at odds with and the strictures of eighteenth-century gentility, with its emphasis on matching sets and elements working together appropriately and harmoniously. Moreover, the clothes may not have "fit" properly by the normative standards of the day. Either extreme sartorial refinement or unusual stylistic amalgams might give away a self-emancipated slave or servant. A person could draw unwanted attention if her mix of styles seemed too unusual or outlandish, or if that person lacked the modes of speech and carriage that validated a suit of genteel attire. On the one hand, men and women who fled their masters hoped to blend in and avoid detection, to "pass" as free persons and move across the social and actual terrain as smoothly as possible. On the other hand, their clothes created new subjectivities, through which they might insert themselves into free communities. Either inclination could invite the kind of surveillance that might get a person caught. The choice was whether to attract visual attention of the correct, socially approving sort, which might then instigate a fuller inspection of one's speech, carriage, and manners, or command the gaze through a hybrid and necessarily circumscribed look that might generate suspicion.

In the attire of self-emancipated slaves and servants, the politics and poetics of fashion collided. Successfully navigating the social and economic landscapes of the port cities confronted both the practical, material limitations of being poor and relatively unconnected, and the desire for individual expression within those confines. The dilemma was how to facilitate social and economic mobility in unfamiliar environments while employing visual signs of social distinction. To put it another way, how could one blend in enough to be safe from capture without sacrificing the material gain that fashionable clothing might generate in the underground economy, the social opportunity to appear free, or the possibilities for expressing individual style?

The published notices that serve as windows onto this dilemma also created it. Designed to promote the capture and return of material and human "goods," they supplied information that was easily comprehended, about dress that was, presumably, easily recognized.[50] The advertisements attempted to "fix" runaways visually as a means of locating them both geographically and socially. They harnessed the power of print in order to disseminate knowledge about the subjects' physical persons, part of a trade in goods and bodies supported by print, and vice versa.[51]

Securing freedom meant escaping detection and defying description. Newly free people must have suspected they would be sought through newspaper notices—described in order to be identified, dissected into physiological and sartorial parts, only to be visually reassembled. A man might wear a fashionable coat for a time until a notice forced him to get rid of the item because, after its publication, the coat would give him away; he would henceforth be identified by it and with it. Although he might exchange the coat for another garment, the newly acquired item might be a local stolen good, easily recognized as not legitimately belonging to its new owner, whereas the coat from his former household was, like the former slave, new on the scene. Perhaps, suspecting that such a notice was likely to appear, he considered unloading the garment quickly, knowing that to do so meant foregoing the social possibilities the coat might afford. If worn rather than traded or sold, it gained him no economic capital; if it was pawned, he sacrificed its potential social capital, however compromised by the notices.

Ultimately, the advertisements also worked to modify the very concept of fashion in colonial cities by associating it with colonial society's "lower sorts." This was also accomplished by juxtaposing the fine attire worn or stolen with physical characteristics such as complexion, hair, gait, and physiognomy. Some self-emancipated persons were described as having straight or "curl'd" hair, natural or a wig; a "down look" or "thin visage"; a "black complexion," or one that appeared "swarthy" or "pockfretten." Alice Dodd was ostensibly tall, slender, and fair of complexion, with a "left eye lower and less than the other."[52] The notices set "unusual" physical characteristics against the stolen attire, presenting them as "tells" or clues to the person's true identity, no matter how he or she appeared. In so doing, they made high status into a total package that included a particular physicality, making fashionable dress without other visual markers seem suspect.

Inverting the meaning of a fashionable appearance also had a gendered dimension. The propertied men who placed the notices were chiefly interested in providing accurate descriptions in order to ensure the return of their chattel, and assumed that readers knew a fashionable coat from one that was not. Yet by employing variations on the theme and term "fashion," they feminized their male targets. Associating aspiring, disorderly "runaway" men, often men of color, with fashion entailed using words freighted with gendered meaning in order to literally and figuratively restore social order. By making a fugitive's low status apparent through his attempts to be fashionable, the notices made him symbolically feminine. They turned fashionability from an indicator of high rank into a marker by which the subject might be recognized, apprehended, and returned to his rightful owner and place in society. The language of the notices compounded the violation of social boundaries and legal contracts with gender inversion. At the very least they warned people not to be fooled or let their eyes be deceived, suggesting that a fashionable coat alone told one nothing about a man's position.

By contrast, rarely did explicit references to fashion appear in descriptions of female "runaways," who numbered far fewer than men.[53] Was the women's attire really less fashionable, or did the notices simply not describe it in such terms? If the former were true, it suggests that low-status men, more than women, attempted to exploit fashionable dress. If the latter was the case, perhaps the colonists who placed the ads, mostly men, did not enjoy the same knowledge of women's fashions as men's.[54] Perhaps the connection between women and fashion was so entrenched that it needed no articulation, or perhaps fashionable dress was more prevalent among women of various ranks than among men, so that a woman who appeared fashionable would not necessarily be marked as of high or low status, although other characteristics such as speech, carriage, or complexion might give her away. Conversely, a "fashionable" man was immediately recognizable as disreputable, even dangerous.

Practices of sartorial distinction could reflect but might just as easily confuse social hierarchy in the port cities. While the purchase of fabrics from retailers supported the idea of fashionable privilege, the presence of an underground economy showed such exclusivity to be elusive. Fashion in dress both set individuals apart from one other and marked people as members of particular social groups. For elite colonists this was relatively unproblematic—fashion caused an individual to stand out among his or her peers while unmistakably associating the person with those same peers, although too much distinction was a gamble. For those lower on the social ladder, the appropriation of items designated as "fashionable" possessed both greater social possibilities and higher potential risks. They could use the garments to facilitate social mobility, but their very fashionability could give them away. Although access worked to discredit fashionability as a reliable indicator of social position, colonists did not respond by rejecting *la mode*. Rather, theft and pawning rendered the acquisition of the very latest and finest styles, and entrée to the genteel settings in which they were displayed, all the more essential. Thus, the continuing adoption of rapidly changing fashions served to limit the socially transforming potential of "fashionable" goods for those who hoped to exploit it. Once a style was widely regarded as the fashion, and could be called such, it had all but lost its currency among people who enjoyed social rank that amounted to more than merely the performance thereof through attire.

Calico and the Colonies

Examining a particular item, calico, demonstrates how a particular style could travel both geographically and socially, oscillating between high and low status associations as well as from metropole and colony. Cultural forms did not always flow in one direction only; the imperial "periphery," whether in terms of social or actual location, was also a site of cultural production. Although in American collective historical memory calico is often considered the cloth of the frontier, in the late seventeenth and eighteenth centuries it was the literal and metaphorical fabric of an emerging British empire. Portuguese sailor Vasco de Gama first introduced calico, a lightweight cotton cloth produced in India (its name derived from the port Calicut) and printed with designs, to Europe in 1499. It reached France by the late sixteenth century, and English privateers discovered it in their raids of Spanish ships. The first shipment of India calicoes and chintzes arrived in London in 1619 via the British East India Company, which soon launched a campaign to promote India textiles. After the earliest cottons failed to generate desired demand, the company directed its painters and printers in India to produce English floral patterns; they returned transformed into fanciful patterns, "exotic" in appearance to English eyes.[55] The look of the east influenced and was appropriated by the west.

Consumers on both sides of the Atlantic responded enthusiastically, and by 1680 India cottons had all but supplanted European textiles in the British market. A disdainful Daniel Defoe sniffed at the "fansie of the people," especially women, for the cloth. Samuel Pepys purchased a flowered calico dressing gown, or banyan, for himself in 1661, and calico items populate the 1696 inventory of wealthy New Yorker Margarita van Varick. Its popularity stemmed from the fact that calico was as vibrantly colored and densely patterned as French silks and brocades but far less expensive, generating what historian Beverly Lemire has called a "calico craze."[56]

The English nobility, however, continued to prefer fine European fabrics, suggesting the distinction between fashion and luxury and the court's somewhat ambiguous role in defining them in a consumer culture. Not content with the growing popularity of the cloth, the East India Company worked to ensure that it would find reception among the "better sorts," giving "voluntary contributions" to King Charles II in exchange for his agreeing to wear a waistcoat of India cotton.[57] After a cargo of calico arrived from India via an English merchant ship, the finest and most brilliant piece would be presented to a monarch such as Charles II as an example of the spoils of his burgeoning commercial empire. Fashions changed, but luxury, represented nowhere better than the court, lasted. Whereas English consumers had demonstrated an appetite for calico first, the East India Company hoped to control the meaning of the cloth by stamping it with the imprimatur of the court, making it luxe. Their actions suggest the court's role in the fashion system, as this particular style "trickled up." It was not where the "calico craze" originated, yet it remained the acknowledged seat of the mode in the late seventeenth century, and the nobility's patronage might solidify other markets.

Solidify them it did. The fabric became so sought after that English wool and silk producers began to regard its importation as a threat to their industry. Parliament severely limited its importation several times over the first two decades of the eighteenth century, but legislation did little to abate actual demand for calico, which continued to find its way into England.[58] In fact, the proscription likely stimulated appetites for the cloth, which became all the more desirable in its illegality. The issue reached a critical point in 1719 when riots erupted in Spitalfields, England. Two years later, Parliament banned painted, printed, flowered, and checked cottons, even those of native origin, making the wearing of them illegal.[59]

The prohibition on cotton cloth, which lasted until 1774, when the domestic cotton industry began to achieve prominence and profitability, was essentially a sumptuary law. Although enacted partly to stimulate England's wool production, more than mere protectionism of the wool industry drove the legislation. Calico, a widely adopted fashion, transcended social class. And while certain garments for men were made of calico, women stood as the chief consumers of India cottons. In the Spitalfields violence, enraged English weavers tore calico gowns off women's bodies; if the market or the government could not be counted on to regulate women's consumption, then people would take matters into their own hands. Some men even complained that the widespread wear of calico dresses caused them to mistake their housemaids for their wives, a convenient if somewhat tongue-in-cheek means of explaining men's cross-class sexual indiscretions.[60] But enforcement of the act made its adoption dangerous; therefore, the production, importation, and adoption of calico tapered off for a time. Although it was not swept entirely from the market, calico never fully regained its original popularity in England.

What did this proscription mean for calico in the colonies? Philadelphia's *American Weekly Mercury* printed a section of the act just a few months after its passage, calling it a "remarkable Clause . . . for prohibiting the Use and Wear of Calicoes."[61] The law itself did not apply in the colonies—in fact, British America became the primary market for India cottons. In 1726, Mary Alexander ordered ten types of printed calico, requesting not only more varieties of calico—printed and plain—than any other type of fabric but also greater quantities. Unless she greatly overestimated demand, residents of New York must have desired the fashionable cotton textiles. In the short term, this redirection of a popular fabric put the colonies "ahead" of the metropole, where calico's proscription made it more desirable and exclusive. Mainland Britons might gaze at their colonial counterparts with sartorial envy. But ultimately calico's affordability and accessibility in the colonies, coupled perhaps with its declining use in England, rendered the cloth less desirable as "the fashion," although it continued to be advertised and sold in the port cities throughout the eighteenth century.[62]

The fashionable calico gowns of the early years of the century became the work dresses of the early 1730s, moving from fashion to function. By that time, slaves and servants were donning calico, probably items acquired secondhand or handed down in their households. One "negro woman," aged fourteen or fifteen, "had on when she went away . . . a callico wistcoat with a large red flower and a broad stripe and a pettycoat with small stripes and small red flowers." In addition to the finer callimanco articles, twenty-four-year-old Sarah stole a calico suit of clothes, probably a woman's riding habit that she would don rather than attempt to resell. In 1736, the runaway English servant woman Sarah Sembler wore a "calico gown, red quilted petticoat lined with blue, and new pumps."[63] These women donned and stole what they imagined would serve them well as free persons—after all, calico ranked several notches above homespun or oznaburg, a rough cloth of German origin sometimes called "slave cloth" and used in the garments of bondspeople. But those very items, finer though they were, then became associated with servants. Pilfered, not purchased, they adorned those female members of society, often women of color, who sought to exploit the social fluidity of colonial urban environments.

Associated in England with disorderly women of all ranks, and with inappropriate economic expressions of women's power in general, calico in the late 1720s and early 1730s became the cloth of the colonies through a combination of parliamentary legislation and changing tastes in England. Yet it also became associated with certain women—no less disorderly than their English counterparts but defined as much by status, and perhaps color, as gender. Still, the meaning of calico was never entirely clear or fixed. While the men who robbed Samuel Belden's shop in 1735 took plenty of what was termed "fine calico," clearly deeming it saleable to those who would patronize peddlers such as themselves, Belden had hoped to sell it legitimately, to retail-paying customers. Both in terms of its geographical associations and its social connotations, calico became a fashion that was difficult to "read."

The Colonies and the Court

Just as fashion in dress served as a system, albeit an imperfect one, for distinguishing among groups and individuals in colonial cities, it also provided an important means of connecting—to England. For men and women alike, particularly those with means, certain styles and the settings in which they were displayed represented access to the taste, refinement, and imagined order of the "fashionable world" within the disorderly universes of colonial cities. Challenges to clear markers of status waged through practices of sartorial distinction and access to fashionable attire made the performance of social position reliant on displays of imperial connection. In printed advertisements and narratives of the English court, as well as through colonial assemblies and the adoption of mourning dress, colonists might proclaim their place in the British empire. Fashion played a central role in these texts and contexts.

Scholars of consumption in British North America have noted that England loomed large for colonial consumers seeking fashion.[64] Just as the term "fashionable" served as a selling point, so too did "London" or "English," and retailers often linked the adjectives in advertisements that established the connection between the metropole and fashion. In 1736, the first advertisement for fabrics in the *New York Gazette* promoted the "best London and Bristol Shalloons." The following year, John Inglis, a Philadelphia shopkeeper, heralded the arrival of "ENGLISH Brocade silks" and a few years later more specifically noted the fabrics "lately imported from London." John Wallace, who, like Inglis, kept a store on Front Street, touted the "London fashionable superfine broadcloths" that had just arrived in the summer of 1742.[65] However, it is not clear whether this language indicated that the styles of cloth were worn there, produced there, or simply came from or through that port, especially given the mercantilist political economy of the British empire and the subordinate place of the colonies in it. Colonial consumers could read their own meaning into the notices.

The years in which advertisements for fabrics began to populate newspapers also saw the appearance of another component of colonial print culture—reports of the activities at court. Periodically, any literate New Yorker could metaphorically consume the highest of styles, those set at Windsor Castle. Detailed descriptions of court fashion dominated coverage of court events. When Princess Anne married the Prince of Orange in 1734, the *New York Gazette* reported that she wore "robes of silver tissue" adorned with lace and "rows of Oriental Pearl." At Queen Caroline's birthday in 1736, the ladies appeared "variously dress'd, some in Pink Sattins, Ducapes, or Unwater'd Tabbies, others in a new-fashion'd white Lutestring Diamond Spots, either of Pink, Purple or Green." Still others chose brocaded and flowered silks that looked "different from last years Forest silks." The article went on to chronicle the women's gown sleeves, hoops, jewelry, stockings, and shoes.

Not to be outdone, the gentlemen donned "Deer coloured flower'd Velvets," several sporting "gold brocaded waistcoats," although the editor devoted far less space to male attire.[66] Recounting of the opulent clothing, rather than attention to the food, music, or décor, filled almost two columns.

The descriptions were usually front-page items. Narrative in style, as well as richly descriptive, they might have been read aloud around the tea table or, perhaps with a touch of mockery, at more plebian and male-dominated sites of sociability such as taverns and coffeehouses.[67] On one hand, they reinforced a sense of provincialism, for even the most lavish of affairs in the port cities could never match a royal birthday celebration at court. Yet the columns also provided an imaginative connection to the seat of high fashion. To know what the nobility wore was to know of *le monde*, the fashionable world. That knowledge could make one feel included, a part of that universe; but mere knowledge without actual participation marked one as an outsider.

Often the descriptions of royal and noble dress practices contained less-than-subtle patriotic urgings that served to encourage loyalty to the Crown and remind colonists of their place in the political economy of the British empire by connecting fashion and nation, the personal and the political. Reprinted from English newspapers, the pieces acknowledged that some of the reading public—not to mention some members of the court—wrongly looked to Paris for the lead in fashion.[68] When the Prince of Wales married Princess Augusta in 1736, a description as extensive as the one penned following the famed birthday lauded that "most of the rich clothes were the Manufacture of England, and . . . the few which were French did not come up to these in Richness, Goodness or Fancy." To the sin of disloyalty the report added that of unfashionability. The clothes worn by the royal family themselves were "all of the British Manufactures." The piece describing the queen's birthday noted that the ladies' heads "were dress'd chiefly *English* . . . Lace." Emphasis on the origin of fabrics became all the more crucial since women of means adopted both the *robe à la anglaise* and the "sack back," or *robe à la française*. The difference between the two styles was a length of material that draped from the neck of the gown in the back of the French sacque, meaning that it required even more fabric.[69]

Focusing on the fabrics rather than the forms of dress allowed the newspapers to praise the example the Crown set for others, particularly during periods of conflict with France. In 1739, the year conflicts leading to King George's War began, one writer heard that in Bath people intended to follow the royals in wearing muslin rather than fine French cambric. According

Woman's Dress (Open *Robe à la française* and Petticoat), American and French. The length of fabric that draped down the back of the sacque gown created an elegant line and showcased luxurious materials. Philadelphia Museum of Art: Gift of Thomas Francis Cadwalader, 1955, 1955-98-6a, b.

to his information, they counted it "as a meritt to be included in the number of those that endeavour to save their country three hundred thousand pounds a year."[70] In combining the dress of the royal family, the decisions of the "fashionable" folk who inhabited or visited the resort town of Bath, and the economy, the writer made choosing English fabrics over French ones both fashionable *and* good for the nation. Yet anti-French sentiment failed to produce a wholesale rejection of Parisian styles and goods in England or the colonies. One writer for the *American Magazine and Historical Chronicle* professed disdain in 1746 for the "frenchify'd Air" and fashions he encountered on the streets. "It is amazing to me," the pseudonymous Will Downright continued, "that at a time when we are, or ought to be, seriously engaged in a War with France . . . that we are giving the French all the encouragement we can by consuming their commodities."[71] Downright knew French fabric when he saw it, and its adoption distressed him. Fashion played an important, often disturbing role in imperial conflicts.

The relationship among fashion, status, and British identity appeared most clearly, and quite literally, on display during colonial balls and assemblies. Usually held to mark occasions of state, at least in the first few decades of the eighteenth century, they supplied settings in which the colonial elite performed their gentility, established their connection to the English court by replicating some of its rituals, and secured their place in the empire. These exclusive events, held in New York as early as 1713 when a "ball for peace" celebrated the end of Queen Anne's War with France, became more frequent in subsequent decades. As celebrations both of state and of polite culture, they provided distance from colonial plebeians.[72]

As they attempted to reinforce status hierarchy, assemblies complicated gender ideologies with actual gender relationships. The events relied on gendered difference—on a notion of men and women as complementary partners in dances—but created a shared space based on social class. Still, distinctions of gender permeated the celebrations. On November 1, 1733, in Philadelphia, William Penn hosted a celebration in honor of the "anniversary of His Majesty's birth-day." The mayor and aldermen of the city, along with "several other Gentlemen of distinction," attended. At noon the revelers drank toasts to the health of various members of the royal family. Dinner followed, and, later, "bonfires and illuminations" ignited around the town—quite a display for the Quaker City. Capping off the evening, the "men of distinction" ostensibly joined with equally distinctive women for a ball given at the governor's house "for the entertainment of the ladies."[73]

In the paper's description, the event seems a mere afterthought, a convention designed to appease female members of the colonial elite. But such language belies the increasingly heterosocial nature of a version of gentility deeply implicated in forging a connection to empire. Balls required the equal participation of men and women. Yet they provided prime forums in which women could and did put their supposed "natural" inclinations toward dress and display to great social use. Assemblies acted as mock contests that an elite woman might "win" by appearing the most beautiful, the most fashionable of all.[74] Ostensibly secure in social position, a woman attending an assembly competed with theoretical social equals to be regarded as the best among her sex. In attempting to attain such recognition, perhaps some women hoped to emulate the court fashions they had heard or read about. But social distinction acquired through such fashionable display also situated a person and his or her immediate social circle in a much larger hierarchy.

Whereas balls were accessible to only elite colonial women and men, the adoption of mourning dress provided a more attainable means of participating in court culture. The demise of a member of the royal family usually signaled the fashion of mourning, which had come under attack in English periodicals. Social critics cast it as a pretentious and ridiculous means of commemorating death—mere display that perverted expressions of deeply felt grief. Yet the practice persisted, proving as popular in the colonies as in England.[75]

In January of 1737, Mary Alexander received a letter from Roderigo Pacheco, a London merchant, who wrote that "the death of the Best of Queens that ever was in England occasioned a vast demand for mourning goods."[76] Late in 1736, just months after her lavish birthday celebration, Queen Caroline died suddenly, probably the result of an internal injury sustained during childbirth.[77] Hearing the sighs of grief around the city and seeing the people all dressed in dark colors made him imagine that "the loyal subjects of New York will certainly imitate London."[78] Pacheco found himself in a uniquely appropriate position to make such a determination, having operated a mercantile business in New York until 1726.[79] He had considered whether or not to send some material in advance of an actual order but decided to do so. Along with the goods, Pacheco included a description of exactly how the fabrics were worn, of what the ladies and gentlemen of London donned in mourning: "the ladys chiefly wear bombazeen and silk . . . headcloths of cambrick with broad hems." He did not think they would "go in colours for the first six months." Likewise, the men sported somber shades of black, blue, and gray.[80] The performance of mourning thus manifested itself in masculine and feminine attire.

Around the time Alexander would have received Pacheco's missive, twin notices, reprinted from the *St. James Evening Post* of November 24th, appeared in the New York and Pennsylvania *Gazette*s. They stated that Lord Chamberlain's office had issued the following directions concerning the dress that "peers, peeresses, and privy counsellors" should adopt for Queen Caroline's mourning: "The Gentlemen to wear black cloth, without buttons on the sleeves or pockets, cambrick cravats and weepers broad hemmed, shammey shoes and gloves, crape hatbands, black swords, buckles and buttons. The ladies full dress, black bombazeens, broad hemm'd cambrick linnen, cape hoods, shammey shoes, and gloves and crape fans. Their Undress, dark Norwich crape, and glaz'd gloves."[81]

Although the notices appeared in the popular press, they clearly prescribed the attire and accoutrements for nobility. Pacheco made no such distinctions in his letter to Alexander, instead referring generally to "loyal subjects of New York." In the eighteenth century, the Crown dictated two types of mourning—one in which only members of the court participated, and another for "all persons," observed by those within the court's orbit but also more generally.[82] The description that appeared in the newspapers, which echoed Pacheco's letter, seemed to indicate the former. But the merchant apparently imagined the colonial city, lacking its own court, as a stage on which all inhabitants who could afford to do so would perform the drama of royal mourning. Perhaps he had reason to believe so; after all, he had previously resided in New York. His comment suggests a foreshortened social hierarchy engendered by access to goods, but it also reveals the power goods possessed to seemingly camouflage yet actually express provincialism. Where else but in the colonies would non-nobles presume to participate in royal mourning? Yet from an economic perspective, perhaps in pushing the dress of high mourning on Alexander and her clientele he was simply trying to sell more cloth.

Alexander herself must have realized that not all New Yorkers would "imitate London" by donning the garb of mourning, though some undoubtedly would. Her June 1737 invoice from the Collinsons included a number of colored and patterned fabrics, not mourning cloth alone. But she did request some eighteen pieces (of various qualities) of "Norwich mourning crape," the fabric recommended for the undress of grieving ladies.[83] However, she might have ordered the crape to provide for local, family mournings, since by the time the goods arrived in the fall the official mourning period would have ended. Well into the following year, retailers advertised their "choice sortments of all Things necessary for mourning, both for men and women,"[84] demonstrating that demand for such goods persisted. Local mournings may have acquired greater significance given that it was difficult to beat the royal clock that set mourning times. But even if British colonials could have wholly and swiftly replicated the styles of the beau monde, it is not entirely clear that they always sought to do so.

"Lately in fashion here": Colonial Distinction

Just as provincial balls were not court affairs, and mourning in the colonies fell a trifle behind the curve, New York City was not London, or even Bath or Bristol for that matter. Urban markets in British North America differed from their English counterparts, as merchant correspondence demonstrates. A combination of imperfect supply, the speed of the fashion cycle, and stylistic preferences accounts for the difference.

One problem for colonials who hoped to dress *à la mode* was physical as well as metaphorical distance from the place in which "the fashion" originated. Sometimes styles did not arrive quickly enough to meet demand. Although no order exists, Alexander must have requested at least some of the fabrics that Roderigo Pacheco recommended for mourning attire. In a letter to her the following June he apologized that the "quantity of black things sent... arriv'd too late."[85] What good was it to have the very latest in mourning attire after its use had become obsolete?

At other times the desired fabrics simply did not arrive at all. Two years before their exchanges about mourning fashions, Pacheco regretted the "sundry omissions and mistakes" in Alexander's order. The rapidity with which fashions changed accounted, in part, for problems of supply, exacting limits on fashionable replication in colonial markets. In February 1737, Pacheco was again forced to explain that he could not procure some of the fabrics Alexander requested, "more especially the patterns of callico which can not at this season and at such short time be printed."[86] His comment suggests that the impediments to supplying Alexander's demands were time and distance, not the prohibition of calico. The patterns may have existed, but perhaps Alexander's requests were "off" the production cycle. If so, then the varieties of calico she desired had already been produced and consumed in another colonial market, or styles had changed. Or maybe her desires were distinct from existing patterns, and by the time Pacheco had them printed she would no longer want them. Some twenty years later the firm of David Barclay and Sons wrote to Alexander, "There are wanting to compleat thy order, a few of the printed goods, taffaties and persians." The former had not yet come from the printers, they claimed, while the latter two were simply not "at present to be had."[87]

Sometimes suppliers attempted substitutions. In 1758, Barclay and Sons informed Alexander that she could expect to receive very little crape, "on account of the great demand . . . occasioned by the late mourning." What a change from Roderigo Pacheco's hard sell of mourning cloth to Alexander twenty years earlier. To appease her, they sent printed handkerchiefs and Russian linen.[88] In the fall of 1753, New York merchant James Beekman's suppliers professed to have adhered as closely as possible to his order yet substituted another kind of calico for the one he requested. For this they gave no reason, only insisting that the two were "hardly distinguishable." The following spring the firm lamented, "It gives us concern that we have not been able to conform to your orders for the printed callicoes . . . we had no callicoes two colours and blue of any sorts."[89]

Examining fabric orders from one year to the next establishes the annual, even seasonal shifts that typified the fashion cycle. Merchants tended to place two large orders per year, one for autumn goods and another for spring, the cloth varying in weight and pattern. Consider the fabrics Alexander "desired of Peter and James Collinsons to come in the Fall of 1735." She ordered several bright colors of lustring, grazette, and worsted, as well as nine pieces plain and fifteen "lively" striped callimancoes. If the money sent exceeded the goods requested, she noted, the Collinsons might send more callimanco. In June 1737, however, Alexander requested mostly flowered rushells and cambleteens.[90] In the space of only two years, not only the prints and patterns but also the materials themselves differed significantly. The wheel of fashion turned quickly.

Yet even if merchants could consistently keep pace with London fashions in fabric, evidence suggests that colonial markets did not necessarily stand ready to consume the "latest" styles, no matter how they were advertised, and did not seem intent on following the court. Alexander ordered neither French cambric nor India muslin in 1739, the year royals and patriotic inhabitants of Bath began preferring the latter to the former, according to the piece reprinted in the *New York Gazette*. The year after news of flowered gowns worn at the queen's birthday appeared, however, she requested flowered rather than striped fabrics. But the connection seems tenuous at best, particularly considering that sheer emulation almost never informed her choices.

The specificity of merchants' orders demonstrates that they knew local retailers and customers were particular in their tastes. Alexander rarely relied on swatches, however obvious in their visuality, to speak for themselves. In the 1726 order, her editorial comments break up the collagelike pages like written directions for a traveler perplexed by a visual map. The text modifies the images and artifacts. For the crapes, Alexander wanted "nothing blewish." As for the silver lace, she desired the pattern of the first but the narrower width of the piece immediately to its right. Furthermore, Alexander had particular patterns in mind. For some of the swatches, the colors, mostly muted reds and blues, were accurate, but she wanted the figures "smaller and thicker." Comparing two of the samples, she noted, "I would have a broad strip[e] with a flower between of these colours, [and] the cloath better."[91] The specificity of her demands reflected the tastes of her market. Likewise, Robert Pringle of Charleston indicated at the beginning of a 1738 order, "Goods proper for So Carolina." The Italian gauzes he received two years later took so well that he requested more, but he wanted blues and greens, "those colours being best liked here." Yet the velvet sent in 1742 was not the "right sort for this place." The following year, Thomas Hutchinson sent Pringle some ribbons that "stick on hand, the women having alter'd their fashions which are very changeable in those sort of things."[92] Did Hutchinson send them because they were not selling in Boston? Or were they popular, yet surplus, in the northern port, but not in Charleston? Modes could be quite local.

Sometimes colonial merchants grew openly frustrated in their attempts to have their requests for color, pattern, and quality met. Perhaps no one was as exacting in his specifications as James Beekman. After the firm of Pomeroys and Streatfield failed to fill his order for spring fabrics in 1754, they must have received an angry letter or two in response. Later that year they wrote, "We have sundry of your favors before us . . . complaining that the printed callicoes were not so large flowers as you could have desired." Then, in a missive dated only four days later they claimed in exasperation, "We have endeavoured to conform to your orders . . . but it is impossible to be so exact in patterns as your orders would bind us to." They attempted to assuage Beekman's inevitable anger with the accompanying, and somewhat hollow, insistence that the fabrics sent were "the newest patterns."[93] Certainly that would satisfy him. Yet two years later, Pomeroys and Streatfield again expressed difficulty filling Beekman's order. No longer desirous of the large flowered prints of two years earlier, he now wanted small-figured calico. "It was impracticable to conform exactly to have Your patterns so small as an inch diameter," they noted, "but [we] have chose the smallest patterns we had and hope that the goods now sent will please."[94]

Robert Pringle was deeply unhappy with two fabric shipments he received late in 1738, mincing no words in his response. "I must desire leave to inform you," he wrote, "that the goods are not to my liking as they are not according to the memorandum or invoice I sent." As if the bait-and-switch were not enough, he continued, "Neither do I think them fresh and good in quality, but rather appear to be old shopkeepers that have been often handled, especially some of the calicoes which are very old and unfashionable patterns which render them unsalable here." The other fabrics, of equally low quality, were "chiefly for the summer season" and thus "entirely unsaleable."[95] Philadelphia merchant William Pollard was likewise displeased with the nature of the fabrics he imported, though his displeasure did not translate into his advertisements. He wrote in 1764 that the quality of the calicos, which he characterized as "ordinary," was particularly distressing since, if they had suited his order, he might have sold them "in a fortnight, being much wanted." The durants also proved so unsatisfactory that Pollard testily proclaimed them to be "the last I shall ever have from Yorkshire." Within two months, he had received a fall shipment, this time from Liverpool, for which he placed an ad in the *Pennsylvania Gazette* describing the "neat assortment" of fashionable fabrics in rich colors.[96]

While any self-respecting merchant would attempt to procure the highest-quality items at the lowest prices, merchant correspondence reveals something more: not all styles that were in fashion in London sold well in colonial cities, although suppliers provided colonial consumers, via merchants, with the opportunity to purchase the styles. Before Alexander prepared her June 1737 order for cloth to arrive that coming fall, the Collinsons had sent a few additional sample pieces. In a nota bene, she thanked them: "I very well approve of your sending the Sprig'd Damasks for a tryal, and when any new fashioned thing is in vogue, a piece of it may be proper for a tryal." But when she indicated flowers in her current order she did not "mean sprigs but . . . large running flowers." She further elaborated, "By a white flower I mean large running white flowers thro the whole piece." Whether the sample "sprig'd" damasks would sell Alexander did not know, but the other fabrics, the rushells and cambleteens "which have come lately here in fashion take very well."[97] Robert Pringle observed that "the women here come very much into wearing bone lace," noting that a box "for a trial might be worth while," perhaps because he was unwilling to place a large order.[98]

Other merchants also encouraged suppliers to wait for their word before shipping quantities of fabric. In an order dated 1739, Philip Livingston insisted on large-flowered calico, "none small single flowers as you sent me last year which I can't sell" because they were "in no demand." And when William Pollard received "dull brown" fabric instead of the claret cloth he had requested, he explained that it simply would not sell. Teetering precariously between firm and rude, Pollard wrote, "I would not have you advise any of your Friends to send a large parcell of goods here . . . without first consulting me."[99] On one hand, merchants expressed the desire to present their customers with "fashionable" fabrics, trusting suppliers to send the latest modes and encouraging them to do so. Yet in noting that certain fabrics were in fashion "lately here" or "in no demand" they acknowledged the particularity of colonial markets. Small batches of fabrics had to be tested with local consumers.

Colonial merchants such as Mary Alexander, Robert Pringle, Philip Livingston, James Beekman, and William Pollard possessed a unique transatlantic perspective. They almost certainly knew more about London fashions than did colonial consumers, but they were also far more familiar with colonial tastes than were their English suppliers. Some suppliers even acknowledged the difference; Barclay and Sons hoped that the substitute Russian linen sent to Alexander would "suit [her] market." What accounted for stylistic differences? For example, why were large flowers popular in New York at a time when small "sprigs" were worn in England? Did colonists prefer showier patterns? Apparently New Yorkers displayed a penchant for appearing *à la mode*. Traveler Sarah Kemble Knight wrote in 1704 that the English there looked "very fasheonable in their dress," contrasting their attire with what she regarded as the peculiar styles of Dutch residents.[100]

But fashionability in the colonies did not necessarily require looking exactly as the smart set in London did—in fact, something too novel might mark one as ostentatious or, worse, a pretender to social status, interpretations that tended to coincide as the eighteenth-century progressed. Therefore, even if merchants could reliably acquire the latest styles in a timely manner, despite the constraints of supply, time, and distance, colonists did not necessarily seek the brand new.[101] Colonial consumers turned first to the tried and true, developing a vocabulary of fashion that responded to the unique social and sartorial world of port cities. The trick was to distinguish oneself within acceptable standards of attire—to don the most recent pattern or color of large flowers rather than be the community risk-taker who would first wear small flowers—while still appearing distinctive enough within a varied and confusing sartorial landscape. William Smith Jr. reflected in his *History of the Province of New York . . . to the Year 1732*, "In the city of New York we follow London fashions; though by the time we adopt them they become disused in England."[102] Yet it was perhaps difficult to determine whether the men and women who populated port cities were behind the curve or on a different path altogether, and what this indicated about their social position.

The sheer variety of fashions in colonial cities over the first half of the eighteenth century, from Quaker plainness to colorful calico, and leather breeches to assembly wear, reflected the increasing diversity of their populations and the variety of arenas for display. Individual expressions confronted social hierarchy, and metropolitan mandates, whether commercial or sartorial, collided with colonial location. The meaning of fashion, rather than fixed and discernable, was shifting, contested, and ultimately unclear—as changeable as styles themselves. Increasing imports, as well as theft and pawning, made fine attire accessible to people who could not necessarily afford it, whose social rank did not validate it. Yet at the highest social echelons, men and women used in-group knowledge of fashion in their displays of gentility and imperial connection. As long as elites performed for one another in exclusive spaces, fashion's role in securing social status was fairly unproblematic, and even desirable. However, such emphasis on *la mode* granted high-ranking women great influence, which, considered alongside the presence of consumer goods among the not-so-beau monde, made fashion a flash point of gender relations.

Fops and Coquettes

GENDER, SEXUALITY, AND STATUS

Stopping in Staten Island along his journey from Maryland to Boston in 1744, Dr. Alexander Hamilton observed, almost without irony, that the gray moss that hung heavily from the trees might "if handsomely oild and powdered and tyed behind with a bag or ribbon . . . make a tollerable beau-periwig." Ever casting a keen eye toward things genteel (or just as often ungenteel), Hamilton knew a thing or two about the styling of wigs, preeminent markers of status and masculine identity for men in eighteenth-century British America. Yet he did not limit his observations to the adornment of trees, always having much to say about the physical appearances of the people he encountered. Hamilton was unsparing in his critiques, his journal a veritable compendium of mid-eighteenth-century fashion dos and don'ts.[1]

In particular, the doctor clearly considered himself to be a connoisseur of women, seldom missing a chance to comment on their looks and taking particular notice of their dress. For instance, he found the ladies of Albany "ugly" and the Dutch women he encountered there clad in a "comicall headdress" and "short petticoats." By contrast, the pretty, well-dressed women he observed in the cities of Philadelphia, Newport, New York, and Boston looked more to his liking. There was the lady of "masculine make" who was dressed *à la mode*, which would have meant wide skirts supported by panniers, or side hoops intended to display sumptuous fabric. Hamilton juxtaposed this woman's physiology and perhaps demeanor against the modish feminine fashion. He identified a "coquette" by way of her "gay tawdry dishabille" consisting of a "robe de chambre of cherry coloured silk laced with silver round the sleeves and skirts."[2] Hamilton's description of a flirtatious young lady sporting a fashionable red chamber robe (or bed gown) adorned with sparkly trim and worn without a hoop or stays presents the very picture of a loose woman. From Hamilton's elite Anglo-American male perspective, clothes made the woman—or rather, various types of women, as he utilized a gendered social taxonomy defined by modes of dress.

Like Hamilton, many British Americans were preoccupied with sending sartorial messages and "reading" other people correctly amid an emerging consumer culture. Concerns about the relationship between dress and identity were particularly pronounced in the growing, increasingly heterogeneous, and socially fluid port cities. As illustrated in Chapter 1, a person's attire was supposed to facilitate these tasks of social discernment but might just as easily confound them due to the variety of sartorial expressions, competing ideas of what constituted fashionability, and the mutability of fashion and its meanings. Set in this milieu, Hamilton's journal expresses an attempt to make people socially legible by using fashion in dress to explicitly connect ideas about gender and sexuality to detemations of social position. Confident in his own powers of discernment, he used dress as a form of social shorthand that conveyed at a glance who a person was, inside and out. For Hamilton, dress *revealed* rather than performed identity, and what it disclosed might stand in contrast to what its wearers hoped it conveyed. Primarily, he equated certain forms of fashionability with disposition toward members of the opposite sex. A "gay tawdry dishabille" bespoke the coquette beneath, while a "fop" was known by his excessive attention to modish dress and high-status women. In Hamilton's eyes, fashion in dress became an index of how people behaved romantically and thus where they stood socially—and vice versa. Such critiques served as a way of calling out and ultimately dismissing social climbers, male and female.

Fashion in dress served as a primary site for negotiating the intersection of gender and status for two reasons: first, fashion was conceptually feminized, but particular styles à *la mode* were either for men or women.[3] Fashion in general was feminine, but certain fashions were masculine, creating a tension between idea and practice. Second, fashionable appearances could facilitate social and romantic relationships between men and women that helped secure or enhance social position. The adoption of *la mode* performed elite masculinity and femininity, visually and materially expressing rank-specific gender identity. But fashion could also expose its followers to ridicule and castigation on those very terms, attacked for eroding the gender and social boundaries that high fashion was, in theory, supposed to maintain. Although *la mode* in the abstract, and sometimes specific styles, provided ready targets, such concerns were as much about what fashion indicated about relationships between the sexes as they were critiques of how men and women looked. Put another way, focusing on men's and women's appearances served as a way of assessing their interactions and relative power. Fashion was the subject, but gender relations and their ability to undermine proper, gendered social order was the object. Yet even the strictest warnings and the most biting satires could not drain the pleasure out of fashion, could not wholly devalue its social currency. "Fashionable" was a term of social approval or opprobrium, depending on who applied it to whom. It was a description that captured the tension between performances of gender and social status and helped generate new ways of expressing and connecting the two hierarchies by midcentury.

The Feminization of Fashion

In England and British America, fashion was associated with women and was therefore metaphorically "feminized." Yet it also signified the scope and masculine power of British commerce and trade with "exotic" lands,[4] and presented opportunities for colonial men to feel less colonial and more metropolitan. Thus fashion in dress was both an acknowledged form of feminine power and important to men and women alike as a site for expressing social status.

To a large degree, fashion became ideologically feminized through English periodical literature such as Joseph Addison's *Spectator*.[5] Its feminization depended on three related premises: first, that the consumption of fashionable goods was women's activity; second, that attention to dress and display was not merely an observable but an inherently female preoccupation due to women's natural vanity and insatiable appetite; and, finally, that the very concept "fashion" possessed symbolically "feminine" traits such as unpredictability and fickleness. The formulation was predicated upon an unexamined and seemingly unproblematic tautology: fashion was feminine due to "natural" propensity for display and novelty among females, and women pursued fashion because it was innately feminine.

The very circularity of an equation in which fashion was feminine because women pursued it, and women pursued it because it was feminine, represents a general trend in the western world of the late seventeenth and early eighteenth centuries toward the reinterpretation of sex and gender categories. Whereas scholars of anatomy had once viewed male and female as essentially similar, inverted versions of each other, over the course of the seventeenth and eighteenth centuries they increasingly came to regard the sexes as incommensurably different, although complementary. With the divergence of male and female came the hardening and reification of the categories "masculine" and "feminine," and attendant suspicion of individuals who belonged to one sex but displayed characteristics of the other.[6]

As an integral part of this gendering process, Joseph Addison's censorious Mr. Spectator and Richard Steele's sly Tatler, among others, marked out a public, political, economically productive role for men and a private, domestic, space for women.[7] Supposedly removed from bastions of male power such as the legislature and the marketplace, a woman was to adorn herself and her home, and thereby appropriately ornament her husband or father. It is unsurprising that the gendering of fashion proceeded through print, for in England, a bourgeois public sphere predicated on rational, dispassionate, theoretically disembodied communication emerged in purposeful opposition to unstable, irrational, embodied fashion and its status-obsessed adherents. Opinions held by individuals or the public might change, but they did so through thought and reason, not whims and desires. Even as male participants in this "sphere" continued to pursue *la mode*, they employed fashion as a foil, associating mindless pursuit of it with those members of society who threatened the integrity of the masculine British social order: fops, fools, the French—all grotesquely effeminate in their characteristics.[8]

The gendering process was bound up in the era's social flux, as the concept of social rank slipped its chains of noble lineage.[9] Status tensions produced by expanded access to luxury goods contributed to the solidification of gender categories into a dichotomous model, which acquired status-specific trappings. Although, or perhaps precisely because, men participated equally in consumer culture, it became marked as a feminine phenomenon and displaced onto women's behavior. If consumption engaged in for the sake of appearance and display could be "culturally coded as part of women's nature,"[10] then fashionability might be divorced from social status. However useful in theory, this was difficult to accomplish as long as masculine performances of rank depended on sartorial splendor. The ideological feminization of fashion belied its obvious pursuit by men, pursuit that had much to do with women.

Social critics in the colonies also articulated the connection between women and fashion, feminizing the concept and cementing a binary gender order. Writing in 1732 from his "house on Manhattan Island," the cleverly pseudonymous Callamancos asserted that women were generally "more solicitous" about attire than men, which he regarded as indicative of their "superficial, wavering and inconstant" natures—likening females to the changing nature of fashion itself.[11] Likewise, a letter to the editor of the *New York Gazette* penned in 1739 near the beginning of the War of Jenkins' Ear, addressed the "female passion for dress and show" by reproducing a paragraph from Addison's *Spectator*. The excerpt discussed a tale from Virgil about the Roman female warrior, Camelia. Although an "Amazon" who had rejected many of the characteristics of her sex, including fine dress, Camelia possessed one inherent and unavoidable female trait, her capacity to be dazzled by finery. After defeating a Trojan enemy in battle, as the story went, she became entranced by his "embroidered tunic, beautiful coat of male [sic] with a mantle of finest purple, golden bow hung upon his shoulder . . . golden clasp and . . . helmet of the same." Overcome by a "woman's longing for the pretty trappings that he was adorned with," her "heedless pursuit after these glittering trifles" spelled her eventual destruction.[12]

As a warrior, Camelia had transgressed gender conventions, yet her "natural" female inclinations belied her. The moral was that women's passion for display was not easily repressed and would always exert its sway. Moreover, in this instance, it generated passion for a man who was nonetheless her political and military enemy—such were the wages of effeminacy. Thus, it was best indulged by and expressed on the female body itself and segregated from venues of male power. If not, disastrous consequences followed for women, but more for the masculine institutions they invaded, for men, and for society.

Women's supposed taste for fashion symbolized a binary gender system, while in practice it challenged the social order that the ideology ostensibly underpinned. Personal adornment of any sort necessitated a degree of economic power and choice for women, even as they spent their fathers' or husbands' funds, one of a wealth of sticking points that plagued an articulation of commerce as masculine but consumption as feminine.[13] When the woman who adorned herself in toilette became a woman on display in public, as she inevitably did—in the streets, in church, at the theater—she threatened to undo the logic of separate spheres as well as confuse status distinctions. Bernard Mandeville, no opponent of commerce, observed the "scores of people, especially Women, of almost the lowest rank, that wear good and fashionable clothes," scapegoating poor women for the "vice" that "turn'd the trade."[14] In colonial port cities, these women of low rank were often slaves and servants.

As social critics reacted to and attacked women's consumption, they recognized that fashion served as an expression of power over status from which women would not be thwarted.[15] As the "Busy-Body," the latter-day colonial cousin to Addison's Spectator, wrote in 1729, women who attempted to "purchase the reputation of fashionable" through "modish extravagances" disdained those who attempted to "controul them in the pursuit of their darling pleasures."[16] Men were forced to tread lightly on feminine proclivities and pleasures lest they suffer rejection. While free colonial men of various ranks enjoyed many means of expressing social status and participation in British culture—politics, trade, coffeehouse conversation, the production of print—fashion was a primary way for women to signify their importance and involvement.[17] Yet the idea that reputation and position might be purchased by women, and then reflected onto the men in their lives, threatened both the notion of a contingent, relational feminine identity and the idea of masculine status—meaning both position as a man and social position—as independent.

Men and Women, Hoops and Wigs

Although fashion in general highlighted concerns about gender and status, particular styles became lightning rods for such debates around the turn of the eighteenth century. The hoop petticoat, an element of female dress that persisted in some form through the nineteenth century, asserted women's economic power through its purchase and social power through the ways in which it commanded attention.[18] Thus the hoop stimulated anxieties over female display, consumption, and sexuality in Old and New England alike and provided a focus for those fears. In colonial Massachusetts, controversy over a male fashion, the periwig, joined concerns over the female hoop.[19] The attention hoops and wigs received in print suggests their popularity. Together, the two modes provide a case study of the ways in which fashion created "gender trouble," as critics charged them with confusing expected performances of masculinity and femininity and undermining the assumptions behind those categories.[20] Embedded within the attacks lay concerns that men and women cultivated themselves for one another but that, paradoxically, such preening led them to forsake proper gender positions. Finally, writers used the language of gender to discipline status seeking.

Appearing during the reign of Queen Anne in the early years of the eighteenth century, the hoop was descended from the farthingale, an element of Tudor-era fashion designed to hold women's skirts in a particular shape. Its geographic origin is uncertain; although some English writers considered the hoop to be a European invention, it may have appeared first in England rather than on the continent. Used to display luxurious and often heavy imported fabrics to their greatest advantage, hoops were initially fashioned of whalebone culled from the waters around Greenland—a product of transatlantic trade. Cane, wicker, and wire eventually came to compose lighter-weight hoops, which could easily accommodate the delicate silks from France and cottons from India that became popular in the eighteenth century. These fragile, flexible hoops were more easily dislocated by wind or interpersonal contact than their predecessors; thus the bodies beneath might become visible at a moment's notice, supplying some men with their first-ever public view of the female leg.[21]

Yet even as large hoops and their unpredictable motions grabbed the gaze, they also protected their wearers. The shape of the hoop petticoat shifted over the course of the century, but its original form was half spherical or domed, creating a bubble of space around the figure underneath equal on all sides, lifting the skirts it supported off the ground to reveal feet and ankles. Although hoops' movements threatened at times to expose women, hoops generally made female bodies *less* accessible, surrounding them with a large and forbidding "machine" of wire and fabric that could fend off unwanted physical advances even as it attracted attention.[22] It was this dynamic of attraction and repulsion, one that bespoke women's control over their bodies—and perhaps the bodies of others who were jostled, invited, or put off by the contraption—that so frustrated the hoop's detractors.

These sexual anxieties dovetailed with concern over the hoop's expense and thus with expenditure engaged in for the ends of women's appearances. Critics satirized the hoop petticoat mercilessly, attacking its size, its immodesty, its inconvenience for wearers and danger to others. Such attacks demonstrated extreme unease with women's control of money and sexuality and command of the gaze—power that needed to be checked. The *Tatler*'s cultural critic Richard Steele, writing as Isaac Bickerstaff, went so far as to put the hoop on trial, devoting a full week to the topic. Despite arguments proffered on the hoop's behalf, such as its encouragement of the woolen industry that produced cords for stiffening it, its stimulation of Atlantic trade, and its potential for safeguarding female chastity, the fashion was "convicted" as an extravagant one that produced personal indebtedness.[23]

One English engraving titled "The Review" put not the style but its wearers on trial—and, to an extent, its viewers. The scene is a city street, and the print comprises two vignettes. The focal point is the backside of a woman wearing a large hoop. To the woman's left another lady's hoop, perhaps caught by the wind, appears to blow up in the front, while in the background, at the image's center, a hoop-clad woman is lifted out the top of her carriage with the assistance of ropes and pulleys. The text beneath the engraving addresses women readers, promising:

> Ladies for you this ample scene I vend
> A new invention by your sexe's friend
> With which you may securely trip along
> Each narrow lane, or shun the rustic throng.[24]

The writer, cheekily acknowledging but also lampooning hoop-wearing women's high status and urbanity, gives credence to charges that hoops are unwieldy and incommodious to such genteel ladies. By way of remedy he promotes "a new invention" that will help women manage the motion of their hoops, explaining: "With silken cord to guide the huge machine / On such occasions as above is seen (see the black doing his office)."[25]

Closer inspection reveals that the woman on the far left is actually lifting the front of her skirt using rope handles. She emerges from Long's Warehouse, where she has ostensibly acquired the device (as the building's frieze depicting a hoop-clad woman suggests), into a crowd of approving, mostly female, spectators. The figure whose wide-skirted back faces us gazes with admiration at the woman, as a friend gestures toward her as if to say, "You see?" The invention of hoops with handles meant that women might control their uncontrollable skirts more easily. They would protect themselves from exposure and avoid bumping into people—surely desirable outcomes. Yet the image suggests the various problems associated with such theoretical and imperfect control. For one thing, how would women use it? Was empowering them to move their hoops up and down, left and right, really better than leaving things to the wind or the "rustic throng"? And how might others, particularly men of low rank, exploit the invention? Toward the center of the scene, a smiling, turban-clad, and caricatured servant of African descent lifts the skirts of his mistress ("see the black doing his office") so that a well-dressed English gentleman may take a peek. The jab expresses anxieties over domestic, perhaps intimate, relations between Englishwomen and men of African descent. Yet it also raises the specter of black men not merely enjoying access to the bodies of Englishwomen for themselves but providing other men with such contact. The text promises that women can use the "new invention" to protect themselves and others, but the image suggests that they will only reveal themselves more easily, at times and places of their own choosing; or, perhaps worse, be exposed by their equally libidinous servants. The hoop with handles is under "review," but in actuality, women's bodies are being reviewed.[26]

Yet if measures were not taken to manage hoops, the distressing scene filling the right half of the engraving was inevitable. There, a jury of gen-

"The Review," printed by Carrington Bowles, London, ca. 1770s. Courtesy, The Winterthur Library, Joseph Downs Collection of Manuscripts and Printed Ephemera.

teel men and women gathered under the huge canopy of a hoop renders its verdict while the defendant cries and pleads. As the text beneath this scene explains,

> The wide machine aloft in Nikey's court
> Displays its orb to public jeer and sport
> The weeping maid while she her sentence hears
> Wails her lost hoop and melts in pearly tears.[27]

The contest, almost militaristic given the reference to Nike, ends in a loss for the defendant. Her punishment: to remain defrocked of her hoop, hanging above the jury as exhibit A, mocked and turned into the kind of humiliating public spectacle it deserved to be, not one engendering admiration. Like Bickerstaff's trial, "The Review" lampoons the hoop in particular, and fashion in general, by casting them as issues of legal importance. How ridiculous that something so trivial would command the attention and intrusion

FOPS AND COQUETTES 55

of the state. Yet by endowing the hoop with such consequence, both Bickerstaff and the engraving backhandedly acknowledge the style's significance. Demonstrating how hoops operated in public, on crowded city streets made even busier by the commotion the style generated, "The Review" visually established concerns about Englishwomen's bodies and their adornments in urban, consumer environments. Anxieties about women's display, sexuality, and power that needed to be checked by a court of public opinion, if not the state, were all projected onto the hoop's wide, spherical screen.

Just as critics tried to regulate the hoop petticoat fashion in England by impugning women's status and sexuality, so too did issues of social and sexual power animate satire printed in British North America. In Boston, the hoop, representing fashion itself, became a battleground in conflict between men and women of various classes in the early decades of the century. The initial salvo, *The Origin of the Whale Bone Petticoat: A Satyr*, appeared in 1714. Its author hoped to "recall the wan'dring fair from traveling too far in whale bone gear."[28] Yet the writer was quickly interrupted by Madame Alamode, her name an obvious reference to French fashion, who claimed that he had neither the strength nor the sense to defeat a foe that had bested even the Tatler:

> Did we not valiantly maintain the fight
> 'Gainst mighty Bickerstaff's immortal wit?
> We did, we did, we bravely kept the field
> His wit and conqu'ring reason both did yield.[29]

In the immediate wake of Queen Anne's War, Alamode used military metaphors to protect her chosen fashion and to describe its successful defense, insisting that the author quit his arms, sue for peace, and "wage war no longer with our darling dress."[30] If Bickerstaff had gone down to ignominious defeat when confronting the hoop in England, could the colonial critic hope for more? Here the satirist accomplishes two ends: he unites Alamode with women in England against their common foe Bickerstaff, and intimates that he will do better. Women such as Alamode framed the matter as a war; very well, the author would marshal every weapon at men's disposal.

The author began by attacking fashion in general on all the standard fronts: it signified vanity, pride, appetite, and even stupidity. Particular styles failed to serve much practical purpose, he claimed, citing muffs that were too small to keep hands warm in New England's "blustering northwest station," and movable hoops that would cause women to run for cover in winter: "when northwest storms come thundering at your feet, how you snails half frozen will retreat," he rhymed.[31] Fashions frequently failed to suit the persons on which and the places in which they were displayed, he asserted, citing the wet and chilly New England environment as a reason to reject impractical modes.[32] Still, such styles persisted. Seeking to supply an explanation for the emergence of fashions generally, the author claimed that they served to remedy various "natural" deficiencies in women—huge ruffs disguised ugly necks or high hairstyles made "pigmy"-sized women appear taller. To the implied question of where fashions came from he supplied the answer female vanity and desire, echoing the circular reasoning connecting women and fashion: modes arose from female proclivities and then reproduced them. With the relationship between fashion and female appetite securely established, he launched into a bawdy tale of the hoop petticoat's ignoble origins, spinning the following yarn illustrating the connection between hoops and women whose desires knew no bounds.[33]

In the court of Versailles there lived charming Belinda, the toast of France and the taste of many suitors. When she contracted a virulent case of the clap that caused her to waddle around in obvious pain, her doctor prescribed a cure that would incapacitate her for a fortnight. Protesting, and rattling off a list of potential conquests soon to arrive at court, she offered the doctor ten thousand livres for a quicker fix, something that would get her back in the game of love toute suite. Inspired by the tidy sum, he replied,

> Order your mantua makers to attend
> Tailors, et caetera, for I intend
> Deep within circling ambuscade to hide your straddling gate
> Madam I'll built you like a pyramid!

He then advised her to pile on several layers of petticoats, and thus

> By this device you'll walk without much pain
> And shine triumphant in Versailles again
> If you but wear it all the bubbl'd nation
> Will soon admire and bring it into fashion.

Not only could Belinda be restored to her licentious ways, spreading her legs and disease with impunity, but she would be further celebrated as an innovator in fashion. Lest a reader miss the message about the hoop's genealogy, he concluded the tale:

> whale bone petticoats had their rise
> to hide a filthy strumpet's foul disease

> And now fair ladies view well your monstrous dress and recollect
> Think on the whore that was the architect.[34]

That her greedy doctor, not Belinda, was the "architect" was of no consequence when the point was to equate hoops with whores. It is unsurprising that the satirist perhaps wrongly looked to France for the odious hoop's emergence, considering the Francophobia that pervaded New England in the eighteenth century, the association of the French court with fashion, and popular assumptions about French corruption of a political and sexual nature.[35] Women who thought themselves grand and beautiful in hoops would be seen as harlots, the piece implied—dirty, spoiled, and attractive to no man.

In case the equation of hoops with French prostitutes failed to dissuade hoop-wearing women, the poem concluded with the exclamation, "Your next extravagance will be our breeches!"[36] This dire prediction suggested the gender trouble at the heart of the matter. Accusing a woman of "wearing the breeches" meant that she inverted gender roles and behaved like a man.[37] The feminine extravagance and excess symbolized by a particular mode, in this case the hoop, led to gender bending in the service of usurping male prerogatives, both inside the household and out. Paradoxically, the more distinctly and desirably "feminine" hoop wearers tried to appear, the more masculine they became. Hoops were ominous portents of things to come, the satirist warned. If left unchecked in their appetites, women would remain unsatisfied not merely until they possessed the world but until they encompassed it—male and female, public and private—beneath their spreading skirts. In claiming power through what was given them ideologically and socially, fashion, women exposed themselves to ridicule, derision, and the potential loss of their status as women.

Yet hoops were not the only fashion to receive censure in colonial Boston. The male periwig garnered its fair share of negative attention and also signaled gender trouble. Associated with the court of Charles II, and worn to display wealth and position, periwigs were long and curled. For English Puritans, they recalled the stylistic distinctions of roundhead and cavalier that marked anti- and pro-monarchy camps during the English Civil War of the 1640s. Although Puritans triumphed, dismantling the Crown and establishing England as a commonwealth, the monarchy's restoration in 1660 not only toppled their control but ushered in a new era of luxury and excess, which the periwig came to represent.[38]

As historian Richard Godbeer has shown, prominent Puritan divines in New England such as Samuel Sewall and Nicholas Noyes abhorred the wigs. Sewall railed against them in his copious diary, while Noyes published a tract denouncing them as vain, extravagant, unnatural, and effeminate. Although men donned periwigs in order to visually establish identity, critics charged that the perukes confused designations of age and rank; it was, quite simply, difficult to determine whether a periwig wearer was old or young, wealthy or middling, they claimed. Furthermore, the wigs ran counter to God's will for clear social order and suggested dissatisfaction with what God had supplied. Finally, scripture reserved long hair for women, they asserted, so periwigs not only visually confused gender but signaled that men might be acquiring dangerous, Eve-like characteristics such as vanity and frailty.[39]

In addition to gender confusion and its power to threaten other forms of order, periwigs, like hoops, indicated a crisis in gender relations. In his 1722 pamphlet *An Answer to Cases of Conscience Respecting the Country*, minister Solomon Stoddard railed against all forms of worldliness "not instituted by God," taking aim at periwigs. According to Stoddard, in addition to being wasteful and extravagant signs of pride and discontentedness with the provisions of God, they were "contrary to masculine gravity," making men "look as if they were more disposed to court a maid" than to ponder God's kingdom.[40] Men in periwigs performed for women, not for God or even for earthly magistrates. It was not so much that periwigs visually made men into women but that the style's effeminacy signaled an uncontrolled, Eve-like appetite for women and a desire for their attention. Such a need to be seen and judged attractive gave the intended audience great power.

Fashions such as hoops and periwigs indicated indulgence of bodily appetites and unrestrained passions; therefore, Stoddard felt compelled to mention the former style in a tract about the latter. Although throughout the jeremiad he resisted addressing women and their modes directly, he concluded, "There be many other practices that are plainly contrary to the light of nature. HOOPED petticoats have something of nakedness; mix'd dancings are incentives to lust." Stoddard not only referred to hoops in the same breath as wigs but in doing so revealed his concern with how men and women interacted, and with what drove and facilitated such interactions.[41] Fashion was, in part, to blame.

In places other than Boston, writers also linked wigs and hoops, casting them (and fashion itself) as expressions of carnal desires. The following poem appeared in Jacob Taylor's almanac for 1726, published in Philadelphia:

> Now Madams with French Fashions must be fooling
> And wear a hoop as if their tails want cooling
> Our spruce gallant too, struts and looks so big
> With empty scull, pulls off unnatural wig.

Here the hoop is a French mode, and hoop-wearing women are indecent, practically exposing their bottoms, whereas wig-wearing men are brainless. Both possess an excess of sexual appetite, evidenced by their sartorial choices. The poem concludes by directly connecting desire and fashion, paradoxically and in Calvinist terms characterizing styles as "unnatural" and ungodly, yet all too suggestive of human nature: "Thus wretched man is to his lust a slave / Wearing what God or nature never gave."[42]

Critics of hoops and periwigs suggested that such fashions produced not only unnatural appearances but also unnatural relationships that hailed the downfall of society. But not all British Americans sympathized with such dire predictions. A young Benjamin Franklin, already chafing at Boston's social and religious mores, wasted little time sending up these ideas in a pamphlet titled *Hoop-petticoats Arraigned and Condemned by the Light of Nature and the Law of GOD*, particularly taking on Solomon Stoddard's contention that the hoop had "something of nakedness" in it. He satirized the minister's pamphlet but also English satires of the hoop while using their very conventions and content. Like the *Tatler*'s Bickerstaff, Franklin laid out his "charge" against the "vain, sinful, and immodest fashion" of the hoop, namely that it contradicted the "ends of apparel." These included covering nakedness, protecting the body from harm, and adorning the body. But in Franklin's treatment, a reader could clearly see that the hoop, in its size and construction, achieved all three; so that rather than being contrary to the ends of apparel, it served them rather perfectly. The notion that women were rendered "almost naked" by huge hoops seemed little short of absurd, the idea that they endangered themselves and others nearly as foolish; and, finally, who could reasonably argue that hoops failed to "adorn," or cover, the body? In a final jab at Stoddard's fears of nakedness, Franklin quoted Isaiah's call to the daughters of Israel that they tremble and "strip ye and make ye bare and gird sackcloth on your loins." If the hoop did in fact promote an unclothed state, was that not in line with the scriptures?[43]

Primarily, Franklin strove to suggest the absurdity of viewing the fashion, or any fashion, as cause or evidence of society's downfall, slamming jeremiad-happy Puritan divines along the way. He facetiously recommended several steps that persons in positions of authority might take

[15]

Quest. X. IS not a spirit hankering after Ceremonies that are not Instituted by GOD, a Provocation?

A. YES, because it is contrary to the Second Commandment: Exod. 20. 4. *Thou shalt not make to thy self any graven Image*, &c.

1. THIS is an Arrogating a Power that GOD hath not given to Men. It may be said to them that do it, *Who gave you this Authority?* Decency, and Order may be without any new Ceremonies: *Jeroboam was taxed for assuming a Power that did not belong to him*: 1 King. 12. 33. *So he offered upon the altar which he had made in Bethel, the fifteenth day of the Eighth Month, even in the Month which he had devised of his own heart* ———.

2. IT is a Reflection on the Wisdom of GOD; as if they could Mend His Institutions: As if they could find out a Better way of Worship, than He hath Appointed, Col. 2. 23.

3. IT is a Presuming on a Blessing without a Divine Warrant: Math. 15. 9. *Teaching doctrines [which are] commandments of men.*

THERE be many other Practices that are plainly Contrary to the Light of Nature.

𝕳𝖔𝖔𝖕𝖊𝖉 Petticoats have something of Nakedness; Mixt Dancings are incentives to Lust; Compotations in Private Houses, is a Drunken Practice.

F I N I S.

BOSTON in New-England :
Printed by B. Green: Sold by Samuel Gerrish at his Shop near the Brick Meeting-House in Corn Hill. June 25: 1722.

A page from Solomon Stoddard's pamphlet *An Answer to Cases of Conscience Respecting the County* (Boston, 1722), p. 15.

to suppress the hoop and thus forestall God's impending wrath. Parents should steer their children from it, ministers their congregants, and husbands their wives, he prescribed. How ridiculous, he implied, that a fashion would compromise these relationships of hierarchy, power, and control. Yet even as he attacked these concerns as ludicrous, Franklin's satire lent them a certain credibility. In particular, he remained discursively bound by the gendered terms of the controversy, particularly the association between hoops and women's unbridled sexuality. He concluded, "If the wearing of hoop petticoats were the punishment of such as have proved themselves to be whores, it might probably suppress two great sins at once"—the hoop petticoat recommended as both a sign of and a punishment for prostitution.[44]

Despite the controversy—or perhaps because of it—the wearing of hoops and wigs persisted until the final decades of the eighteenth century. In fact, hoops grew in size into the 1740s, when panniers, or side hoops, reigned supreme. By the 1760s the hoop had returned to something approximating its initial domed shape but in the 1770s grew sideways again.[45] Frankly, nothing could match the hoop for its capacity to display fabric, the chief indicator of fashionability. And although long, curled periwigs fell out of fashion, they continued to be worn at court and by professional men—indicators of position and yet still targets of ridicule. Engraver William Hogarth produced "The Five Orders of Perriwigs as they were Worn at the Late Coronation and Measured Architectomically," which satirized the wigs and their wearers by creating a scholarly model for comprehending the various styles as if they were architectural features such as columns. The "orders" of wigs included "Episcopal" (clergy), "Old Peerian or Aldermanic" (peers and city officials), "Lexonic" (lawyers), "Composite or Half Natural," and "Queerinthian," each diagrammed to show its faces and architectural components.[46] The image made wigs and their wearers seem ridiculous, and inverted the serious attention and deference both received.

Although wigs for daily wear by ordinary middle- and upper-class men became shorter and straighter across the first half of the eighteenth century, they remained important to the performance of masculine gentility. Increasing in popularity were bob wigs, a plain chin- to shoulder-length style curled under all around. Oliver Delancey of New York acquired a wardrobe of wigs in the early 1740s from peruke maker William DeWitt, who enjoyed the clientage of other prominent residents such as Samuel Bayard and William Livingston. The bob wig, or what DeWitt recorded as "boob wigg," was his best seller. Delancey purchased three perukes late in 1742, another "dark" one in February of 1743, and still another "pale boob wigg" in March.

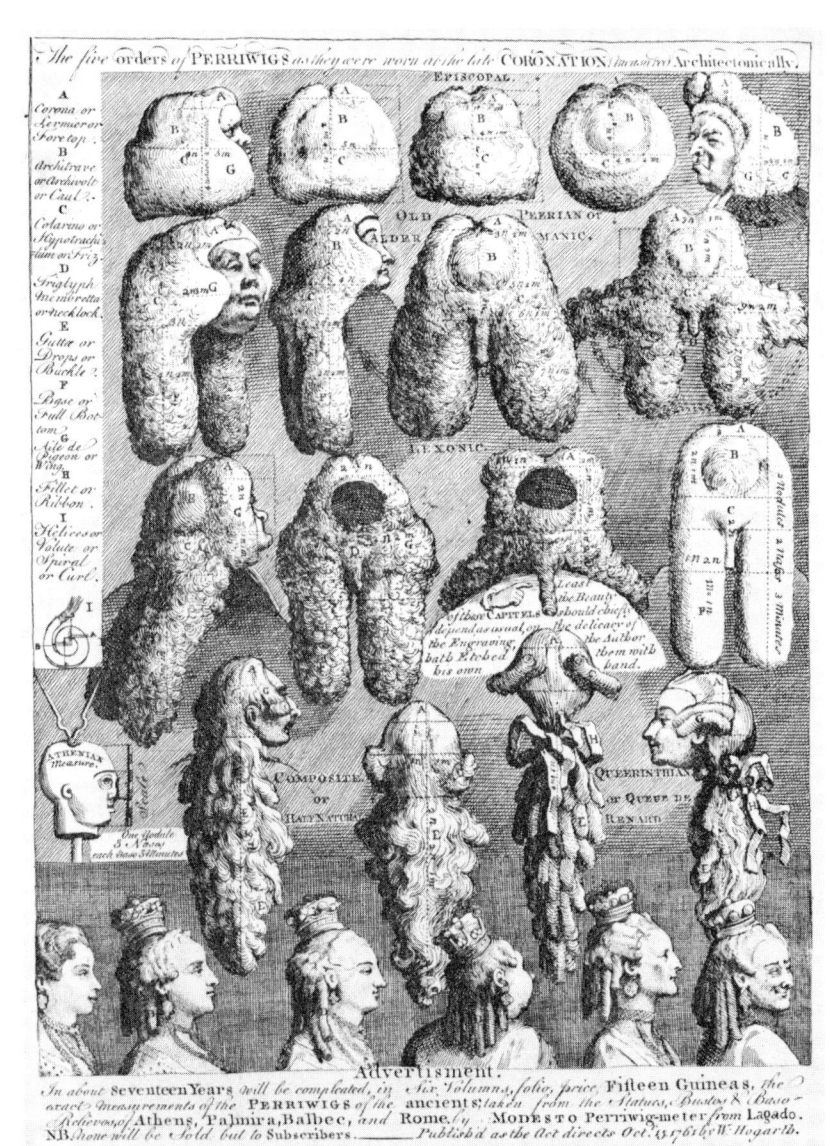

"The Five Orders of Periwigs," by William Hogarth, London, 1761.

At times DeWitt specified whether the wigs were "of englesh haire," as these were the most expensive and sought after.[47]

To ensure English hair, perhaps, Robert Pringle of Charleston procured his wigs directly from London. In 1739, he purchased a "good light collored bob wig and a light colour ramelie wigg," which he wanted "pretty full of hair" and made "very neat and fashionable." The ramelie style had full sides and a braided tail in the back with bows at the top and bottom. The bob wig cost three guineas, and the other was cheaper at fifty shillings. In 1744, he requested a "fashionable light periwig . . . either a good neat bobb or tail wig, I mean a bob major." As was the case with his attire, Pringle had not enjoyed a new wig since he received the previous ones from London because "there are none good for anything to be had here." Unfortunately, the wig did not suit him as well as the clothes. It was too large and full, but could be easily disposed of in Charleston, he reasoned. He then asked for another made with less hair and of a color not likely to turn yellow in South Carolina's hot sun. Thomas Bradford also recalled that wigs were ubiquitous—"universally worn," he claimed, as preeminent markers of gentility.[48] Styles changed, but the social significance of wigs for men did not. No man of rank preferred natural hair until late in the century, whereas fashionable women sported their own locks until the late 1760s.

Women's hoops, men's wigs, and the debates surrounding them exposed tensions between gender positions and gender relations in Anglo-America. In theory, dress was supposed to perform and establish identity—one's position as a man or woman as well as one's social rank. But particular fashions could undermine notions of fixed identity because, like fashion itself, position was always situational and relational, created through behaviors and practices. Focusing on fashion became a means of regulating relations between men and women through the disciplining of appearances. These styles gave material, visual, and economic expression to a kind of power that lay outside institutional regulation, one that existed in the space of social and romantic relationships between the sexes.

Pursuing the Mode

Although fashion as a concept was feminine, particular styles were masculine or feminine, and men and women alike pursued the mode in British North American cities. However they may have tried to distance themselves from attention to personal adornment and its associations, following fashion was by no means insignificant to men of various ranks. Dr. Alexander

Hamilton acknowledged the power and importance of fashion after dining one evening "in the company of two Philadelphians who could not be easy" because they were underdressed for dinner by Boston standards. "What strange creatures we are, and what trifles make us uneasy!" he marveled. "It is no mean jest that such worthless things as caps and wigs should disturb our tranquility when we imagine they are wore out of season," he continued, noting the importance of seasonal propriety. Yet he too felt out of place that night, having discovered a "great hole" in the lapel of his coat, "to hide which employed so much of my thoughts that, for want of attention, I could not give a pertinent answer when spoken to."[49] Fear of appearing inappropriate tied his tongue in mixed company, behavior that might then mark him as ungenteel. A hole in one's coat could rend the delicate social fabric woven by gentility and put a person's reputation at risk.

In theory, a man of rank need consult no one; in reality, tailors, wig makers, and the world of public opinion, of which women were very much a part, often literally and figuratively shaped the male figure. As "Poor Richard" poetically put it in 1745:

> Nothing exceeds in Ridicule, no doubt,
> A Fool in Fashion, but a Fool that's *out*.
> His Passion for Absurdity's so strong
> He cannot bear a Rival in the Wrong
> Tho' wrong the mode, comply; more sense is shown
> In wearing others Follies than your own.
> If what is out of Fashion most you prize
> Methinks you should endeavour to be wise.[50]

The verse suggested the fine line that a gentleman trod when it came to attire. Although fashion might be folly, to be hopelessly out of fashion was the worst misstep, marking a person as a socially inept.

Helping to generate tension between performances of social status and gender identity was that masculine display in attire rivaled feminine in the early eighteenth century. Men's fashionable wear was as sumptuous and visually arresting as women's. High-ranking men of Restoration England not only sported long, curled periwigs but wore suit coats that nearly covered the breeches, giving the appearance of a skirt. One prominent scholar of costume has even described men's formal suits of the 1740s as having a "feminine silhouette"—by modern standards, perhaps, but not necessarily those of the day. The sleeves of men's coats and women's gowns were full and cuffed, with ruffles peeking from beneath.[51] Likewise, men's and

Daniel Parke II, by John Closterman, 1706, oil on canvas. Daniel Parke II appears as the epitome of English masculine power in the Stuart period. Virginia Historical Society (1985.35).

women's fashionable dress shared in the rich colors and patterns of costly textiles, finished with a high degree of ornamentation. Women often chose floral-patterned fabrics, and men's garments also sported flowered embellishments. One man's silk needlework purse, bearing the embroidered inscription "John Smith's Pocketbook, 1744," was decorated with apple trees, flowers, mushrooms, a bird, and a goat.[52] This is not to suggest that gender distinctions in attire—suits versus gowns, aprons versus waistcoats—did not exist. But many elements that to modern western eyes might be coded "feminine" were, in fact, hallmarks of masculine status. As the portrait of Daniel Parke attests, elite men were the peacocks, using attire that was obviously costly in terms of color and pattern to announce social rank and attract attention.

Although wigs and coats alike shortened as the century progressed, eye-catching attire for men continued to reign supreme. Thomas Bradford, an octogenarian who supplied material for John Fanning Watson's *Annals of Philadelphia* in the 1820s, recalled of the 1750s that "red cloth coats were considerably worn" and that "waistcoats were made of silk velvet with flowers," sporting "great descending pockets." Coats had "large cuffs with big skirts," and shirts were ruffled. Breeches, adorned with "paste-gem" buckles, hit at the knee, showing off the well-formed leg. "Shoe buckles and knee buckles of silver were general," he remembered, and "big broaches in the bosom."[53] Flash and dash was the order of the day for the man looking to cut a figure. Fashion may have been theoretically "feminized," but it was essential to the performance of masculine status. Even the "poorer classes," Bradford claimed, donned "gold and silver sleeve buttons set with stones of paste." They may not have been real gems, but from a distance who could tell?

As the volume and variety of imports to British North America increased in the 1740s and 1750s, expanding access to former luxury goods, acquiring items in London, directly from London, or through social connections there became a mark of distinction for colonial elites.[54] Although the influx of fashion tradespeople, many claiming London training, meant that colonists might be assured of the most fashionable fits (or so advertisements claimed), attaining true sartorial distinction entailed going to the source of *la mode*.[55] The wellborn continually raised the status bar, requiring fine manners, speech, carriage, conversation to validate fashionable dress, but dress itself remained an important means of performing position in front of those within and without their social circle. Men pursued the mode for themselves and for their "ladies" at home. The procurement and adoption of the latest styles connected men and women in the colonies and across the Atlantic, as they used fashion to cement the social and romantic connections so essential to the performance and maintenance of rank.

England held a prominent place within the expanding fashion trades in the port cities, as tailors and seamstresses who claimed to work in the "newest" or "latest" fashion touted not only their modish skills but the acquisition of such training in London. For example, "Nathniel Bowser, taylor from

London," opened a store on Hamilton's Wharf in Philadelphia in 1748. For "further encouragement" of new business, he brought with him a "choice assortment" of fabrics, all purchased "at the best hand in London." In New York, mantua makers Mary Wallace and Clementia Ferguson promoted the "fixed correspondence" that allowed them to know from London "the earliest fashions in miniature," likely referring to small fashion dolls whose dress reproduce the mode. Likewise, New York tailor John Forrest, operating under the "sign of the Gold-Lac'd Waistcoat," a dazzling example of elite men's dress, announced in 1755 that customers found his work "as much to their satisfaction as in London."[56] The growing presence of the fashion trades in British North American cities indicates the importance of skill in creating fit, of knowledge in creating styles, and the importance of both in the creation of fashionability.

Yet not all colonial men believed the claims of colonial tailors, or felt them worthy of patronage. The wealthy merchant James Beekman expressed his low regard for all fashion tradesmen in New York City when he composed a lengthy epistle to the amusingly named Robert Doughty in 1749. Along with detailed instructions, Beekman sent a coat and breeches of his own, since there was "no Depending on our taylors to take the measure." He wanted one coat "of the very best broadcloth . . . a good Black and lined with a superfine shelloon" (likely a piece of mourning wear), another "cloth coat the same colour as the enclosed pattern," and a blue one. He was especially particular about fit, cautioning, "I have a further desire of you of which I would not have you fail and is often neglected." "Take particular care," Beekman continued, "to take in anuff of the Cloth at the Sides and Sleaves that In case any of them Should Prove two Narrow by my growing Lustyer they may be Lett out and made Larger."[57] Clearly, James Beekman's girth was expanding along with his business. Although he did not wish to expend the energy and funds necessary to obtain London-made attire for some time, the prospect of fine tailoring was worth the hassle and expense.

Robert Pringle of Charleston also patronized London tailors almost exclusively. In January of 1739 he sent a lengthy order to David Glen with the instructions that the clothes be made "in the best manner you can." Like Beekman, he advised that they "not be made scanty but in every way large and full," for garments too big could be altered whereas nothing could be made larger. Pringle continued, "All the cloaths you have hitherto sent me having been too little and scanty for me which hope you'll take care to prevent in the future." In addition to fit, Pringle was particular about fabric and trimming but deferred somewhat to the knowledge of the tradesman in determining modishness. He requested a riding coat of a "fashionable middling colour," a superfine scarlet broadcloth waistcoat with "gold buttons and a full lace with best gold lace or gold arras and fashionable," and a banyan made of "very fashionable worsted damask of the finest and best sort" with "the two sides . . . of different colours." He also asked for extra buttons since there was "no matching them here."[58] The port cities might be flush with consumer goods, but not all things could be had.

When the items finally arrived in April of the following year, Pringle was pleased to note that "everything fits me well," but he observed that the coat had too much wadding for Charleston's warm climate and thought the banyan rather "dear." Again in 1744 he ordered a black suit of clothes from David Glen. Asking his brother Andrew to deliver the missive, Robert claimed that he had only had one suit made in Charleston since 1739 because the "workmanship [is] very bad." Given that several years had passed he also instructed Andrew, "If he should be dead you'll please employ whoever you think proper."[59] Clearly, any London tailor was preferable to one in Charleston.

Even Poor Richard himself seized the opportunity to patronize a London tailor during his sojourn in the city. On three occasions in 1757 Benjamin Franklin paid tailor Rob Christopher for unspecified work, shelling out over 133 pounds total. He also purchased two pairs of sterling silver shoe and knee buckles. The previous year, Franklin had included in his almanac the advice, "When you incline to have new cloaths, look first well over the old ones and see if you cannot shift with them another year." The maxim urged readers to remember that a patch on a coat was preferable to empty pockets.[60] Franklin did buy some plain black ribbon and had some shoes and hose "mended" in keeping with his waste not, want not maxims—but these items and services were for his servants.[61]

While Franklin cultivated his own appearance in London, he also purchased items to send home to Philadelphia, a standard practice among men of means. Colonial distance from the seat of the mode created interdependence between men and women. Although contemporary wisdom held that women were the ones most knowledgeable à la mode, acquiring the latest fashions from Europe meant that elite British American men, more likely to travel, might transmit items even in advance of the dry goods trade, seeing firsthand what was worn by the ladies of London. Male travelers hoped to please and helped to dress fashionable women in the port cities, working to ensure that their wives, sisters, and daughters would be the most stylish in their communities. In 1741, Eliza Lucas's father sent her "a piece of rich yellow lutestring" consisting of nineteen yards of material, "ditto of blue for my mama," as well as a piece of holland and cambric.[62] Years later, Eliza's own daughter Harriott received from an English lady a "very gentile present" of a fan, which her mother approvingly pronounced "a curiosity," and a pompon, "the prettiest we ever saw." Pinckney wrote that the little girl was delighted, since they were "the first that have reached this part of the world, so she has the opportunity of setting the fashion."[63] Although a wealthy Englishwoman was undoubtedly a reliable source for *la mode*, in general, men did the supplying of tokens from abroad. While Anglo-American women depended on these men to convey the stuff of distinction, the men burnished their own reputations through reflected glory. Yet men also distanced themselves from the mode by denying their own knowledge and agency, or by legitimating the tendering of goods as expressions of sentiment rather than status. Women, however, might disdain the items, the men's taste, and even the men themselves.

Henry Livingston of New York revealed such anxiety when he wrote to his brother Robert from London in 1744, explaining that the "sample padusoy," a heavy silk brocaded fabric that his sister had given him, had been lost, perhaps in transit. This was unfortunate because Henry had intended to use it as a guide for purchasing a larger piece of something similar. "Unwilling to rely" on his own judgment, he turned to "some ladys to make choice of a fashionable colour." He included twenty-two yards of the cloth in his package to Robert, but not without some trepidation. "In case sister does not approve of the colour," he clarified, "Mr. Cheese has promised to change it for me."[64] Livingston, a man of wealth and taste, solicited and deferred to the opinions of a group of knowledgeable urban women in choosing a fashionable fabric for his sibling. Furthermore, he gladly acted as his sister's London broker in her pursuit of fashionability—appropriateness of which for her environs *she* would ultimately determine.

Other men felt more secure in their abilities to choose wisely. In 1754, two cousins engaged in a similar correspondence in order to obtain an elegant gown for a female relative. As Michael Gratz was preparing to leave London and join his brother in business in Philadelphia, he received a letter from his cousin Hyman Gratz. The Gratz brothers had acquired not only the essentials of commercial training during their London education but also certain notions about "fitness in dress and address," from which Hyman hoped to benefit. In fact, Michael Gratz's appearance was fancy enough to cause another cousin, Solomon Henry, to worry that his tastes marked him as a "nabob," an epithet levied at West Indian planters trying to cut figures in the metropole. Likewise, Hyman wrote, "From appearances you wish perhaps to become an English nabob. I certainly think it is your duty first to ask my opinion." Hyman's tone teased, for in actuality he wrote to take advantage of his cousin's expertise in fashion, explaining that his daughter recently became engaged, and encouraged Michael, before he departed for Philadelphia, to "look for a rich dress for . . . the bride."[65] Hyman wanted his daughter to appear elegant and fashionable on her wedding day, as he gave her to another, and implicitly trusted Michael's taste. Although his cousin's days must have been full of preparations for the journey to Philadelphia, the father of the bride considered the selection of a gown important enough to broach the favor.

Whereas Livingston's sister had requested the paduasoy, we know not whether Gratz's daughter wanted a wedding gown from abroad. Given the prized nature of London goods, we can imagine her delight; but what if the dress was simply "wrong," whatever the reason? Anglo-American men traveling abroad could claim a fair degree of authority with respect to the mode, but the women back home for whom they procured goods also had a say, men realized. Benjamin Franklin's letters to his wife and daughter in Philadelphia serve as explanations about his choices—preemptive strikes of a sort. In 1757, Franklin promised to buy a "crimson satin cloak . . . the newest fashion" for his wife, Deborah, and a "black silk" for daughter Sally, and throughout the following spring he continued to send gifts. The accompanying letters reveal the degree to which "fashionability" trumped all other considerations in his choices, including personal aesthetics or preferences. He sent Sally a "new fashion'd white hat and cloak" and a pair of shoe buckles "made of French paste stones," which he claimed were "next to diamonds in luster." Amid his assurances about the fashionability of various items, and the authority that such claims established, Franklin distanced himself from *la mode*. He drolly stated that the four silver salt ladles he sent Deborah were "in the newest but ugliest fashion," and included with them a tea table cloth, explaining that "nobody breakfasts here on a naked table."[66] Whether or not Franklin approved of a covered table, or appreciated the design of the salt spoons (clearly, he did not), they were "the fashion," and thus desirable. Better to be a fool in fashion than a fool that was out, he supposed. The goods were not his taste, he implied, but simply what was in vogue, separating his powers of discernment from that of the throng. Thus Franklin could at once keep feminized fashion at arm's length and accept less responsibility for what his wife might deem a poor choice.

Letters exchanged between William Templeton Franklin, Benjamin

Franklin's son from an extramarital relationship, and Elizabeth Graeme of Philadelphia suggest the role that items of fashion, and concern over their appropriateness for the recipient or in a colonial setting, might play in courtship and romance. "Billy" Franklin, as he was called, claimed that Graeme, whom he sometimes addressed "thou dear Tormentor," excelled all the "ladies of distinguished rank and merit" with whom he shared "intimacy." As a token of his affection, he sent "one of the newest fashion'd muffs and tippets worn by the gayest ladies of quality," drawing a direct connection between adoption of the latest style and social position. The fur boa, worn around the neck, and the purselike covering for the hands were in imitation of a gift the rakish protagonist of Henry Fielding's 1748 novel *Tom Jones* gave to his love Sophia. In a lengthy, pleading letter, Franklin half-seriously bemoaned the "contemptuous reception she gave a small present [he] sent her, particularly the muff and Tippet which, though worn by People of the first fashion in England she sneeringly treats as a gawdy Gewgaw." He had attempted to win her affection through the gift of a fashionable item, citing a "tenderer motive" in giving it than perhaps she imagined: "As she was often pleased to liken me to Tom Jones, and express herself much delighted with the Story of Sophia's Muff mentioned in that novel, I could not help flattering myself that this might, in the same manner, tend to raise or keep alive some soft emotions in my favour. But now, alas, I see there is not intrinsic merit in a Muff."[67] Franklin was being a bit cheeky—he knew it would take far more than a muff and tippet to win the learned Graeme—but he also seemed to hope that the muff and tippet would at least impress her and begin to bind her heart to his.

Yet for all his efforts, this Tom did not wind up with his Sophia. Who ended the relationship and why remains uncertain; one theory runs that Franklin, surrounded by attractive and sophisticated women in London, took up with another and married her before returning to the colonies. In any case, a few years later Graeme's father "thanked God" that his daughter had "escaped him."[68] Ultimately, according to her relatives, Graeme had not been fooled by Billy Franklin's pretty words and presents, the weapons he used to win her. Despite his apparent desire for her, made manifest in his gifts that recalled sentimental fiction and promised to heighten Graeme's fashionable distinction in Philadelphia, he was, it seemed, a man "of fashion" in the worst sense. Perhaps Sarah Drinker of Philadelphia put it most clearly in a poem copied into her commonplace book that made explicit the relationship between fashionability and unsuitable, even destructive, courtships:

> Thus many waste their precious time
> And fool away their youthful prime
> And spend their money too
> In following every foolish fashion
> That's newly brought into the nation
> And some themselves undo
> For gay with gay acquaintance take
> And oftentimes such matches make
> As ruin both at last[69]

Drinker connected expenditure with relationships that were as gay and insubstantial as the "foolish fashion" that both stimulated and signified them. Both men and women would be ruined, but the former faced economic downfall while the latter could expect sexual degradation.

Despite the association of fashion with women, to be a man in fashion was desirable. Colonial men seeking to polish their appearances and reputations procured items from fashion's source, claiming for themselves authority "back home" while giving the women to whom they sent items a leg up on the mode. Yet these men often relied on the judgment of others—whether London ladies, tailors, or their own wives, daughters, and sisters—to validate their choices. Thus pursuit of the latest styles from London connected genteel men and women, affording each a measure of power within the cultivation of a fashionable appearance. This mutual dependence, however, generated as much anxiety as pleasure.

Other Pursuits

Fashion was feminized, yet pursued by men and women; necessary to express gender identity, yet feared to undermine it as well as proper gender relations; desirable as an indicator of high rank, yet disdained as a sign of pretension. As Anglo-Americans turned to stock types to help them locate people on the social landscape, extreme fashionability served as the marker of a suspect figure, someone of whom to be wary. Recognizable "persons of fashion" such as fops and coquettes insinuated themselves with members of the opposite sex, turning innocent sociability or romantic courtship into sexual conquest and social climbing. Thus fashion's power might disrupt legitimate relations between men and women and a smoothly functioning "marriage market" among social equals.[70]

Newspapers such as the *New York Gazette* took up the problem of how fashion negatively influenced relationships between men and women. Print was increasingly the institution for regulating and disciplining appearances in the eighteenth century, even as it served as a forum for promoting the consumption of fashionable goods. As one fictional exchange claimed, fashion had the power to forestall proper unions. In the summer of 1731, a group of male "petitioners" wrote that they stood in need of wives, but the "gay and splendid appearance" that women of their "station" affected made it "very difficult to distinguish them from People of the best Estates in Town." All they desired, the men claimed, were "spouses of their own rank." As rough, simple men, unschooled in the ways of fashion, they dared not approach the women "thus guarded with an Air of Quality . . . and covered with Silk and Satin without."[71] Two weeks later, a response from the "Court for Reformation of Manners" appeared. The "Court," likely a triple reference to law, courtship, and the Crown, agreed that the splendid style of young women did indeed discourage the petitioners. It also concluded that the ladies did seem to esteem themselves above those men who were actually their social equals. But in issuing its "verdicts" the Court excused the women's appearance (if they could reasonably afford to maintain it, it stipulated) on the grounds that they only wished to attract "beaus," most of whom valued external artifice more than internal worth. Such fashionable men likely enjoyed a plentiful stock of money, "which is the aim of these Ladies."[72]

Several themes mingled in the satirical exchange. The petitioners blamed the women for dressing and acting in such a way that confused social hierarchy and therefore thwarted appropriate courtship and marriage. The Court then rejoined, chastising the women for snubbing the men but not for the goal of marrying "up" in rank that caused them to cultivate their appearances. Men, certain men in particular, rendered a fashionable appearance necessary on the marriage market. Rather than suggesting that the women "lower" themselves, the Court cheekily advocated bringing the men up to their standards. This could be accomplished through paid education under the tutelage of polite women. Knowledge of politeness and the ability to impart that wisdom supplied an avenue toward economic gain—perhaps a more direct route, the piece implied, toward what the social-climbing women, tricked out in the garb of performed status, sought in the first place.

Likewise, a man who appeared too fashionable had one thing on his mind—if he possessed much of a mind. Fashionability bled all too easily into foppery, code for a host of behaviors and social practices open to ridicule. A character that first emerged on stage in the Restoration era, along with new forms and levels of consumption, the fop embodied a slew of distasteful characteristics, all of which possessed gendered meanings that expressed status anxieties. Fops possessed the easily discernible trait of vanity demonstrated through their excessive attention to dress and appearance. The juxtaposition of finery with behavior that seemed either too rough or too affected revealed the fop.[73]

The association of foppery with foolishness is perhaps the oldest.[74] The meaning dates to a period when "fool" indicated a man kept around the court to provide amusement and entertainment, a jester at whose expense members of the nobility enjoyed laughter. It suggests that the man preoccupied with cutting an elegant figure never succeeded, appearing ridiculous and yet entirely unaware of it, setting himself up as the target of jests and becoming the object of satire. A fop's laughable appearance derived from the premise that he already was a fool—a person who possessed no sense or judgment, and who lived only to please others. Yet fops were not merely foolish; they were downright stupid, often described as having ornamented yet empty heads. A poem appearing in the *New York Gazette* lamented a world filled with "so many fops, for one that wise is."[75] By midcentury, Poor Richard proclaimed, "Vain are the studies of the fop and beau who all their care expend on outward show." Fine clothing, he continued, signified a "light and empty mind" devoid of content.[76]

Above all, the fop was effeminate.[77] Since passion for finery was the hallmark of women, writers insisted that "such men as appear fondest of being remarkable for a shewy and glittering outside" were "vain, empty, and effeminate." Two adjectives commonly associated with women described the fop: "fawning" and "servile."[78] Yet this effeminacy, evidenced by the fop's appearance and appetite for display, manifested itself in an appetite for women. According to one 1738 poem, the fop shunned manly pursuits such as war, preferring other conquests:

> Thus the soldier, seeking glory
> Courting death in rude alarms
> Finds at home, the usual story
> Some spruce fop in Chloe's arms.[79]

The term "fop" replaced "gallant," suggesting that the pursuit of women, as well as of fashion, characterized the fop.[80]

Although fops were appetite-driven, like women, they were not women. Rather, men of fashion inhabited an ambiguous gender position. "Fribble," a common eighteenth-century term, demonstrates the uncertain gender of fashionable men. The *Dictionary of Love* deemed this "great critic in dress" a "no species"—neither male nor female."[81] To call a man a fribble was a gross insult, Philadelphian Thomas Bradford remembered, recalling that silk umbrellas appeared only "after the arrival of Dr. John Moran who wore one and was deemed a *Fribble*."[82] During a period in which the line between male and female was hardening, fops and fribbles were liminal figures.[83] Fashionable men represented the tensions of an Anglophone world in which fashion was feminine in theory but heterosocial in practice, and extending to persons of all ranks besides.

Effeminizing predatory men, suggesting that men surrendered their status *as men* in pursuit of fashionability, becoming dependent on dress and on society's opinions of it, was a means of expressing perhaps the most bothersome characteristic of the fop: his social aspirations. A fop was "a pretender of wit, wisdom, or accomplishments."[84] Upon leaving New York City, Hamilton spoke of the number of "fops" there who had "high ideas of themselves," never having observed "different ranks of men in polite nations" in order to know "what constitutes that difference of degrees."[85] Hamilton's fops imagined themselves to be socially prominent when they were, in fact, simply ignorant of their low status, a function of their parochialism.

To what or whom did fops owe their inflated senses of self and status? Women served as the primary instruments of a fop's ascension, as culpable in "making" the man of fashion as tailors and wig makers. Since fondness for clothing and display marked women's nature, fops played upon this supposed proclivity as they sought the company of "the fair," seeking feminine approval. As a letter to the editor of the *New York Gazette* noted in 1732, "Tom Tinsel," who "thought himself undrest in a plain suit of clothes," did not care to be valued by "men of sense"; the ladies were his "chiefest concern."[86] According to a 1738 poem, the man of fashion turned himself into a "lady's lap dog," a "happy fopling of the fair." His success clearly showed "what some women's fav'rites are."[87] Another verse speculated on the causes of foppishness thusly:

> His wit is spiritless and void of Grace,
> Who wants th' Assurance of Brocade and Lace,
> Whilst the gay FOP genteely talks of Weather—
> The Fair in Raptures doat upon his Feather
> He dresses, fences: What avails to know?
> For Women chuse their Men, like silks, for Show.[88]

As fops courted social approval, they preyed on women romantically, resembling another stock character, the rake.[89] When the soldier trod off to war, the fop insinuated himself with "Chloe."

Yet women needed to beware, for true love and affection never guided a man of fashion's behavior. He loved himself far better than anyone else. While in Newport, Dr. Alexander Hamilton met Dr. Keith, who "passed for a man of great gallantry." Keith showed him a drawer full of "trophys of the fair," mementos such as "tore fans, fragments of gloves, whims . . . and other such trumpery." Keith did not really care for women; he wished only to mark his conquests with pilfered goods that fill what he termed his "cabinet of curiosities." He was a "man of fashion," which the *Dictionary of Love* defined as "one who has insinuated himself into the hearts of two or three women."[90] The wealth of entries describing fashionable types, as well as definitions for "fashion," "dress," and "toilette" in a book ostensibly devoted to the language of love, suggests the relationship between passion and fashion. Both stemmed from appetite yet disappeared quickly, leaving nothing of substance behind. They came together most clearly in a fop's appetites for fashion, women, and social status, and the mutually constructed nature of those desires.

The man of fashion's exploits invested women with great power but also assigned them serious blame. An essay appearing in the *American Magazine and Historical Chronicle* in September of 1745 put it very clearly: "If then it be true that Men . . . become wise men or fools, brave or effeminate, independents or prostitutes, as the Ladies they converse with would have them to be; how severe a satire is a fop . . . on the particular fair one he is devoted to?"[91]

Certain women, such as the "airy and frocklicksome" ones so taken with Newport's Dr. Keith, engendered foppery. Others, such as "Miss Modish," a *New York Mercury* essay claimed in 1757, downright required it. The piece recounted the tale of a "bachelor" and his long quest to woo a belle who held the opinion that "one might be as well out of the world as out of the mode." She sorely used him by demanding that he follow every latest and absurd fashion in dress and address, the essay claimed, yet continued to reject him no matter how he appeared. Instead, Miss Modish admired "Mr. Foppington," the essayist lamented.[92] Rather, women should refine their tastes in such a way that men would not need to appear overly fashionable or "foppish" in order to gain their attention; to mind the proscription of the 1744 poem "To a Lady Who Ask'd What Is Love" and know that love was not "centered in the Beau . . . who all consists in outward show, And want of Wit by

Dress supplies." Or to be like the subject of "The Lady's Choice," who required that her husband be "neat, yet not foppish."[93]

Although faint was the sartorial border between fashionable and foppish given mid-eighteenth-century high fashion for men, the onus was on the ladies to distinguish the genteel gentleman from the preening and predatory fop or his cousin, the rake. Women's supposed inherent inclinations toward finery made them the best arbiters of fashion but the least suitable judges of men; they had to be trained lest worthy men fall short. Fops, fribbles, coquettes, and other persons "of fashion" threatened to ascend the social ladder through social and romantic conquest, bending the rules of gender along the way and giving women the lion's share of social power.

When Dr. Alexander Hamilton reflected on the peccadillo of a minister in Boston, he wrote, "The wisest men have been led into silly scrapes by the attractions of that vain sex, which, I think, explains a certain enigmatic verse: Diceti grammatici cur mascula nomina cunnus Et cur Famineum mentula nomen habet." According to Hamilton the maxim translated as, "the first is masculine, because it attracts the male, the latter feminine because it is an effeminate follower of the other." In this formulation a woman who attracted "the male" was masculine, and the man who was thus attracted was the "effeminate follower." The hierarchy of gendered power and of rank was inverted. The "unfortunate" clergyman was too taken by the woman, the daughter of his landlady and thus beneath him in status, to care. His desires caused him to impregnate her and thus "lose his living."[94] Hamilton prided himself on knowing a coquette when he saw her, but apparently the minister did not.

The dual attraction of men and women to fashion and to one another could produce power inversions with respect to accepted hierarchies of gender and rank. Fashion in dress could help inhabitants of the port cities "know" one another and form legitimate social, filial, and romantic connections. Yet, some feared, it might also undermine this project, facilitating improper relationships detrimental to social order. Thus, the desirability of fashion and its pursuit by men and women alike proceeded alongside unflattering, highly gendered depictions of the mode and its adherents. The fact that no one placed himself or herself within the categories of opprobrium helped account for the gap between discourse and practice. A fop or coquette was always someone else.

The tension between social relations and social order acquired a gendered dimension through fashion, and the strain between gender relations and gender order was expressed through the language of social status. Beneath the disciplining of appearances lay anxieties about behaviors that such appearances indicated and the consequences of those actions. If social position could be performed through fashion in dress, which could result in the achievement of actual status through securing the right kinds of connections, then it was important either to hone one's powers of discernment, like Hamilton, or to decouple fashion from status entirely. A fashionable man thus inhabited an awkward position—socially esteemed but potentially suspect, depending on who was judging, as writers warned women of fops who preyed on their position and their virtue.

The ideological feminization of fashion, coupled with fashion's role in social and romantic life, meant that women enjoyed a great deal of power in social relations. Although in the colonial context women sometimes depended on men who traveled abroad to supply them with the "latest," women remained acknowledged arbiters of fashion. The desirability of fashion bespoke two forms of dependence: of men on women and of colonists on England. The world of fashion was not, however, segregated from other arenas of power but intersected with transatlantic commerce and even politics. By midcentury, the gender and status politics of fashion helped produce new forms of masculinity and femininity, new gendered expressions of status, and ultimately, new fashions.

Country Modes

CULTURAL POLITICS AND
POLITICAL RESISTANCE

3

During the spring of 1766, Robert R. Livingston, a lawyer and member of the prominent Livingston clan of New York, took on the persona of a wife in a piece of satire he likely intended for publication. The "letter," a missive from a woman in the city to her husband in the country, gave the following "melancholy account" of the social scene in New York in the wake of agreements among local merchants and retailers not to import English goods. Livingston's female narrator complained that the town's beaux, "whose brains like their hearts" she regarded as "too much devoted to nothing ever to have suffered any idea . . . but such as we or their glass inspired," had become "so infiltrated with politicks" that she scarcely ever heard "a clever thing said (unless indeed by the gentlemen of the army)." The fashionable men of New York engaged only in the "tedious recital of the cabals of the statements in the ministry, the downfall of liberty, and a thousand other such insignificant subjects," she complained. Furthermore, the "lady" lamented, turning to her own "sex," the women had become "so infatuated with this modest dulness that many are resolved to resign the charms of dress and let a horrible homespun covering (which can become none but a country wench) take the place of rich brocade." Although she had repeatedly attempted to convince her cohort that "womans better part is dress and that their empire depends upon it," she feared she would not be able to prevent the wholesale rejection of imported finery. "Must we in nothing be distinguished from meer country dowdies?" she queried. If her husband visited her in the city, she concluded, he would find her "shrowded in a cloud . . . of filthy homespun and homeweave cambrick which it is resolved we must wear because forsooth it is of our own manufacture."[1]

Appropriating the voice of a woman of fashion, one who was living it up in the city, away from her husband, Livingston pitted high-minded masculinity against mindless, foppish effeminacy, and domestic, "country" womanhood versus urbane, artificial femininity. He did this to serve a political end: promoting the renunciation of the fabrics that were the British empire's stock in trade and encouraging the attendant adoption of domestically produced homespun in their place. By lampooning and shaming those colonists, particularly Anglo-American women, whose dependence upon and adherence to metropolitan fashion trumped their sense of domestic as well as political duty, he employed a version of gentility that required throwing off traditional, feminized trappings of social status. His female narrator, although ostensibly of high rank, was vain and selfish in her preference for brocade, not genteel. Her form of social life was empty, frivolous, and feminized, while discussions of politics were meaningful, serious, and masculine.

Livingston engaged in a cultural trend that reenvisioned social status in gendered ways and, in turn, remade gender ideals in class-specific terms. Around midcentury, a set of domestic discourses, meaning both household and colonial, about social and gendered propriety coalesced in response to the growing volume of consumer goods available in the port cities and the power Anglo-American women exercised through fashion.[2] This revisioning of status had its roots in literary sentimentalism, the culture of sensibility, and the Scottish Enlightenment,[3] and was visually embraced by colonial elites in their increasingly understated yet still luxe sartorial choices. The emerging categories and hierarchies underpinned and informed the resistance movement of the 1760s. Crafted in a climate of widespread consumption, putting relations between men and women at its center, and drawing on an existing taxonomy of fashionable types, Livingston's satire reveals the ways in which the contests over fashion that unfolded during the first half of the eighteenth century shaped the imperial crises of the 1760s. The colonial resistance movement became a crucible of contests over relations between the sexes and social hierarchy, and the intersection of the two.[4]

Indeed, the imperial crisis seemed to magnify attempts to police urban social landscapes and their practices of fashionable display. Resistance to Parliament's acts supplied a new context for old fashion-focused contests over status and gender, loading prescriptions of modesty, virtue, and sense and accompanying proscriptions of vanity and artifice with political weight and making their enforcement quasi-institutional. Likewise, discourses intended to discipline appetites and curtail expenditures found a new raison d'être in a climate of political resistance. Men of means and influence such as Robert R. Livingston and Benjamin Franklin used the crisis to enforce a vision in which men and women of sense and virtue, not of fashion, comprised colonial society—particularly elite circles—checked one another when necessary, and set the example for others. In fact, nonconsumption served as a useful political tool due, in some measure, to the contests and cooperation between the sexes that had long animated social relations.[5]

Although the rejection of imported goods could be an inclusive practice in which colonists of all ranks might participate, the printed encouragements of nonconsumption promoted emulation and utilized hierarchies of rank and gender. In the hands of colonial resisters, the renunciation of fashion and embrace of homespun relied on much the same forms of social order as did adoption of *la mode*—ones in which elite men and women performed for one another and then set the *ton* for others. In this idealized world, however, women maintained social influence only if they hewed to certain gender ideals that at once distinguished them from men and earned them a place in political discourse—namely productive (yet polite) domesticity. Moreover, they had to forgo a former source of power: personal choice in attire. As fashion became a flashpoint of political resistance during the 1760s, nonconsumption campaigns proved to be a handy means of reconciling a movement toward home rule with concerns about who would rule at home, as resisters struggled with how to foment popular resistance without sacrificing social and gendered hierarchy. Yet social arbiters and political agitators consistently confronted practices that flew in the face of their prescriptions and proscriptions, suggesting that the period during and immediately after the Seven Years' War witnessed contests over cultural authority, conflicts that the resistance movement tapped into and furthered. Who, in the end, claimed the power to define what social status and gender identity looked like, and what would this mean for fashion's cultural capital in the port cities?

No "Gewgaws": Domestic Discourses

Hannah Callender of Philadelphia was a woman of sense and taste, not of fashion. Born in 1737 to William and Katharine Callender, Hannah entered the ranks of the city's Quaker elite. She possessed means, family, and education, attending Rebecca Birchall's school for girls during her adolescence. There she formed friendships with other refined and well-read—and of course well-bred—young ladies.[6] Callender and her circle embraced a constellation of traits that comprised an ideal of genteel femininity for young, privileged women of her generation—"the fair." The mores communicated by the diary she kept as a young woman closely match values prescribed in printed materials, chief among them a rejection of any behavior or appearance that might be regarded as showy, and a close connection between external display and internal worth. Callender thus participated privately in a public discussion that used fashion to reassess the relationship between gender and status, creating new standards of feminine gentility that subverted the art of fashionable display to the domestic arts.

A campaign insisting that rank should rely upon distinctions of merit rather than wealth had been under way in the colonies since the early 1750s, led by men such as Benjamin Franklin. Constructing and implementing such a philosophy required several tactics. Dismantling women's "empire" of fashion and display through lauding a modest and domestic feminine ideal was one tactic, a project in which some women themselves participated. Discrediting metropolitan culture through promoting the consumption of American-produced or "domestic" items served as another strategy; and casting appetite in general—and the desire for luxury goods in particular—as dangerous and effeminate was a third. The creation of a supposed meritocracy based on inherent rather than acquired traits and internal rather than external qualities actually masked attempts to maintain social hierarchy by drawing clear lines around what constituted propriety. Yet the tenets of virtuous femininity and masculinity inadvertently paved the way for formerly "unfashionable," rustic provincials, particularly women, to claim a new kind of power, grounded in a newly valued set of distinctions, even as older models persisted.

Prescriptions of genteel femininity cast Anglo-American women as wives or potential wives, instructing them to be simple in address and appearance and cultivated in mind but not artificial in manner in order to secure or keep good husbands. These traits, rather than ornamentation and affectation, were the true markers of femininity and high status, as well as the path to both through making a legitimate match. Such rhetoric was, in part, a reaction to the social power women exercised through fashion and display and concerns over what that influence might mean on the marriage market, as well as within the marital household itself. Gentility had to be made domestic, and women's dependency had to be reinforced.

Yet women like Callender and Eliza Pinckney of South Carolina, although of different regions and religious backgrounds, embraced and promoted the tenets of genteel, domestic womanhood for their own motives of distinction, and thus had a hand in forging the class-specific ideal. They rejected ostentatious display, predicating their feminine identities on characteristics such as taste, education, and piety. No "women of fashion," they forged sentimental rather than vain attachments to the goods that were abundant in their lives, however *à la mode* those items might have been. Such women seemed too secure in their status to rely on mere fashion to express it; yet, because of their social position, being fashionable in the "appropriate" ways came naturally. As practices of consumption engendered prescriptions and proscriptions encouraging women to shun display in favor of sense and taste, defining objects of fashion as objects of sentiment allowed some women to set themselves apart by embodying the qualities so vaunted in the period's print culture, from newspapers and almanacs to sentimental fiction.[7] Their decorous femininity consisted of refinement, sensibility, and virtue, all of which ran counter, discursively, to fashionability.

Beneath the seemingly liberating prescriptions of simplicity and education that some genteel women embraced lay conservative messages about how best to attract a good man and how to be an even better wife. The emphasis on controlling appetites, disciplining desire, and above all eschewing artifice and display in the pursuit of a husband and the maintenance of a household indicates that the developing midcentury rhetoric of genteel femininity possessed a decidedly domestic component. Parliament's Marriage Act of 1753, which required formal, public ceremonies and official licenses to establish economic ties between a couple further entrenched the dependence of a women's material status on marriage.[8] Sexually active women had to be wives in the new legal, public sense, or else they were whores and their offspring bastards, not entitled to any support from the father no matter what private promises of union had been made. As a cultural component to this legal reform, the ideal of genteel, domestic femininity made a woman's social status and very womanhood dependent on her marital status. It was a moral stance responding in part to increasing consumption of goods, the spread of "fashionable" practices, and women's economic and social power in both.

Yet the concept of genteel domesticity was not entirely a reaction to women's consumption per se. It had much to do with the function of fashionable display within the so-called marriage market and the complicated operation of coverture, the legal philosophy whereby a woman's economic identity merged with her husband's within the institution of marriage.[9] When women resorted to show and affectation to attract men, some feared, they threatened to corrupt potential worthy, honest mates whom they might then spend into ruin once netted. Yet when women themselves possessed means, unseemly courtship behavior could lead unworthy, undeserving men into positions of wealth and power; in fact, this was the rationale behind the

Marriage Act of 1753.[10] Therefore, regulating women's appearances, and the behaviors that they suggested, proved critical. Perhaps as troubling to some men, more women in Philadelphia were choosing to remain single, the combination of education and property allowing them to do so.[11] In the face of women's growing independence, be it actual or expressed through spending, a strain of printed prescriptions required the "softer sex" to behave and appear in particular ways in order to prove themselves worthy of being courted by men of sense. Still, certain women possessed their own notions of taste and refinement, for instance, the long-unmarried Elizabeth Graeme, who chose to run a European-style salon out of her ancestral home in the mid-1760s. Independent of means and well educated, Graeme felt little need to marry in haste, although she did, ultimately, wed.[12]

The rhetoric of genteel, domestic femininity responded to women's consumption, the power some women exerted in sociability and courtship, and elite and middling colonial women's "public" lives in salons, assemblies, and the streets. Yet even as it attempted to contain women's behavior in the service of social hierarchy, domestic femininity opened a door for certain women to attract attention and attain status through the cultivation of virtues that existed independent of wealth and its trappings, at least in theory. A lengthy description of Betsey Brook, a Maryland woman Callender met in the fall of 1758, reveals what the twenty-one-year-old diarist admired in a young woman:

> Her person tall and genteel, her complexion fine, her features admirably well proportioned . . . tho not brought up in a city delivered herself with ease and becoming freedom. . . . I never see a more engaging manner than she was mistress of when addressed by a stranger. Her dress was plain and something particular from us: yet coud not be altered in her, without robing her a beauty which seemed intirely her peculiar. A cambletee riding gownd, stomarger of the same, a white silk lace . . . a round eared cap with a little black silk hood, graced as innocent a face as I ever see.[13]

Callender first took note of the woman's form and face, praising her graceful carriage and balanced features. In the diarist's opinion, Brook's physical attractiveness lay in these "natural" attributes above all. Callender then described the decorous and easy way in which she handled herself in company, although she was bred in a rural rather than a cosmopolitan, urban environment. Brook was not artful but seemed polished in a completely genuine manner, an extremely important quality in the journal keeper's opinion. Finally, Callender approvingly noted Brook's "plain" dress, which was nonetheless comprised of camblet, lace, and silk. Although her attire appeared "particular"—different, not in the Quaker style or any other recognizable mode—it imparted an innocent beauty to the girl that was all her own, Callender marveled.[14]

Scottish-born Anne MacVicar Grant, who moved to New York with her family in 1758, lavished similar praise on the daughters of Superintendant of Indian Affairs William Johnson, likely the offspring of his common-law marriage to Molly Brant, a Mohawk Indian. "Never was anything so uniform as their dress, their occupation, and the general tenor of their lives," Grant began. During the day, these "amiable recluses" plied their needlework "for the Ornamental parts of dress, which were the fashion of the day, without knowing to what use they were to be put, for they never wore them." These young women were domestically productive but not fashionable, she noted approvingly. Rather, their dress was as "simple and uniform as everything else; they wore wrappers of the finest chintz and green silk petticoats and this the whole year round without variation." Impervious to changes of mode or even of season, the daughters had a genteel look all their own, and an expensive one at that, considering the fabrics. Crowning this look, their long, beautiful hair was tied with a single ribbon and each wore a calash to shade them from the sun.[15]

Betsey Brook's and the Johnson daughters' physical and behavioral virtues, as chronicled by Callender and Grant, found encouragement in the prescriptive literature of the mid-eighteenth century. Some years earlier, in 1747, Poor Richard presaged Callender's approving description, promoting the happy consequence of such a simple aspect and issuing a caution against appearing otherwise:

> Girls, mark my words and know, for men of Sense
> Your strongest Charms are native Innocence
> Shun all deceiving Arts; the heart that's gain'd
> By craft alone, can ne'er be long retained
> Arts on the Mind, like Paint upon the Face
> Fright him, that's worth your Love, from your Embrace
> In simple Manners all the secret lies
> Be kind and virtuous, you'll be blest and wise.[16]

Prescriptions such as these began to appear in the 1740s in the colonies, marking a departure from earlier printed poems and jests that satirized scolding wives and cuckolded husbands.[17] Instead, the maxims emphasized blissful unions between virtuous, modest women and men of sense who displayed unaffected yet refined tastes and manners—code for the construction of a particular status position that was high but not aristocratic, humble but not low or rough.[18] They guarded against those who attempted to "buy" gentility or fake it with airs, affectations, and goods, comparing face "paint" to internal "arts." They insisted that women be transparent selves or suffer the loss of worthy men's love. Women—or rather a particular elevated class of women—became the "softer sex" or "the fair" to be honored by men "with courteous style and gentleness of manners" that matched their own.[19]

If a woman hoped to attract a good and virtuous man, prescriptive literature instructed female readers, first she must cultivate her own virtue. Of course, virtue and innocence by their very natures could not be cultivated, accepted wisdom held; they simply existed in good women and were theirs to lose. While reading Samuel Richardson's novel *Clarissa; or, The History of a Young Lady*, Callender displayed little sympathy for the "fallen" fair, writing with disapproval that "from the cradle" women received warnings against such loss of virtue.[20] Clarissa's own virtue is unimpeachable, yet in rejecting the wishes of her family that she marry a man whom she does not love, the heroine exposes herself to dishonor. Robert Lovelace, the suitor with whom she corresponds in secret, rapes her, yet still she refuses to marry him. Instead, she retreats to die in solitary shame. She suffers for the wanton fulfillment of her own desires, for disobeying the dictates of her wise family. Even virtuous women such as Clarissa could "fall," rendering themselves ineligible for a proper match, whereas Richardson's heroine Pamela, in his novel *Pamela; or, Virtue Rewarded*, trades the gifted finery she receives as a lady's maid for her original country wear, and eventually marries the master.[21]

Appearing and acting in ways inappropriate for attracting a man of sense signaled potential trouble to come, and some "ladies" did not always behave as demurely as prescriptions directed. In fact, some young women were downright uppity. Hannah Callender noted that "two celebrated beauties" sat near her one day in meeting. While she praised the demeanor of the "daughter of Doctor Shippen," she noted that Patty Loyd had evidently been "brought up to think she can have no action or gesture that looks amiss, when on the contrary," Callender proclaimed in verse,

> I hate the face, however fair
> that carries an affected air . . .
> And fopperies which only tend
> To inspire what they strive to mend.[22]

Like a fop, Miss Loyd was so full of affectation that it marred her natural beauty. And such haughtiness in a woman was particularly unseemly, because it exposed the lack of gentility it attempted to cover and could only attract the wrong sort of man—perhaps himself a fop or rake.

Excessive consumption, ostentatious display, and illicit sex were linguistically conflated through terms such as "ruined," which could signify financial distress or sexual downfall.[23] Some women, it seemed, had only two things on their minds—fashion and courtship. In July of 1758, when Callender attended the funeral of a neighbor's child, the behavior of some "ladies" who attended made her "think of a satire cast on the sex," and so she remarked, "The generality are pretty trifling gew gaw things, entirely wronged in their education, made to believe they were formed for man." The subtext of domestic femininity was certainly that women were "formed for men" as wives, but it rejected anything that smacked of coquetry—flattery, wheedling, and flirtation. Callender not only emphasized the quality of women's education but also echoed a characterization of women who lacked proper instruction as fashionable but useless items, "trifling gew gaw things" fit only to be toyed with and tossed aside, like a coquette.[24]

Callender's assessment mirrored prescriptions for women that directly juxtaposed "dressing the mind" with adorning the body and indulging its pleasures. The championing of internal rather than external refinement was a product of the Scottish Enlightenment and its insistence upon reason, sentiment, and authenticity.[25] As Eliza Pinckney cautioned her daughter, "The danger arises from too frequent indulging of our selves which tends to effeminate the mind" so that "rational faculties are more and more inactive and without doubt for want of use will degenerate into downright dullness."[26] By linking self-indulgence with effeminacy and dullness, Pinckney recalled the traits of a fop. Vanity in particular, represented by excessive consumption and display of fashionable goods, stood in contrast to virtuous sensibility. Since young women were equally capable of "improvement and perfection" as young men, a writer for the *Universal Spectator* observed in 1751, why then were girls so "neglected" in their training? Little wonder that they imagined "dress and diversion to be the most important affairs of Life," since "to be drest, to be flatter'd, to be diverted" composed "almost the whole business of those early years wherein they ought to be instructed," the piece continued.[27] How could women help but indulge their vanity, the author implied, given their training? Poor Richard offered a related query in 1761: "Do you, my fair, endeavour to possess an Elegance of mind as well as Dress?" and lamented that some women's "supreme ambition" was "to be fair." "For this," he continued, "the toilet ev'ry thought employs."[28] An exchange between Esther Edwards Burr, daughter of minister Jonathan Edwards, and John Ewing, a tutor at the College of New Jersey, shows the umbrage she took at the characterization of women as interested only in dress. In a round of "smart combat with Mr. Ewing about our sex" in which he expressed "mean thoughts of women," she asked "what he would have 'em talk about—whether he chose they should talk about fashions and dress." He replied, "Things that they understood," implying that fashion more or less comprised that category.[29]

Proper education was essential if parents wished to match their daughters with men of sense, the *Universal Spectator* claimed, so that women's husbands would not be "asham'd of them in Company or weary of them alone."[30] Education in the ways of virtue, not in the world of fashion, formed a woman for marriage. When Joseph Shippen, second son of the merchant Edward Shippen and secretary of the province, penned his "Lines Written in an Assembly Room," a paean to certain young women who attended the Philadelphia Assembly in 1764, he assiduously paid no attention to attire. Instead, Shippen praised Katherine Inglis's "conduct free from art," and the "true index of her mind" seen in Sally Coxe's form and face.[31] These fine ladies, although almost assuredly fashionable in appearance, needed no artifice. In Shippen's depiction, it was their sensibility and virtue that radiated beauty, not satins or jewels.

Prescriptions also connected education with chastity, lauding learning as a means by which women became virtuous, and the lack thereof as the certain means to an uncertain fate at the hands of fops and rakes. A 1761 piece from *Poor Richard's Almanack* titled "On Female Education, by a Lady of Quality" bemoaned the fates of uneducated women. "Strangers to reason," taught to use dress and airs to catch men, they were "left to their passions and by them betrayed."[32] Such women, born to flatter and be flattered, attracted only coxcombs, which Callender termed the "most disagreeable things in nature." After politeness forced her to spend the afternoon visiting with such a man at friend's home she wrote:

> Monkeys in action peroquets in talk
> They are crowned with feathers the cockatoo like
> And like camelians daily change their hue.[33]

These were not men to marry. Inconstant at best, they only flattered and made fine—or in Callender's assessment, outlandish—appearances by which women might be dazzled and to which they might fall prey.[34] Young

Harriot Pinckney of Charleston wrote a friend with this advice from her mother, Eliza, about marriage: "Let neither comet nor blazing stars dazzle your eyes . . . look through the glitter and the glaze till you find that inestimable jewel, a virtuous man's heart." Although she "was not such an enemy to a fine coat to persuade you ladies that grow toward marriageable to dislike a pretty fellow the worse for wearing one," acknowledging that appearance was not *un*important, inner fineness counted most.[35] As a contemporary maxim held, "No admiration will be lasting, no happiness secure, which is not founded on the basis of virtue."[36]

But neither was it acceptable for educated women with means to remain unmarried. Some moralists placed women's education firmly in the service of household management; training in "arithmetick" formed women to better "regulate the expenses of a family," the *Universal Spectator* insisted in 1751, "the want whereof is often times apparently the fatal cause of extravagance and ruin." Sarah Powells, a young girl living in the unmarried Quaker Deborah Morris's household in 1763, learned numeration and arithmetic in part through keeping an account of the articles of clothing washed and ironed by a servant named Lidia.[37] The labor of Lidia's body contributed to the cultivation of Powells's mind in the Morris household economy. Not only did the market go "to the heart of family life" through commercial unions and the participation of men and women from merchant families, as Margaret Hunt has argued,[38] but also vice versa; *Poor Richard's Almanac* consistently tied the operation of the household to the larger economy. In a society increasingly flush with goods, the domestic economy lay at the center of a market driven by demand and consumption,[39] putting wives into positions of economic influence. The combination of marital constraint and material sway was put into rhyme in 1760:

Small is the Province of a Wife
And narrow is her sphere of life
Within that sphere to move aright
Should be her principal Delight
To guide the House with prudent Care,
And properly to spend and spare.[40]

The poem's emphasis on proper expenditure, and the purchasing power it suggests as the key to domestic maintenance, somewhat undermines the verse's insistence on the household as "small province" and "narrow sphere."

According to one observer, at least some women in the colonies were already quite domestic—unimpressively so. Andrew Burnaby, an English man who toured much of British America in 1759 and 1760, remarked on the extravagance and ostentation of Virginians but then found the ladies of the region too reserved and unrefined for his liking, particularly compared to his English kinswomen. They cared only for country dancing and pastimes such as barbecues, he noted, and otherwise "chiefly spent their time in sewing and taking care of their families; they seldom read or endeavor to improve their minds; however they are in general good housewives (and) . . . make as good wives and as good mothers as any in the world."[41] This he admired, but he also implied that such domestic skills developed at the expense of other forms of cultivation. Burnaby much preferred the "sprightly" and "accomplished" women in Philadelphia and New York. His opinions, however they may have reflected urban social life in practice, generally ran counter to the prevailing, prescriptive notion that women's education and cultivation should be pursued for the betterment of marriage and domestic life.

The sentiment shaped a parallel rhetoric that began to emerge in the 1750s emphasizing the importance of frugality and consuming what was produced domestically, "at home," even as the colonies grew more enmeshed and invested in Atlantic commerce. As the Seven Years' War raged in North America in the late 1750s, so did appetites for imports, suggested by lengthy advertisements and merchants' accounts alike.[42] The abundance of goods that flowed into the colonies by midcentury helped spawn a native rhetoric that encouraged thrift and the consumption of domestic—meaning American—items. "Don't after foreign food and cloathing roam, but learn to eat and wear what's rais'd at home," Poor Richard advised as early as 1748, the dual meaning of "home" connecting colony and household. Such habits would improve health and increase wealth, he continued, and keep minds "sedate and uncorrupt."[43]

Anti-luxury discourse was not new in British culture, but some in colonial port cities began to contemplate ways to replace finery's siren song with the hum of domestic production, linking industry, good judgment, and financial security. A pamphlet appearing in Boston in 1753 titled *Industry and Frugality Proposed as the Surest Means to Make Us a Rich and Flourishing People* lauded a "Linen Manufacture . . . as tending to promote These among us." After King George's War, Boston's economy fell into a slump. In 1751 the town fathers embarked on a scheme to put poor widows to work spinning, linking "poverty and pastoralism."[44] Two years later they appealed to readers' "patriotism" and "love of country" in order to engender support for the construction of a physical plant. They even staged a spinning exhibition of several hundred women, including a number of "daughters of the best families" who "made a handsome appearance," demonstrating that domesticated female labor was compatible with both high rank and comeliness.[45] Yet the pamphlet also targeted consumer appetites. "I shall not attempt to compute what Quantity of Linen we import, nor what Sums are sent out in Payment for it," the author stated; however, anyone with eyes could see that colonists' "Bodies are covered with it." The "greatest Part" arrived from "foreign Countries." "If we are now poorer than we were thirty years ago," the pamphleteer declared, "we are at the same Time finer." Defying all logic, people's "ornaments" had increased along with their "poverty," as appetites overcame reason and debt generated social currency.[46]

The piece exposed a vicious, twofold trap: indulging high tastes led to poverty, causing people to desire even finer appearances in order to counteract suspicions of financial dearth. That people often purchased fine goods on credit allowed those without "means" to acquire them. One writer claimed New York's port to be so rife with "Galic spoil" in 1757 that the "jolly tar's feet shines with silver buckles, cambrick and brussels Lace adorn their nuckles; And on each head you'll see a gold-lac'd Hat."[47] The common seaman, in short, had turned Frenchified, be-ribboned fop.

The spoils of war were spoiling society, some feared. Social critics observed that people no longer knew their places, a problem signified by excessive consumption and the mounting debt produced. The dire socioeconomic consequences of consumer fever seemed of particular concern to Benjamin Franklin, writing as Poor Richard. He had spent time visiting friends in the Jerseys who complained of lack of money, although colonists unwisely spent "two hundred thousand pounds" annually on European and East Indian commodities. Franklin found this statistic as astonishing as it was dismaying, responding, "When you incline to have new cloaths look first well over the old ones and see if you cannot shift with them another year." Or more strongly urging, "When you incline to buy . . . India silks or any other of their flimsy slight manufactures, I would not be hard with you as to insist on your absolutely resolving against it," inverting the assumption that imported fabrics were of high quality.[48] Colonists behaved as if "a little tea" or "clothes a little finer" were "no great matter," but Franklin claimed to know otherwise, pointing to the slippery slope of financial ruin in morally charged terms. "You call them goods," he admonished, "but if you do not take care they will prove evil to some of you." Too many colonists, for the sake of finery on their backs, caused their families to endure empty bellies, he claimed. They preferred outward show to inner satisfaction, and served individual rather than colony desires, which would ultimately result in their personal undoing. "Silks and sattins, scarlet and velvets" were not "necessaries," according to Franklin, yet even wellborn colonists were seduced by their luxury. By such extravagance, "the genteel are reduced to poverty and forced to borrow of those whom they formerly despised, but who through industry and frugality have maintained their standing."[49]

Franklin's social world-turned-upside-down supplied a cautionary tale but not necessarily an apocalyptic vision. It constructed, rather, a meritocracy in which those possessed of good sense and moderate habits triumphed over spendthrifts, no matter how wealthy or wellborn. Yet given the rise of sensibility, one might assert that the truly wellborn did not pine for luxury while those with extravagant tastes did not tend to be of high rank.[50] And at the center of the new social taxonomy stood good wives who managed themselves, both in appearance and behavior, and their homes modestly and moderately. An example put forth in the Boston broadside of 1753 spelled out the inverse: "With an ill grace must that Tradesman complain of hard Times and the Difficulty of getting a Livelihood, whose Wife and Daughters are cover'd with Scarlet and Velvet."[51] The showy women in the family both incurred debt and increased his poverty, while their appearance belied his artisan status. Yet their showiness was also made to indicate it. He needed to better control them and their appetites, or suffer the fiscal consequences in silence.

One means of exercising such control was to get women spinning. The author of the 1753 Boston pamphlet praised the "liberal Benefaction of the Ladies, by which the managers have been able to open a new School, where Spinning will be taught our female Youth." Waxing melodramatic, he wrote that it pleased him "to see a number of modest Maidens, furnish'd with the Means of gaining an honest livelihood, who must otherwise, perhaps, eat their Bread at the expense of their Innocence, and having once enter'd upon a Course of Vice, must have gone on in the same, during a Life continually increasing in Wretchedness."[52] Virtuous production of cloth would prevent the production of American Clarissas, and by maintaining their virtue, the women would keep themselves pure and marriageable. Moreover, the fruits of the women's labor, domestic cloth, would promote and represent the frugality of all who consumed it. As one *Boston Gazette* item from 1750 asserted in a verse originally "published among us in the year 1702, which perhaps might do very well again as a proper and seasonable caution . . . The Loom, the Comb, the Spinning Wheel, would much promote this country's weal."[53]

Hence, a discourse that divorced femininity from outward display dove-

"Let sloth adornd with splendid arts, / Another's labour own . . ." E. Martin, engraver, London, 1790. This print depicted the ideal woman as domestic, genteelly productive, naturally attractive, and, although pictured with a child, whom she instructs in needlework, chaste. Courtesy The Winterthur Library, Joseph Downs Collection of Manuscripts and Printed Ephemera.

tailed with one that cast restrained propriety as the true signifier of high status. Intersecting with voices calling for increased colonial and household production in the 1750s, it advocated the rejection of imported finery as an indicator of true gentility. But for this vision to be effected, women in particular would have to become properly domestic—wise in their selection of goods as well as husbands; sensible in their expenditures, appearances, and behaviors; productive, rather than consuming. It was an ideal that some colonial women began to perform through self-fashioning as well as enacting the visions of husbands and artists, even as their understated finery showed them to be no less followers of fashion than women of lower rank.

Midcentury Modes

Several stylistic shifts marked the middle of the eighteenth century, a period of great demographic, economic, and imperial transformation in British North America.[54] As the populations of the port cities swelled due to natural increase as well as migrations both voluntary, from Scotland and Germany, and forced, from Africa, the new ideas about and ways of defining social status acquired a new "look": a country or pastoral mode for elite men and women, displayed in portraiture. An import in terms of style and substance, looking much like visual depictions of the English gentry in the same period, the country mode nonetheless could have colonial resonance.[55] It was joined by another, more obviously indigenous sartorial expression, one typified by leather jackets and breeches. The look of the backcountry came to town on the bodies of militiamen as the period saw urbane places like Philadelphia, the emerging "fashion capital" of the colonies, beset with frontier conflicts as well as frontier modes. Yet the Seven Years' War also spurred the arrival of thousands of British soldiers in uniform, signaling the power of the metropole and heralding the rise of a military mode. Taken together, these martial styles provided alternative and accessible expressions of masculine status and power.

In contrast to the periwigs and ermine memorialized in paintings of powerful men of the late seventeenth and early eighteenth centuries, by the 1740s styles had become less elaborate and ornamented, although no less costly and fine. The British colonial portraiture produced by artists such as Joseph Blackburn, Robert Feke, and Jonathan Singleton Copley illustrate the trappings and self-fashioning of colonial elites across regions.[56] Renderings of men and women displayed attention to sumptuous fabrics and details of dress yet depicted relatively simple attire. The images were characterized by pastoral settings, genteel poses, and direct gazes. They presented a vision of colonial gentility that partook of fashion, quoting the modes of the day while at the same time advancing a more timeless image in order to portray people whose status and position were perpetual and did not depend on the caprice of *la mode*. Of course, high rank "allowed" a person to be fashionable in both economic and cultural terms. The concept of gentility encompassed certain styles worn by certain people, wellborn and well-bred yet not aristocratic, allowing only some colonists to be both fashionable *and* genteel. Among the wealthy and wellborn, fashion was a subset of gentility; for others, it ran counter.

As colonial elites, whether made so by slave-labor agriculture or through trade, came into a sense of themselves in the mid-eighteenth century, they used art to depict and secure that sense, suggesting much about an idealized relationship of attire to social status. Although they often lacked the combination of old family names and landed estates that characterized the English gentry, untainted by participation in trade, men in the port cities made their occupations into an expression of social position.[57] Isaac Winslow, a wealthy Boston merchant, had his three-quarter-length portrait painted by Robert Feke in 1748, perhaps to commemorate his marriage to Lucy Waldo a year earlier. Focal points are Winslow's serene and confident visage and his waistcoat of ivory silk, sporting dense gold embroidery, on which the light falls. His hair, likely a wig, is powdered, curled at the sides, and tied at the back. His coat, from beneath which ruffled sleeves peek out, is of brown broadcloth or silk and cutaway in the fashion. The movement of the viewer's eye down the length of the portrait, pausing to note that the waistcoat is unbuttoned just so to allow the fine linen shirt to peek out, leads to Winslow's hand, which points toward the tiny scene in the background of a boat landing. With water to Winslow's left, and a tree to his right, he is firmly and comfortably situated in the outdoors, not a countinghouse or parlor, although his fine dress would have been suitable for an assembly.[58]

Seven years later, how Winslow's life had changed. Now the father of two daughters, Winslow commissioned a painting of his family from Joseph Blackburn. The work conveys the refined cosmopolitanism that marked genteel heterosociability while representing the gendered, filial order of patriarchy through the height of the figures—Isaac is standing, his wife Lucy sits, little Lucy stands but beneath her mother, and the infant Hannah sits in Lucy's lap, almost an extension of her mother but with enough independent will to reach out for the fruit the elder daughter bears. All but the baby gaze out at the viewer and wear slight smiles. Isaac's expression is

Isaac Winslow, by Robert Feke, about 1748, oil on canvas, 127 × 101.92 cm (50 ⅛ × 40 ⅜ in.). Museum of Fine Arts, Boston: Gift in memory of the sitter's granddaughter (Mary Russell Winslow Bradford, 1793–1899) by her great-grandson, Russell Wiles, 42.424. Photograph © Museum of Fine Arts, Boston.

Isaac Winslow and His Family, by Joseph Blackburn, 1755, oil on canvas, 138.43 × 201.29 cm (54 ½ × 79 ¼ in.). Museum of Fine Arts, Boston: A. Shuman Collection—Abraham Shuman Fund, 42.684. Photograph © Museum of Fine Arts, Boston.

notably more relaxed than in his individual portrait; so, too, is his stance less stiff and formal than before, as he places one hand on his hip, seems to lean slightly on a pillar with the other arm, and crosses one leg in front of the other. This is a powerful man comfortably in control, his left hand gesturing not at the distant indicators of his vocation but at his fecund wife at the painting's center. The background contains a swan pond and a brick gate, suggesting the entrance to an estate within which the family is happily contained.[59]

The palette of this painting is more vibrant than Feke's, yet it appears that Isaac wears the same cream-lined brown coat as in the 1748 portrait. However, he now sports an entire suit with matching waistcoat and breeches, which are visible because of his stance, the fact that Blackburn has portrayed more of his body, and the greater cutaway of the waistcoat. Gone is the embroidered silk waistcoat, and the shirt ruffles at the neck and sleeves are more understated. Isaac's look is in keeping with the fashion of the day, but the use of the coat from the earlier work helps to give the figure the desired timeless quality. Complementing the sober yet rich brown of her husband's suit, Lucy Waldo Winslow wears a gown of rose-colored silk, the fabric beautifully rendered, as was Blackburn's style, the hue picking up colors from the sky. Lucy Jr.'s dress is somewhat unusual, with its gathered sleeves, and fruit tumbles from her overskirt as a sign of abundance. She is almost nymphlike, the ageless spirit of the pastoral.[60]

Perhaps unsurprisingly, young women were made to embody the pastoral aesthetic that was so central to the colonial elite's self-fashioning in art.[61] This was accomplished through landscape settings and the liberal incorporation of natural accessories. Some artists even depicted women as shepherdesses; in 1754 Blackburn painted Mary Sylvester of Long Island out of doors, with a crook in her hand and a lamb at her side. Two years later John Singleton Copley depicted Ann Tyng of Boston in similar fashion. These young, unmarried women could be portrayed as country lasses, tending their flocks with the "native innocence" so praised in almanac verse before taking on the obligations of marriage and motherhood for which, the depictions suggested, they were well suited.[62]

Twelve-year old Jane Galloway was years away from marriage when Benjamin West painted her portrait in 1757, but the image nonetheless deployed pastoral motifs to encourage admiration. A Quaker from Maryland who spent much time in Philadelphia, Galloway appears in a kind of "fancy dress" used by artists in London, her jaunty hat and lace kerchief (blown by the wind) two of its hallmarks.[63] Although she was not depicted as a shepherdess, such a rendering might have suited her, for the same year Galloway copied into her commonplace book a "Pastoral Song" lamenting that she had left "Amynta," abandoning "my sheep and my sheephook" to fruitlessly roam the world in search of love.[64] But even without lamb and crook, the portrait inspired adulation of its subject. One male admirer penned the following verse, capturing the important triumph of "nature" over art in feminine beauty:

> When Jenny's Picture was by Damon seen
> Drest in the Graces of the Paphian Queen,
> Transported with the piece, he said, that Heav'n
> To mortal Nymph had ne'er such beauties given;
> No maid on Earth could boast so fair a face,
> And vanquished Nature here to Art gave place,
> But when he saw fair Jenny's lovely form,
> Where sweetness wins us, and where beauties warm,
> Superior far he found her blooming face,

Ann Tyng (Mrs. Thomas Smelt), by John Singleton Copley, 1756, oil on canvas, 127.32 × 102.55 cm (50 1/8 × 40 3/8 in.). The unmarried Ann Tyng is portrayed as a genteel shepherdess. Museum of Fine Arts, Boston: Julia Cheney Edwards Collection, 39.646. Photograph © Museum of Fine Arts, Boston.

> Adorned by Heav'n with each celestial grace;
> Raptur'd the youth awhile the Fair beheld,
> Then cry'd to Nature vanquished art must yield.[65]

Comparing Galloway's image to the goddess Aphrodite, he is at first dubious that a mere mortal could hold such charms, regarding the portrait as "artful," which is to say inauthentic. But upon seeing Galloway in person, in particular her "blooming face," he realizes that the real thing is more beautiful than the representation; that nature is in fact superior to art. Just as the prescriptions of the day instructed.

Galloway's senior by several decades but no less wellborn, forty-year-old Rebecca Boylston appeared in a portrait that combined the pastoral and the neoclassical to indicate the prerogatives of a wealthy, unmarried woman of sense and taste. Boylston wears a Turkish-style robe of rose-colored velvet, trimmed in gold, over a loose gown of ivory silk with lace trim. Her simple hairstyle is adorned with a few strands of pearls, and she holds a basket of flowers, gazing out with some bemusement at the viewer. The portrait, which depicts Boylston in a park, combines the relaxed refinement of the colonial "aristocracy" with the pastoral aesthetic that characterized depictions of young women. Six years later Boylston married Moses Gill after his first wife died; perhaps the cosmopolitan pastoralism of her portrait helped to attract at least one suitor.[66]

A similar relaxed yet luxe cosmopolitanism shaped a new vision of masculine power as well in the 1760s. The same year Copley painted Rebecca Boylston, her brother Nicholas also sat for his portrait. In what has become one of the more famous portraits from eighteenth-century British America, Boylston wears a heavy blue and green silk banyan and rose-colored nightcap over a bare head—no wig. Clad in such luxurious but informal dress, he sits with one arm resting on two large ledgers. He is the image of learned, leisured repose, a man comfortable enough with his wealth and position in the world that he can "afford" to be painted in a dressing gown, seated.[67] This was but one of the several ways in which Copley's generation defined "model masculinity," according to art historian Margaretta Lovell. In addition to the relaxed opulence of Boylston, other types included sensitive, thoughtful men, artisan men such as Paul Revere, and military men.[68] The options for representations of male power and status seemed to be expanding.

Although the military portrait was a long-standing element of British art, by the 1760s a martial look began to influence men's fashionable and everyday dress. The frock coat, with its downturned collar, close cut, and

Rebecca Boylston, by John Singleton Copley, 1767, oil on canvas, 127.95 × 102.23 cm (50 3/8 × 40 1/4 in.). Museum of Fine Arts, Boston: Bequest of Barbara Boylston Bean, 1976.667. Photograph © Museum of Fine Arts, Boston.

contrasting buttonhole stitching recalled military jackets, and its popularity likely resulted from the Seven Years' War. In the summer of 1764 John Tabor Kempe, the attorney general of New York, procured several items from the Norfolk tailor John Swick. In the letter that accompanied the shipment of attire, Swick flattered his client, writing, "Your taste just suits the present fashion . . . your laced cloathes are made, what we call here, french frock fashion," which he described as somewhat more relaxed than traditional coats yet still formal enough "for an Assembly."[69] Having recently defeated France in the contest for North America, perhaps it was now acceptable, even desirable, for Britons to adopt what Swick considered a French mode; this was most likely a particular, ornamented version of the frock coat.

Military style itself seemed to be changing in British North America as a response to the challenges of colonial, frontier warfare. Memoirist Anne Grant recalled that General William Howe "forbade all displays of gold and scarlet" in preparation for a rugged march "and set the example by wearing himself an ammunition coat, that is to say one of the surplus soldiers coats cut short." The most powerful man in the British army in North America was dressing down. And although "hair well dressed and in great quantity was considered as the greatest possible ornament," whether worn in a bag or a queue, Howe cropped his hair short and ordered everyone to do the same. Others also dated changing hairstyles for men to the Seven Years' War. From the perspective of the early nineteenth century, Thomas Bradford remembered that when members of General Edward Braddock's broken British colonial army returned to Philadelphia after their crushing defeat at the hands of the French and Indians in the summer of 1755, they did so sans perukes, ushering in the fashion of "natural hair" for men. He deemed it "a fashion suitable to the military and thence adopted by our citizens." Coincidentally, he noted, the king of England had around this time just "thrown off his wig," turning a deaf ear to the remonstrances of London's peruke makers. Colonial advertisements, Bradford continued, confirmed this "change of fashion" and the subsequent "ruin of our wigmakers."[70] His tale, perhaps a function of his imperfect memory, begs the question of whether wigs declined in popularity in colonial cities as the result of a stylistic shift in the court of George II or because of the decisions of some beleaguered soldiers. Of course, men could still find "uniform English gold and silver lace for hats" and other martial finery at shops such as the Hat and the Helmet in Boston, but the frontier war and its often violent aftermath seemed to usher in a more informal military mode.[71]

Even as the backcountry served as a bloody battleground in the 1760s, colonial elites made the countryside their genteel playground. Venturing forth from town or the country homes of wealthy urban families, "pleasure parties" composed of men and women embraced pastoralism by selecting bucolic settings for events such as "barbecues" in Virginia and angling or fishing expeditions on the outskirts of Philadelphia.[72] Particularly for city dwellers, escaping to the country signaled the virtue and independence that commercial activities, and the fortunes and status they generated, seemed to compromise in the eighteenth century. Moving beyond the ballroom, country houses and settings provided spaces for elite heterosociability, just as genteel country modes came to characterize elite self-fashioning.

Promoting Resistance, Maintaining Order

After the economic boom of war, the port cities experienced slumps in the early 1760s, widening the distance between rich and poor and sharpening gradations among the ranks. Boston's recession was most pronounced. Philadelphia was plagued not only with economic woes and social tensions but also with internal political turmoil connected to clashes and uprisings in the backcountry, most notably the march of the Paxton Boys in 1764. In 1760 and 1761 the city saw a rash of individuals cutting women's gowns and petticoats with razors, making it "dangerous for [women] to appear without protection," according to one nineteenth-century recollection.[73] "Rough" elements were influencing Philadelphia society even as the assembly danced on and salons gathered. Of New York City, one observer noted, once the army departed, the "ephemeral adventurers" who had prospered as a result of the soldiers' presence had to face "clamorous" creditors and often fled town.[74] Even amid the thrill of victory over France, it was a time of commercial contraction and social tension.

Contributing to the anxious economic, social, and political climate was an item in the *Pennsylvania Gazette* that reproduced debates in Parliament over the terms of the Revenue Act.[75] The first piece of legislation explicitly designed to raise funds through colonial consumption, the act taxed certain goods while forcing all trade through legitimate channels, clamping down on smuggling. Although the law, also known as the Sugar Act, chiefly concerned a duty on molasses, it also taxed several luxury items such as coffee, Madeira, and "all wrought silks, bengals and stuffs. . . . of the manufacture of Persia, China or East India, and all callico painted, dyed, printed or stained there; and for and upon all foreign linen cloth called Cambrick and French lawns."[76] One purpose of these now-doubled duties was to enlarge the market for British merchandise by raising the cost of manufactures from other countries.[77] And whereas calico had once been practically forced on the colonies, now the appetite for the fabric was to be exploited. Only four years earlier, Benjamin Franklin had argued that the key to unifying and expanding the British empire was to put the colonies on an equal commercial footing with Great Britain. Now it seemed as if Parliament hoped to profit from colonial demand for fine and imported goods at a time when colonists already lived beyond their means.[78] The tax on fabrics from the East and France, making them even costlier, also seemed to punish colonial cosmopolitanism, since it was directed at the tastes and habits of those with means.

Merchants in Boston expressed the first sign of indignation toward the act and its implication by deciding to "curtail many superfluities in dress." They pledged to entirely forego lace and ruffles and not to purchase English cloth "but at a fixed price."[79] The resolution's focal point was mourning dress, long a symbol of connection to and participation in court culture in the colonies yet one that had inspired a tradition of critique in the English press. Merchant *men* forged the agreement, which regulated only men's attire. "No part thereof but the crape in the hat is retained," the news item continued, yet even that was altered, for "instead of which a piece of crape is to be tied upon the Arm, after the Manner of the military Gentlemen." Partaking of the military mode, the look was to be less fop, more soldier, the resolution clearly indicated. In rejecting an "effeminacy of dress" Boston's merchant elite, the "principle" men of the town, made sartorial understatement a political performance, one that expressed status-based masculine virtue. The city's tradesmen also got into the act by pledging to wear "Nothing by Leather for their working habits . . . and that to be only the Manufacture of this Government."[80]

The New York Assembly followed with a petition to the House of Commons in October of 1764. Thanks to the provincial press and American agents in London, most colonists knew that a duty on paper rode closely on the heels of the Revenue Act; perhaps the petition was intended to forestall the Stamp Act's eventual passage. It insisted that Parliament possessed inflated notions of the colony's wealth based on its burgeoning trade with the Spanish and French West Indies during the Seven Years' War, when "luxury advanced upon us slower than our Gains." But now trade was both generally diminished and confined to its traditional channels, and British merchants would soon be convinced that their "splendor was not supported by solid riches."[81] The disjuncture between the appearance of wealth and its actual existence echoed the very issue Franklin's Poor Richard addressed in his maxims about immoderate consumption. Furthermore, New York's merchants were in a position to comment, Lieutenant Governor Cadwallader Colden believed, since many had risen suddenly "from the lowest Rank of the People to considerable fortunes, and chiefly by illicit Trade in the last War."[82] Colden's comment expressed the threat that both commerce and its spoils posed to traditional social hierarchies.

The Revenue Act's focus on the consumption of "feminized" luxury goods, especially fabrics, provided the anxieties of social commentators with a political focus; reactions to the odious commercial policy displayed impulses of social control and status gatekeeping. As John Watts noted in a letter to Moses Franks, the Revenue Act threatened to destroy "the very means" by which colonists were able to purchase imports, "which no doubt the colonys themselves will repine at when 'tis first felt, as they have too much run into the habits of luxury." Although Watts regarded the legislation as unfortunate, he felt it was the "right medicine for all that," claiming "it must from necessity bring us into a state of frugality, and oblige us to cloathe ourselves with the plain manufactorys of our own country."[83]

With the act's passage, the discourse of domestic production and consumption that budded in the 1750s began to flower. A news item from Annapolis, Maryland, appearing in the *New York Gazette* lauded the manufacture of stockings with "America spelled sideways." A group of merchants in Philadelphia established a linen manufactory in 1764, which, like the Boston institution a decade before, employed poor women in the production of domestic cloth.[84] In November of 1764 a notice from Philadelphia, reprinted in New York and Boston, proclaimed that "yesterday was brought to this city, a quantity of fine homespun broadcloth made this fall . . . immediately purchased by some gentlemen for their own wear," emphasizing the high quality of the fabric as well as its consumption by high ranking men. Another notice from Boston printed in New York proclaimed, "There are many articles of dress manufactured" which "exceed in strength and beauty" any that came from London.[85] The merchant William Lux realized by July 1765 that "the Stamp Act is likely to oppress us so much that it behooves us to think in time of getting a warm coat for winter manufactured here, as I am sure we shall not be able to purchase one from our mother country."[86]

Yet despite praise for domestically produced fabrics, or realistic resignation in the face of their utility, demand for imports continued largely unabated in 1764 and 1765. As the firm of Pomeroy and Hodgkin instructed

John Keteltas after they failed to send the right sort of checked cloth in the winter of 1764, "It will always be much to your advantage to send your spring orders earlier in the winter, as the demand for North America is very large."[87] Imported cloth was of higher quality for the cost than domestic. Moreover, imports remained "fashionable," a quality still very much valued.[88] For example, New York's high-end merchant and retailer Samuel Deall enjoyed a brisk business in luxury items in the mid-1760s. Oliver DeLancey spent £92 in 1764 and £104 the following year at Deall's shop alone, purchasing everything from various colored "ribbands" and trimmings to Barcelona handkerchiefs and French kid gloves. William Bayard was a similarly loyal customer, updating his account several times a month to acquire items such as "Brussels lace" or "pink persian."[89] The business of tailors also provides a measure for assessing the persistence of taste for imported fashions. The Philadelphia craftsman John Reedle emphasized that his "correspondents" in London and Paris kept him abreast of the "change of mode," while George Griffiths noted that he had trained with Mr. Lloyd, "one of the most eminent master tailors" in England.[90]

As elite men's consumption of imported fashions persisted, colonial newspapers turned their attention to the "ladies" to set an example for and tutor the men in the ways of taste and virtuous consumption, particularly after the passage of the Stamp Act.[91] The prescriptions, which alternately doled out shame and approval, were underpinned by ideas of social hierarchy and the theory of emulation. The *New York Mercury* claimed that the bengals, lillepusias, and broglios produced in Boston's manufactory had been "bought by some of the principal ladies in their Town." Versions of the fashionable eastern fabrics were being produced in America and were receiving the patronage of high-ranking women. "As the ladies have set the example," the piece continued, "I hope the gentlemen will follow this laudable custom"—implying that they had not yet done so—"as they may be supply'd in the spring with several sorts of summer wear." An item in the *Pennsylvania Gazette* stated that it was "high time to explode that ancient proverb, which has been so long regarded by Gentlemen, to the great injury of the continent," that "'Far fetch and dear bought is fit for Ladies.'"[92] On the contrary, the piece implied, the "ladies" were proving themselves restrained and virtuous in following calls for consumption of domestic goods. In a letter to New York's Society for the Promotion of Arts, Agriculture and Economy, "Sophia Thrifty" claimed that while some of the town's young ladies might appear "smitten with the charms of gaiety and dress," she could assure readers that the "matrons," mistresses of their families, would not hesitate to throw off the mode, claiming the mantle of virtue for married women and casting young ladies as coquettes seduced by fashion.[93] Whether or not the items accurately characterized displays of female virtue, the papers rhetorically impressed genteel, domestic femininity into the service of domestic consumption for the sake of political resistance.

As for men, the *New York Gazette* reported that "a quantity of fine Homespun Broadcloth" had been brought to Philadelphia and "was immediately purchased by some Gentlemen for their own wear."[94] The *New York Post Boy* declared that many "principle gentlemen" were "clad in country manufactures" and that the "fashion of funerals and mourning is in general much altered from the late troublesome and expensive method."[95] Yet an editorialist for the *Pennsylvania Gazette* observed that gentlemen insisted on continuing to deck themselves with fine mourning attire. The author was "sorry to find that expensive funerals still continue" in Philadelphia, and that men continued to dress up when a mere badge should have been enough to signify mourning. The writer hoped that the city's residents "whose fortunes will admit, and whose stations seem to require this expense, will begin this custom, especially when they consider how much their example will affect their inferiors, who are fond of supporting this outside grandeur, though conscious, at the same time, they will 'ere long want those seventy or hundred pounds they so foolishly lavish away, in this unnecessary conformity to fashion."[96] The people of fashion, those of high rank, had to be involved in fashion's rejection up and down the social scale. The dilemma, as Andrew Elliot observed in 1766, was that members of this crowd, the "people of fortune," were all "in trade" and could not necessarily be relied upon to follow suit.[97] Still, the nature of printed encouragements of nonconsumption worked to create bonds of political resistance while maintaining status and gender hierarchy.

In the face of continuing consumption, newspapers worked both to contain actual behaviors and to craft a new social reality better in line with prescriptions and political goals. Even as it stimulated desire for goods through advertisements, print could serve as a vehicle of social control. The Stamp Act's duties on paper hit printers particularly hard; they therefore had a serious stake in promoting and lauding, perhaps even exaggerating, the behaviors that might hasten its repeal. In September, the *Pennsylvania Gazette* assured its readers that "a number of merchants in this town have wrote to England for goods to be sent upon condition ONLY that the Stamp Act is repealed." This might have held true for certain merchants, but others such as William Pollard continued to generate orders for goods through the winter. One week later, the *Gazette* stated that the city's tailors were experiencing "cucumber times" because "most of their customers have declared they will have no new clothes made" until Parliament repealed the Stamp Act.[98] Printers such as Franklin did not object to goods and commerce per se, as advertisements supplied a portion of periodicals' profits. But nonimportation provided a way to both quash the unsavory stamp tax and replace the trade in imports with one in domestic goods, if only the local products would sell. It was a big "if." Continued consumption of imports in the wake of the Sugar Act demonstrated that printed prescriptions had far to go in regulating behavior.

Perhaps in an effort to make the tail of commerce wag the dog of nonconsumption, in the fall of 1765 the northern port cities' merchant communities forged agreements not to import goods until the Stamp Act was repealed. The newspapers expressed their approval by printing the entire texts of the agreements.[99] Although the cities were experiencing economic downturns, the resolutions were not driven by financial difficulties. Rather they served as political strategies that located masculine virtue, understatement, and self-control at the center of resistance to an unjust act.[100] Socially prominent merchants such as Thomas Willing, who had headed the Philadelphia Assembly ten years earlier, expressed his independence from trade and its spoils by signing.[101] *He* would not be to blame for the persistence of mourning garb, finery, and frippery among men. The resolutions made moneyed, potentially suspect commercial men appear virtuous and principled.[102] Having declared their politics as well as their masculinity to the public, merchants might continue to pursue gentility within their own circles.

But colonists such as Benjamin Franklin went to great lengths to prove colonists' willingness to embrace domestic manufactures and forgo luxuries, presenting a narrative of self-sacrifice and self-sufficiency to Parliament in 1766. Whereas before the Stamp Act colonists had displayed a "fondness" for the fashions of Britain that "greatly increased the commerce," he proclaimed, they had now lost respect for the mother country.[103] When questioned about the colonists' dependence on imported goods, he replied, "I do not know a single article imported into the *northern* Colonies but what they can either do without or make themselves." The exchange continued:

> Q. Do you not think cloth from England absolutely necessary to them?

A. No, by no means absolutely necessary; with industry and good management, they may very well supply themselves with all they want.
Q. Will it not take a long time to establish that manufacture among them; and must they not, in the meanwhile, suffer greatly?
A. I think not. They have made a surprising progress already. And I am of the opinion that before their old clothes are worn out they will have new ones of their own making.[104]

Drawing on his own established discourse of industry, frugality, and self-sufficiency in order to score political points, Franklin went on to insist that "the people will all spin and work for themselves in their own houses," perhaps exploiting British notions of the majority of colonists as country bumpkins. Attempting to hit Britain where it hurt—commerce—he pressed his point, and perhaps his luck, further:

A. You will find that if the Act is not repealed they will take very little of your manufactures in a short time.
Q. Is it in their power to do without them?
A. I think they may very well do without them.
Q. Is it to their interest not to take them?
A. The goods they take from Britain are either necessaries, mere conveniences, or superfluities. The first, as cloth, etc., with a little industry, they can make at home; the second they can do without till they are able to provide them among themselves; and the last, which are much the greatest part, they will strike off immediately. They are mere articles of fashion, purchased and consumed because the fashion in a respected country, but will now be detested and rejected. The people have already struck off, by general agreement, the use of all goods fashionable in mourning, and many thousand pounds' worth are sent back as unsalable.[105]

How precarious was the commerce and thus the stability of Great Britain, he implied, if it depended on "mere articles of fashion." The interrogation concluded thusly:

Q. What used to be the pride of the Americans?
A. To indulge in the fashions and manufactures of Great Britain.
Q. What is now their pride?
A. To wear their old clothes over again till they can make new ones.[106]

Franklin may well have believed what he proclaimed, although it is more likely that he, with the assistance of like-minded members of Parliament, exploited fears of diminished markets in order to secure repeal. In any case, he vastly overstated his claim of colonial sacrifice in the face of a just cause. The truth was that consumer habits were not so quick to change; neither sellers nor buyers of goods uniformly embraced nonimportation and nonconsumption. Some merchants, ever mindful of profits to be gained and demand to be exploited, looked ahead to the scarcity of goods that would render their own shipments more valuable. Writing just days after the nonimportation agreements officially took effect, Evert Bancker acknowledged that the countermanding of orders would make "English goods in great demand and sell well when the Stamp Act is put aside." In case his meaning was unclear, Bancker parenthetically added, "so that there will be a great advantage in having goods here." Likewise, William Pollard wrote, "We have no spring goods this year. I expect a good demand for mine in the Fall if they come in time as many people have not ordered this year." By contrast, Benjamin Franklin, writing an editorial for a London paper and again exploiting the issue of quality, claimed that no American pined for "Norwich crapes or any of the expensive, flimsy rotten black stuffs and cloths which you used to send us."[107] Even if some Philadelphians who lived "handsomely" were "going to a degree into homespun," as Lord Adam Gordon noted while traveling through North America late in 1765, they did so because the province "got specie" through that "branch of Trade . . . enabling them to make remittances for British manufactories."[108]

Baltimore's William Lux realized how continued colonial demand might be interpreted in England. "I suppose you'll be apt to blame us for sending our orders for goods continually if the act is repealed," he alleged in a letter to a colleague, but for the time being Americans had to be "content to live as forefathers did, and cover ourselves with bearskins till we can learn to make clothing for ourselves, which we shall soon do." As proof of his claims, Lux sent along a pattern of a coat and one of his wife's gown, "both of which she is now spinning."[109]

During nonimportation, the *performance* of women's production took on enhanced meaning. What was really being performed and publicized, however, was refined and virtuous femininity. Historians have aptly described the ways in which such attention politicized women's activities,[110] yet the reverse was also the case: the political climate provided new and legitimate social opportunities. When eighteen "daughters of liberty," reported to be "ladies of good reputation," gathered at the house of Doctor Ephraim Bowen in Providence, the hosts served an "elegantly plain" supper. According to the news item, the guests tarried little in dining, omitted tea, and proceeded to spin through the night. The piece turned what sounded like a social event that might have rivaled an assembly (albeit an all-female one) into a sober and industrious gathering. The women "of reputation" who attended agreed not to purchase any British manufactures and furthermore not to "admit the Addresses of any Gentlemen" who did so.[111]

The focus on high-status and middling women reforming men through bestowing or withholding affections and social approbation persisted after merchants officially adopted nonimportation, though men were enlisted in policing women's consumption and appearances as well. Indeed, debates over nonconsumption took the form of social and romantic parry and thrust between the sexes, as a complicated blame game took shape. "Sophia Thrifty" chastised the town's men who avoided retrenchment of expenses on the grounds that their extravagant wives would not allow it. She insisted that many women were full of frugality and "publick spirit" and that the ones who displayed "gaudy plumes" and succumbed to other "modish expenses" did so not so much to please themselves as to "dazzle" some duped members of the opposite sex. "While you men will be silly enough to admire a brilliant figure beyond a prudent girl, and prefer external ornament to intrinsic Merit, we women will be politic," she declared. Men's tastes and desires were to blame. "But remove the cause (as my grandfather used to say) and the effect will cease—In a word, down with your Beaux, and Belles will instantly decrease," the letter continued in its attempt to control the behavior and consumption of men and women through forcing them to police one another.[112]

Robert R. Livingston's "letter," likely composed in the spring of 1766, highlighted heterosocial relationships as well, implying that at least some women adhered to nonconsumption more closely than men. "I shall live in the hopes that we like the gentlemen shall rather chuse to talk than act," his fashionable narrator declared. However, "this at last I am sure of," she continued, "that the many Ladies who want that sprightliness of wit or that bloom of beauty which is necessary to distinguish them when all are reduced to so meek a level and whose fortunes (and as the gentlemen say pride) sett them above all schemes of oeconomy will never consent to so mortifying a degradation" as to don homespun. In this formulation, wealthy women were unattractive, possessing means but no wit or beauty; they needed finery in order to be attractive. But if society were leveled through the rejection of luxury goods, the true cream would rise, the satire implied. Although, the narrator insisted, people would not choose to "herd with that part of the sex" if they could help it, the women made up "no inconsiderable part of this town."[113]

These women's prominence in the social scene produced the dilemma: cutting a figure sartorially and socially required "herding" with women of fashion, often women of fortune. Perhaps Livingston was inspired to write, in part, by the actions of his own twenty-year-old son Robert R. Livingston Jr., who John Jay, writing in March of 1766, warned had acquired "every qualification necessary to form a Buck" and deserved the title "man of Pleasure." Jay apologized for sounding so grave yet felt concern for his friend and law partner's well-being and rejoiced that Robert Jr. was now "in the country, separated from temptations." He judged that Livingston had lost by "playing the buck," gaining "nothing but every uncertain prospect of advantage" from his dalliances in the realm of the fashionable.[114] Certain of the town's "beaux," whose minds previously had been filled only with what women "inspired," according to his father's letter, had turned to sober discussions of politics, managing to break free of supposed feminine influence. Jay hoped that Robert Jr., away from the city and under the salubrious influence of the country, would do the same.

An ideal society in which merit of mind and "natural" rather than "artificial" beauty trumped display was simply not the way the world worked. Yet if women could make homespun the fashion, then other social arrangements might follow. Drawing on a long-standing tradition of blaming women of low rank for social confusion, Hannah Prudence imagined that "Maids" would cease trying to "exceed their Mistresses in Dress," forgoing demands that they be supported "in their Cambricks and Lawns."[115] Going beyond such sartorial leveling to recast social hierarchy through dress, Livingston's letter offered the following vision, in the form of a nightmare the narrator had suffered. She "went to a ball dressed in the prettiest and richest brocade, having at least half the beaux to my share, when I found Miss ____ and Miss ____ (whom you know the gentlemen are pleased to dignify with the title of bells) and many others dressed in homespun" surrounded by gentlemen while she, "dressed in the usual manner," stood "unattended by so much as one gallant." This perplexed her not a little, and her confusion deepened upon noticing that those in homespun were "placed nearer the head in proportion as they were frightfully clothed." She asked the manager of the assembly what accounted for the strange arrangement, and he replied, "You cannot be surprised, Madam, that in an American Assembly we should give the highest place to such Ladies as have the greatness of soul to prefer their countries interests to the vain desire of dazzling the eyes of fools, nor that the lowest place should be given to those whom that vanity has urged to contribute to its ruin." The manager, the narrator continued, began to place her at the bottom of the table when she awoke with a start, relieved that it had only been a very bad, very vivid dream.[116] An assembly in which the coarser the cloth the more refined its wearer was an inverted one indeed.

For others the bad dream was that American homespun was simply not fashionable, certainly not by London standards, and therefore proved a hard sell. The challenge for Franklin, Livingston, and others who supported nonconsumption was to cast fashionability as a vice while creating a new "fashion," to exchange one sartorial regime for another while not disrupting social order too greatly. Yet in order to promote compliance, they had to suggest that those who failed to follow the new modes, no matter how elite, would fall socially and that other, more virtuous men and women would take their places. In this context, sober masculinity and domestic femininity became more charged than ever, and obvious adherence to them more essential. Yet as advertisements, merchant orders, account books, and personal purchases demonstrate, ways of performing status that relied on fashion in the European mode persisted.

Most colonists seemed only too happy to pick up their consumption of imports where they left off. By April 7, 1766, William Lux rejoiced to William Molleson over the repeal of the Stamp Act. Lux intended to celebrate by attending a "grand Ball Illumination" planned for the occasion. He then included a list of items needed for a wedding: twenty yards white satin, sixteen yards white trimming, a hat, flowered gauze, lace, three dozen women's lamb gloves, two dozen men's, and a French necklace and earrings.[117] In May, the *Pennsylvania Gazette* proudly heralded the act's repeal, declaring "that to demonstrate our affection to Great Britain . . . each of us will, on the fourth of June next, being the Birth Day of our most gracious Sovereign George III, dress ourselves in a new suit of the Manufactures of England, and give what HOMESPUN we have to the POOR."[118] If anything suggested homespun's abiding association with lower sorts, it was that. The item proclaimed that men (and women, presumably, although the reference to a "new suit" is clearly gendered male) should feel free to doff domestic cloth and don finery once more.

But something had changed by the mid-1760s: fashion itself. And given the political climate, no more would lace and ruffles on a man or homespun on a woman be regarded in quite the same way in the colonies, no matter the mode. The consumption of consumer goods engendered cultural responses that redefined Anglo-American masculinity and femininity in the service of maintaining social distinctions. Prescriptions seemed to promote a meritocracy in which the most virtuous men and women would be accorded due attention and respect, rather than a hierarchy based upon display. Yet knowledge of one's elevated station, combined with some anxiety over the preservation of it, made it possible for women such as Hannah Callender to selectively adhere to prescriptions, and for men such as the merchant John Watts to criticize uncontrolled appetites for imports the very year in which his own wife spent a small fortune on an array of fashionable goods, from fabrics to face patches.[119]

During the 1760s, the language of imperial contest overlay gendered social tensions produced by consumption, increasing their visibility and locating them at the center of political resistance. Assessing the causes of nonconsumption, as well as the ambivalence toward and incomplete adherence to it, requires understanding the relationship between the world of fashion and the sphere of print, between two increasingly divergent courts of public opinion. While the Revenue, or Sugar, Act exploited appetites for feminized luxury items, the Stamp Act threatened to dismember the very arm of masculine rationality that worked to contain those desires. Fashion in dress became a political tool precisely because it remained a powerful marker of status in an intellectual climate that increasingly regarded gentility as a behavioral commodity—that is to say, not really a commodity at all. Yet the favoring of certain kinds of ruggedly masculine and rustic feminine appearances opened a door for the likes of colonial men and women to attain status by a different definition. Although the revolution in gender ideologies, particularly genteel femininity, appeared largely complete, gender relations and social practices continued to undermine attempts to redefine social status in accordance with the virtuous "domestic" politics of the American resistance and revolutionary movements.

New Duties and Old Desires on the Eve of Revolution

4

On November 2, 1773, Sarah Eve reflected in her journal on the time she had spent with Mrs. Brayen, the wife of a doctor, a "man of fortune" from Trenton, New Jersey. The day began well enough—that morning Eve had called upon friends who insisted that she accompany them to visit the woman. She agreed, not wishing to seem "one of the inflexibles." Upon arriving at the Brayens' residence, the visitors found the lady of the house occupied with someone who was to frame a picture for her. Closely observing Mrs. Brayen, Eve mused, "How soon one may discover some people's passions." "Though by appearance fond of show and gaity," the twenty-two-year-old diarist continued, "*she* is mistress." She elaborated on this point, explaining that her hostess had just returned from buying wine for her husband, who "preferred her taste before his own!"[1]

Once Mrs. Brayen had ended her discourse on how to properly frame a picture, she donned her cloak and bonnet and the group went shopping. Eve complained that the woman "wanted a hundred things, cheapened everything, and bought *nothing*."[2] After the exhausting yet unproductive outing, Mrs. Brayen trotted off to dress for midday dinner; an hour and a half later she returned, and the group sat down to eat at three in the afternoon—a more fashionable hour? "I should have thought Tea full as proper," Eve wrote, "my impolite appetite unaccustomed to be so served had left me two hours before." Her lack of interest in eating, however, did provide ample opportunity for her to observe the "shallow elegance" and equally thin conversation that plagued the gathering. Almost immediately the "doctor's Lady" inquired of one of her companions, Mrs. Hayes, how she managed to acquire everything "so much handsomer and so much finer than anybody else . . . a proper stress to be laid on the word *so*," Eve reported archly. The flattered woman, "with pleasure sparkling in her eyes and a consciousness that this was no more than her due," proclaimed Mrs. Brayen to be "very polite and very obliging, and in this entertaining manner," Eve drolly noted, "we passed an hour and a half at the table." They then drank tea "at candlelight," the silver candlesticks handsome and much admired. As soon as she could politely break from the group, Eve excused herself and headed home, "thanking fate I had so little to do with high life and its attendants!"[3]

In keeping with Adam Smith's *Theory of Moral Sentiments*, Eve, lest she be regarded as difficult, grudgingly succumbed to the prevailing desires of the company to visit Mrs. Brayen. But she went to great lengths to distance and distinguish herself from the odious woman and others whom she deemed consumed by attention to material goods and desire for empty flattery. Eve juxtaposed "appearances" and "passions"—outward display and internal merit. On the one hand, Mrs. Brayen's love of display revealed her shallow character.[4] On the other hand, Brayen's stereotypically feminine preoccupation with "show and gaity" belied her assumed and inappropriate position as master of the house—the de facto husband. It was a complicated formulation in which a woman's appearance at once clearly established her character, thereby fixing social and moral order, yet in Mrs. Brayen's case upset the very gender hierarchy on which that order relied. The juxtaposition of vanity and authority evident in the hostess encouraged Eve not to mistake a "feminine" orientation toward consumption and display for lack of influence or power.

Far more than a cache of catty commentary, Eve's journal situates the relationship among fashion, social status, character, and gender at the center of a familiar tale about the years preceding American independence from Great Britain. Such a focus helps shed new light on this pivotal moment by showing how people crafted and responded to renewed political upheaval in a climate of urban commercialism and consumerism.[5] The significance that fashion, and with it formulations of masculine and feminine propriety, had acquired during the Stamp Act crisis increased and grew more fraught after the passage of the Townshend Acts in 1767 and into the early 1770s. In particular, focusing on Philadelphia, which had become the most cosmopolitan city in British America by 1770, and which saw unique social and political struggles over nonimportation and nonconsumption, highlights the relationship between the cultural politics of fashion and political culture.[6] The marriage of gentility and sacrifice, of politeness and plainness served as a strategy deployed by certain merchants, tradesmen, and printers seeking to discipline commercial interests and consumer appetites that threatened the efficacy of resistance to Parliament's agenda of taxation. Positive encouragements reported the ostensibly virtuous behavior of the "people of fashion" while denigrating fashion itself, employing a new set of social norms. Yet this time, not only were the virtues of modesty, industry, frugality, and sensibility used to further political goals, but the goals themselves acquired a new social dimension: middling men, be they small-time merchants or artisans (who stood to gain customers for their own local goods), could theoretically regulate the appearances of their social "betters."[7] In particular, attacks discursively used fashion to target high-status women and wealthy men of commerce, the latter by questioning their masculinity through impugning their republican independence. The projects of self-discipline and the regulation of appetites begun decades earlier in prescriptive literature began to acquire a distinctly republican cast.

Still, demand for the stuff of fashion persisted, as there was little agreement on what high status looked like. The so-called quiet period, 1770–73, witnessed an escalation in conspicuous consumption in the port cities, as imported goods were plentiful and styles extravagant for men and women alike, from the male "macaroni" mode to high hairstyles for women. In this consumer milieu, men in the fashion trades such as tailors and hairdressers, upon whom colonists relied for the latest styles, increased their standing and authority yet also met with derision. Tailors in particular engaged in professional organization, economic protection, and political agitation. In response, some Philadelphians cast them as foppish pretenders to status who were responsible in part for the odious presence of macaronis, the credit crisis, and the confusion of social hierarchy. But their patrons, among them perhaps the very men who dragged their feet on nonimportation, were also to blame.

Ultimately, a fashionable appearance would need to be rendered antithetical to success in society and courtship for any new political or social vision to succeed, for as long as men and women stood to profit socially, romantically, or economically, appetite for *la mode* would persist. Even as genteel English publications such as the *Lady's Magazine* validated fashion as a legitimate pursuit for its female readers, producers of local almanacs continued to construct a version of femininity that rejected fashionable display in favor of wifely modesty. The ideal strove to divest high-status women of the power and legitimacy of fashion while ostensibly preventing lower-ranking women from emulating them. But fashion itself, not to mention its devotees, would not be so easily governed.

New Duties, Politeness, and the Pose of Plainness

Although widespread rejoicing followed the repeal of the Stamp Act in 1766, some colonists suspected that Britain's program of imperial reform would continue. Indeed, approximately one year later, the Townshend Acts swept through the houses of Parliament (although not without marked contest) and into the port cities of British North America. Designed, like the Sugar and Stamp Acts before them, to raise revenue, the acts levied duties upon a handful of articles, mostly staple supplies such as glass, lead, and paint rather than "luxuries," with the notable exception of tea. They differed from the Navigation Acts by regulating trade within the British empire itself. However, an assessment of the value of china exports to the colonies led Charles Townshend to formulate the duties, which suggests that the consumer habits of colonists influenced the plan.[8]

Philadelphia merchants, compared with their Boston brethren in particular, hesitated to adopt measures of resistance to the Townshend Acts. Scholars have suggested that they were not faring as poorly as merchants in other cities, and that, for some, Quakerism militated against such decisive and potentially disruptive action.[9] Perhaps the most compelling explanation is that these successful commercial men were deeply implicated in the smooth functioning of transatlantic commerce and the profits it engendered. How, then, was nonimportation effected in a merchant community where resistance to it was strong and nonconsumption rendered an attractive choice within a consumer culture? How did tradesmen, printers, and certain merchants encourage certain behaviors, both consumer and political, in a social environment that so often rewarded others? How did they inspire people toward sacrifice?

Those who touted nonimportation, namely John Dickinson and Charles Thomson and their supporters, crafted a two-pronged strategy: gentle encouragement of nonconsumption—perhaps hoping to make the tail wag the dog—and increasingly fevered insistence that merchants reinstate nonimportation. The latter tactic assailed merchants by characterizing them as rapacious, contrasting them with plain and virtuous farmers; the former relied primarily upon recounting the behavior of high-status women and lauding their salutary influence on men. The images of genteel "ladies" who sought sense rather than stuff and made industry their watchword and of "gentlemen" farmers inspired by patriotism over profit were powerful ones indeed. We should be wary of taking such notices at face value or reading them as unbiased reports of events, however. Rather, they were strategies crafted to encourage certain kinds of behaviors—advertisements that, like others among which they appeared, peddled an image as much as an item.

The primary piece of encouragement toward nonimportation in Pennsylvania, and chief charge against those who resisted it, made use of what many Quakers regarded as a distinctive quality and drew upon expressions of masculine understatement in dress. A "pose of plainness" characterized polemical appeals to and attacks on merchants. And it was indeed a pose, for a wealthy, urbane, yet landed attorney named John Dickinson sounded the clarion call.[10] "Letters from a Pennsylvania Farmer" was no more penned by an average eighteenth-century farmer than was the 1714 "Satyr" on hoops written by a woman. The letters clearly demonstrate how far the pose of plainness had come in swaying the court of public opinion toward particular political and social goals. No longer did a different sort of "court" marked by politeness and imperial pomp necessarily reign supreme; something of equal design, contrived to seem uncontrived, now challenged its sway.

Plainspoken, and ostensibly plain in appearance, was the "farmer" who argued for nonimportation. Consider Dickinson's opening appeal to his readers: "I am a farmer . . . I received a liberal education and have been engaged in the busy scenes of life but am now convinced that a man may be as happy without the bustle as with it." No country bumpkin, the farmer was a well-educated man of the land, as his portrait indicates. He had known town life, contrasting its "bustle" with the pastoral quiet of his bucolic surroundings. Furthermore, the farmer professed that he wished for no more in the way of wealth, and therefore remained "undisturbed by worldly hopes or fears relating to myself." Through such self-abnegation he contrasted country life with mercantile interests, playing upon the hypocrisy of Friends' doctrine that called for shunning worldly trappings in a town replete with obvious Quaker wealth.[11] Dickinson's straightforward tone, profession of civic goodwill, and rejection of self-interest and aggrandizement lent his arguments credence and pushed Philadelphia merchants into a defensive stance.

Yet those who supported nonimportation and nonconsumption could not lay exclusive claim to plainness. A "Chester County Farmer," probably the merchant Joseph Galloway, questioned the efficacy of nonimportation, claiming that those who invested in and produced domestic cloth had been burned by the repeal of the Stamp Act and the ensuing return to (or continuation of) consumption of imports. Dickinson retorted with an even stronger letter from a Virginia "gentleman" to a "Philadelphia merchant," claiming that commercial men had simply passed the burden of the Townshend Acts on to their customers and cared little for questions of liberty and rights.[12]

The figure of the plain and simple farmer made an appearance in Boston during celebrations of the Stamp Act's repeal publicized in the *Pennsylvania Gazette*. One notice proclaimed that "all ranks of People" demonstrated "joy and satisfaction" as flags were hoisted, cannons fired, a "number of houses decorated with streamers and a liberal entertainment provided." Filled with "decent and rational joy," the day concluded without "the least shew of disorder or riot." Revelers drank toasts to the "Royal Family" and to "the FARMER."[13] In this way Bostonians as well as Philadelphians who applauded their demonstration could have both gentility and rusticity—a democratic display attended by people of "all ranks" without messy, plebian behaviors such as those on display during Boston's anti–Stamp Act crowd actions. The account situated aristocracy and simplicity in harmonious coexistence.

As Philadelphia's merchants dallied into 1768, rhetoric grew increasingly inflamed, its authors attacking them as self-interested shades of men. As consumers as well as suppliers, displaying appetites for goods as well as the profits that procured them, commercial men embodied the problem. One "freeborn American" submitted a particularly impassioned plea to the "respectable merchants and citizens of Philadelphia" to act in concert with Boston and New York's resolutions. If they failed to act, choosing to protect trade over liberties, they would soon degenerate from "the opulent merchants of Philadelphia" into a "miserabile vulgas!—a miserable mob!"; from men of means and sense to mere rabble. Not only did the writer threaten the social position of commercial men, but he also questioned their morality. "It is well known," he continued, "that in France to say a man is a merchant is to give him a most odious character; it is to say—he is a rogue!" By classifying merchants as Frenchified "rogues" the author cast them as effeminate ruiners of fortunes, and of women. He attacked their status as well as their manhood. "But alas," he concluded, referencing bucolic virtue, "some of us in the country surmise a more formidable reason than the mighty, the monstrous evil of being—out of fashion!"[14] Some were willing to put the public good before their own desires for gentility.

The conflation of "plainness," sensibility, and masculinity marked even those encouragements couched in allegory and rhyme. *Hutchins Improved . . . for the Year 1768* featured the poem "The Bullfinch and Sparrow: A Fable by the King of Prussia." The piece told of a plain sparrow who, although the "fav'rite of each female bird" due to his learned and engaging ways, envied the brilliantly plumed bullfinch who lived in a gilded cage. When the latter overheard the sparrow lamenting his own fate and wishing he had been born a bullfinch, the golden warbler proclaimed:

What is there in this fine gilt cage
So much your fancy should engage?

> These wires my prison bars, where I,
> A Splendid Slave, must live and die!
> Go hence, content, and learn of me,
> How vain the finery you see.
> Forbear my joys true bliss to call:
> thy LIBERTY is worth them all.[15]

The bullfinch was a "splendid slave," the contradictory phrase conjuring the image of a liveried bondsman common in plantation homes and immortalized in eighteenth-century paintings. The message and moral were impossible to miss: the stuff of show, of ornamentation, constructed a gilded, imperial cage no less confining than bars of iron. "Vain" finery would deprive a man of his freedom and thus of his manhood, just as Parliament attempted to deny colonists' rights and free trade. Happier by far lived the sparrow who, although plain in appearance, possessed the cultivation of mind and manners—as well as the independence—to "win the feather'd fair-one's heart."[16]

Such "fair ones" were not dazzled by display, nor sought it for themselves, promoters of nonconsumption insisted. They lauded high-status women's tastes as expressions of their noble sentiments and unblemished characters. During the Townshend Acts crisis, printers such as David Hall and William Sellers of the *Pennsylvania Gazette* brought the full weight of polite domesticity and refined sensibility to bear on the cause. In the winter of 1767–68 the paper continually praised members of the "fair sex" who had thrown off their luxurious habits. No ordinary women, these "very agreeable ladies" from the "best families in this town" pledged to forgo finery. "How agreeable will they appear in their native Beauty, stripped of these ornaments, from the prevailing motive of Love to their Country," one piece predicted. The *Gazette* reported that a "Number of ladies" dressed "without ribbons" were "genteely treated by the Lady of the house (who was in the same habit)." In Providence, three "daughters to a gentleman of fortune . . . clothed themselves in garments of their own spinning, from the noblest of all motives—LOVE TO THEIR COUNTRY."[17] A passion for the good of the land stirred these women's hearts more strongly than the attention of beaus gained through a fashionable appearance. Prescriptions of modesty and the rejection of artifice found a vehicle in nonconsumption. If fashionable women rejected imports, perhaps the merchants who supplied their appetites would as well.

Encouragements connected feminine gentility, industry, and domesticity.[18] In New York, an "extract from a letter sent from a Gentleman at Amboy" insisted that "industry was so prevalent in this Metropolis" that one "lady of distinction" had knitted thirty-six pairs of stockings, despite being infirm and caring for a large family. One Philadelphia woman of "good Fashion" had "laid aside all foreign Goods, especially Cloths of a foreign manufacture." So endowed was this lady with a "noble Spirit of Freedom, Liberty and Frugality," the notice professed, that she gathered up all the fragments of imported fabric in her house—some 137 in all—and sewed them into a petticoat. In a further connection of gentility to industry, and of both traits to innocence and virtue, the *Pennsylvania Gazette* praised the eighteen "young ladies of as good families as any" for producing forty skeins of yarn during a "spinning entertainment." The productive diversion concluded with an evening of such "innocent mirth as might neither counteract the work of the day or blemish the characters of sober and virtuous ladies."[19] No fashionable entertainments leading to debauchery there.

Also of serious concern were the ways in which women's examples and behaviors influenced men. As one editorialist put it, "We must, after all our efforts, depend greatly upon the Female sex for the introduction of oeconomy among us."[20] Fortunately, their supposed examples were taking hold. One "gentleman" in Portsmouth reportedly held a "genteel entertainment" in which the men *and* women appeared "all clad chiefly in the manufactures" of the town. Even merchants got into the act, one dressing his child entirely "without ribbons." "Many gentlemen in Town of Figure and Fortune," another piece proclaimed, "are determined to cloath themselves and Families for the future with the manufactures of this country." The notice gave the following example: one "gentleman," a "hearty friend to the government and the proposed scheme for encouraging frugality, industry and manufactures," desired a winter coat. He wished it to come from Pennsylvania but, failing that, would "have no objection if it comes from a neighboring one, if it be good." A person need not forgo quality in order to embrace domestic goods.[21]

However, some observed that American "ladies" were not adhering to nonconsumption. An "extract of a letter from a Gentleman in London" published in May of 1769 stressed that whatever the merchants decided, "people ought to enter immediately into the strictest associations... to discourage by every lawful means in their power the importation of European manufactures." The writer noted that although many had already sacrificed "pride and vanity" by appearing in homespun, "there seems a necessity of inspiring the softer sex with an equal spirit of patriotism." He claimed it "surprising" that while women in England displayed their "love of liberty, . . . so little of the same spirit appears in the Fair in America." "We find at present very little alteration in the demand for Tea, Silks, ribbons, Lace and every other expensive article of female vanity," he continued, "though that for the coarsest woolens seems considerably abated."[22] The author thus accomplished two goals: first, he unfavorably compared American to English "ladies," the latter of whom were setting a fashion of simplicity and virtue that the former failed to follow; second, he contrasted the "vanity" of women of means and fashion with the virtue of the lower sorts, who rejected even cheap, coarse wool in the support of a cause. Fashion's trajectory moved from English ladies to the colonial "masses," cutting out female provincial intermediaries whose selfish vanity put them, paradoxically, quite behind the curve.

Fashion itself and its adherents came under direct attack as writers addressed the problem of demand and appetite. A letter to the editor of the *Pennsylvania Gazette* lamented that colonists had, in their fondness for England, "foolishly and unguardedly adopted her customs, mode and manner of living even to an extreme."[23] "Nations will not think until they feel," a "freeborn American" insisted, linking the head and heart in sensibility. He then crafted an appeal based on plebian, masculine roughness: "A homemade coat is not such a terrible thing! The skin of a son of liberty will not feel the coarseness of a homespun shirt!" The writer thus acknowledged that homespun could be coarse. But colonists—men in particular—should not *feel* so much that they cared, becoming soft seekers of luxury. Finally, the author took aim at the underlying problem: adherence to fashion. "The resolution of a Pennsylvanian be made of sterner stuff than to be frightened at the bug bear—fashion!" he insisted. If only people would unite in wearing and using domestic goods they would not be "censured," but rather "imitated" and "admired."[24] Ironically, the virtuous would become the fashionable by rejecting fashion.

A notice appearing in December 1768 provided perhaps the starkest example of this inversion. The "genuine relation" recounted an evening one "stranger" had spent among some persons of fashion. After the "tea equipage was removed," one of the company produced tickets for a play that the gentleman, although professing to possess "no taste for theatrical performances," felt obliged to accept. Yet some of the group had already planned to attend worship at St. Paul's that same night and now found themselves "much straitened to put their pious resolution in practice"—the author casting a barb at "worldly" Anglicans. A "division of sentiment," which could not be settled by reasonable discussion, resulted in the cutting of cards to decide the matter, and "giddy chance" favored the theater. "Good God, Gentleman, what a degenerate Age we do live in!" the author railed, continuing, "Into what State of Apostacy are we fallen when our Zeal for Religion is actuated by the turn of a card and the Mimicry of Buffons is put in Competition with the sacred oracles of truth!" The writer might have ended his tale on such a fever pitch, but as a supposed postscript he continued, "I almost forgot to tell you." He gave his ticket to a "Negroe who attended me at tea," but the "virtuous slave" immediately sold it for half the price and purchased a prayer book. The piece concluded, "An example of Virtue in a Slave worthy the Imitation of the Greatest Ruler upon Earth." The lowly slave had overtaken persons of wealth, power, and fashion.[25]

Despite such world-turned-upside-down formulations, the recognition that the few set the fashions and the many followed informed most inducements not to consume. One proponent appealed to the "people of fashion" in a point-by-point, almost geometric proof of nonconsumption's validity. The writer professed surprise at the "insensibility" of Philadelphia's citizens in resisting nonimportation and nonconsumption. He then directly addressed the town's "societies, companies and clubs"—likely the Philadelphia Assembly among them—directly: "It is not the many that spread and support a fashion, and may not these several societies . . . introduce and establish the glorious fashion of wearing none but American manufactures?"[26] The pieces linked virtue in the form of support of domestic goods—and the rejection of imported ones—with high social standing, ironically engendering a democratic movement through the exploitation of social hierarchy. They made sacrifice and plainness into a fashion set by those of the best breeding and greatest fortunes.

This is not to say that boycotts did not ultimately possess a genuinely democratic appeal and significance.[27] But they were promoted largely by playing upon notions of social hierarchy, not egalitarianism. To a degree, it worked. Peter Oliver, a judge and brother of Massachusetts tax collector Andrew Oliver, whose house had been attacked during the Stamp Act protests, recalled that it was "highly diverting to see the names and marks to the Subscription of Porters and Washing Women" agreeing not to purchase "silks, velvets, clocks, watches, coaches, and chariots" in Boston.[28] The rejection of those items began to signify the gentility they had once expressed, for why bother to eschew luxuries that one had never enjoyed?

Popular pressure proved difficult to resist, particularly after New York's merchant community adopted measures even stronger than Boston's.

There, tradesmen agreed to withhold business from merchants and retailers who refused to sign. Still, Philadelphia's commercial community continued to seek other resolutions to the problem of the Townhend Acts, mainly through petitions to Parliament. Their success in the election of October of 1768, which supplied a kind of referendum for the debate over nonimportation, demonstrated that "Whigs" had failed to generate widespread support for a boycott. Two Quakers, James Pemberton and John Ross, both staunch opponents of nonimportation, won the assembly seats, retaining the support of mechanics. For the moment, both Quaker political hegemony and the nonimportation question seemed settled.[29]

Yet by the spring of 1769, the two-pronged approach of "polite" encouragement and "plain" appeal succeeded, shored up by pressure from the other northern port towns. With propaganda encouraging the city's residents, women in particular, not to consume with or without nonimportation, merchants decided to act.[30] Once Philadelphia's merchants had agreed not to import, they, too, embraced the pose of plainness. The signatures reveal that fewer elite Quakers signed and that the participants possessed less wealth than those who joined the Stamp Act boycott.[31] However, John Reynell, one of the town's wealthiest Quaker merchants, signed, somewhat drolly declaring that he would "give up his beloved article of tea and put on a leather jacket"—the prosperous merchant turned humble tradesman. Furthermore, his wife had purchased a new wheel and was happily spinning away, he claimed.[32]

But the handwriting was on the homespun. Dry goods merchants in particular, watching their counterparts in the perishable trades continue to profit and sensing continued demand for imports, were anxious to resume trade. Five Quaker and three Anglican importers withdrew from the merchant committee overseeing the boycott in the winter of 1769–70.[33] By that point, Henry Drinker, of the dry goods firm James and Drinker, wrote that he doubted "more than ever" that merchants would hold to their agreement. "Interest, all powerful interest, will bear down on Patriotism," he predicted, continuing, "Romans we are not as we were formerly, when they despised Riches and Grandeur, abode in extreme poverty and sacrificed every pleasant enjoyment for love and service of their Country." Drinker used the language of civic virtue to contrast participation in the Stamp Act boycotts with the lower level of enthusiasm that plagued the current agreement. Although he regarded Spartan sacrifice as preferable, Drinker knew that the combination of merchant "interest" and consumer appetite, the twin engines that drove a commercial, consumer society, would work together to render it unappealing. In New York, a "public opinion poll of consumers" indicated that people were ready to rescind the boycott.[34] Through the poll, a collective voice spoke out in favor of individual expression.

Many examples of continued consumption of imports can be found, particularly among the elite men and women who supposedly set virtuous examples. Undeterred by the Townshend Acts, Charlestonians retained their fondness for high fashion and generally turned deaf ears to critiques.[35] In June of 1768, George Washington requested a suit of clothes of "fashionable coloured cloth" from a London tailor, and for his wife, "two handsome stomachers, with sleeve knots made of ribbons," a "green satin quilted coat," and a "handsome grane Winter Silk (but not yellow) . . . to be made into a saque and a coat."[36] Ever concerned with cutting a genteel figure, he likely donned such finery for his many trips to the theater in 1772 and during his attendance at the Philadelphia Assembly in 1773. Although nonimportation agreements had not yet been forged in Virginia, talk of them was widespread. Likewise, Thomas Jefferson ordered imported broadcloth, cotton and silk stockings, and "scarlet cloth for waistcoats." Such tastes did not prevent him from including in a group of maxims that he recorded below the list of goods: "moderation in all respects is best."[37]

We might expect such extravagant habits from members of South Carolina's and Virginia's gentry, who were renowned for their opulence, but consider the purchases of one prosperous Philadelphia couple, John and Elizabeth Lloyd Cadwalader. In 1768 the newly married merchant and his wife, daughter of Maryland's Edward Lloyd, one of the richest men in the colonies, began to refurbish a townhouse on Second Street. The following year, with nonimportation in effect and nonconsumption vigorously promoted in the public prints, John Cadwalader purchased the most prestigious and expensive kind of carriage from a London craftsman, and by 1770 owned two smaller buggylike phaetons.[38] As for attire, from January of 1768 through May of 1769 John purchased £77 worth of imported fabric from one retailer alone, including scarlet and green cloth, Persian, gold buttons, black serge, and mantua. Also oblivious to calls for nonconsumption or dismissive of them, Elizabeth Cadwalader bought from the same retailer in May of 1769 £23 worth of goods, including calico, Durant, silk, and many varieties of gloves and ribbons. Much of what she chose was black.[39] Perhaps Mrs. Cadwalader purchased items in the increasingly visible Quaker plain style, or perhaps a great deal of mourning wear.

Although mourning dress had been targeted for reform since the Revenue Act of 1764, other mourning rituals seemed to escalate. Peter Oliver penned the following sharp critique of funereal practices in Boston: "Under the pretense of Oeconomy, the Faction undertook to regulate Funerals, that there might be less Demand for English Manufactures." For years, he continued, sensible people had attempted to curtail the expensive practice of mourning, but now the "Demogogues and their Mirmidons" who controlled the government had corrupted those reforms so that "what at another Time would have been deemed oeconomical was at this Time Spite and Malevolence." "One extreme was exchanged for another," Oliver claimed, as "a funeral now seemed more like a Procession to a May Fair, and processions were lengthened, especially by Ladies, who figured a way in order to exhibit their Share of Spite and their Silk Gowns."[40] Oliver thus linked the performance of sentiment with that of status, questioning the motives of those who organized nonconsumption, as well as the authenticity of those who supported it. For Oliver, the pretense of economy masked the real agendas: for men, the desire for political power, for women, the desire to see and to be seen, even in an environment of supposed plainness. Thus performances of loyalty to the colonial cause became like social assemblies, as colonists molded a vestige of imperial culture to their own anti-imperial uses.

Oliver concluded his biting review with one final turn of the supposed inverse relationship between appearance and reality, display and artifice on its head. Quoting Richardson's *Clarissa*,[41] thereby subtly impugning the women's chastity by reference to the fallen heroine, he wrote, "There is no inconvenience without a convenience." Oliver explained, "Whereas formerly a widow, who had been well rid of a bad Companion, could conceal her Joy under a long black Vail, she was now obliged to use what Female Arts she was mistress of in order to transform her Joy into the Appearance of a more decent Passion, to impose upon the Croud of numerous Spectators."[42] In his observation, the rejection of imported goods made people, women in particular, all the more artful and less authentic. Forgoing the material trappings that expressed or disguised sentiment forced them to actually perform grief. The "convenience," however, was that at least throwing off fashionable veils required women to discipline their expressions.[43] In this respect Oliver echoed the desires of patriot men, who lauded performances of frugal and industrious female behavior that they insisted—or hoped—reflected authentic sentiments.

The campaign to get colonial consumers to "buy into" asceticism was not particularly successful. The collapse of nonimportation in 1770 revealed the economic power of Philadelphia's merchants, the persistence of consumer demand for imports, and the triumph of an individualistic identity that adherence to fashion fed. Parliament's repeal of all duties but the tax on tea provided the necessary excuse for abandoning the boycotts. As the *Pennsylvania Chronicle* noted, "There will always be importers of English goods while there are buyers."[44] Attempts to make plainness and sacrifice fashionable could not succeed so long as the people of fashion continued in their habits, so to speak. The pose of plainness and aesthetic of understatement was still literally comprised of imported cloth, meaning that the political economy supporting such styles undermined their symbolic value. And the "people of fashion" in port cities were, by and large, the commercial elite, whose position relied not only upon the appropriate consumption and display of imported goods but on the fortunes that trade in them created.

The "Loud" Period

Although some historians have called the months between the so-called Boston Massacre of March 1770 and public outcry over the Tea Act in the fall of 1773 the "quiet period," the early 1770s proved anything but tranquil in terms of consumption, display, and rising social and political tensions in Philadelphia.[45] It was, quite simply, a period of conspicuous consumption among many urban denizens, as an influx of inexpensive imported goods and the adoption of extravagant, eye-catching styles for men and women alike widened rifts between artisans and merchants. Grudging agreements among the town's men of trade not to import British goods forged in response to the Townshend Acts fell apart once Parliament repealed the taxes, with the exception of the duty on tea, in 1770. The breakdown of nonimportation angered many artisans, who envisioned new markets for their own wares that might result from declining imports.[46] Likewise, pledges to renounce imported goods, and to choose domestically produced items such as cloth and tea, were similarly compromised. Nonconsumption movements had proven largely unsuccessful in attempting to permanently discredit the imported goods and styles that influenced the identities of persons and places. A gesture of conformity masquerading as individuality, following the mode as set in European circles, expressed personal distinction as well as social belonging to local and Atlantic communities, helping to establish Philadelphia as the colonial center of culture and refinement.[47]

Although John and Elizabeth Cadwalader were Whigs, their consumption continued unabated into the 1770s. In 1770 she began to patronize milliner Mary Symonds, giving her hundreds of pounds worth of business in gowns, caps, ribbons, lace, and accessories, including six pairs of purple gloves in

September of 1770, twelve rows of French beads in April of 1771, and twelve pounds of hair powder in June of that year.[48] The following year, Charles Willson Peale painted a family portrait in which John and Elizabeth Cadwalader and their daughter, Anne, look very much the fashionably genteel family. He sports a gold-laced waistcoat, a ruffle peeking from the sleeve of his burgundy coat; she wears a lavender silk gown overlain with lace or embroidered muslin and replete with three sleeve ruffles, a fan folded primly in her lap as she gazes up at her husband. Even their daughter, seated on a mahogany table and reaching for the peach her father offers, wears a dress of peach silk overlain with muslin.[49]

Indeed, the high style of the late 1760s and early 1770s suggests a certain disregard for, even outright defiance of, Whig insistence on sacrifice and asceticism, demonstrated by the level of consumption and appetites for fashion. Imports flooded Philadelphia, prompting the merchant William Pollard to note in 1772 that "in the dry goods way people seem more infatuated" than ever. "If possible," he continued, "larger quantities are imported than the province can consume." Auctions, or "vendue sales," that sold goods directly and cheaply to the public became increasingly common. And merchants and shopkeepers were not the only ones profiting from demand for the latest styles. Esther De Berdt Reed, who had recently arrived from London after marrying Philadelphian Joseph Reed, remarked in November of 1770 that one woman was "making a fortune by going to England and bringing back new fashions" and that "articles for gentlemen's use" were particularly desirable. Hungry for new modes herself, Reed later asked her brother to procure for her a "handsome spring silk, fit for summer and new fashion," but then found that she could have one made to her liking in fashion-conscious Philadelphia. Reed and Pollard both pointed to a glutted market, she noting that "the country will soon be overstocked" and he remarking that "people in order to sell off their goods undersell each other and many sell under the first cost."[50]

Not only were more goods available at lower prices, meaning that even "lower sorts" could potentially afford fine things such as silks and fans, but certain fashions in dress for both men and women grew quite remarkable, even extravagant, attracting attention and stimulating debate. One novel item that received both positive and negative attention was the umbrella. Already in use in warmer climes for protection from rain and sun, and introduced in England in the 1760s, the umbrellas of the late eighteenth century, although large and clumsy by modern standards, were items of fashion, brightly colored and made of oiled silk.[51] Debate quickly erupted on

Portrait of John and Elizabeth Lloyd Cadwalader and Their Daughter Anne, by Charles Willson Peale, 1772, oil on canvas. 128.3 × 104.8 cm (50 ½ × 41 ¼ in.). Philadelphia Museum of Art: Purchased for the Cadwalader Collection with funds contributed by the Mabel Pew Myrin Trust and the gift of an anonymous donor, 1983, 1983-90-3.

their merits—for whom were parasols best suited, if suitable at all? Were they necessary, especially outside the tropics? Discussion unfolded in the public prints, the forum best suited to prescribe or proscribe certain styles and behaviors for a wide audience of readers. Some regarded umbrellas as ridiculous and frivolous, serving no purpose that a good hat could not supply. Others called them effeminate, appropriate only for use by women. Defenders of the umbrella, such as one writer for the *Pennsylvania Gazette*, mentioned style and substance—not only was the parasol a "graceful part of dress in many countries," but it was also a tool for protecting people from "vertigoes, epilepsy, sore eyes, fevers," and other maladies resulting from exposure to the sun. To the charge of effeminacy, the writer responded that to follow such reasoning to its absurd conclusion would be to argue that since "the ladies wear shoes, let the men therefore go barefooted!"[52]

The umbrella debate demonstrates the ways in which men's fashions in particular troubled some Philadelphians, who felt that they undermined masculinity, confused designations of social status, and were economically irresponsible. The author of the satirical pamphlet *The Miraculous Power of Clothes and Dignity of the Taylors, Being an Essay on the Words Clothes Make Men, Translated from the German*, shared such preoccupations, taking aim at tailors and their patrons.[53] In addition, he targeted the upstart immigrants that poured into the city after midcentury—hence the title's inauthentic reference to the essay's original publication in German. The piece attacked people so preoccupied with appearances that they mistook fine clothes for a fine person beneath. It facetiously insisted that only clothes could "effect that which virtue, honesty, merit and love for our country in vain try to perform." The virtuous but plainly dressed man, no matter his station, would be refused by polite company, the author claimed, while all rushed to greet the "gilded fop" who dazzled their eyes. "Now our honest plain man is entirely forgot," the writer continued. "Simpleton! Why has he not better clothes and less merit?" he queried, juxtaposing style and substance. "How can the world help it that a great soul hides itself in a mean garment?" he asked sarcastically, skewering people for valuing appearance above all.[54]

Warming to his other target, he continued, "Since then to our clothes we owe the decision of our merits, I frankly confess that there are few persons of the world for whom I have so much veneration as I have for my taylor." He often experienced awe upon observing how "merit, virtue, ingenuity, sense, wit, etc.," emerged from a tailor's crafty hands. "By a stick of his needle," he claimed, "worthy men spring out of nothing." His final point was that since tailors made clothes, and clothes made "men and merit," people should not claim for their persons the honor rightly afforded to their attire. The language of compliments would be altered in order to obliterate the conflation of external display and internal worth. People should accurately say, "Sir, I have the honour to assure your waistcoat of my humble respects. I recommend myself to the favour of your embroidered suit. The merits of your rich trimmings are the admiration of your country. May heaven long preserve your velvet coat for the good of church and state!"[55]

Underneath such absurdity lay a serious economic argument about the social perils of extravagance. All too often such finery expressed neither merit nor wealth, purchased as it was on credit. Credit flowed from English to colonial merchants, who readily passed it along to their customers until 1772, when the market abruptly contracted.[56] In his "postscript," the satirist advocated a law that "no person of the male sex" could don a rich, fashionable suit until it had been paid for in full. Men would be required to wear the receipt on their person as evidence of payment—proof of purchase as accessory, serving as the truest status symbol. By this method, "a great many who possess neither money nor merit and who have hitherto kept up their esteem merely at the expense of their tailors and creditors would, by being stripped of the borrowed pomp and clothes, lose at once all that made them preferable, amiable and important." He wondered what would become of these people and of Philadelphia's "grand assemblies" if a social hierarchy based on substance rather than show took hold, if clothes were no longer allowed to make men.[57]

And what of the men who made the clothes that made the men, equally a concern of the author? Apparently not all tradesmen had suffered from the collapse of nonimportation; some, namely those in the fashion trades, were increasing their economic and political clout in an era of "conspicuous consumption." On August 20, 1771, sixty-eight tailors signed their names to a document that professed the "necessity of uniting and coming under proper regulations respecting our business." Although clearly a professional organization, the Taylors Company of Philadelphia also served as an institution for sociability. The participants strove to cultivate the "advantages that may arise from frequently meeting together and conversing on usefull and entertaining subjects," being "desirous of cementing a lasting mutual friendship betwixt us." The organization's bylaws included provisions requiring attendance at regular meetings, with fines for absences and tardiness; dining together once a year (funded by such fines) to preserve "harmony and friendship"; complete freedom of religious conviction; and fixed prices on all work. Article 8 plainly stated: "If any person belonging to this society should be found out charging a lower price for workmanship than what is specified in our printed agreement, it shall be deemed proper to inform against such a person." A "fair hearing" would follow, and the offending tailor, if convicted, would be reprimanded and required to ask the pardon of the group. Failing this, he would be expelled from the society and "treated as an Underminer."[58]

The formation of the Taylors Company marked an upwardly mobile class of men who aimed to secure certain wages and suppress competition. Economic protectionism enforced through democratic, legalistic means provided the company's raison d'être. Furthermore, they sought to regulate the entire profession, agreeing "not to pay any journeyman more than four shillings per day." Yet lest they be accused of merely pursuing self-interest, the society made regular sociability central to its existence, seeking to establish themselves as men of sense as well as skill. By the spring of 1773 the Taylors Company was faring so well that they could "hire someone to serve notices of meetings."[59] By 1774, one writer hoped to wrest power from the tailors who presumed to direct the "sensible inhabitants of the city."[60] Although intended as a sneeringly sarcastic phrase suggesting their utter indignity, the "dignity of the tailors," socially and politically, was indeed on the rise, and some Philadelphians considered these men as upstart as some of their clients.

Just as the pamphlet's author worried about extravagance in male dress generally, so, too, did Edward Duff, a College of Philadelphia graduate who delivered a commencement address on the "extravagance of the present Modes of Dress" in the summer of 1773. But others had a more specific style in mind. Duff's speech was followed by another titled "On the Character of a Macaroni," given by Joseph Harrison.[61] "Macaroni" referred both to particular short-lived fashion for men in the early 1770s and to a certain kind of man. Often derisive, the term applied to elaborately powdered, ruffled, and corseted men of fashion, successors to the Restoration-era fop and predecessors to the nineteenth-century dandy. First appearing in London in the 1760s, macaronis were wealthy young men who had taken a grand tour of the continent and returned to England bedecked with European, particularly Italian, fashions—hence the moniker "macaroni" that soon came to describe a fashion. The macaroni cut a fantastical figure, donning a tall wig crowned by a comparatively tiny cap, with a long queue in back. His suits were opulent and closely cut, their silhouettes incredibly slim, his padded and silk-stocking-clad calves disappearing into high-heeled shoes.[62] These were the hallmarks of the macaroni mode, but a series of lampoons from the London print shop of Matthew and Mary Darly depicted a host of macaronis,

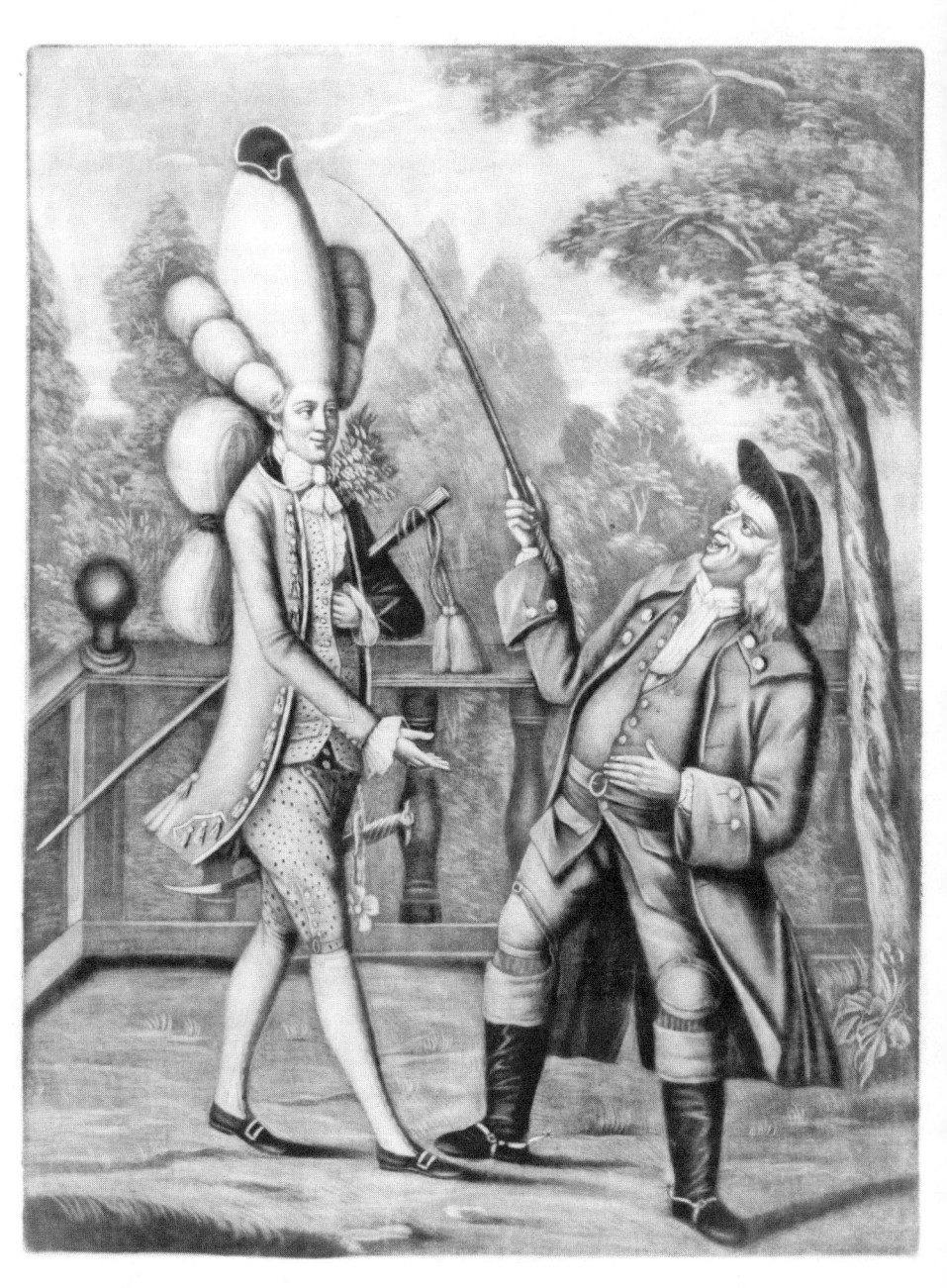

"What is this my Son Tom," mezzotint, 1774, printed by R. Sayer and John Bennett. A plainly dressed father makes sport of his son's macaroni style, in particular the tall wig and small cap. Courtesy Library of Congress, Washington D.C., Prints and Photographs Division, LC-USZ62-115003.

from farmers to barristers.⁶³ Thus "macaroni" could apply to any man who followed fashion in order to ape high status, who was all style and no substance. Harrison's commencement address suggested that a macaroni's character might be visually apprehended.

Duff's and Harrison's commencement addresses were timely, in that the previous year colonists saw perhaps the fullest fictional elaboration of the upstart man of fashion in John Trumbull's *Progress of Dulness*, a satire directed at the fellows of Yale College. In the creation of Dick Hairbrain, the "country fop" come to town, Trumbull continued the long tradition of the fop character in English letters, looking back to his literary predecessors from the metropole while illuminating a distinctly provincial context through the character and his foibles.⁶⁴

The scion of a Connecticut farmer, Dick decides to attend college, where he quickly transforms into a man of fashion. Through description of the character's supposedly fashionable attire, Trumbull emphasizes his stupidity, lampooning "the modish hat, whose breadth contains the measure of its owners brains"—equating his tiny macaroni cap with his small mind.⁶⁵ In fact, Dick's big hair takes the place of a brain, as Trumbull makes such external display a signifier of internal emptiness. Dick attends college to acquire not the learning and sense but rather the fashionable education, refinements, and gentility necessary to legitimate his family's new, ill-gotten wealth. He fails, however, to triumph over his upbringing in "distant woods." In finding a "college suited to his mind," Dick pursues the wrong sort of education. He becomes a fop of the first order with a slew of fashionable vices to accompany his pseudo-modish garb—the "proud displays of awkward dress that all the country-fop express." Though a student of the ways of fashion, Dick never gets it quite right:

> The suit right gay, tho' much belated, Whose fashion's superannuated; . . .
> The silver buckle, dread to view, O'ershad'wing all the clumsy shoe
> The white-glov'd hand that tries to peep From ruffle, full five inches deep.⁶⁶

Dick styles himself in the macaroni fashion in an attempt to ascend the social ladder, perverting a setting intended for cultivation of the mind to serve his own bodily desires. At each rung he cruelly uses women, making a fool of himself, and landing deeply in debt—as well as in jail. Bungling his attempts at gentility, he proclaims his low breeding. Through extensive descriptions of Dick's ridiculous attire and affected behavior, Trumbull catalogs the ways in which those merely aping status could be discerned and unmasked. Readers could not help but realize the wrongheaded futility of Dick's tasteless "receipt to make a gentleman."[67] So, too, should they accurately "see" real fops for the empty pretenders they were.

Although Trumbull's Dick Hairbrain was but a lampoon, actual macaronis roamed the streets of Philadelphia, as some men continued to perform social position through fashionable display, aided by tailors and hairdressers. They symbolized the climate of display in the extreme in early 1770s Philadelphia, although elites likely sniffed at such pretense. The same Sarah Eve who disdained Mrs. Brayen also noted in her diary that Dr. Curry, visiting from Montego Bay, where her father, Oswell Eve, was doing business, waited three full days after arriving in Philadelphia to call on her family. They heard he was sick with a cold but then learned, as the daughter Eve supposed, that "he entertained so high an idea of our *quality* that the poor Doctor thought his clothes were not good enough to wait upon us in." "Therefore," she speculated dryly, he "delays his visit until he gets fitted up in the macaronia taste, I suppose."[68] If that were the case, Philadelphia tailors and hairdressers almost certainly assisted him. By dressing to impress, the doctor failed to do so, but only because Eve was secure enough in her own social status, yet wry enough about what her family's financial straits might mean for that position, to sense a poser in the good doctor.

Since the male head of the Eve household was away, Dr. Curry came to pay his respects to the ladies of the house; perhaps this was why he adopted the macaroni mode. A hallmark of macaronis, according to proscriptive literature, was their incessant courting of female favor, as well as adopting appearances and behaviors that confused the very categories of masculine and feminine. An essay in the *Universal Almanack* for 1773 mocked "that taper, trim, two legged Bagatelle, that soft-faced, soft-hearted thing with a great head and nothing in it, thy well-beloved macaroni." "Bagatelle" meant a trifle, an unimportant and insignificant bauble, but also indicated a French game played on a table with a cue and balls, a reference rife with sexual imagery. The macaroni had male "parts," but his appearance and behavior belied them, making him all the more dangerous. Devotees of fashion and of women, macaronis bowed and scraped before the altar of fashion before gathering "round ladies knees." At once an inveterate pleaser of women, yet himself effeminate, the macaroni "quits his manhood," becoming an "amphibious despicable thing," neither clearly male nor female.[69] Among the macaroni's more recognizable and distasteful gender-bending features was his large powdered wig.[70] One description from 1772 that deployed the androgynous pronoun described the "vast quantity of hair on its head . . . loaded with powder and pomatum,"[71] a look that mirrored fashionable hairstyles for women.

In the early 1770s, fashions for women expanded in literal and figurative ways—to fill more space, and to adorn more bodies. Lower prices resulting from the glut of goods meant that a greater number of women could afford to don high styles, as advertisements competed not only to sell the greatest array of fashionable items, from fine fabrics to tea equipages, but to do so on the "lowest terms," as William Pollard had observed.[72] What was more, styles themselves became larger and more elaborate. At tea tables, assemblies, and even in the city streets, ladies' hoops grew wider and heads climbed higher with the appearance of the high roll.

Fashionable hairstyles for women began to grow in the late 1760s, and with them rose the ire of social critics. While some editorials appearing first in London periodicals decried the large headdresses that English ladies all too eagerly copied from their French counterparts, other printed treatises described in detail the latest hair fashions from France and how to achieve them with the assistance of a *friseur*.[73] These instructions, coupled with the presence of hairdressers hailing from England and France, helped speed the spread of the high roll to colonial cities. Philadelphia wig makers Launier and Robison made "ladies frizets in the neatest manner" and "in the Paris mode, if agreeable," while Matthews from London made "new inverted tupees . . . ladies brains and cushions . . . and all other fashion wigs now wore in England."[74] Parisian Louis Fay, whose shop was located in Strawberry Alley, advertised that he dressed ladies hair in fifty different ways and men's in thirty. His services could be retained by the month or by the style at four shillings for men and a pound for women.[75]

British American women who considered themselves fashionable quickly adopted the high roll. Some elite ladies of Philadelphia, such as Elizabeth Lloyd Cadwalader, chose to have their high rolls preserved for all posterity in portraiture.[76] Sarah Eve also wore her hair high, complaining in 1772 that the social kissing practiced by Edward Shippen "disorders one's high Roll."[77] According to one description provided by twelve-year-old Anna Green Winslow of Boston in her diary, high rolls were composed of "red cow tail, horsehair, and a little human hair . . . all carded together and twisted up." She noted with delight that, with the "roll" perched atop her young head, she measured a full inch longer from the roots of her hair

"Coiffures," France, ca. 1780s. Contained in a pack much like playing cards, these coiffure cards allowed women to use the enclosed busts or their own miniature likenesses to try on different headdresses, and to show hairdressers exactly what styles they wanted. Courtesy The Winterthur Library, Joseph Downs Collection of Manuscripts and Printed Ephemera.

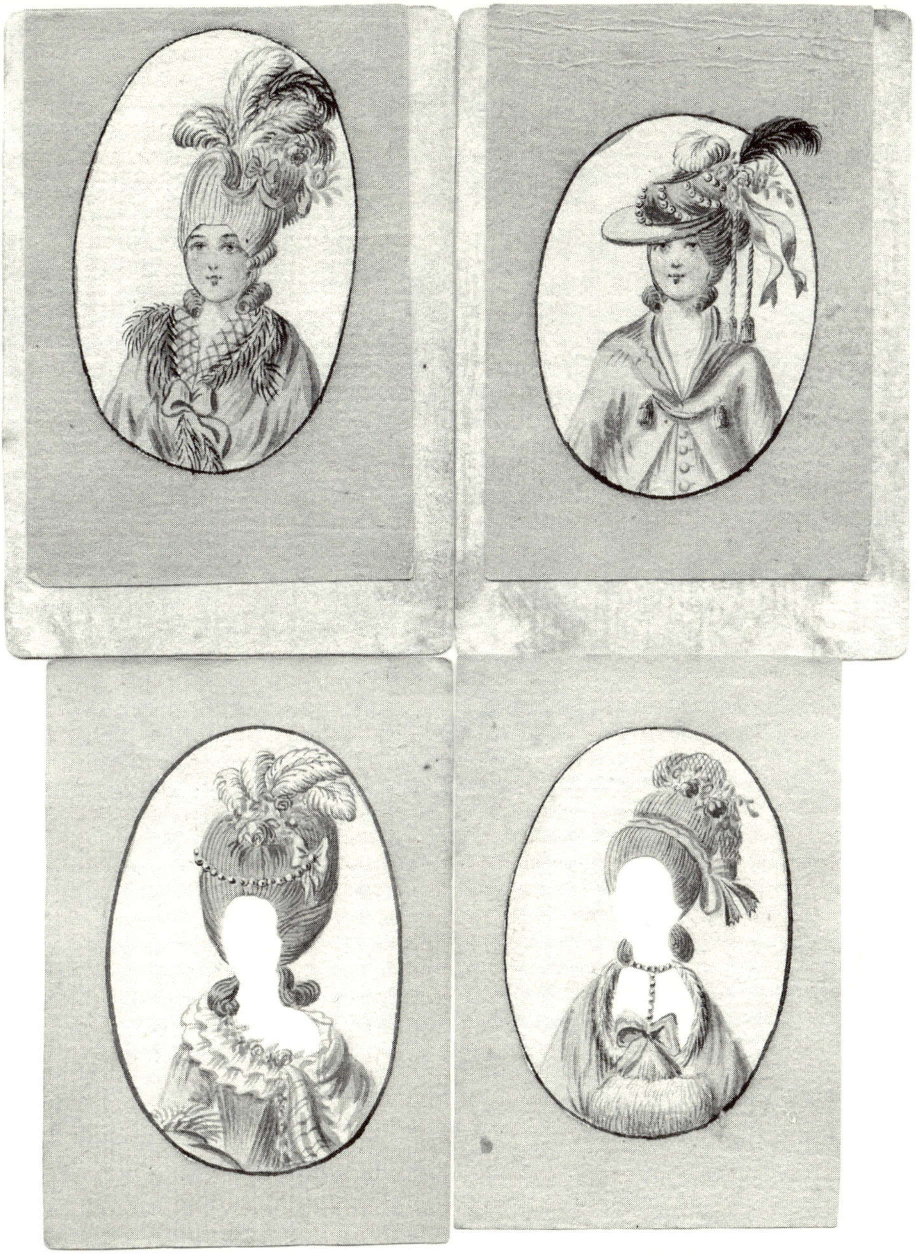

Anna Green Winslow, frontispiece in Alice Morse Earle, ed., *Diary of Anna Green Winslow: A Boston Schoolgirl of 1771* (Cambridge, Mass., 1894). In this portrait miniature, Winslow is memorialized in her much-desired yet much-maligned and uncomfortable high roll hairstyle.

up to the tip of the style than from her forehead down to her chin. Usually a side curl was brought down over one shoulder, and the roll then festooned with pearls and flowers. But Winslow's pleasure at her appearance was tempered by the fact that the style made her head "itch and ach and burn like anything," probably because such rolls often weighed more than a pound.[78] Furthermore, it took some time, perhaps hours, for a hairdresser to create such a style, so having it "disordered" by an overzealous greeting was of no small inconvenience. The amount of time involved in achieving the elaborate look meant that wearing a high roll signified high social status in two ways: by replicating a style worn at court and the beau monde in England and by requiring plenty of spare time in order to have it constructed.

Achieving the high style required women to spend hours more or less alone with male hairdressers, often of European origin. Charges of inappropriate sexual encounters with their coiffeurs, attacks that conflated sexual and consumer appetites, served as another means of discrediting women who sported high rolls. The advertisement that parodied "Lewis Fay" noted that his many feats of dressing hair "in the newest ridiculous way," which including making hair to grow in bald spots, were performed "near the sign of Queen Charlotte, a dollar's the price for bawd, strumpet or harlot."[79] Anxieties over relationships between men and women of different social ranks, the potentially illicit exchanges that were occurring, and the dependency of women with means on men without informed attacks on hairdressers and their clients. Perhaps genteel patrons were raising them up socially and economically even as *friseurs* sexually compromised female customers. Hairdressers and other purveyors of fashion shared the strange fate of producing markers of high status within a social hierarchy that assigned them low rank.[80] Although a patron of hairdressing, Sarah Eve mused that a person of worth was often too soon forgotten in death while another was "remembered and his name handed down to posterity for having been the best hairdresser."[81] Yet like tailors, hairdressers claimed more than a little authority in the 1770s, power derived from the ability to create status, in part by making customers attractive to members of the opposite sex. As the parody of Lewis Fay noted, *friseurs* could help men ensure that "the Ladies ye ardently love shall admire thee."[82] Even men who did not fashion themselves as macaronis relied upon the expertise of hairdressers. Jacob Duché, assistant minister at Philadelphia's Anglican Christ Church, had his hair "curl'd and powder'd" every day.[83] And he carried an umbrella besides.

The increasing consumption of fashionable items and high styles of the early 1770s bespoke continued economic and cultural dependence on England, and a social landscape marked by status seeking and gender bending. How could Philadelphians reconcile high-rolled women with the image of demure "daughters of liberty" that Hannah Griffits sketched in her 1768 poem "The Female Patriots," genteel ladies who eschewed imported goods and fashions for love of country?[84] Unfortunately for the resistance movement, it seemed that the former were the "ladies" of the "first families," the "best taste," of "distinction." Or square the presence of macaronis with men of sense and taste who secured position and the affections of women by renouncing fashionable display? The image of a high-haired woman of leisure, sitting for hours in the service of her own vanity, and a ponytailed, big-wigged, brocaded macaroni flew in the face of prescriptions featuring the modest, domestic colonial woman virtuously spinning cloth to support an independent domestic economy and the homespun-clad man who rejected fashion as a form of social currency. But such ideals were just that, as disregard for and backlash to the rhetoric of resistance suggests. Umbrellas, macaronis, and high rolls stood as symbols of appetites for and adherence to high fashion. What was more, money spent in procuring the styles increased the fortunes of tailors and hairdressers; perhaps it was only a matter of time before the latter formed a professional organization. As residents asserted the city's, and their own, stylish, cosmopolitan character through fashion within a shifting local and imperial political climate, social life, sartorial practices, and politics became inextricably intertwined even as they jockeyed against one another.

Quiet Wives

When Anna Green Winslow sported her high roll in 1772, one of her disapproving aunts said the roll ought to be made smaller and another drolly rejoined that it "ought not to be made at all." To appease them (for she often read her journal entries aloud), Winslow penned the following: "Nothing renders a young person more amiable than virtue and modesty without the help of fals hair, red cow tail or D___ (the barber)."[85] It reads like a maxim plucked directly from a conduct manual. The tugs of filial duty and fashionability, Winslow found, were powerful and often contradictory. Such was the tension between high fashion and feminine propriety in the early 1770s, between expressions of status dependent on the mode and its proponents and those based on inherent "taste." On one hand, publications such as the *Lady's Magazine* validated fashion. Yet in the face of "loud" styles such as wide hoops and high rolls, local almanacs urged women to keep quiet. Concerns over the intersection of status hierarchy and gender relations continued to shape the messages male writers sent to colonial women about appearance and behavior.

In 1770 the *Lady's Magazine; or, Entertaining Companion for the Fair Sex* began publication in London, being advertised the following year in the colonies. The preface to the inaugural issue wondered why women continued to be "neglected by the learned" as they were reading more than ever. Although many women possessed elegance of mind, "as external appearance is the first inlet to the treasures of the heart, and the advantages of dress, though they cannot communicate beauty may at least make it more conspicuous," the periodical would "inform distant readers with every innovation that is made in female dress." It planned to catalog "the fluctuations of fashions" through patterns and engravings. In the following two issues, however, the magazine fell silent on fashion. Finally, in volume four of the same year the editors assured readers, "We have not lost sight of our promise to the Fair Sex of giving them the most early intelligence of the revolutions which shall be made in fashions." Since "the stage" set the "standard of taste," they presented readers with a "genteel undress, in which Miss Catley appeared in the character of Rosetta in Love in a Village."[86] For the readers of the *Lady's Magazine* at least, the theater was an acceptable setter of trends.

Yet even as elite and middling women might read of changing fashions and their importance in the highbrow *Lady's Magazine*, writers of almanacs sought to discipline such appetites among their readers.[87] Styles considered outrageous received as much negative attention as macaronis. *Father Abraham's Almanack* for 1770 included the following poem titled "To the Ladies, on the Present Fashions":

> If our Grandames of old,
> From their Graves could behold
> How their Daughters like mad Women dress,
> As they lie in Tombs,
> They'd repent that their Wombs,
> Ever bore such a whimsical Race.[88]

Casting "Ladies" as "mad women" made them the opposite of women of sense. Their mothers and grandmothers would be ashamed to have produced this "race" of people who had become inherently "whimsical."

The continued promotion of a modest, not a modish, appearance was most common. *Poor Richard's Almanack* for 1773 included a poem titled "Real Beauty." The piece contrasted the "blaze" of diamonds and rubies with the subtle and therefore far more attractive "soft tear" and "sweet blush of modesty" in a female face. Real beauty lay in sentiment, not show. Similarly, "The Country Lass" praised the virtuous rural maid who "never loses life in thoughtless ease." Instead, she knew true contentment through unaffected tastes: "her home-spun dress in simple Nature lies, And for no glaring equipage she sighs."[89] The verses implied that women should appear without affectation in dress as well as manner.

A pantheon of ideal traits that rendered a woman most eligible for marriage—modesty, sense, and "natural" beauty—replaced fashionability. Almanacs insisted that a humble appearance was the surest means of attracting a husband. "The Way to Get Him, Addressed to the Fair," encouraged women to reveal their beauty "by degrees." "We soon grow surfeited with those, who all their charms at once disclose," the poem continued. As a final piece of advice, the verse closed:

> If Girls, to Admiration prone,
> would only let themselves alone . . .
> Their Prudence would be well repaid
> By every conquest which they made.[90]

The poem suggested that if women would only cease their fussy, endless hours at toilette, and stop trying to attract men through display, their virtue would be rewarded with a fine "catch." "Rules for the Choice of a Wife," which appeared in the same volume, also connected a modest mien with entrance into matrimony. The guidelines read, "If much of her time is destroyed in Dress and Adornments, if she is enamoured with her own Beauty and delighted with her own praise, if she laugheth much and talketh loud . . . turn thy face from her charms."[91] Men of sense, the "rules" indicated, preferred unadorned, simple maids to showy women of fashion.

Jests took aim at women who did not adhere to prescribed standards of beauty and behavior. Father Abraham's allegorical tale "The Fox and the Goose" promised readers knowledge of "the nearest road to woman's heart." Through flattery and show, the fox, a "connoisseur in female failings," convinced the vain goose to elope with him. He then maneuvered her into a position to be devoured.[92] The joke drew no distinctions between groups of women, referring instead to the general weaknesses of females, in particular their susceptibility to flattery. It suggested that women were extravagant and vain and that such traits would prove their sexual downfall, even death.

Another essay in *Father Abraham's* for 1772 singled out individual, if fictive, women, with similarly misogynist results. The piece purported to explain "the reasons why Miss Jenny Tinderbox, Miss Squeeze, Miss Betty Tempest and the sagacious Sophronia remain unmarried." The first lady waited in vain for a "man of quality," disdaining good men of her own modest station in life. Miss Squeeze, by contrast, had a moderate fortune and was determined to marry someone who could match it penny for penny. Betty Tempest possessed "beauty, fortune, and family" but acted like a silly, vain coquette who preferred fools to men of sense. Finally, Sophronia was simply too learned. Her love of Greek and "exquisite sensibility" caused her to reject every suitor, until in old age "without one good feature in her face she talks incessantly of the beauties of the mind."[93] All four characters held opinions of themselves—whether of their beauty, fortunes, or brains—that, like women's hairstyles, were too high. The result was a life consigned to spinsterhood.

Juxtaposing fashionable living and wifely contentment suggested that one was compatible with the other, thereby undermining fashion as a tool in courtship and a route to the happy union of marriage. The pursuit of fashion fueled a social hierarchy dictated by women and, in flush times, when fine goods could be had cheaply, by women of various ranks. Fashion vested a "race" of persons castigated for their inherent love of display with the power to set and apply standards. These women bestowed attention on men who appealed to their senses and ignored or reproached those who did not. Macaronis literally embodied the extreme—"amphibious despicable" things who lisped compliments; they were merely ridiculous. But according to "Reflections on Gallantry, and on the Education of Women," even men of sense often appeared and behaved in particular ways to please and attract women in courtship. They did so because, like Father Abraham's allegorical goose or the "mad women" of verse, women did not possess sense enough to reject glitter and show.[94]

Thus prescriptions and proscriptions generated by men attempted to discredit fashionable display at a time when fashion's presence and social currency could not be denied. It was not enough to make fashion unmanly or effeminate—that association had existed since the early decades of the century.[95] As long as signifying status and success in courtship relied on the styles that tailors and hairdressers produced and the heterosocial spaces that women arbitrated, targeting female behavior and proclivities remained the best means of ensuring that clothes would not make the man.

Poor Sarah Eve

What then of Sarah Eve and her embrace of modesty and simplicity to distinguish herself from other women? Her diary demonstrates one way in which a woman constructed a protective wall around her social position and founded it on the bedrock of feminine propriety and internal merit. Sarah Eve separated the performance of genteel femininity from material display, much as Hannah Callender had done some years earlier. It was essential that she do so, for Eve possessed personal as well as political reasons to disdain the affluent and ostentatious Mrs. Brayen and her circle. Although she never mentioned the political climate in her diary, Eve was as invested in its consequences as any Philadelphia resident. The conclusion of her tale reveals how the imperial crisis could affect relationships between financial success and social hierarchy and had a negative impact on the Eve family in particular.

Early in 1773, Eve reported an evening spent reading Richard Cumberland's *The Fashionable Lover*, which she praised as a "prodigious fine comedy."[96] It is a typically confusing eighteenth-century comedy of manners in which the title character attempts to seduce the virtuous and beautiful orphan girl Augusta Aubrey, who lives by the leave of the unethical, social-climbing Bridgemore family. The designing rake Lord Abberville sneaks into Augusta's room with the assistance of daughter Lucinda Bridgemore's maid and is discovered there by none other than Lucinda herself, who just happens to have designs on the man Augusta loves. Aspersions fall on the heroine's virtue, but in the end her innocence is revealed and her good name and true love restored. Her redemption coincides neatly with the reappearance of her equally virtuous father, who has regained his once-lost, sizable fortune.[97]

Like other tales of its day, *The Fashionable Lover* delivered the message to audiences and readers that money could serve to temporarily confuse, but in the end did not mask, the equation of legitimate social status and virtue. At the center of his moral, Cumberland placed a clear prescription for women: truly virtuous, modest women triumphed, and always would. Paradoxically, their rejection of social fame and wealth would be rewarded with material comfort. The play's epilogue, aimed specifically at the "ladies," the nation's "ornament and pride," drew a sharp distinction between scenes of gaiety and those of domestic bliss. The playwright called upon women to renounce Soho, the "fashionable" section of London, in favor of time with their husbands.[98] In referencing the area of town, he indirectly warned of the short distance between fashionable living and lost virtue, for Soho was also a haven for prostitutes. Women who ignored the caution and continued to pursue their own pleasure not only proved easy prey for men such as Lord Abberville but actually encouraged and were therefore responsible for men's rakish behavior.

In the play's final lines, after mocking the amount of time women spent at their toilette, the author speaks through a female character to fire the following parting shot: "Save me, just heaven, from such a painful life, / And make me an unfashionable wife!"[99] Although fashionable audiences might titter at the earnest didacticism, the pursuit of fashion in dress and diversions emerged as incompatible with status as a virtuous wife. Cumberland made the very phrase "unfashionable wife" into a tautology; being a wife required the rejection of fashion. By contrast, the "high life" was a "painful," lonely one.

Yet Sarah Eve was no stranger to the so-called high life herself. Born in 1750 into an Anglican family, her father, Oswell Eve, a sea captain and shipping merchant, became prosperous enough to partially own twenty-five vessels. They lived in a "large stone house," and Eve maintained a particular style of appearance and carriage. A handsome young woman, according to her contemporaries, she possessed a "stately" manner and red hair that was often "fashionably dressed" in the high roll style.[100] She did not really believe her own appetite to be "impolite," as she deemed it in her tale of the midafternoon meal—quite the opposite. Another account from her diary further confirms her status. On November 17, 1773, Eve and two female friends walked to the commons to take in a review of troops. They had expected to catch up with her brother and two other male friends, but did not, and "to [their] great mortification found [them]selves . . . surrounded by people of all ranks."[101] Her remark reveals that she did not usually mingle with Philadelphians whom she considered beneath her own social position.

But while the early 1770s may have proven boom times for some Philadelphians, the Eve family, however prominent, enjoyed no such luck. In May of 1768, Sarah's father suffered financial losses and left Philadelphia to conduct business in the West Indies. Much of her journal looks forward to his eventual return.[102] Although born into comfort, by the time she wrote her diary in 1773, Sarah Eve felt impoverished, much like Jane Austen's fictitious heroines of the next generation. Her situation contained not a little irony, for the consumer habits of women such as Mrs. Brayen drove dry goods trade; in a period of stagnation, Oswell Eve's business collapsed. Eve despised the very kinds of people who were, in part, responsible for her father's success or failure, and by proxy her comfort and condition. The imperial crises of the 1760s had created a new social reality for the Eve family.

Eve described her sentiments in a entry dated June 3. "Will fortune never cease to persecute us?" she ranted. "But why complain," she then philosophized, "for at the worst what is poverty? It is living more according to nature—luxury is not nature but art." Poverty might also allow a person to more fully ignore the opinions of others, she noted. Yet Eve could not meet her own criteria, could not discount the judgments of her neighbors. She continued her entry with the story of a childhood friend who acted "as if poverty were really infectious," cutting down side streets or "walking herself into perspiration" to avoid having to confront Eve. Although the two young women had once been "almost inseparable" and had suffered no official disagreement, they had not spent "ten minutes together" for over two years. Eve then turned introspective, commenting, "People when deprived of the goods of fortune are apt, I believe, to be jealous as well as suspicious of their reception by those who enjoy them."[103]

Eve had known the power of "goods of fortune"; now everyone knew of her family's misfortune. How could she feel secure within a social environment that valued the very items to which she enjoyed little access? Although she felt envious of those women who still enjoyed the good life, Eve shaped a feminine identity, and thereby a social status, based on good taste and modest behavior rather than wealth and material display. Women such as Mrs. Brayen had the goods, but their showy tastes and actions were precisely the kind to be disdained and rejected. Eve described her day with the woman in critical and condescending terms—the references to her own "impolite appetite" and unfamiliarity with the "high life" read not only as irony-laden indicators of her gentility but also as signs of insecurity. Constructing a virtuous, sensible, but refined femininity served as means of defending rightful social position from encroachment by the gaudy but wealthy Mrs. Brayens of the world on one side, and from vagaries of fortune created by imperial agitation on the other.

Sarah Eve died young, as a result of illness in December of 1774, not long before she was to marry Benjamin Rush. The notice of her death and burial described her as a paragon of the feminine virtues that she had tried to embody. It praised her "correct" taste and "polished" manners, which were never "put on, and laid aside, like a part of dress." She had borne her ailment with magnanimity, possessing a "delicate sensibility of the soul." Though not yet an "unfashionable wife," Eve had heeded Cumberland's prescriptions. Yet unlike the heroine of *The Fashionable Lover*, the play she so enjoyed, Eve died before recovering lost wealth or making a fortunate match. The obituary made oblique reference to her financial circumstances, noting that "family occurrences" had obliged her to withdraw from public life at a time when she was "perfectly qualified to appear before it with advantage."[104] Paradoxically, the very modesty she exhibited in shunning the public eye best suited her for its gaze. Sarah Eve, who suffered trying economic straits in life and was now deceased, could afford to be praised. Unlike women of fashion who paraded their hoops and headdresses about the streets of Philadelphia, in her relative poverty she had been no more offensive in life than she was in death.

WITH THE PASSAGE OF THE Townshend Acts, the resistance strategies and their promotions begun in 1764 expanded but also evolved. Proponents of nonimportation and nonconsumption attempted to make the rejection of imports and the embrace of local products not only signs of virtue but also of gentility embraced by people of "the first fashion." Yet as merchants seemed reluctant to agree to nonimportation, they faced attacks on their love of country, fellow feeling, and masculine independence, critiques that wedded the visual and material trappings of social status to political ideology.

Yet despite such campaigns, the aesthetic of understatement, whether composed of indigenous or imported materials, had not wholly triumphed. As fashions changed across the Atlantic to the macaroni mode and the high roll, styles in port cities shifted with them. Many colonists, from merchants to those in the fashion trades, remained deeply implicated in the consumer economy and in stimulating as well as supplying the demand that drove it. While versions of gentility that relied upon sacrifice might have been effective for encouraging political resistance in the form of boycotts, they threatened an economy fueled by consumption of imported goods—an unfortunate contradiction. And although prescriptive literature continued to cast wifely domesticity as antithetical to urbane fashionability, some women continued to exert social power through the latter. Not until 1773, when Parliament took a step that threatened to undercut commercial profits, establish a monopoly, and further democratize a taste and practice arbitrated by women, the drinking of tea, would Whigs have their day. In the wake of the Tea Act and the series of events that followed, the imperial crisis would come to a head and erupt into open conflict. The resulting attempts to make sartorial choices hew to political proclivities suggests that the politics of fashion fit uneasily with the changing fashion of politics.

A Contest of Modes in Revolutionary Philadelphia   5

From the hoop controversies of the early eighteenth century and the sumptuary restrictions of South Carolina's 1740 slave code to the homespun campaigns and backlash of the 1760s and early 1770s, the port cities of British North America saw continual contests over fashion in dress. Fueled by a variety of sartorial styles and attempts to define their meanings, these conflicts often concerned the ways in which social order intersected with gendered power in a robust consumer culture. In the midst of a period in which *la mode* itself was beginning to change, becoming more country (however refined) and less courtly, the imperial crisis magnified the already contested cultural politics of fashion, making fashion a critical site of power struggles social, economic, and now political. Resisters-turned-patriots combined new social imperatives regarding dress and display with old ideas of hierarchy to support their goals. It comes as no surprise, then, that fashion was the center of political and cultural battles from 1774 to the conclusion of the American War of Independence.

In particular, the city of Philadelphia, cultural center of British North America and eventual capital of the new American republic, served as the site of culture wars that both responded to and helped produce the revolutionary contest.[1] Although nonconsumption campaigns of the 1760s had attempted to supply social distinction and romantic conquest with new visual and material markers, they failed to fully undermine European fashion's appeal. Marked by increasing socioeconomic stratification, by the early 1770s Philadelphia stood as the largest, most refined and fashionable city in the colonies, its position signified in part by the rise of conspicuous consumption and high style—the ruffled, heavily powdered "macaroni" mode for men and large, elaborate hairstyles for women. Whereas in Boston, Whigs engaged in "macaroni making," as one English print cheekily called the practice of tarring and feathering, to make gruesome sport of high-status Tories such as John Malcolm, Philadelphia had not been such a hotbed of radical activity. In addition to high styles, the city was home to pacifist plain-style Quakers who formed part of an aesthetically understated social elite. Having emerged as a cultural center, the city also became the locus of colonial resistance and political power with the sitting of the Continental Congress in 1774. Two years later it became the seat of the newly independent republic and was by turns controlled by Continental and British forces alike over the course of the war. Thus Philadelphia played host to battles for the character and "look" of the new nation, contests that pitted calls for republican simplicity, itself a fashion of sorts, against the "timeless logic of signs of power, brilliant symbols of domination and social difference."[2] And at the center of these struggles lay fashion.

At the heart of revolutionary contests over fashion, as in many culture wars, lay the power to define gender identity and control relations between the sexes. With the outbreak of armed conflict, men could adopt a military mode that was at once masculine, legitimately patriotic, and outwardly impressive, negotiating the twin requirements of republican virtue and formidable display by using a soldier's dress to forestall charges of foppery. But women's expressions of femininity and material, visual, and social power through fashion were politically embarrassing and dangerous, according to Whig men, insofar as they signified disloyalty to the American cause in the nation's very capital. There seemed little way to bring the logic of power based on personal display and distinction into line with patriot prescriptions of homespun simplicity and conformity.

As revolutionaries and loyalists alike tried to locate people in one of two binary political positions, they attempted to make fashion, and with it gendered subjectivity, visually and materially circumscribe those stances. The problem was that many Philadelphians, elite women in particular, refused to remain "fixed," rejecting the equation of sartorial expression with political allegiance and its options, according to Whigs, of debauched or virtuous femininity. In a divided city, the stakes of the long-standing problem of reading people accurately through dress, and their consequences for gender, sexuality, and state politics, rose higher and higher. During the British army's occupation of Philadelphia in 1777–78 and its aftermath, the Whig style of politics confronted the Tory politics of style, the former repeatedly and unsuccessfully attempting to destroy the latter. The early 1780s saw a city determined to maintain the cultural prominence signified by fashionability, as well as political preeminence and legitimacy, the crucible of a similar dilemma facing the new nation.

"A New Method of Macarony Making, as Practiced at Boston," mezzotint, 1774. Two somewhat oafish and roughspun Sons of Liberty, indicated by hats bearing the number forty-five and a large cockade, tar and feather a customs officer. The print's caption plays on the notion of the "feathered" macaroni. Courtesy Library of Congress, Washington, D.C., Prints and Photographs Division, British Cartoon Prints Collection, LC-USZ62-45386.

Making a Republican Capital and a Capital Republican

With the sitting of the Continental Congress in 1774, which convened in response to the Coercive Acts passed by Parliament to punish Boston for its resistance to the Tea Act, Philadelphia became not only the largest and most refined city in Britain's North American colonies but also the seat of colonial political power. How would these identities coexist? The influx of wealthy, influential men and their families from other regions of British North America enlarged the ranks of the city's elites and further enhanced the cosmopolitan character of the place, even as the Continental Association enacted colonywide nonimportation and nonconsumption, pledging to "encourage frugality, economy and industry" and "discountenance and discourage every species of extravagance and dissipation." Among these they included the masculine gentry pastimes of horse racing, gaming, and cockfighting, as well as heterosocial fashionable amusements such as "exhibitions of shews, plays, and other expensive diversions and entertainments" such as balls.[3] Furthermore, the association recommended the election of committees of observation and inspection to enforce the boycott in each colony. These groups of men kept close watch over merchants and consumers, men and women, monitoring consumption, display, and participation in leisure activities. They hailed from wealthy as well as artisan ranks; the "sub-committee" for the north side of Philadelphia included John Bayard, Owen Biddle, Richard Bache, and the printer William Bradford, as well as five lesser-known men. They kept a log of "attempted importations" through May of 1775; for example, one ship arrived on December 17, 1774, carrying among its freight four crates of "coffee . . . which will come under Notice of this Committee." According to the "memoranda," merchants signed away their cargos left and right, turning them over to the committee rather than doling the goods out to retailers and their customers.[4]

As a cloud of surveillance settled over the city, high styles of foreign origin collided with homespun republican rhetoric. Elizabeth Cadwalader's spending proceeded apace when in 1775 she purchased, among other items, a "fashionable cap," "fashionable stomacher and bows," India dimity and muslin, 22 yards of brocade, and 125 yards of Chinese ribbon.[5] The chasm separating rhetoric and reality was apparent to commentators on both sides of the Atlantic who targeted women and their dress. An "invitation to Spinners" appearing in the *Pennsylvania Gazette* in the summer of 1775, after the war had begun, pled with women to forgo their "toilets and balls," their "modes of dress and tinsel garbs forsake, and useful cloathing for your country make"—to trade consumption and display for production, in other words.⁶ In the Darlys print shop, high-rolled American women replaced English macaronis in a series of lampoons with titles such as "Bunker's Hill, or America's Head Dress," "Miss Carolina Sullivan, one of the obstinate daughters of America," and "Oh Heigh Oh, or a View of the Back Settlements."⁷ The cartoons suggested that upstart America was like a pretentious woman of fashion, a mere pretender to status and legitimacy located far from the center of power and content simply to copy its style.

Furthermore, the images sent up American women as the standard-bearers of such absurd mimicry, which undermined Whig rhetoric of republican independence and highlighted divisions of sentiment that were increasingly clear and disturbing in Philadelphia—new capital of the infant republic, center of culture and refinement, and deeply divided city. Many of the town's elite women, Quakers in particular, were unenthusiastic about the war for independence.⁸ When a letter printed in the *Pennsylvania Gazette* reported on the "folly in the extreme" displayed by London women whose heads were "drest as high and as broad as is possible . . . with two or three yards of different colored gauze, interspersed with feathers, artificial carrots, radishes and salad," further attesting that one lady ornamented her head with a miniature sow and six pigs, the message to Philadelphia's ladies was clear: avoid such folly and its association with the enemy, or be castigated. And not only did such a style call one's loyalties into question; it also called into question one's very status as a woman. A poem titled "On the Preposterous Fashion of the Ladies Wearing High Plumes of Feathers in Their Heads" in the *Pennsylvania Evening Post*, reprinted from the *London Evening Post*, ironically called women who donned the plumes a "feather'd race (for sex, alas, is fled)" and lamented the ways in which feathers "martializ'd each grace."⁹

Whereas women stood accused of treason to their country and their sex for adopting certain fashions, men enjoyed a more legitimate, even celebrated way to access the external trappings of status, power, and appeal to the opposite sex—the military mode, where fashion and politics merged most explicitly. In July of 1775, John Adams wrote of the "military spirit" that pervaded the Quaker City, filled with "Rifle Men, Indians, Light Infantry, lightHorse, Highlanders . . . and German Hussars." Likewise, Esther Reed observed, "Everything in this city bears a warlike aspect. Two thousand men in the field, all in uniform, make a very military appearance," while Eliza Farmer described a "pretty uniform of sky blue" among "six or seven different sorts" adorning companies hailing from Philadelphia.¹⁰

"Bunker's Hill, or America's Head Dress," 1776. Caricature and Cartoon File, PR 010, negative number 39757, Collection of The New-York Historical Society.

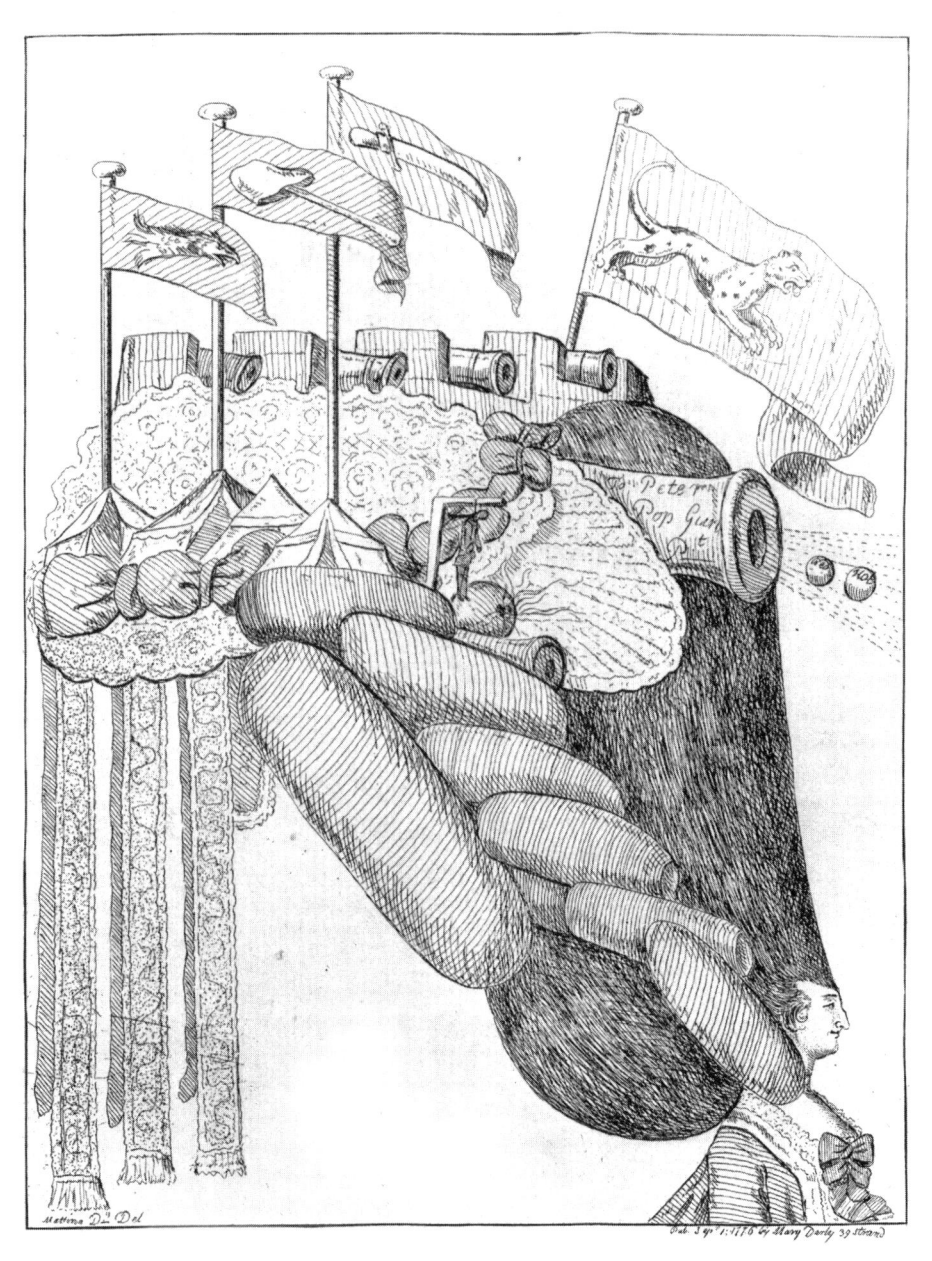

"Miss Carolina Sullivan, one of the obstinate daughters of America," printed by Mary Darly, London, September 1, 1776. Caricature and Cartoon File, PR 010 #1776-3, negative number 39754, Collection of The New-York Historical Society.

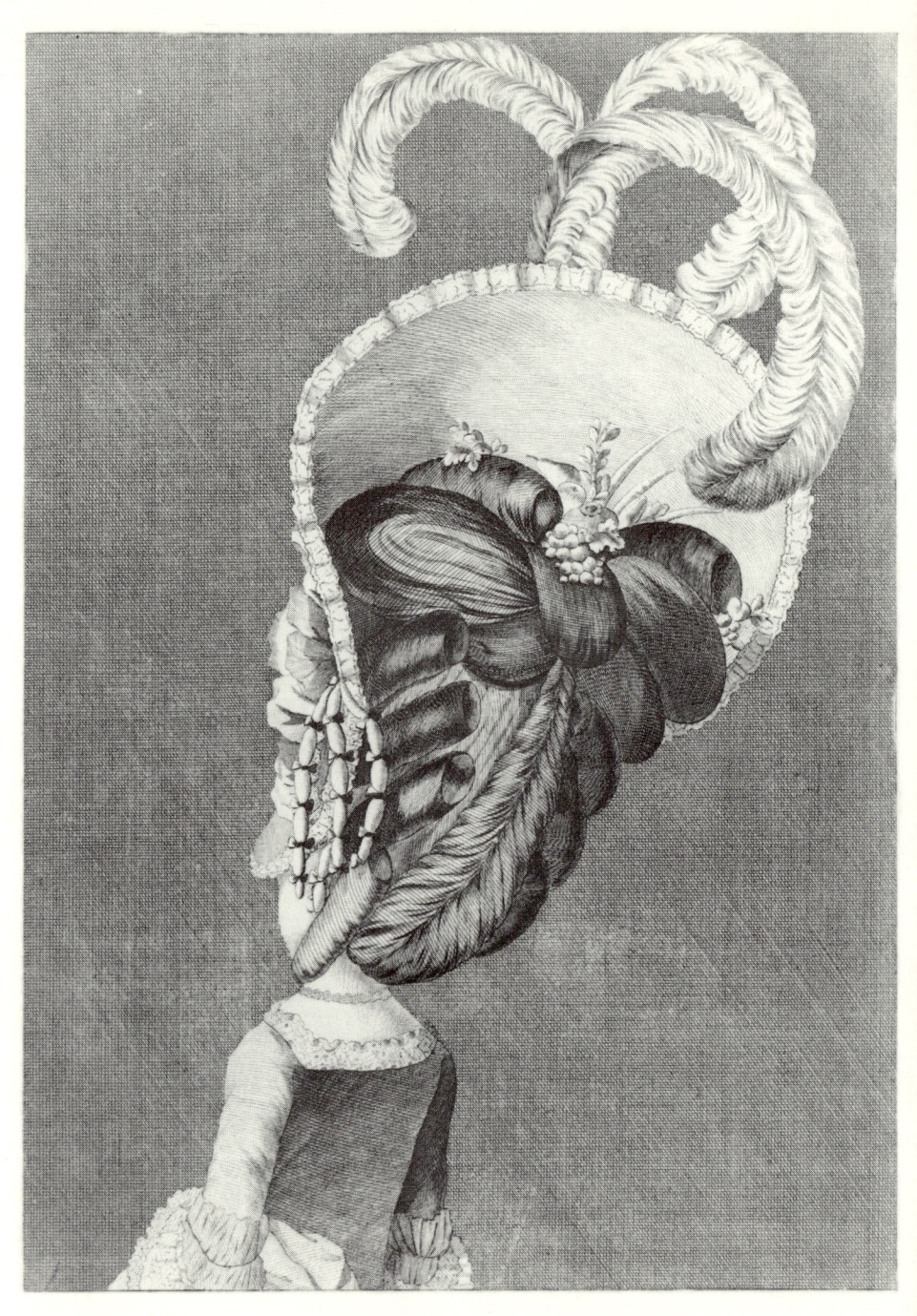

"Oh Heigh Oh, or a View of the Back Settlements," printed by M. Darly, London, 1776. Library of Congress, Washington, D.C., Prints and Photographs Division, British Cartoon Prints Collection, LC-USZ62-115004.

Fine martial attire particularly impressed Adams, who was notable for his tortured fondness for display that constantly threatened to undermine his republican principles. In a letter to William Tudor, he carefully chronicled the uniform of a soldier who appeared before Congress, "his errand to show us the dress and armour of a German Hussar." With his large, beribboned cap decorated with a death's head, cloak "ornamented with gold cord, lace and fringe," scarlet waistcoat, and "Turkish sabre by his side," the soldier cut "the most formidable military figure I ever saw," Adams declared.[11] He badly wished to be a soldier, moved by the glamour of wearing a uniform, bearing arms, and appearing formidable, even as he claimed that the "pride and pomp" of war held no attraction for him.[12]

Adams put his finger on the dilemma surrounding how American soldiers should look—formidable but not foppish. Respect for provincial soldiers was a problem that dated at least to the Seven Years' War, when New Englanders chafed at the general superciliousness with which British regulars regarded colonial troops.[13] Americans well knew in what low esteem British officials held the collection of "farmers, dry goods dealers, and slave drivers" that comprised revolutionary militias.[14] For the purposes of inspiring respect and intimidation, colonial soldiers, particularly of the emerging Continental army, needed to look like proper military men, not a ragtag bunch with bad clothes. But neither would it do for them to appear too fashionable. Versions of martial masculinity competed as the leaders of the new nation, the army, and even militia companies pondered how to appear at once virtuous, legitimate, and formidable.

When the first troops assembled in Pennsylvania, Associators and militia wore hunting shirts in various shades, a style that persisted through the war among many of the state's companies.[15] Made of deerskin for the winter and linen for summer, these tunic-style garments, often worn over leather breeches, reached the knees and were open down the front, kept closed by a leather belt that held a knife or hatchet.[16] Hunting shirts suggested frontier savvy, expert marksmanship, and homespun simplicity. Esther Reed observed that the riflemen who "dress themselves like Indians" made "a very formidable show."[17] In fact, a congressional committee called to design a medal to commemorate the surrender of Boston decided on an image that included a rifleman clad in hunting shirt with tomahawk in hand, a dress that John Adams had thought "peculiar to America" but learned that it was like that of Roman soldiers—attempting to turn a "savage" style into something "civilized."[18] But what impressed Reed, recalled the Roman republic, or had currency on the frontier might not inspire the same fearful respect in well-trained British officers, regulars, and European mercenaries. French observer Abbé Robin remarked that hunting shirts looked "well enough" but that their chief advantages were their light weight and the range of motion they afforded.[19] And, according to one broadside addressed to the Associators of the City of Philadelphia, accessible and economical hunting shirts possessed the added benefit of serving to "level all distinctions." Although deeply democratic, such a visual leveling might not lend itself so well to social deference and the exercise of military discipline.[20] Samuel Adams cautioned the recipient of a letter that its bearers were "sons of wealthy farmers" and "friends to our cause" who commanded military companies in their home counties. "Though they are not dressed like fops," he explained, "I dare say you will show them due respect."[21]

Adams's directive demonstrates that cutting a powerful figure could not be entirely separated from the dictates of traditional gentility. John Cadwalader, who later received a commission as a brigadier general, purchased a pair of silver epaulets in May of 1775.[22] Martial dress, though theoretically somewhat timeless and lying outside the mode, both responded to and produced fashion, as gold-laced martial-style caps became the rage in Philadelphia in 1775. The infantry were soon clad in British-style uniforms, and wealthy Philadelphians organized the so-called silk stocking light horse company, commanded by Cadwalader. At issue were two things: the way the forces appeared to outside observers and designations of rank within the army. Although William Paca wrote from Congress to the Maryland Council that, by May of 1777, the army had begun to "make a very formidable figure" and stood "handsomely uniformed," three years later a congressional committee persuaded General George Washington that outfitting the army in one uniform would "tend to inspire foreign troops with a more respectable opinion of ours than would be maintained were they to continue in their present motley dress."[23] In this instance, respectability required uniformity.

Anxiety over expressions of power and legitimacy on the world stage dovetailed with individual men's desire to maintain a certain martial fashionability. William Whipple, a delegate to the Continental Congress from New Hampshire, signer of the Declaration of Independence, and officer in the army, noted with alarm that Robert Treat Paine, delegate from Massachusetts, had begun to dress his head in the "true Macaroni Stile."[24] Although Whipple disdained his colleague's fashion choice, he did not question Paine's authority to make it. Not so within the army, as the hairstyle became the focus of conflict and contestation, threatening to confound military discipline. Officers attempted to forbid soldiers to wear their hair à la macaroni, a style they regarded as unmilitary, unmanly, and unsanitary in its excessive use of powder and pomatum. Yet soldiers resisted and the mode persisted. Officers hoped to regularize and homogenize the appearance of those who served under them in order to inscribe military as well as social hierarchy, expressing the authority of their higher rank both within the army and without, and maintaining expressions of distinction for themselves alone.[25]

Correspondence between Henry Laurens, the wealthy South Carolina planter and president of Congress, and his son John, who served as a colonel in the army, demonstrates the importance of measures of distinction among officers in the Continental army. The elder Laurens feared that John did not possess the right sort of clothing—which, given the dearth of supplies, he likely did not. He sent scarlet, blue, and yellow fabric in the hopes that his son might find a tailor in the army to make something of it.[26] But more than articles of sheer necessity such as coats and breeches, the Laurens men discussed hair powder. No doubt they would have agreed with Sarah Eve's remark that the item was as necessary to Reverend Duché "as to a soldier, for it gives a more significant shake to his head and is as priming to his words and looks."[27] Henry repeatedly attempted to locate some powder to send to his son, and when this proved impossible, he advised John, "My hairdresser recommends to you to substitute flour until he can by his art procure a better article for your hair."[28] Bent on achieving a particular appearance was the man who, lacking powder, floured his head.

Yet Philadelphia printer Philip Freneau claimed repudiation of display to be the hallmark of the colonial soldier, comparing him to the British regular in verse:

> No fop in arms, no feather on his head
> No glittering toys the manly warrior had
> His auburne face the least employ'd his care
> He left it to the females to be fair.[29]

Freneau cast the British army as effeminate fops, devoted primarily to their toilettes. By contrast, rugged, ruddy colonial men left such trifling concerns to the "fair sex," and by doing so became all the more attractive to them in their martial masculinity. As historian Charles Royster has observed, public expressions of patriot military sentiment portrayed women eagerly sending the men they loved off to fight, withholding their approbation from those who did not or from men who joined the wrong side.[30] A notice in the *Pennsylvania Gazette* applauded the women of Amelia County, Virginia, who, on

"Dress: The most distinguishing mark of a military Genius," P. Price Jr., publisher, Philadelphia, ca. 1813. This early-nineteenth-century image lampooned the soldier who proudly considered his festooned appearance an indicator of martial prowess. Courtesy The Winterthur Library, Joseph Downs Collection of Manuscripts and Printed Ephemera.

the first anniversary of independence in 1777, resolved "not to permit the addresses of any person (be his circumstances or situation in life what they will) unless he has served in the American armies long enough to prove, by his valour, that he is deserving of their love."[31] Whig rhetoric laid claim to women's affections in such ways, claiming that they preferred respectable politics to respectable social standing, indeed, insisting that the former would produce the latter, with the assistance of female attention. Martial attire allowed men to appear virtuous, brave, and dashing. They could legitimately bedeck themselves in the finery that supposedly so captivated women without exposing themselves to charges of foppery or effeminacy, although a fine line had to be trod, for as Freneau suggested, a soldier might yet be a fop in arms. Still, a soldierly appearance proved a far more acceptable means of garnering attention than did other fashions. And so for American men the military mode, whether rough-and-tumble hunting shirts and leather breeches, or laced coats and hats, proclaimed and achieved it all—status, power, elegance, virtue, attention, and affection. Women, however, to appear appropriately patriotic, were left with bland homespun and flat heads.

The Persistence of Finery and the Power of Women

The military mode and country look did not mean that other expressions of finery had disappeared; on the contrary, according to John Adams, they were alive and well and threatening the cause. Adams, reacting to the luxury he perceived all around, repeatedly waxed hyperbolic about the need to inculcate the citizenry with proper republican tastes. In a letter to James Warren, he pronounced, "We must change our palates, our taste in dress, furniture, equipage, architecture." In another missive to Warren dated the following day he continued to stress the need to "sacrifice some of our appetites. . . . Silks and velvets must be dispensed with." Such gewgaws, he claimed, were mere "trifles in a contest for liberty." Yet he seriously doubted that people possessed "virtue" enough to bear even such small sacrifice indefinitely. How long would people submit to the "mortification of their appetites, passions, and fancies," particularly when the "mercantile interest" was so "complicated with the landed interest," forming one large self-aggrandizing group who both desired and benefited financially from the spoils of trade? Targeting men, he wondered "whether our people have virtue enough to be mere husbandmen, mechanicks and soldiers," calling forth the images of pastoral farmers, artisans, and men in uniform.[32]

Such figures, among which Adams could hardly count himself, stood in marked contrast to men such as fellow Bostonian and loyalist Jonathan Sewall. In a letter to Abigail, Adams commented on the burning of Sewall's home, which gave him "some pleasure." He considered its destruction the wages of Sewall's political and social sins, ominously warning that "whenever vanity and gaity and love of pomp and Dress, Furniture, Equipage, Buildings, great Company, expensive Diversions and elegant Entertainments"—in short, the trappings of fashion and the beau monde—"get the better of the principles and judgments of men and women there is no knowing where they will stop, nor into what evils, natural, moral, or political, they will lead us."[33] Sewell and his family had suffered for their unchecked appetites, habits that signified moral corruption. Making these into a symbol of loyalty to Britain served to displace the behaviors Adams fretted about among fellow republicans onto monarchists, and served as a kind of visual shorthand by which loyalists could be known.

Yet when Adams lamented in September of 1776 that simplicity and virtue were not "in fashion," he had reason for concern. Philadelphia's city's role as the seat of republican government had not undermined the cosmopolitan fashionability literally embodied by its ladies. In 1777 in his account of the town's society and culture, an unknown Frenchman expressed amazement at the "twenty or thirty different styles" of headdresses spied in Philadelphia. Overall, the author praised American women's virtue and "charming modesty," touting the "youthful freshness" owed chiefly to their "way of dressing." They wore "short gowns covered in the front by an apron . . . so like those of our chambermaids that one would take all the Anglo-American women for servants out on errands or hairdressers on their way to a customer," he marveled.[34] For this author, the combination of courtly hair and domestic dress that was perhaps unique to British America confused class distinctions; his account contained both admiration and mockery.

In contrast to their appearances on the street, for attendance at church or meeting women donned "extravagant finery," the Frenchman noted. "If the dress of Anglo-American women on weekdays suffers a little by comparison," he described, "nothing is more elegant, more splendid or more beautiful than their Sunday gowns." "You would not recognize them," the author declared: "Hair, ribbons, hats, fichus, aprons—everything is so tastefully chosen and looks so neat that a Frenchwoman decked out in all her finest silks and pompons cannot compare with an Anglo-American in her ordinary Sunday dress." He lamented that such display was limited to attendance at church alone. Philadelphia's "fair," he claimed, returned home to strip off all ornamentation, ending the day "in the deadly boredom of an evening spent all alone in pious meditation."[35] Another Frenchman, Abbé Robin, also observed that piety was "not the only motive that brings the American ladies in crowds to the various places of worship." Having no places of public amusement, no fashionable promenades, they went to church to display their fine dress, he explained.[36] The accounts suggest that, given the city's political and social climate of surveillance, church remained the only safe haven for display.

Or perhaps there existed one other: funerals, which the French writer described as an "occasion for ostentation," when "all the men and women . . . dress up as elegantly and stylishly as they can." Free of traditional mourning attire, which signified participation in imperial culture and rendered the commemoration of death yet another means of performing social position, American funerals had become regularized, limited, and simple. Yet the "vigorous simplicity" of the services themselves belied the fine attire, as well as the ornate coffins, which were carved, painted, and "decorated all over with funeral ornaments made of tin plate for the poor and of silver plate or heavy gilt copper for the rich."[37] The rituals surrounding death remained arenas of distinction.

Threats to sartorial and behavioral expressions of republican virtue came also from the public sphere of print. Even as *rage militaire* swept the colonies, the Earl of Chesterfield's *Letters to His Son* became a best seller.[38] Instructions on how to ascend the ranks of the polite and the fashionable by affecting certain modes and manners, Chesterfield's *Letters* were published in Philadelphia in 1775, being reprinted annually in America until the turn of the nineteenth century. The book chiefly concerned cultivating gentility in the attainment and maintenance of social status. To this end, Chesterfield stressed the importance of taste, and of women as arbiters of it.

The earl cautioned his son to dress carefully and with measured flair to please the ladies. "Pray not only be well dressed but shining in your dress," its "taste and fashion," he instructed. Women not only appreciated but "required" such an appearance. Why meet their exacting standards? Because "it is the women who stamp a young man's credit," Chesterfield asserted. Within women's natural ability to judge gentility, he argued, lay the key to status and renown. He thus acknowledged their tremendous power within the social realm. Women's opinions could make or break a man; his fate depended on remaining in their good graces. They could "establish or destroy" a man's reputation. At all "events," therefore, a man "had better talk too much to women rather than too little."[39]

Yet in the competition to "rise in the world," Chesterfield clearly regarded the courting of feminine approbation as mere strategy—a means, not an end. The object, ultimately, was to increase one's standing among men. He baldly stated: "If you do not make yourself agreeable to the women, you will assuredly lose ground among the men."[40] Putting it another way, he explained, "all this I do not mean singly with regard to women as the principal object; but with regard to men and with a view of you making yourself considerable."[41] In Chesterfield's opinion, men should exploit women's proclivities and social currency for personal gain. Underpinning his advice on how best to appeal to and exploit feminine attention lay profound disdain for women and their abilities. He called them "children of a larger growth" who occasionally displayed "entertaining tattle and sometimes wit" but never "solid reasoning [or] good sense." Women were fickle creatures who could not act sensibly for "twenty-four hours together," and their whims always disrupted their "best resolutions," he maintained. Susceptible to the lowest forms of flattery, placated by trifling presents such as fans or ribbons, women were but gewgaws themselves. "A man of sense only trifles with them, plays with them, humours and flatters them, as he does with a sprightly, forward child," Chesterfield declared, "but he neither consults them about nor trusts them with serious matters, though he often makes them believe that he does both."[42]

Such were the sentiments that characterized the colonial best seller, opinions that few men would "dare openly avow" for fear of being "almost universally shunned as the pests of society," insisted an essay in the *Lady's Magazine* that took issue with Chesterfield.[43] Needless to say, not all praised the earl's wisdom, in particular women who regarded themselves as persons of sense. Mercy Otis Warren regarded his descriptions of women as fashion-conscious creatures, easily swayed by men's flattery, as unfair and inaccurate. She was particularly perturbed upon receiving a letter from her son that declared how thoroughly he enjoyed reading Chesterfield. Warren attempted to disabuse him of his admiration for the earl's insights in a letter written in December of 1779 insisting that "it is the race of fops and fribbles, the half-learned sceptic . . . who are devotees of a man bold enough to avow himself the champion of every species of vice, only cloathing it decently."[44] She well knew that as fops courted the social approval of the fair sex, they preyed on women's virtue. Gentility and high rank masked the low rakishness of a Chesterfield.

Yet Chesterfield had ascribed to elite women of fashion a power that could not be denied, one brought to bear during the British occupation of Philadelphia in 1777–78. After two hard-fought battles, General Howe's army captured the city, occupying it for eight months. It was a time of want—high prices for food, fuel, and goods—and of deep patriot dismay over the fallen city and the uncertain loyalties of its Quaker residents, women in particular.[45] Continentals were no longer the only desirable men in uniform in the region; they were joined by redcoats, sparking a contest for the loyalties of the town's "fair" even as the women themselves also strove to command attention.

Close friends Sally Wister and Debby Norris, both born in 1761 to wealthy Quaker merchant families and educated at Anthony Benezet's school for girls, responded with great excitement to the influx of eligible and entertaining young men. During the British occupation, the Norris family remained in their mansion on Chestnut Street in Philadelphia while the Wisters fled to their country home in Germantown.[46] On September 26, 1777, a group of soldiers appeared at the Wister estate. Sally supposed them to be British due to their dress, but "to our great joy," she wrote, "they were Americans," linking her political and personal preferences.[47] Continentals apparently looked good to her, perhaps because they appeared as dapper as the British soldiers she initially took them to be.

The Wister-Norris correspondence demonstrates not only the young women's attention to the soldiers but their preoccupation with their own appearances in front of the men. Wister took particular care to tell Norris how she was dressed when greeting officers, often expressing deep displeasure over her attire. A group stopped in for "refreshment" one evening, catching Wister unawares in a "green skirt, dark short gown." The following day, however, she reported looking "smarter than the night before" in a chintz dress. Yet despite her careful measures, she whined, "When will Sally's admirers appear," wondering "why Sally has not charms sufficient to pierce the heart of a soldier," sensing that her appearance held her back in conquests. Again in June of 1778 Wister donned what was likely the same odious "green skirt and dark short gown" and again stood surprised to find men at the back door. This she deemed simply "Provoking."[48] Embarrassed by her plain appearance before the officers, in the five days that followed Wister described her attire for Norris, constructing imaginary exchanges with her friend in order to validate her fashion choices. When June 4th proved uncomfortably warm, Wister altered her dress to accommodate the high temperatures, explaining that although she did not "make an elegant figure," she did not expect to see anyone. But the following day she dressed in "light chintz, which is made gown fashion, kenting handkerchief, and a linen apron." A mock conversation with Norris followed: "Sufficiently smart for a country girl, Sally. Don't call me a country girl, Debby Norris. Please to observe that I pride myself upon being a Philadelphian."[49]

Wister worried about looking unrefined, banished as she was to the country, and declared that she was still a denizen of the city. No longer a girl but neither a grown woman, she sometimes felt "awkwardish," a problem compounded by removal from her urban social network and the polish it signified and supplied.

Although undoubtedly preoccupied with her own dress, Wister took similar notice of the soldiers whose attention she so desperately sought. Of the two captains, Lipscomb and Moss, who dined with the Wisters in February of 1778, Sally wrote, "How elegant the former was dress'd and how pretty he look'd," captivated by Lipscomb's figure. Especially revealing of the ways in which fashion facilitated relations between the sexes are the occasions on which the men apparently altered their appearances to please the young women. The evening before the morning that found Wister provoked by the early arrival of soldiers, she conversed with Captain Dandridge, whom she regarded as "the handsomest man in existence." While "chatting upon dress," he expressed little patience for officers who wasted precious time having their hair dressed and powdered, to which Wister replied that she was "excessively fond of powder" and found it very becoming. In response, Dandridge rather bashfully branded himself careless about such things. But the next morning, according to Wister, he appeared "powder'd very white." She queried, "Will I be excused Debby, if I look upon his being powder'd in light of a compliment to me?" To which the Norris in Wister's head replied, "Yes, Sally, as thee is a country maid and don't often meet with compliments." "Saucy Debby Norris!" Wister retorted.[50] But clearly, her opinion had some influence on Captain Dandridge's toilet, who found himself caught between his rejection of a fashion he deemed frivolous and adherence to a genteel martial mode that so captivated Wister. Likewise, in December of 1778, Norris reported meeting "two beaus" while out with Sally Logan Fisher, who then invited them over for tea. Norris learned that one of the men, Lieutenant Barker, who "made a very good figure," had served in the army, and the next morning Sally Fisher observed Barker dressed in his best regimental coat—"to look agreeable to herself, I say," Norris concluded.[51] The lieutenant dressed to impress the ladies.

Although ostensibly politically neutral during the revolutionary conflict, in terms of their social and romantic inclinations Norris and Wister seemed to prefer Continentals to redcoats. Not so with other Philadelphia belles. In the midst of the occupation, an engraving titled *The Wishing Females* suggested what at least some American men feared and loathed: that high-status women of Philadelphia directed romantic interest toward and threw their social weight behind the occupying army, not Whigs. The image depicts two women in high rolls and "undress," or at-home attire, gazing longingly out their parlor window at British officers and regulars. One smiles knowingly as she peers through a looking glass, closely inspecting the troops in the field. The other dreamily contemplates the men, chin on hand. They appear to be sexual predators, ready to leap from the interior, domestic space to cavort lasciviously in the external realm of military men.[52]

Whig suspicions of romantic or perhaps more threatening "alliances" between Philadelphia's ladies and British soldiers were further confirmed by the Meschianza, an elaborate fete staged in May of 1778 to honor the de-

"The Wishing Females," c. 1778–81. These Philadelphia women of fashion ogle and wish to be with the uniformed men outside their window. Courtesy American Antiquarian Society.

parting British army, held on Joseph Wharton's impressive estate just outside the city. Many of Philadelphia's most elite and eligible young women participated in the eighteen-hour extravaganza, each attended by a British officer or "knight" who competed in medieval-style jousting tournaments in her honor and to secure her affection. The ceremony tempered violence with gentility in counterpoint to the image of an American army in which "officers were not gentlemen but merchants with swords . . . farmers and mechanics."[53] Hannah Griffits poetically cast the Meschianza as a "shameful scene of dissipation, the Death of sense and reputation," regretting that "ladies joined the frantic show." Major John André orchestrated the event, down to circulating a sketch of how he wanted the women to appear.[54] Sketched also by Pierre DuSimitiere, who painted a portrait of Willy Smith in her elaborate Meschianza attire, the festooned and turbaned high roll served as the outfit's focus.[55] By costuming white women and enslaved black men in pseudo-Turkish costumes, André intended to signify imperial, cosmopolitan values as well as subservience to the Crown.[56] It seemed to some that Philadelphia's ladies were taking fashion directives from a British officer, molding their very bodies to his desires and specifications, although they had already embraced the modes from which he, quite literally, drew his vision. Yet Josiah Bartlett, delegate from New Hampshire, devalued the women's influence, along with their morals, echoing the chastening message of *The Wishing Females*. In a letter to his wife composed in the summer of 1778, he wrote that when Congress arrived back in Philadelphia, "they found the Tory ladies who tarried with the Regulars wearing the most enormous high head Dresses after the manner of the Mistresses and Whores of the British officers."[57] Worse, according to Timothy Pickering, Whig women were as fond of the hairstyle as Tories.[58] Philadelphia's ladies were not about to let politics proscribe a fashion they preferred.

The high roll had come to signify political loyalty for Whig men, even more so in 1778, with *rage militaire* subsided and the city recently occupied. When high-haired women dared to appear in public on the second anniversary of independence, the high roll took on a starring role in street theater against the backdrop of a city rife with social and political tension. In the words of Josiah Bartlett, "Some Gentlemen purchased the most Extravagant high head dress that could be got and Dressed an old Negro Wench with it." The woman was then "paraded around the city by the mob," making "a shocking appearance to the no small mortification of the Tories and Diversion of the other citizens."[59] In his diary, William Ellery recorded that "a crowd of the vulgar" escorted a "noted infamous doxy" through the streets.[60] Employ-

Sketch of a Meschianza belle, by John Andre, drawing with watercolor, 1778. John Fanning Watson, manuscript of "Annals of Philadelphia," 242. Courtesy The Library Company of Philadelphia.

ing a sexual epithet but no racial designation, Samuel Holton also supposed the woman to be a "strumpet," while Richard Henry Lee described her as a "woman of the town" whose head was "elegantly and expensively dressed, I suppose about three feet high and of proportional width."[61] At the expense of a single victim, a prostitute, the episode mocked women who sported high rolls, casting them as politically disloyal, unchaste, and of low status, completely inverting the wealth and feminine beauty that women who wore high rolls felt the style signified. Yet it was also designed to humiliate loyalist men and British soldiers on the social battlefield by attacking the characters of women associated with them. According to Bartlett, "gentlemen" who could afford to purchase such a headdress perpetrated the incident. These men, perhaps members of Congress who celebrated decorously inside the statehouse that day, bought the roll, but a mob did the dirty work. A masculine alliance that transcended rank allowed Whig gentlemen to chasten and control women of their own rank without sullying their own hands. Perhaps high-rolled women embodied anxieties about their own vanity and dependence. No doubt they besmirched the capital of the republic and the radically democratic state of Pennsylvania with old-world fashion, luxury, and social hierarchy that the events of July 4, 1778, attempted to invert.

Yet two of the Philadelphia ladies whom the incident ridiculed made countermeanings of the episode. According to Richard Henry Lee, the "tory wife of Doctor Smith," mother of memorialized Meschianza belle Willy Smith, facetiously christened the victim "Continella or the Duchess of Independence" and "prayed for a pin from her head by way of relic." She distanced herself by making the figure symbolize the ridiculousness and low breeding of Whigs, mocking them with the language of aristocracy and reinverting the episode. Lee, of course, claimed that women were "very much mortified notwithstanding" Smith's bon mot, insisting that the incident had "lessened some heads already and will probably bring the rest within reason." Josiah Bartlett also observed that "head dresses are now shortning."[62] According to these delegates, the ladies of Philadelphia were sufficiently chastened by the parade of Continella. The Whig style of politics had bested the Tory politics of style. But perhaps the final word was had by Rebecca Franks, who, to Colonel Jack Stewart's jest that the victim was "equipped altogether in the English fashion," replied, "Not altogether, colonel, for though the style of her head is British, her shoes and stocking are in the genuine Continental fashion."[63] Just as the independence day mob had figured high-rolled women as prostitutes, Franks compared the ill-clad American army to a woman of the street—dolled up, perhaps, but still low bred and bound by humble origins. So much for the military appearing respectable and well-ordered within, formidable to enemies without, and attractive to women. The contest was not over yet.

The Demands of Nationhood

The 1778 American alliance with that master of modes France further complicated the relationship between fashion and political allegiance. The women of Philadelphia turned out in their "most brilliant attire" to welcome the French army.[64] Once despised by British Americans as popish, foppish, and libidinous, French men became saviors. What then of French fashions? After all, if high rolls were "in the true French taste," as one French man told Timothy Pickering,[65] who could reasonably argue that the style paid tribute to the British enemy?

The problems, similar to those plaguing military dress, were two: balancing republican virtue against expressions of national legitimacy, which required pomp and display during a time of economic crisis, and acknowledging distinctions of rank in the midst of political division. Fetes, however grand, needed to follow a particular script.[66] Samuel Adams expressed consternation over the way in which the celebration held to welcome the French army to Philadelphia had unfolded. For example, a toast to the king of France preceded one to the Congress of the United States. Adding insult to injury, revelers then drank to the French forces before the Continental army. None of this suited Adams. "Nations and independent sovereigns," he exclaimed testily, "do not compliment after the manner of belles and beaus," as he juxtaposed the freedom and independence of a republic with the simpering dependence of men and women of fashion.[67]

As for negotiating social relations among the actual belles and beaus of Philadelphia, the French ambassador, according to keen observer the Marquis de Chastellux, received company of all political persuasions except the warmest of loyalists, alienating no lady of rank, and pleading ignorance when a Tory woman offended a Whig in his presence.[68] His arrival inaugurated a series of balls in which Whigs, requiring accomplished dancing partners, had little choice but to incorporate genteel loyalist-leaning women.[69] In a letter to her mother, Mary White Morris, wife of financier and signer of the Declaration of Independence Robert Morris, wrote that at the many balls and entertainments, the "military gentlemen were too liberal to make any distinction between Whig and Tory ladeys," and "if they made any, it was in favor of the latter." "Strange as it may seem," she continued, "it is the way those things are conducted at present in this city.[70] However, Sarah Franklin Bache, daughter of Benjamin Franklin, regarded the time as a "season of friends to the wigs," who "spent it gayly," though she assured her father that she dressed not with "singularity" but only in such a way as did credit to her family, and that balls were "the only reason that the (spinning) wheel is lay'd aside."[71] Indeed, accompanying her letter was a piece of homespun silk intended for the queen of France, material proof of Bache's industry and patriotism. Yet a concerned "correspondent" to the *Pennsylvania Gazette* queried, "What opinion must the public entertain of the political principles of the Honourable Congress of the United States of America" when some of its members undertook "the management of balls, graced with Messienza Ladies, equally noted for their tory principles and their late fondness for British debauchees and macaronis."[72] The author felt that the women's politics, signified by their taste in corrupt men and vice versa, rendered them unsuitable for sociability with the nation's leaders.

Feminine fashions remained of serious concern, particularly the big hair that the Philadelphia mob failed to bring low. Part of the ostensibly rational and disembodied public sphere of print, figuratively located far from both the raucousness of street theater and the play of fashion, the *U.S. Magazine* published a series of satirical exchanges debating the propriety and attractiveness of the high roll.[73] Pitted as a contest between male and female contributors (although both writers may have been men), the pieces served as both a series of ironical inside jokes for well-bred readers and a means by which they jabbed at one another. The discussion took the coiffure seriously while mocking the gravity with which it invested a feminine hairstyle. A "Defence of the Female HeadDress at Present in Fashion" deemed it the clearest expression of virtue—that is, the dictate to love thine enemies, skewering pretensions to piety and ostensible neutrality. Drawing a direct connection between the style and the fate of the patriot cause, the author continued, "Neither the scarcity of the materials . . . the enormous expence attending their purchase, nor the unparalleled hostility of our enemies have damped the eagerness with which our females have imitated the dress of (England's) virtuous ladies. Their heads, like the palm tree, have grown under oppression. They began to swell at the beginning of the contest, they took a farther rise upon the captivity of the garrison at Fort Washington, and their growth bore some proportion to the famine that starved and wasted our unfortunate soldiery."[74] Even "republican ladies" fell under the style's spell. The "Retaliation" that appeared the following month pointed out that gentlemen were equal "imitators of their enemies" when it came to fashions of the head. Its author queried, "Does not your hair, cherokee'd, toupeed, raised in form of a pyramid, pinned, curled, frizzled, buckled, platted, ramelied, cued, clubbed, confined in a bag or loosely flowing on the shoulders, revolve thro' as many varied a whimsicality of modes as any females on the continent?" Indeed, neither love of country nor hatred of foes had prevented large-brimmed hats, currently "extended to the size of my tea table," from replacing the smaller, martial hat à la General Washington. Yet the piece also skewered women's supposed frugality as a mere sham concocted to legitimate the adoption of revealing modes of dress. Such measures, its author insisted, proceeded not from willingness to expose oneself to the "scrutinizing eyes of the gentlemen" but rather "from principles of frugality only, and on honest desire to avoid as much expense as possible."[75] Thus with a wink the writer mock justified an eye-catching fashion through claims of economizing.

Some women tried to have it both ways—to attract attention for impressive looks and commendable actions. In the spring of 1780 Congressman John Fell wrote that women's dress in Philadelphia was "quite equal to the dress of the ladies that I have seen in the boxes in the playhouses of London" and "even along the Streets resembles in a great degree the Actresses on the Stage."[76] In 1780, genteel women were turning the very streets of Philadelphia into theaters—of fashion and patriotism. Sarah Franklin Bache, who attended assemblies and spun silk, led a group of women in making up linen shirts for Pennsylvania regiments. She was, according to Chastellux, not only an "admirable female patriot" but "THE agreeable woman of Philadelphia . . . an enthusiast to excess for all the French fashions [who] waits only for the terminato of this little revolution to effect a still greater one in the manners of her country."[77] Whigs must have been dismayed at his comparison of their "little" political upheaval to a "greater" one in fashion. But while Bache attempted to be fashionable and patriotic, women such as Esther Reed, the wife of Pennsylvania's president Joseph Reed, publicly set the two in opposition, displaying her loyalty by leading women of high social standing in collecting money for American troops while calling for "clothing more simple" and "hair dresses less elegant."[78]

Yet Abbé Robin, who accompanied French troops to Philadelphia, noted the high hair that persisted among the town's female denizens. Although he "had no expectations of discovering the traces of the French modes and fashions" in America, he found otherwise, describing dresses made of the finest silks "overshadowed with a profusion of the most superb plumes." The hair these feathers adorned was "raised and supported upon cushions to an extravagant height, somewhat resembling the manner in which the French ladies wore their hair some years ago." In Philadelphia "the head dresses of all the women, expect Quakers, are high, spreading and decked profusely with our gauzes."[79] North Carolina congressman Hugh Williamson wrote that he considered providing his correspondent with "a description of a true city lady in full dress, head, hoop and all, but I don't love caricature and to draw after the life might obtain that name."[80]

Williamson's equation of the actual style with caricature and Robin's account of outré big hair gave credence to fear that Americans appeared foolish to foreign eyes. John Fell bemoaned that "our extravagance is look't on abroad with contempt," while Virginia congressman Arthur Lee wrote that Philadelphia had "broke suddenly loose from the simplicity of Quaker manners, dress and fashion" and was instead "affecting the vanity and nonsense of French parade."[81] Samuel Adams feared consequences more dire than foreign disdain. "Should . . . foppery become the ruling taste of the Great," he warned, "the Body of People would be in Danger." Harking back to Restoration England, when the figure of the fop first appeared, he recalled that during the reign of Charles II those in positions of power considered ways to turn the minds of the people away from attention to their liberties. "The Answer was," Adams readily supplied, "by making them extravagant, luxurious, effeminate." Yet Congressman Samuel Huntington realized the necessity of appearing "decent in dress" when receiving "foreigners of distinction" and petitioned Congress for two thousand dollars toward his fashion needs.[82] One man's extravagant effeminacy was perhaps another's merely "decent." Who decided?

While some delegates fretted about the republic's reputation for luxury and others contributed to it, foreign observers applauded the city's refinement. The exclusive Philadelphia Assembly continued its balls, Chastellux recording that the dances, like toasts, had "some relation to politics"— for instance, the Defeat of Burgoyne or Clinton's Retreat. The assembly's managers were "chosen from among the most distinguished officers of the army," who ran the balls with military sternness.[83] Congressman Hugh Williamson seemed rather blasé when writing in 1782, "To say that balls and dances are frequent is to say little, for we have them every night."[84] That year the city witnessed a particularly grand fete thrown by the French ambassador to honor the dauphin of France's birthday. Benjamin Rush recorded that "for ten days before the entertainment nothing else was talked of in our city." Those in the fashion trades benefited: "Hair dressers were retained, tailors, milliners and mantua-makers were to be seen, covered with sweat and out of breath, in every street." According to Rush, the day of the event "was ushered in by a corps of hairdressers occupying the place of the city watchmen." The image suggested an army of *friseurs* marching through the streets of Philadelphia. In order to supply demand, they dressed heads beginning at "between four and six o'clock in the morning."[85] This was the Franco-American Meschianza, a republican assembly that nonetheless included dancing and the display of fireworks and high fashion.[86]

Thus wealthy residents of Philadelphia, both native elites and transplants, embraced their roles as new national elites, favorably comparing their city—particularly its fashions and women—to other American towns.[87] In particular, a rivalry developed between Philadelphia and New York that would inform debates about the location of the nation's capital. Elizabeth Wister found the "New York stile not equal to the dear Philadelphia fashions," while Anna Rawle, maintaining a lively correspondence with her mother, Rebecca Shoemaker, in Philadelphia about fashion, claimed that although "the extravagant and singular dress of the York ladies" was much vaunted, she was rather "disappointed" in her "high idea of New York girls." Rebecca Franks wrote to her sister Abby that, while the women of New York excelled those of Philadelphia in their hair, few knew how to entertain without the help of playing cards, and none could "chat above half an hour, and that on the form of a cap the colour of a ribbon, or the set of a hoop-stay or jupon." She continued, "I will do our ladies, that is in Philadelphia, the justice to say that they have more cleverness in the turn of an eye than the New York girls have in their whole composition." But dress was still important to Franks, for she had spent one morning "trying to dress a rag baby in the fashion" and, failing, instead provided a written description of the modish pinning of a handkerchief around the throat.[88] Franks disdained fashion as adopted and discussed by others while pursuing it herself. Philadelphia women followed fashion but were not consumed by it like vapid New Yorkers, Franks implied, and a city's reputation was only as good as its ladies. Hence, Philadelphia possessed the style *and* the substance so essential to the seat of national power.

By 1780 the log book discussed earlier in this chapter, in which the Committee of Inspection and Observation recorded its seized merchandise in 1774, was being put to very different use. On the slim volume's back cover is a list of "expenses" recorded monthly from May through November. These include an array of fashionable goods and services: fine clothes, powder and pomatum, dressing hair, Windsor chairs, Madeira, gloves, silk stockings, queen's ware plates, and a teapot and tea board, the prices extremely high.

The list-maker incurred the expenses in preparation for social visits such as "attending New Town Court" or "attending Easton Court."[89] By 1780, someone—perhaps one of the very men appointed six years earlier to enforce the resolutions—thought little of nonconsumption, choosing instead to heed the cultural politics of fashion.

By the early 1780s, with the war ended and the martial mode with it, there seemed little agreement on how to reconcile the new republican political order with traditional displays of power and prestige. The nation's culture, its "look," was still up for grabs. Had old-world style, from high rolls to hair powder, trumped Whig politics or merely been made to serve them? Fashion in the European mode had thus far survived the Revolution, despite repeated attempts dating from the 1760s to sound its death knell; for some, the question was whether the American republic could survive fashion. Arthur Lee, so misled about Philadelphia's austere character, felt that men who had enhanced their fortunes during the war through trade "employ their wealth in a manner not very consistent with that un-ostentatious virtue which ought to animate an infant republic." Perhaps they were not effeminate macaronis, but for many of the city's men of wealth and influence, cultural proclivities toward extravagance continued to chafe against political prescriptions and proscriptions. Echoing the Continental Association's language from almost a decade earlier, Lee sniffed, "Extravagance, ostentation and dissipation distinguish what are calld Ladies of the first rank."[90] How grossly unjust, he implied, that women so immodest, unvirtuous, and unrepublican ranked so high on the social ladder.

Yet it was the refinement of these beaus and belles that pleased and impressed foreign visitors, and gave Philadelphia the polish required of capital cities. Was the cultural and political center of the new nation a national embarrassment or the jewel in the republic's uneasy crown? What did its appearance suggest about the rest of the newly independent nation? The struggles of the revolutionary era demonstrate that exercising political power proceeded through attempts to control the material, social, and gendered influences that fashion alone combined—its cultural politics. Fashion brought these political modes together, but never smoothly or easily. Like the period's contesting styles, they collided, clashed, and structured the revolutionary contest itself. In this sense fashion was not merely political, having to do with the state and a person's relationship to it; fashion was a form of power politics with consequences for the relationship between state and society, linking the personal and the political in ways that characterized the debates of the 1780s.

Fashion and Nation

In the 1780s, Americans faced dilemmas both sartorial and political. Having won independence from Great Britain in a contest that not only pitted an imperial power against a nascent republic but also set ways of signifying power, legitimacy, and authority against one another, inhabitants of the United States faced the vexing question of how the new nation would appear in the eyes of the world and to itself. Fashion in dress focused the tension of being freed from political dependence on Britain while still economically tethered through commerce, exposing the de facto colonial position of the republican polity.[1] Observing that independence had not resulted in a clean break, some argued that political transformation should signal a change in culture, and that an independency of dress was a place to start. Yet independence had been won through the assistance of the acknowledged masters of modes, the French, whose ministers arrived in the United States with all the pomp and circumstance befitting an ancien régime, inspiring a series of balls and fetes in which displays of fashionability were paramount.[2] Such was the power of visual and material signifiers of identity, whether national or individual.

In fact, the personal and the political sometimes found themselves at odds. The cultural politics of fashion, through which people created but also challenged hierarchies of gender, status, and empire, acquired a national cast in the 1780s. The issues that sartorial practices had long expressed and highlighted became American republican problems of social order, gendered power, and political economy. In the early years of the republic, Americans balanced traditional expressions of position and authority against new, nationalist prescriptions and proscriptions and attempted to reconcile them by appearing at once appropriately republican and legitimately powerful to various audiences—local, national, and international.[3] It was a tall order, one that Americans seemed unable to fulfill, always erring on one side or the other of the parochial/cosmopolitan divide, according to foreign observers.

Expressly linking the personal and the political, anxious proscriptions in newspapers and magazines insisted that too many Americans remained slavishly loyal to *la mode* at the literal expense of their pocketbooks, their reputations, and their country. Increasing understatement in men's fashionable dress may have served the needs of both social distinction and republican simplicity, but this did not mean that the look was not imported both in form and in fabric—it was. Moreover, Anglo-American women of various ranks remained the chief arbiters of refinement in dress, which remained necessary to ensure success in courtship and social life; thus men of the republic were dependent not only on "feminized" fashion but on the "fair sex," many of whom, despite attempts to discipline them into artless simplicity, followed fashion's dictates and their own desires.

Alongside fashion's continued power to perform social distinction emerged a line of argument that asserted fashion's threat to the national political economy, one that served as a way both to mobilize particular political agendas and to disdain the appearances of haughty women, aspiring men, and the realm of fashion they inhabited. Once threats to proper social order and gender relations, men and women of fashion now jeopardized the very health of the nation, writers claimed. Yet the behavior of elite Americans demonstrates that such messages were intended chiefly for others, although they possessed their own, in-group concerns about the relationship between fashion and propriety. Part of the problem of republican governance lay in the conflation of feminine social influence and masculine economic and political power that adherence to fashion had represented throughout much of the eighteenth century. In the new political order, one that empowered and rested on a disembodied "people," social and political realms, or the embodied personal and the (theoretically) disembodied political, would need to be broken apart, at least in theory, and fashion was the wedge that would do it.

"For the Good of My Country":
Ambivalence and Necessity among Elite Men

For nine months stretching from November of 1783 to June of the following year, Annapolis served as the temporary capital of the United States. Here Congress ratified the Treaty of Paris and George Washington dutifully resigned his commission. To mark the latter occasion, Congress arranged for an "elegant public dinner," in the words of Rhode Island representative David Howell, followed by a ball held at the Maryland statehouse attended by some two hundred elected officials and elite residents of the town. The following day's somber ceremony saw the statehouse turned into a far graver stage, though still "crowded with people of the first fashion," many of whom wept tears of affection and loss at the leader's leave-taking, resigned to the resignation.[4]

Yet after hosting such a display of solemnity, Annapolis, a town known for its politeness and sociability, seemed to return to its former gay self, inspiring comment from some congressmen. John Beatty from Pennsylvania wrote to his brother in March of 1784 that his situation was "tolerably agreeable," noting that the inhabitants were exceedingly hospitable and that every species of amusement, including dancing assemblies, plays, and concerts, could be found. Fellow delegate Charles DeWitt from New York claimed he had never seen a people so "totally devoted to pleasure, dress and extravagance" as Marylanders, while French traveler Abbé Robin observed that "female luxury here exceeds what is known in the provinces of France." Putting a fine point on it, Beatty wondered whether "through the all powerful influence of fashion we Congressional republicans or plebeians may not shortly assume the dress and manners of the patricians and nobles of Annapolis."[5]

Although likely written half in jest, Beatty's comment acknowledged that fashion was socially potent and infectious, so much so that a person who desired to fit in to a particular society would almost inevitably find himself susceptible to prevailing modes. By contrasting the style of elected political leaders with the established local elites through categories drawn from the classical republics, Beatty characterized himself and his fellow public servants as plebian, members of the common people. Yet they might acquire the dress and air of patricians, the aristocracy. Whether they would be compelled do so—would *choose* to—or would adopt the fashions almost unthinkingly as a consequence of circumstances remained unclear. Beatty elided the conscious, volitional element of dress, granted agency to fashion itself, and removed himself from responsibility. On the one hand, this was dangerous, for what truly independent man fell under the spell of fashion? Yet independence would be reasserted when the patrician finery was thrown off, no longer needed, or simply disappeared when the situation changed and the true plebian characters of Congress were again revealed.

Charles DeWitt, so taken aback by the appearance of Marylanders, used the situational quality of fashion as a way to legitimate his own sartorial choices, which had much to do with the fraught confluence of political and social propriety. DeWitt had just traveled from his home in Ulster County,

New York, through Philadelphia, a city he greatly admired, where he dined with the French minister Chevalier and the ambassador from the Netherlands. He chanced to meet the latter in the street before the dinner, observing that he was "as plain a Dutchman as I am" and noting with a little surprise and perhaps dismay that "indeed I believe I rather exceeded him in dress." "However, he then explained, "you must know I am rather better dressed on this occasion than usual."[6] DeWitt, the owner of a mill, had been a statesman for many years, serving in the New York Assembly, in the provincial Congresses after 1775, and as a colonel in the Continental army.[7] But he had not traveled beyond his home state, nor met with foreign ministers, even if they were from fellow republics. One would need to be well dressed when treating with ambassadors and perhaps even when en route to occupy a seat in Congress—but *how* well dressed? The audiences and arbiters had changed, which underpinned DeWitt's ambivalence about fine dress and anxiety over his appearance. He was at once relieved to find the Dutch ambassador plainly dressed and a bit embarrassed about his own somewhat finer attire. How should a congressman look?[8]

Virginian Richard Henry Lee, by contrast, seemed a bit more comfortable with his fashionability, perhaps due to his august lineage and English education. In 1785, while serving as president of Congress, he penned a letter thanking his nephew Thomas Lee Shippen of Philadelphia for sending some clothes that Shippen's tailor had made for Lee. Only a few days earlier, having not yet received the clothes, he wrote to inquire about their progress, speculating with humor but also some concern that the tradesman, Mr. Barthold, had "by this time I suppose rigged me out in such a manner as to convert the old president into a young Beau." Lee juxtaposed his age and position of political leadership with a term for a man overly attentive to dress and to women, laying the blame for his transformation at a tailor's feet. The fact that the suit was taking so long suggested that it might not suit the man. Yet perhaps such a look was not to be avoided, and might not be the worst thing in any case. Waxing mock philosophical, Lee sighed, "Very well, if for the good of my country I must be a Beau, why I will be a Beau."[9] People possessed certain expectations about the appearance of the president of Congress, he supposed, and to meet them Lee would shoulder the burden of looking the part. This allowed him to displace responsibility onto the nature of his position and the desires of the people. Yet the letter's familiarity and its joking tone on the issue suggest that such an appearance would be no personal hardship. Despite his advanced age of fifty-three, the old president would gladly cut a fashionable figure.

What might cutting a figure mean for Anglo-American men in the 1780s? What was high style, and did men such as Lee embrace it? In previous months, Lee corresponded with Shippen about a pair of black silk breeches. Although we do not know what his new suit of clothes looked like, given the year we can imagine a close-cut coat and breeches of a dark color and high-quality fabric, worn with a fine linen shirt and a light-colored waistcoat. Men's fashionable dress was moving in the direction of sobriety and under-statement,[10] with emphasis on fit and the contrasting waistcoat. From those made of linen and cotton for daywear to silk vests for formal dress, white and cream waistcoats became extremely popular beginning in the 1780s.[11] Anthony Morris, a merchant and politician who built a grand late-Georgian estate in Pennsylvania, owned at least three white cotton waistcoats, one plain and two printed. The prevailing dark tones of coats and breeches set off the light color of fine silk garments, which in turn highlighted the elaborate, colorful embroidery, usually flowers or other natural motifs, that decorated items of formal dress. American men "could order uncut waistcoat embroideries from Europe and have them cut to fit" in the states.[12] Thomas Roberts of New York sold "fancy waistcoat patterns."[13] French needlework was particularly fine and desirable, and waistcoats of French origin from the late eighteenth century were quite opulent.

While waistcoats had long been an important site of ornamentation in men's fashionable wear, they had competition; vests of the early and mid-eighteenth century were often hidden beneath coats of rich and vibrant fabrics with full skirts. Although they could be left open, such coats buttoned up the front, whereas by the 1770s, coats were cutaway, putting the vest on greater and permanent display—the ever-shrinking focal point of men's dress. By the 1780s waistcoats had shortened to hit at the waist and would become even shorter in the decades that followed.[14] In fact, the clothed, high-status male body itself was shrinking as the look of the country gentlemen came to town and evolved to suit the urban environment. It was the white waistcoat that preserved urbane distinction. For some it was high metropolitan style; for others, republican simplicity. Ideally, it was both at once, especially for the leaders of the new republic. But it depended on who was looking and judging.

Richard Henry Lee and others of his ilk, part of an emerging national political elite with colonial ruling-class heritage, were aware of eyes being cast upon them and the judgments that various audiences might render. The prevailing wisdom held that "as the face is the mirror of the soul, so dress is the index of the mind," according to Poor Richard. Lack of care denoted an "indolent negligence," while a "whimsical habit" suggested caprice. To oppose prevailing fashions, changes in which supported commerce, was "as great a proof of vanity and pride as attempting to be the first who shall introduce a novelty." Here Benjamin Franklin seized the opportunity to insult Quakers, whom he accused of taking "peculiar pride" in diverging from the norm. Since custom had made attention to dress indispensable, the solution was to "neither court nor despise the fashions, but always keep the medium and avoid the extreme,"[15] a prescription with which men such as DeWitt, Beatty, and Lee would likely agree. But who decided what was moderate? Not only did they need to strike a balance between fashionability and taste in a society that often separated the two, but they also had to reconcile dress that befitted their social station with sartorial performances of republican virtue, a politics that was written on the bodies of men as well as women.

When in Paris

The ambivalent posture that characterized the musings of men such as Beatty, DeWitt, and Lee, of acknowledging fashion's inevitable influence while distancing themselves from it, extended to the feelings and behavior of other Americans regarding their newfound friends the French. Britons had long associated fashion with France and vice versa, seeing in both all that was frivolous, effeminate, and debauched.[16] The creation of a cultural foil served English and colonial political purposes in an era of continual imperial contest, though it did not necessarily prevent Britons from adopting French modes.[17] What would be the nature of the United States' cultural relationship to France now that the two nations were political allies, yet one a republic with close commercial and cultural ties to Britain, and the other still an ancien régime? Abbé Robin put his finger on the discrepancy when he observed that "Pennsylvanians differ very considerably from us in the ceremonies of dress as we differ from them in our modes of legislation," drawing a parallel between fashion and government.[18] In the 1780s, some Americans regarded the French and their fashions with exasperation, sniffing at the extravagance even as they were obliged to partake in it.

The well-established reputation of the French beau monde as avatars of fashion was of some concern to Americans abroad, who generally adopted a "when in Rome" (or Paris, rather) stance with respect to French modes. In 1780 George Fox, newly arrived in France, wrote to William Temple Franklin, Benjamin's grandson and a noted bon vivant who lived much of his life there, asking Franklin's advice on what was worn in winter. "As your taste is generally admired," Fox flattered his friend, "please enlarge in your next upon the subject of dress not forgetting the linings and buttons; I should beg you also to enclose a fashionable pattern." Fox's concern extended down to the particulars. Two weeks later he again pleaded, "As the French are extremely exact with regard to the minutiae of dress, I beg you to be particular to those parts which depend on fashion." His desperation suggests that French men and women could be merciless in their judgments. Fox also informed Franklin that since the royal mourning for Prince Charles was almost over, "le monde appears once again in fancy colors," which he called "an agreeable circumstance to those who are not fond of being seen too often in the same dress."[19] Mourning wear was itself a change of mode, but the wheel of fashion had to keep turning to keep the people of fashion satisfied, he observed. Others were more overtly disdainful of French devotion to dress. Mary Norris claimed that her son Joseph was "heartily sick of Paris," because although many regarded it as superior to London, "it is there that fashion has fixed her throne and has the greatest number of votaries."[20] Marie Antoinette may have reigned alongside Louis XIV at Versailles, but *la mode* was the real queen of France.[21]

Abigail Adams also disdainfully commented on the habits of the French while living outside Paris during her husband John's diplomatic stint there. Perhaps surprisingly, she observed that "everything that will bear the name elegant is imported from England and if you will have it, you must pay for it." Having garments made of fabric that was imported and therefore expensive expressed high status, but the French may have also been copying English country dress. Indeed, the only gauze "fit to wear" was English, costing a crown per yard, a price Adams clearly considered high. She railed against what she considered the extravagant costs of niceties-turned-necessities such as hairdressing and mourning dress. To attend to the former she employed a young woman named Pauline whom she had almost dismissed because the girl refused to do much housework, claiming, "It is not de fashion, it is not her business," Adams mimicked. The mistress of the house found that she could not do better, however, and since paying someone else for hairdressing was costly enough to be out of the question given the meager budget Congress had allotted them, she was obliged to keep the coiffeuse on. Pauline knew her worth as a skilled hairdresser and could use it to refuse other forms of labor she felt were beneath her. Still, Adams put her to work sewing in an attempt to make the girl's employment as "useful" as possible.[22]

If English fabric and hairdressing were not enough, the sartorial requirements of court mournings proved an additional, ridiculous expense. Adams recounted that "poor Mr. Jefferson had to hie away for a tailor to get a whole black suit made up in two days; and at the end of eleven days should another death happen, he will be obliged to have a new suit of mourning, of cloth, because that is the season when silk must be left off." However silly it seemed, social and political customs had to be observed, as the worlds of official protocols and seasonal changes in modes overlapped. She continued, "We may groan and scold, but these are the expenses which cannot be avoided, for fashion is the deity everyone worships in this country and, from the highest to the lowest, you must submit." Proving her point that all ranks were subject to fashion's commandments, John and Esther, the household help, were ridiculed by other servants until Adams directed them to have their hair dressed in the fashion. Esther cried and claimed that she felt foolish, but Adams insisted, saying that there was no way "to keep them from being trampled on but this: and now that they are a la mode de Paris they are much respected."[23]

This episode suggests much about the confluence of status, gender, and national context. Faced with an environment in which conformity to a royal mandate was paramount, American servants were dressed up by their employers in the name of social acceptance that adherence to the mode guaranteed—and to avoid the rejection and ridicule that lack of adherence inspired. They were not, however, transformed into members of another class, but rather into people who could be accepted by those of their own rank. Esther seemed to have a greater problem with the makeover than John, perhaps because the risks for low-ranking women who embraced *la mode* were higher; any woman of fashion could be tarred with the brush of sexual impropriety,[24] but servant women were especially vulnerable to such charges, and lacked the protections of higher-status women. Ultimately, Esther and John might not have cared a whit that they were the stuff of sport, but Adams did, probably because it reflected poorly on her, and she had the power to make things right. However disdainful Americans such as Adams and Jefferson seemed of European modes and the societies that required them, they were not comfortable enough to eschew conformity. The reputation of the new American republic demanded otherwise.

Visions of American Women

In 1788, when Congress was sitting in the capital, New York City, delegate Paine Wingate described the city's ladies as "chiefly rumps and heads."[25] Indeed, women's fashions remained a focus of satire and proscription in the wake of the war, as mockery of appearance and suggestions of inappropriate sexuality continued to be the primary means of disciplining unseemly bodies. Lampoons tended to focus on particular fashions, but "outlandish" styles provided permission to mock more generally the public presence women were claiming in the new republic.

The invention and public demonstration of the hot air balloon in Paris in 1783 occasioned a balloon mania that extended to women's petticoats, which must have been round and curved under at the bottom. An item in the *Pennsylvania Gazette* reported from New York that "air balloon dress is so much the fashion in this city . . . that some ingenious temptresses have it in contemplation to establish a balloon petticoat, so constructed as that every person may go up in it with safety." If blaming the fad on "temptresses" was not a clear enough insult to women's virtue, the author made the phrase "every person may go up in it with safety" into a double entendre, suggesting the image of men canoodling with impunity under women's skirts. A writer for the *New York Daily Advertiser* was more explicit about the relationship between female fashion and morality, punning, "When ladies tuck up their petticoats and display their legs, there is an end in view. When ladies put on false rumps, there is an end in view." Women showcased their bottoms as a means to achieve the end of inspiring male desire. The *New York Gazetteer* opted to malign women's bodies from a different perspective, proclaiming that the shape of modern dresses was "calculated to destroy shape altogether," such that a woman dressed "according to the height of fashion may be worshipped without any breech of the second commandment," since (directly quoting the scripture) she appeared like "nothing in the heaven above, the earth beneath or water under the earth."[26]

The hoop petticoat as outlandish "machine" and attention-getting device had long been a target of criticism,[27] but the particular style under review was probably the gown *à la polonaise*, popular in the late 1770s and early 1780s. The polonaise, a reference to Polish dress, consisted of a fitted bodice and round petticoat that hit above the ankle underneath a cutaway overskirt drawn up on the sides or in the back, often draped over pads or bustles.[28] From the back, the gown did appear somewhat unusual compared to previous shapes. The style recalled the dress of milkmaids and other rural women who drew up their skirts to keep them out of the dirt. The look of the country had infiltrated court and town, becoming *la mode*. This might, and perhaps should, have been much vaunted in the United States, considering the appreciation for the "unaffected look" of country girls and approbation

Dress (*Robe à la polonaise*), American, 1780–85, silk; view: ¾ right, from back. Dating from the early 1780s, this yellow gown of hand-painted Chinese silk indicates the persistence of desire for the latest fashions in styles of dress and fine imported fabrics during the Confederation period. The Metropolitan Museum of Art, Gift of heirs of Emily Kearny Rodgers Cowenhoven, 1970 (1970.87a, b). Image © Metropolitan Museum of Art, New York, N.Y., U.S.A.

of homespun that filled the public prints beginning in the 1750s. Perhaps women of fashion felt that they might have it both ways, combining the appearance of pastoral virtue with that of urbane cosmopolitanism, since the former had been transmogrified into the latter. The style, on some level, "trickled up." But of course it had a French name and was neither simple nor homespun nor particularly modest, with its pulled-up skirts. Critics could not help but see it as a grotesque bastardization of rural simplicity.

Moreover, hair was still worn high and dressed elaborately, despite the claims of a letter to the *Lady's Magazine* for 1782. Its author, "A Female Antiquarian" who dated the origin of high heads to Roman extravagance in the time of the Emperor Nero, insisted that they were finally going out of style. Two years later, a "lady of fashion" reported for the periodical that English noblewomen, such as the Duchess of Devonshire, "set the ton in simplicity of dress and superiority of taste," in part by discarding the "false chignon."[29] Yet hairdresser advertisements in American cities suggest that the look of the French court was very much in vogue. L. Marey placed a notice that he had hired "Mr. Derley, who is just arrived from Paris where he has acquired with proficiency (from Mr. Leonard, hairdresser to her Majesty the Queen of France) that elegant and fanciful manner which is so much celebrated in setting off to the best advantage Jewels, Flowers, Feathers, etc etc and making with Ribbons and Gauze all kinds of Chapeaux et poufs upon the French Toque in the elegant taste of the Court of France."[30] Another coiffeur and perfumer in New York promised "cushions and toupees . . . much approved by ladies of the first distinction and taste for head-dress . . . with all kinds of fake hair made in the newest fashion." However, he chose to attract clients with assurances that his work had given "utmost satisfaction" to the "first ladies of taste in London," suggesting that the metropolis retained its appeal and importance to American clients.[31]

The combined emphasis on hairdressing and the use of wires and pads to shape women's skirts inspired Paine Wingate's "rumps and heads" remarks. A delegate to Congress from New Hampshire and son of a Congregational minister from Massachusetts, Wingate seemed at once impressed and repulsed by what he saw in New York. His letters to his nineteen-year-old daughter Sarah in 1788 supply ample accounts of women's fashions in dress, penned for her enjoyment but also her instruction, full of mixed messages about the relationship between cultivation of appearance and propriety. "As you are fond of dress," he began, "I will try to give you some account of the fine girls in this City, tho' I take so little notice of them that I can give you but a poor account." Considering this claim of disinterest, his verbal sketches appear fairly detailed, perhaps since the ladies of New York were "continually taking their pleasure" out of doors and thus often on public view: "The ladies wear large calashes and silk cloaks bordered with ermine when they ride or walk abroad," he recounted. While attending church he noticed that "the old ladies wore hats much like those fashionable ones your way and the young ladies wore yellow straw hats with crowns bound round as yours." Although their hair was "craped pretty large," by which he meant curled or frizzed, "I did not observe any thing very different in other respects from the dress you have been acquainted with."[32] In part, Wingate strove to assure Sarah (whom he called Sally) that she was not sartorially out of step with women in the capital city. Their styles were like hers; she was not a country bumpkin. There is some indication of concern about his own appearance as well, for he seemed relieved in a letter to his elder daughter Mary that "a large number of the Delegates dress as plain as I do." Although "some of the young gentlemen dress very gay," Wingate had company in the more modestly attired representatives and thus would not exceed his budget and be "put out for want of ruffles."[33]

Since Sally "candidly confessed" her fondness for dress in a reply, Wingate felt compelled to provide his daughter with more fashion news, so far as his "inattention to such trifflings" would allow. But his descriptions also grew arch. Although he had not yet attended the assembly, "where is the perfection of dress," he mentioned women "universally" craping and powdering their hair, as well as wearing "abundance of trumpery over their bosoms, which reaches up to their chins."[34] The voluminous fichus to which he referred, tucked into the bodices of gowns and covering the décolleté and neck, inspired ridicule for the inconveniences they presented. A husband who sought his wife's bosom in a tender moment found it "hollow," one satirical "letter" to the *Universal Asylum* claimed. Moreover, followers of the fashion could not see what food they were eating over the "odious puff" of fabric.[35] Ultimately, these so-called modesty pieces were anything but. They covered, perhaps, but transparently, and drew the gaze. As the spring arrived, Wingate noted that "the ladies have still very slim waists with rumpers and plumpers. Very small feet and monstrous large heads. Long trailing gowns and short sleeves."[36] Through this series of juxtapositions Wingate conveyed the styles of the day but also his disdain for them.

Such desirable reports might read like promotions if not qualified by more than just authorial tone. Each description, therefore, served as an opportunity to educate its reader, Wingate's daughter, on appearance and its social and romantic import. Waxing as didactic as the author of a conduct manual, Wingate wrote, "I hope you will learn to consider dress as but of little moment, compared with the ornament of the mind." For although the "most worthless" girl might exceed her in dress, if Sally furnished her mind with useful knowledge, regulated her passions, and was innocent, virtuous, affable, and benevolent, she would be highly esteemed. He continued, explaining, "I do not wish you to be totally indifferent to fashions and the external ornaments of your person, but to allow these a subordinate place in your attention." A shining appearance sometimes hid a less-than-sterling character, but externals were not utterly meaningless. The issue was one of priority—internal cultivation should come first, which would lead to an appearance that bespoke the fine qualities beneath. He hoped, echoing Franklin's adages, that the "good sense" she undoubtedly possessed would lead her to embrace a "commendable mediocrity between the extremes of under and over dress."[37] We can imagine that the idea of "commendable mediocrity" did not exactly fire the young Sally's imagination.

Of course, the chief issue was "the place and company you have to appear in." Here Wingate demonstrated an awareness of the relationship between fashion and the marriage market in a city like New York. For instance, if he met a young man who might make a good match and sent for his daughter, he noted, "I should then think it quite consistent to spend a thousand dollars in your equipment." Such a sum might seem extravagant but was far less so than a hundred dollars spent at home, he explained. Apparently other congressmen were using their political positions and urban locale to socially advance their offspring. One of Wingate's fellow delegates brought to New York his fifteen-year-old daughter, "whom he introduces into the best company and of consequence dresses in the richest manner." Although the girl was neither particularly handsome nor cultivated in Wingate's estimation, her father intended that she should acquire both qualities through attire and exposure to genteel company. Sally, he implied, would likely fare much better, especially if outfitted appropriately. Yet weeks later he mentioned that although "young gentlemen" at times associated with fine and gay women for amusement, they did not "think of submitting to such a heavy tax as to support them for wives." "You will take the hint," he elaborated, "and if you wish to have a husband who is worth having, you will appear in such a manner as will induce him to suppose that you will not be a tax upon him to maintain you."[38]

How confusing this all must have been for Sally Wingate. Keenly interested in fashion, a source of avowed feminine knowledge and power, she received from her father in New York morsels of information that could have only whetted her appetite. Yet in the same breath the dispenser of the tidbits cautioned her not to grow too enamored of dress, which was secondary to other feminine attributes. He acknowledged that a costly appearance was probably necessary to snare a worthy husband, but then claimed that men did not choose fashionable ladies for wives. A young woman needed to be fashionable enough for good society and yet modest in appearance; sociable but not frivolous; talkative but not garrulous; sensible but not overly serious. In the words of Wingate as he cautioned his daughter against the "unfashionable" vice of bashfulness, "a young lady should be very modest in dress . . . and virtuous in her deportment but at the same time when she is in company she will be entirely easy . . . very sociable and familiar upon any trifling subject such as she would be with a brother or sister."[39] In other words, well-bred to at least appear wellborn. Men such as Wingate contemplated filial unions that would benefit all concerned while cementing a ruling class. Appropriate dress had a role in this performance, of course—recall how tongue-tied Dr. Alexander Hamilton became upon discovering a hole in his coat. Yet Wingate's promotion of modesty and virtue in appearance, almost juxtaposed against easiness of address and conversation, shows how precarious the balance for young women who fell constantly under scrutiny.

Foreign eyes could be particularly sharp when it came to assessing American women and their modes. Frenchman Jean Pierre Brissot de Warville generally found both too luxurious, though he took pains to distinguish among the residents of various cities in his printed travel account. Bostonians fared best by prizing "neatness," with women wearing "calicoes and chintzes" not "spoiled by those gewgaws which whim and caprice have added to them among our women." This dig at the women of Warville's own country was often one aim of such travel accounts. He lamented that hairdressing had become so popular, especially among men, but Boston generally escaped rebuke. New York and Philadelphia did not. "If there is a town on the American continent where the English luxury displays its follies, it is New York," Warville proclaimed of the capital city. "You will find here the English fashions," he continued, as women donned the "most brilliant silks, gauzes, hats, and borrowed hair." Philadelphia's ladies sported "hats and caps as varied as those of Paris," preferring French modes, and spent extravagantly on "their toilet and headdress." Even Quaker women curled their hair "with great care and anxiety" and were "remarkable for their choice of the finest linens, muslins, and silks." To find such expressions of luxury among a sect once known for simplicity particularly distressed the author. Casting young Quakers as coquettes, he wrote that "elegant fans play between their fingers." And echoing Wingate's observations about the social consequences of such extravagance, Brissot noted that in New York "the expense of women causes matrimony to be dreaded by men." Of Philadelphia society he concluded, "It is a great misfortune that, in republics, women should sacrifice so much time to trifles and men should likewise hold this taste in some estimation."[40] Not only was the role of fashion in society and courtship a social misfortune, potentially disrupting the marriage market, it was particularly glaring "in republics."

Writers such as Warville put Americans on display. His observations, whether reflected in reality or not, were damning. In them Anglo-American women came across as frivolous and unbecoming in their excess as they aped European modes unfit for a republic. Men were either in thrall to these fine ladies or fearful of their habits, causing them to delay or avoid marriage. It was an old story about female luxury and the ways in which fashion had the power to undermine proper gender relations and compromise sound matches. But now these had become American and thus republican political problems.

Expatriate Ann Head Warder also assessed American modes in the late 1780s but saw things somewhat differently, although no less unfavorably. An English Quaker by birth, Ann Head married John Warder, a wealthy merchant who had fled Philadelphia during the Revolutionary War. Intending to remain in England, the Warders lived in London for a decade before a family dispute over John's father's estate drew them back to the United States and encouraged them eventually to settle in Philadelphia permanently in 1788. Warder first visited America two years earlier, in 1786, and began to keep a journal for the enjoyment of her sister Elizabeth, with whom she was very close. Her diary supplies a unique perspective, an Englishwoman's observations about American customs—and she had plenty of them.[41] Extremely concerned with propriety in dress, her own and others', Warder lost few opportunities to comment on what she regarded as the unusual and often inappropriate styles of Americans compared with the English, even (or perhaps especially) among the wealthy and wellborn.

Warder's first exposure to unbecoming "American" modes occurred in New York City, where she and her family disembarked after their transatlantic journey before proceeding to Philadelphia. Here she began unsparingly to note the "little taste of the New York females with respect to dress which was much more tawdry than genteel." Chiefly, they all wore "short gowns" of "coarse quality," which Warder called "a custom so truly ugly that I am mistaken if I ever should fall into it." Some assured her that she soon would "on account of the heat," which also caused women to use fans incessantly, a practice to which "none objected," despite the association with coquetry. By early July, Warder assured her sister that she had made "no alteration in my dress on account of the weather, though sometimes have felt a good deal oppressed." Yet she dared not adapt after "exclaiming against those short gowns and not stays which when I first came were worn unnecessarily but now in the heat would be truly comfortable." Still, the "indelicacy" of their appearance, which likely referred to the absence of stays as well as the laboring-class associations of the style, would not let her submit. So that Eliza could fully appreciate her claims, Warder promised to dress a doll for her sister in the singular "American short gown," a style that might have been appropriate for the environment but one that did not satisfy standards of propriety in the eyes of this Englishwoman.[42] Warder thus applied national identification to working women's dress.

If on the one hand Anglo-American women appeared too casual in their short gowns, on the other they often looked too "gay," the adjective "tawdry" capturing both missteps. Observing an inconsistency between the garb of children and their overdressed mothers, Warder wrote, "Not a woman has visited me that was not elegant enough for any bride," clearly thinking her guests too showy. Although Philadelphians called "Billy Rawle's wife" the "perfection of America," Warder thought her "drest fantastical" and "wonderfully affected." Polly Vining too was "drest fantastically gay," her face painted a high red. Even at meeting women sported "blue and other gay colours not worn with us," and the men joined them, thinking nothing of donning a "Mulberry coat, nankeen waistcoat and breeches with white stockings," an outfit that "would look very singular in England." Another young man who was getting married she called "very plain and yet a great beau," because he sought something finer than cambric for his wedding shirt. Neither did Warder's niece Hannah's "rather gay" appearance escape a review that deemed the flowers that sprigged her caps "too large to be genteel."[43] No matter how admired for their taste and beauty in the United States, Warder's comments implied, such women would not meet with so much approval elsewhere.

What she considered to be flashy overdressing, either with respect to social occasion, individual position, or family fortune was a pet peeve of Warder's and a faux pas she found particularly common in the States. She wrote that her great-aunt by marriage had "three wondrous gay daughters who dress quite out of character for everything, particularly for their circumstances which I think people in general do here more so than with us." Putting an even finer point on the issue, she mused, "What a shame that some difference should not be shown between those of large and small fortunes." The episode that precipitated this reflection occurred during an evening's visit in which Warder "warmly reprobated the practice of people here" dressing poorly when at home and "when out make such a shew you scarcely know them." A woman in the company "pretended as an excuse," Warder sniffed, that it would be very extravagant to wear long gowns around the house, to which the diarist replied, "If my husband's circumstances would not afford me a good long gown I had rather wear a common worsted one always than . . . set at home not fit to be seen by Man sometimes and when out a Duchess need not be finer."[44] This was a damning critique, for it suggested that fine dress was all for public show, bespoke vanity, and moreover was rarely a true representation of rank. In addition, by choosing to frame her retort in terms of "my husband's circumstances," Warder indicated the economic dependency of wives, chastening those who outspent their spouses' means or resented their inability to dress finer, disdaining a "common worsted" dress as too plain.

Apparently even rural American women fell prey to the allure of fashion. During a visit to the country one man peppered Warder with "curious questions" about London and admired her appearance, "so different to what he ever expected an Englishwoman made." "Is it possible," he queried, that she "should come from London when Jerry's wife a poor country girl makes so fine an appearance?"[45] He seemed flummoxed by this inversion, in which a poor country girl looked finer than a London lady. Yet Warder realized the commonplace nature of the problem and knew how to read the sartorial social codes, her discerning eye recalling Dr. Alexander Hamilton's in the 1740s. But to long-standing proscriptions about status and gender Warder added a national critique, associating problems of sartorial propriety with Americans, and thus casting them as American errors.

Yet Warder, however assured of her superior taste, had to make adjustments to her new society. On a few occasions, she found the tables turned and her own fashion choices under review. While attending church for the first time since the death of her child, she thought a fellow Friend was approaching her to offer words of comfort. But it turned out that the woman "had been told of my getting a whalebone bonnet," which distressed her greatly, and "she beg'd I would be cautious." Warder was too agitated to argue but later resolved not to risk offense by procuring the bonnet. She presented the tale as a "specimen that nothing here escapes the knowledge of anyone." The mere suggestion of her purchase had made the rounds and was enough to cause a stir among some in Philadelphia's Quaker community, who did not wish to see their distinctive plainness threatened by the choices of an interloper from abroad. In other ways, too, Warder decided to go along to get along, dress-wise. For instance, one day in October she thought it not cold enough to don a cloak but put hers on because everyone else was wearing one. And although she never did sport an odious short gown, Warder noted the different colors preferred in America, explaining of her decision to retire one gown that "such light colours [are] of no use here." She then shopped for a "dark gown for this winter they wearing them here entirely." Finally, she directed a bonnet to be "made between English and American mode" as her old one looked "too singular."[46]

Although Warder's remarks must be evaluated carefully in light of her English and class biases, they do suggest that stylistic differences existed on opposite sides of the Atlantic. Her often snide judgments, communicated to a relative abroad, were exactly what some Americans feared—that they appeared ungenteel to foreign observers. It seemed that Anglo-American women in particular were bound to be damned either way, whether too fashionable and luxuriously European or too coarse and distinctively American.

Some seemed to agree with Warder that English styles were superior. William Dillwyn, a Quaker who fled Philadelphia for London during the Revolutionary War, sent his daughter Susanna "a pattern for a silk and another for a calico gown" in April of 1783 and urged her to give him a list of any articles she wanted. He enclosed two more dress patterns in June, again encouraging "Sukey," as she was called, to tell him of anything she might want. The following year her stepmother, Sarah, sent a cloak pattern, and in 1785 William forwarded the instructions for a ducape gown.[47] Although Quakers were not on the cutting edge of fashion, the reference to calico, which was resurging in popularity in the late eighteenth century, and to silk and ducape shows that the Dillwyns were not insensible to fashion or to fineness—supporting Warville's observations about Quaker habits. Surely Susanna had access to dress patterns in Philadelphia, but her parents clearly felt that the styles of dress they were seeing among English Quakers were desirable. Yet it may be that the new patterns, along with the regular correspondence, caused her as much social strain as pleasure. A few years later she complained that her friend Sally Fisher "fatigued" her with "enquires about the customs and fashions and modes in England, which I was by no means qualified to answer."[48] Fisher's queries acknowledged that English modes were probably quite different from what she knew.

Yet difference did not always signal hierarchy; or rather, it depended on one's perspective. Another Quaker refugee, Samuel Shoemaker, saw the difference in styles firsthand during his time in London, according to the diary he kept as a series of missives to his wife, Rebecca, in Philadelphia. But in contrast to the Dillwyns' apparent appreciation of English styles, Shoemaker found himself frustrated by the differences he encountered. His first order of business was to purchase some black paduasoy, probably for a suit. On January 12, 1784, he visited a "great number of mercers" in its pursuit but did not find any he liked. The following day Shoemaker looked again and was told that "the sort I want is entirely out of wear here and that none has been made or can be had." The next day two women Friends procured some for him to inspect; he liked the fabric well enough but resolved to go to a few places more before making a purchase, although he was again assured that there was "not another piece of the sort in London." He then visited the mercer of the queen herself and, sure enough, was informed that "that kind of silk is quite out of wear except among some particular people of our society." Finally, after hearing the same story from a special silk manufacturer and having spent four days hunting, Shoemaker purchased fifteen yards of paduasoy from the women.[49]

Shoemaker then turned his exacting attention to procuring items for family members. He somewhat grudgingly bought two swatches of "fine new pattern printed calico" for his son Benjamin, explaining that they were not "to his order or my mind" but the shop had gone to so much trouble in trotting out an infinite variety of cloth that he was "ashamed to come away without buying something." Fans also flummoxed him—there was a vast array but none that suited. He feared that the "present fashionable fans" would not suit Rebecca's taste, but he purchased one anyway. He was more content with his choice of sleeve buttons for her, brown stone set in gold, which he preferred to the "now fashionable ones."[50] Everywhere he turned, Shoemaker found himself on the fashion outs. This distressed him not because he feared being unfashionable—as a Quaker, his sartorial distinction lay in another mode entirely—but because he struggled to get what he wanted, for himself and for his wife, who preferred her own taste to what was fashionable. On one hand, Shoemaker's taste expressed the social, gendered, and national propriety that some Americans hoped to claim and that others felt they lacked; on the other, no matter the styles sought, it continued to embrace foreign goods.

*Fashion and Political Economy
under the Articles of Confederation*

With the War of Independence ended, and the period of dearth and high prices for goods that proved a challenge to living comfortably (not to mention to cutting a figure) over as well, Americans resumed some of their prewar consumer habits. Imports poured into the port cities, as merchant orders and newspaper advertisements attest. As before the conflict, they emphasized the array, seasonability, and fashionability of wares, particularly fabrics. The notices boasted a "variety of muslins," corduroys and superfines "of the most fashionable colors," printed cottons such as calicoes and chintzes "of the newest patterns," and all "suitable to the season." Fashion's reign in America had not ended with Britannia's rule. Trimmings such as ribbons for women's gowns and, in one instance, feathers likely for headdresses, received particular promotion, as did buttons for men's wear: "horn, mohair, basket, metal, japan'd, pearl, and gold and silver spangled" and "fashionable gilt and plated."[51] James Beekman of New York, after an absence of eight years, returned to the business of trade with a vengeance in the fall of 1784, placing a large order with a London supplier. He, too, desired corduroys and velvets of olive and other "fashionable colors" of "different prices." Also notable in Beekman's order were ladies fans, from low-cost ones to pricey "ivory fans, newest fashion," and huge numbers of buttons of all sorts for men's vests and sleeves, mostly brass but some gilt.[52] Distinction in men's dress had gone minimalist, perhaps, but it had not disappeared, and imported buttons would come to receive their fair share of censure.

The resumption of the carrying trade seemed like a good thing for American merchants, retailers, and consumers after years of stagnation and want. Yet American desire for and dependence on imported manufactures meant that Britain could set whatever terms it wanted for the commercial relationship, shutting its own ports to American products while exporting great quantities of goods. The imbalance of trade that resulted more than replicated colonial hierarchy and fragmentation. States functioned independently of one another and of the union, forging their own ties with British commerce in a confederation powerless to enact national commercial policy. The fruits of domestic manufacturing that had begun to flourish during the war (albeit on a small scale and out of necessity), giving American political independence an economic emblem, could not compete with inexpensive and high-quality imported goods, particularly cloth. The volume of imports meant lower prices and thus widespread access to fine things, but the continuing lack of specie and production of worthless paper money forged a chain of indebtedness that ran from suppliers in London through American merchants and shopkeepers to their customers.[53] At least one Philadelphia merchant, John Shields, wanted his prewar debts repaid, and he took the opportunity to request as much in a postscript to his advertisement, genteelly threatening to "put them in the hands of an attorney for recovery, without respect of persons" if not satisfied. The wealthy and wellborn would not be excepted.[54]

In a climate suffused with personal and national debt, unwanted taxes, and political uncertainty, fashion featured prominently in printed pieces that linked social practices to the United States' status and stability as a nation. Sometimes a synecdoche for luxury—also a popular target—fashion possessed the particular benefit for those invested in American economic independence of being associated with women and fops but also with Europe and appetites for its products. The gender and status politics of fashion were employed to help make arguments about the nation's political economy; likewise, visions of an economically independent and fiscally sound American nation-state could be used to discipline troubling consumer habits through which men of little fortune and women of all ranks might visually and materially threaten social order. Alongside advertisements promoting imported goods, early national newspapers inundated their readers with letters, editorials, and articles that used fashion to do just that.

Connecting national debt and individual expenditures, making the latter responsible for the former, and ultimately blaming people's desires for imports, commentators decried the imbalance of trade that would surely lead to economic ruin. "Though the productions of foreigners may be purchased at very low prices," one writer reasoned, "they are mere superfluities." Therefore, "everyone possessed of republican principles must feel anxiety at seeing such vast hoards of species leaving the continent as remittances." A letter reproduced from the *London Evening Post* also bemoaned the "large orders" that consisted chiefly of "trifles and superfluities" that nonetheless carried the "most fatal consequences" to the national interest. Calls for a return to the practice of nonconsumption resounded, and in one case the *Pennsylvania Gazette* reprinted a set of Boston resolutions from 1767. "The same spirit is now called for!" the paper proclaimed, because "the extravagance and dissipation of late introduced among us are too alarming." Some residents of the town of Newburyport went so far as to reinstate the proscription of mourning dress and extravagant funerals in August of 1785, noting that such rituals encouraged the importation of "unnecessary foreign manufactures," which drained the country of money. Moreover, they contributed to the "ruin of private families," the article asserted, expressly linking public and private calamity. On the bright side, the recent "squandering" of money on "lawns, gauzes, silks and other trifles" created a time for reflection during which the people might wisely decide to "pursue agriculture with assiduity and manufacture more for themselves," another author from Boston scolded, attempting to shame people about their consumer practices and promote a particular, anticommercial vision of American political economy.[55]

Public shaming in the press also served to stifle dissent surrounding debt and taxes by pointing up hypocritical declarations of penury in a consumer society. Indeed, "the cry of scarcity and poverty increases with the appearance of expense and luxury," one observer maintained. While "the refinements of dress" suggested "affluence and prosperity," the "tenor of conversation, the accumulation of debts and the impunctuality of payments" indicated insolvency. Reform of personal habits could serve the public good as well; one New York author calculated that if each family sacrificed a mere four pounds, the national debt would all but disappear. "There is not a family but lays out more money in superfluous (foreign) decorations and luxuries," he maintained. Still, "No money! No money! is the cry of every class of citizens," another writer noted, "yet how well conduct and appearances coincide with the exclamation, every person of observation may be convinced." He directed readers to "inspect the dress of male and female . . . and ask yourself the question, how can this mode of living be carried on without money?"[56] Credit, of course, was the answer, and credit often led to debt.

Underpinning a reliance on credit that facilitated the unnecessary expenditures that harmed both household and nation was the desire to appear of high status, editorials argued. The strategy was to make readers feel foolish for engaging in obvious social emulation while also critiquing the practices of elites: "The city companies make fashions; and as to dress it requires much discernment and knowledge of the town to distinguish between a peer and an apprentice, as all are leveled in this respect by a ridiculous imitation of their superiors." Whether the claim of fashion's culpability in mistaken social identity was true or not, the message—that attempting to perform social distinction through fashion backfired when people could reasonably mimic the appearances of their betters—could not have been lost on readers. Another piece bemoaned that "some of our rulers set the example in extravagance and every class of citizens rapidly follow."[57] Again, whether or not such trickle-down theories of consumption reflected reality, the discourse served the twin purposes of recognizing and preserving hierarchy by naming distinct classes (even as it heralded social order's sartorial erosion) while also disciplining all participants in the consumer economy. But the model of social relations put forth had something for everyone: on one hand, clothes did not make an apprentice into a peer, however confusing the signals; on the other, the suggestive possibilities of dress for social fluidity were preserved.

Some authors reserved special animus for women, framed as the wives and daughters of men who could not legitimately afford to subsidize such fine appearances—or at least claimed they could not. The "Primitive Whig," in a series of essays reproduced from the *New Jersey Gazette*, rhetorically queried, "Who is that yonder honest looking farmer, who shakes his head at the name of taxes and protests that he cannot pay them?" The writer recognized him as the same man who had three daughters training with a dancing master instead of sitting at the spinning wheel; who, "while they should be dressed in homespun . . . now carry half their father's crop in their backs and surpass, in all the foppery and expense of their popinjay habiliments the belles of Jerusalem in the days of Isaiah." Rather than Daughters of Liberty, these women were Daughters of Zion, whose haughty vanity would lead them to be stripped of their finery and beauty and, more ominously, threatened to bring down divine judgment on their nation. In another rant, the Primitive Whig said that men could expect to exist in perpetual dire straits until they obliged their "wives and daughters to dress like the wives and daughters of poor, distressed debtors instead of parading in all the foppery and finery of the most opulent and independent fortunes."[58]

These essays blamed feminine appetites for fashion's social masquerade but placed ultimate responsibility with the husband and father, on whom the women depended financially. Since they could not be relied upon to discipline themselves, it fell to the patriarch to restrain them—if he was prudent enough and man enough to do so. Yet other pieces seemed to give women slightly more credit in the realm of self-censure: "The fair American, conscious of the services she can do her country by a little self denial," one opined, "would surely "dispense with that ostentatious pageantry now so much in vogue when she considers likewise that they are calculated only to give a fashionable grace to want of beauty." If patriotism were not enough to inspire reform, then perhaps a blow to the pride in which fashion cloaked and thus suggested lack of comeliness would do the trick. Recalling older, more virtuous times, the piece concluded, "The softer sex did, during the revolution, display virtues honorary as they were useful." But it could now be said that want and poverty "stalk'd through the country, occasioned by the inordinate desire of its inhabitants for foreign gewgaws."[59] "Fair Americans'" appetites could be the undoing of families and of the nation.

By the same token, women's activities could save their kin and country while ensuring their own sterling reputations. An item from Newport, Rhode Island, sought to correct the rumor "that there was no spinning done in this city" by noting that one family alone had produced two hundred yards of cloth yet "still keep three wheels going: an example worthy the imitation of every lady of sensibility and industry." Yoking the two traits, the prescription in the guise of a report suggested that a woman of sense could be known by her industry, which in turn represented her sensibility, the marriage of head and heart, reason and feeling. Another notice proclaimed that "in most of the counties on this side of the Susquehanna the spinning wheel has become a fashionable piece of family furniture."[60] But not all agreed about the nefarious effects of consumption on the political economy of families and the nation. "If the importation of foreign luxuries could ruin a people, we should have been ruined long ago," one editorialist proclaimed, for Americans had long consumed superfluities "of every nation under heaven" yet still "flourished and grew rich." And on the individual level, appetites for fine clothes tended to incite "labour and industry," producing "greater value than is consumed in the gratification of that desire." "No nation was ever ruined by trade," Benjamin Franklin declared. "Wherever desirable superfluities are imported, industry is excited."[61] Highlighting female industry that might result from appetites for fashion, thereby inverting the association of consumption with lack of productivity, he recounted a tale of the farmer's daughter. Her new-fashioned cap, received as a gift, inspired such admiration that all the other girls in the community went to work knitting mittens to be sold so that they could afford to purchase such a garment.[62] In this vision, the spoils of commerce would not spoil society but would generate labor that could benefit the entire nation.

Fashion and "Federal Sentiments": The Personal and the Political

As the postwar period progressed, general critiques linking consumption, social order, and political economy evolved into more specific calls for reform of the federal government. They used the personal, figured sometimes as collective and other times as individual sartorial practices, to argue for the necessity of political change. Americans had "erred greatly" since the war by "consumption of foreign goods, a great part of them mere gewgaws and needless trumpery," one writer argued. But now people were "smarting from this extravagance and folly" and beginning to mend their ways by increasing their own manufactures and becoming more frugal. This reform, "connected with what our legislatures must and I conceive will soon do," would bring relief, according to one editorialist. Still, "Congress must be vested with larger powers" to "fully regulate commerce."[63]

Other authors were not so heavy-handed but still gestured toward reform. The author of the serialized "Essay on the Means of Promoting Federal Sentiments in the United States, by a Foreign Spectator," which appeared weekly in the *Pennsylvania Gazette* between early August and late September of 1787, before the Constitutional Convention at Philadelphia had adjourned, proposed to examine by what means a "happy federal spirit may be improved and not to hazard any thoughts on the political arrangement of the Confederation, except what are inseparable from my subject." However, a number of Madisonian ideas, such as a critique of the factious localism that produced narrowly interested public servants and was "baneful to the federal constitution," characterized the lengthy, multipart work.[64]

Most importantly, the essay stands as perhaps the most obvious and thoroughgoing use of fashion's gender and status politics to make a case for cultural and political reform, using defects in the former to show the need for the latter. The second installment began, "There is no doubt that a considerable quantity of specie . . . will gradually come out when the federal government has the power to regulate the national finance." In the meantime, the regulation of individual habits would have to suffice, although the material evidence indicated that American consumers had far to go. Quoting Noah Webster, the foreign spectator continued, "The practice of imitating foreign modes of dress cannot cost America less than 900,000 a year. I speak not of the necessary articles of dress, but of changes of fashions." When a new fashion emerged in London or Paris, "let it be ever so unknown and uncouth, we admire its novelty, we adopt it because it is fashionable." Such servile imitation was as socially absurd as it was politically problematic and economically unsound: "We boast of independence, and with propriety; but will not the same men, who glory in this great event, even in the midst of the gasconade, turn to a foreigner and ask him, what is the latest fashion in Europe! He has worn an elegant suit of clothes for six weeks; he might wear it a few weeks longer, but it has not so many buttons as the last suit of my lord—he throw it aside and gets one that has. The suit costs him a sum of money—but it keeps him in the fashion."

Buttons received particular attention from the foreign spectator and others as targets for the practices of men who would place fashionable appearances above the fiscal health of their country and brag about national independence even as they embodied dependence. According to a quote from the *Pennsylvania Packet* that was reproduced in the essay, "300,000 pounds worth of buttons have been imported by the United States from England since the year 1783." In an *American Museum* piece published a few months later and signed simply, "Federal Manufactures," the writer focused on buttons in his prescriptions regarding "winter clothes." He encouraged the adoption of metal buttons, which, though costlier, would last many lifetimes over the short-lived yet popular "Birmingham button." Envisioning a national mode that would proceed from personal choice rather than legal mandate, he submitted, "The silver button, engraved with a continental or federal eagle, would render it a sort of national button by agreement and not by the improper force of law, which should not descend to nor encroach upon such things." Sumptuary laws were not necessary; only prudence and good taste were required to shun the imported buttons that symbolized lack of patriotism, frugality, and, perhaps above all, gentility. Instead of the "silk twist button, called a death head," a button covered with the same cloth of its garment was "neat, modest and genteel." In a letter written from Chemung, a town in upstate New York, to a gentleman in Baltimore, the author claimed that, in England, "a plain button, the colour of the cloth, is esteemed more genteel than any other." Only for the encouragement of English manufactures did Englishmen sport metal buttons, choosing patriotic over fashionable consumption. Yet, according to this piece, American men were rejecting both by continuing to prefer the "ridiculous, octagonal, balloon and frying pan button," though it "disfigured our dress and increases our difficulties."[65] Such haberdashery was not only ugly but dangerous.

However distressing the purchases of men, women did not escape censure for making themselves and their nation ridiculous; their "fantastic fashions" were "matters of contempt and laughter to the very merchants who ship them to us." Waxing increasingly hyperbolic, the foreign spectator warned of economic and political ruin at the hands of fashionable types: "Shall silly women bring their husbands to a gaol or under a foreign yoke! Shall effeminate fops undermine a fabric raised by wise politicians and brave warriors?" Perhaps the only remedy for such political peril was political reform. "If people will not listen to reason and conscience," he argued, "they must be restrained by the hand of government." Although admitting that "Sumptuary laws infringe liberty," the author queried, "but does not every good law check an ill use of it?" If people could not govern their appetites, legal proscriptions would have to do so. Surely "men of sense can be happy without costly buttons and women truly amiable will not sigh for Brussels lace," the author speculated, projecting the image of sensible, decorous men and women.[66]

Of course this was not at all certain, due to the "overdriven principle of equality" that led Americans to disdain any "disadvantage in external appearance" and to the role of fashion in courtship practices that also had the power to confuse social order. The sense that everyone deserved certain outward expressions of status stimulated emulation and made people feel as if hierarchy were eroding, when expenditures actually preserved gradations of rank and fortune, the spectator argued. There would always be socioeconomic distinctions; best to embrace one's station. To encourage this, the author celebrated the honest laborer as a "far greater man than a voluptuous, idle, selfish beau" and vaunted his wife as "infinitely more of a lady than those women of quality who carry a dress twice the value of their husbands' income." Such a virtuous union stood in contrast to practices in the "great towns," where early marriages, the "marks of national prosperity," were on the decline "because women not worth a groat speak with scorn of 200 a year and because pretty beaus and smart bucks prefer English buttons and Madeira wine to the best American girls."[67] Appetites for fashion made men and women unnatural in their desires—women became uppity and men luxurious and effeminate. Proper matches became impossible.

Perhaps the best remedy for social disorder and way to ensure "national happiness" was the inculcation of taste, propriety, and reason, principles positioned against the gaudy show and caprice of fashion. Here the spectator took his examples exclusively from women's attire. While dress that united "convenience, simplicity and neatness" was the most elegant and becoming, "true taste" took account of differences in age, shape, complexion, and season. "The same dress which adorns a miss of 15 will be frightful on a venerable lady of 70," he claimed. Yet the servile and passive reception of styles without regard to such distinctions "sometimes reduces all ages, shapes and complexions to a level." Likewise, "a thin garment ... designed for summer dress in Europe, may just be introduced into America when the frost begins. Yet the garment must be worn, for before the arrival of a proper season there will perhaps be a new fashion." Such imitation without regard to situation was unreasonable. Echoing the environmentalist critique of colonial hoop-wearing women from earlier in the century, Benjamin Rush observed "our ladies panting in a heat of ninety degrees under a hat and cushion, which were calculated for the temperature of a British summer." When would America's fair "awake from this servility?"[68]

The politics of fashion not only fueled social and political dos and don'ts in the "Essay on the Means of Promoting Federal Sentiments," it also inspired allegories in which America itself appeared as an absurd woman of fashion, whether a "painted tawdry coquet" or a "country girl" trying to imitate her grandam Great Britain. Again, hair and head fashions figured prominently. Zeroing in on the headdress in patronizing tones, and deploying Quaker-speak to suggest the importance of genteel plainness, the author pled with a feminized America to "pray, my dear[,] pull off that big, ugly hat, it looks like a market-basket; it hides thy pretty face and snowy neck and makes thy head twice too big for they body." Like a young, comely woman, America did not need to adopt ridiculous modes that only obscured her youth and beauty. What was more, certain styles could prove physically detrimental: "That nasty, heavy cushion will give thee a bad headache in the hot sun," the author claimed, referencing the warmer climes of North America. "Tear off that load of horsehair, foolishly called a bishop, from thy back," he continued. "See how you hobble with it—you can not take one sprightly step in a cotillion—you look humpbacked and frightful." Just as bishops kept ladies from stepping light and genteel and made them ugly rather than attractive, foreign modes encumbered the nation, rendering it immobile, as well as unappealing. Turning prescriptive, the spectator professed to "like that neat bonnet and white robe you wear at meeting, it is an emblem of holy innocence," even more explicitly recommending Quaker modes. Still, he did not intend America to shun the trappings of gentility altogether. "When you go to ball," he directed, "dress with ruffles, ribbons, and a feather or two, but don't encumber they head with streamers, and make it like a peacock's tail."[69] Like a woman of fashion taking the latest headdress to extremes, America trussed itself up for the eyes of the world and garnered attention, much of it negative.

Perhaps these practices had something to do with the nation's newly close relationship with France, who also appeared in allegorical form. "I have seen thee to simper on Frank Sprightly," the spectator noted, "who took thy part in the law-suit and got a bloody nose by the constables," reducing the Revolutionary War to a legal battle and again casting America as an eyelash-batting coquette. "He is a gallant man; be grateful and pay him well," the author advised, "but do not set thy heart upon him; he is too much a courtier for thee—his fine sword knot and embroidered suit coat better for royal dames."[70] Just as a young innocent woman could be seduced and betrayed by a fop or a beau, often distinguished by his sword knot and nothing else, so the American nation should not rely too heavily on France, who would likely always prefer other monarchies to the new republic.

The allegories employed in the "Essay on the Means of Promoting Federal Sentiments" cast the republic as a middle- or upper-class Anglo-American woman, whether a sexualized coquette or a naive country girl, who simply tried too hard. By implication, they scapegoated women for the social, economic, and political problems of the young nation.[71] Their appetites fostered continued dependency; their desires resulted in improper unions. Nowhere were the personal and the political quite so clearly linked.

Contrasts

Print culture was not the only venue in which the politics of fashion informed visions of political and cultural reform. Royall Tyler's *The Contrast*, the first play written and performed in the new United States and staged in the capital of New York City, was an endorsement of "federal sentiments." Among the play's numerous subscribers were George Washington and Thomas Mifflin, governor of Pennsylvania. Although the comedy contained a host of players, its star was fashion. Its labyrinthine plot and stock characters hark back to Restoration theater, but Tyler gave them a nationalist cast by exploiting several ostensibly stark "contrasts"—American versus British, natural versus artificial, sensibility versus appetite, masculine versus effeminate, virtue versus corruption.[72] In the end, the terms from each couplet associated with and signified by fashion were discredited and defeated while two paragons of the other qualities form a stable and prosperous match. But the man of fashion, inimical to happy domestic unions both national and marital, had to get out of the way, be written off the stage.

The Contrast's premise is that Maria Van Rough's father wants her to "mind the main chance" and marry the wealthy, foppish William van Dumpling, known as Billy Dimple. Tyler contrasts Dimple with Henry Manly, ex-revolutionary soldier and "man of feeling," setting up a contest between the two for Maria's affections and hand in marriage. Though her father may be "rough," she embodies homespun sense and virtue. As in other eighteenth-century comedies, the character's names are not subtle, and although people are not always as they seem to the other characters, the audience sees them clearly from the first, aided by dialogue. As the play opens, Manly's sister

Charlotte and her friend Letitia, both women of fashion, discuss the latest styles of hoops and exchange gossip. They reflect on the impending marriage of their friend Maria to Billy Dimple, whom Letitia claims has "now metamorphosed into a flippant, pallid, polite beau, who devotes his morning to his toilet, reads a few pages of Chesterfield's letters, then minces out, to put the infamous principles in practice upon every woman he meets."[73] The foppish predator Dimple learns his artifice and womanizing ways from Lord Chesterfield, a character-establishing tidbit revealed through fashionable chitchat.[74] But why do the women not inform their friend Maria? As women of fashion themselves, they are the objects of Dimple's "pleasing" and thus more loyal to him than to their sensible friend. Only when Charlotte falls victim to Dimple's advances does she learn to repudiate him along with the fashionable world he represents.

The audience first sees Dimple himself at the beginning of Act III, "at his toilet," reading none other than Chesterfield, so that he may better understand and prey upon the fair sex. After he leaves the room, Dimple's equally foppish servant, Jessamy, picks up the volume, noticing that "my master and I obtain our knowledge from the same source." Jessamy looks so "topping" that Colonel Manly's rustic "waiter" Jonathan takes him "for one of the agents to Congress," as Tyler skewered the pretensions of servants and gently mocked the political elite.[75] Tyler exposed the ways in which dependence upon artifice misdirected the behavior of those who enjoyed wealth and stirred the aspirations of those in lower stations. Thus the servant's patronage of his master's guru collapsed the social hierarchy between them. All such men were created equally foolish, and while the servant would likely never rise, the master would almost certainly fall.

Tyler disposed of his fop in much the same manner as Jonathan Trumbull did Dick Hairbrain in *The Progress of Dulness*: through debt. Through various twists and turns of plot, Dimple's extravagant expenditures, gambling debts, and attempted seduction of Manly's sister Charlotte come to light, and with them his corruption. When Van Rough learns that his daughter's intended spouse owes 17,000 pounds to creditors, the marriage is all but off. A fop until the last, Dimple takes his leave in the final scene with the line, "You will please to observe, in the case of my deportment, the contrast between a gentleman who has read Chesterfield and received the polish of Europe, and an unpolished, untravelled American."[76] The audience could only laugh and cheer at this; if Dimple represented polish, then by all means give the United States roughness—but with means like Manly's, of course. The Billy Dimples of the nation, with their fine clothes, debauched English manners, and chronic indebtedness, were drained of their social power through being made ridiculous and economically worthless.

With Dimple literally discredited and socially exposed, the way is cleared for Manly, who, by comparison, lives frugally and retains his wealth. Having fought valiantly in the Revolutionary War, he comes to town merely to place himself and his army colleagues on the pension list. Manly wears not finery but his tattered old regimental coat, much to his fashionable sister's dismay. She and Letitia try to entice him into their circle of amusements with the following exchange, a comparison (rather than a contrast) of fashionable men and women and their erosion of gender distinctions:

LETITIA: Our ladies are so delicate and dressy.
CHARLOTTE: And our beaux so dressy and delicate.[77]

But, as Letitia accurately and disdainfully observes, Manly "is no beau." Thus the Van Rough fortune can be entrusted to him—certainly Maria can not be allowed to control it. No more could it be commended to a daughter, however sensible, than to the effeminate, dissipated Dimple.[78] Ultimately, Maria and Billy occupy a similar position of servility, one to his appetites and the other to her husband. After marriage, however, Maria would legally be Manly, proven more sensible than her father, who was initially dazzled by Dimple's fine clothes and manners. Yet the noble Manly serves as the object of satire as well. His patriotic speechifying and "lofty way of saying things," ostensibly full of feeling but at times overly earnest, would have been comic to the sophisticated New York audience. Although playgoers likely imagined themselves existing somewhere between the poles presented, Colonel Manly gets the girl, winning the virtuous Maria and control of her considerable fortune. The latter, however, is of little consequence to him, since Manly is economically independent and cares little for worldly trappings besides. Thus the match is made, securing virtue and fortune for the next generation of Americans. Status hierarchy has been legitimated through character, and gender hierarchy, in which a married woman's identity was still legally and economically subsumed under her husband's, is paved over through the union of supposed equals in mind, merit, and money.

When considered in light of Tyler's personal life, *The Contrast* acquires another layer of interest. He had recently been engaged to Nabby Adams, daughter of John and Abigail. The match would have been a profitable one politically as well as socially for Tyler, yet rumors about him troubled the Adams family and their circle. Some said he had squandered a fortune, was cavalier toward his studies, and had even fathered an illegitimate son. Still, good reports countered the bad, and Nabby accepted Tyler's proposal. But while living abroad in France, the Adamses continued to hear of Tyler's questionable behavior, namely that he had displayed personal letters from Nabby as trophies, proof of his conquest of her. She promptly terminated the engagement.[79] From all accounts, he was crushed and felt unjustly maligned by the Adamses. Did he draw on his own history in creating the character of Billy Dimple? Was the play an attempt to cast himself in the role of Manly and rewrite the story of his failed romance with a happier ending?

Psychological musings aside, *The Contrast* relied on the taxonomy of fashionable types to teach social lessons that had economic and now political import. Likewise, the play endorsed political reform that would ensure a lasting, proper social and economic order grounded in matches of men and women of sense, no matter if they hailed from different states or backgrounds. Thus Tyler drew a parallel between forms of domestic union. The marriage of Maria Van Rough and Henry Manly served as an allegory for national unity, cultural and political, in which fashion had no place. Dimple represented the dangers of selfish desires and appetites, be they individual or local. Only federal union and the national identity that would follow would ensure domestic happiness in both senses.

A New Fashion(ed) Order?:
Domestic Manufactures and Political Legitimacy

As the ratification debates raged in New York during the summer of 1788, one editorialist advocated the importance of dress in making political distinctions visible. "The members of different parties in foreign country have occasionally been distinguished by different or peculiar dresses," he observed. "Suppose similar distinctions should be made between the federal and antifederal citizens of America. Let American made hats, shoes, buttons, breeches and stockings, etc. be worn by the Federalists." At a time when all Americans were supposed to agree about the national necessity of supporting domestic manufactures (despite people's actual practices), by claiming them for one camp, Federalists damned the other to unpatriotic infamy. "By these means we shall incorporate our federal government in every idea of the mind and blend it with every noble feeling of the heart," the writer promised. Yet he also promoted the wearing of locally made leather breeches by all young boys and servants in the United States.[80] While this may well have been a sartorial dig at antifederalists, who fashioned themselves farmers, how could Americans feel confident that choosing domestically produced products would not relegate their appearances to the ranks of the lowly?

The Grand Federal Procession of July 4, 1788, in Philadelphia, which marked the adoption of the Constitution, attempted to allay fears that American manufactures were not up to snuff by featuring (and thereby promoting) the goods as well as the workers who produced them. Artisans marched by occupational group, and near the front of the parade was the Manufacturing Society. A thirty-foot carriage drawn by ten horses bore a carding machine, a spinning machine "worked by a woman (a native of and instructed in this city) drawing cotton suitable for fine jeans or federal-rib," and a few other looms.[81] Also displayed was "the apparatus of Mr. Hewson, printing muslins of an elegant chintz pattern." John Hewson, a calico printer from England, had been operating near Philadelphia since 1774, and the quality of his work, both in terms of texture and design, was highly touted.[82] Helping to produce the cloth, and also on display in the procession, were Hewson's wife and four daughters, "pencilling a very neat sprigged chintz of Mr. Hewson's printing, all dressed in cottons their own manufacture."[83] Thus the "float" of the Manufacturing Society made calico a national fabric and connected female industry, family economy, and fashion, assuring observers that the three were not inconsonant.

Even as some sought to assure the populace that domestic goods could be fashionable, other writers took pains both to chasten readers for their high tastes and to assure them that the great were, in fact, quite plain in their appearances. A letter addressed "To the Working People of Maryland," penned by Sidney, opined, "I should be sorry . . . if the threads in your garments being somewhat larger might *distress* such men as you who lately, being poorly clad and directed by a Man so plain that almost all his family wear homespun, rescued your children from the high-dressed armies of Great Britain."[84] Whereas working people had grown luxurious in the postwar period, great men such as George Washington retained their humble habits, Sidney claimed. Washington's example was powerful enough to be used by a hatter in an advertisement claiming that the leader, the officers in the Continental army, and most "ladies and gentlemen of consequence in the Untied States" had patronized him for years.[85] Others, however, were not so convinced of the leader's sartorial virtue. Although not mentioning him by name, a piece from New York clearly targeted Washington: "When we see a citizen who has frequently exposed his life in the cause of freedom, dressed in the manufactures of foreign nations, have we not reason to suppose that either he does not understand the welfare of his country or that he totally disregards it?" Despite his eloquence in stressing patriotic duty, "almost every article which he wears is repugnant to his words," the author argued, leveling a charge of hypocrisy at the newly elected president.[86]

Washington responded by donning a suit made of domestic cloth from Connecticut for his inauguration on April 30, 1789, just two weeks after the critique appeared. Newspapers now rejoiced in the hope that "this laudable example in the first and best of men" would make "industry and economy fashionable in the United States." Yet there was no need to sacrifice elegance, for Washington's "complete suit of homespun cloathes" was of "so fine a fabric and so handsomely finished that it was universally mistaken for a foreign manufactured superfine cloth." This was a far cry from saying that people should disregard the weave of their garments; for American cloth to be preferred, at least by the "first and best" of men, it had to be as fine as imported. Likewise, John Adams and several members of Congress were "distinguished by the same token of attention to the manufacturing interest of their country." Perhaps inspired by this, the state of Connecticut intended to bolster ideas of its fabric's quality by presenting every delegate "with cloth sufficient for a new suit of clothes." Although "national dresses and manners as well as principles are absolutely necessary to our becoming an independent people," none of the above could be roughspun, even (or especially) if they were homespun. From Worcester, Massachusetts, to Charleston, South Carolina, and whether corduroy or cotton, producers of domestic cloth insisted on its fineness, "equal to any of the same quality imported from a foreign market," and perhaps even better.[87]

Despite claims of its comparable or superior quality, it seemed that domestic cloth required promotion and protection through political and legal means. The Tariff of 1789 was designed to generate revenue for the federal government, which now possessed the power to enact such measures, but it also protected nascent American manufactures by levying duties on certain imports that competed with them. It was a first step in Alexander Hamilton's plan to shape the United States into an industrial nation in the model of England and wean it from dependence on the former mother country.[88] Supporters legitimated the taxation scheme in two very different ways: on the one hand, they promoted it as necessary since people could not govern their habits and yet would not submit to the tyranny of governmental directives. "Sumptuary laws . . . are needed in this country," "The Observer" argued, but they would not be accepted by "a people with such ideas of liberty." Thus, a better approach was to "discourage foreign superfluities and encourage our own manufactures by duties judiciously imposed." Import

Andrew Brimmer, importer of India and European goods, trade card. This trade card from around 1790 employed the American eagle to sell imported goods. Courtesy American Antiquarian Society.

duties were the sumptuary laws of the liberal state. Others, however, asserted that a change in habits had already occurred, which the promotion of American-made goods through tariffs merely followed and encouraged. While "in 1787 a dangerous passion for European manufactures and luxuries has spread like an epidemic disorder," change soon came in the form of preferring buckskin breeches and homespun, which had "become fashionable in dress." Even "landed gentleman" now saw the virtue in purchasing domestic goods.[89]

Although one approach attacked fashion while the other seemed to celebrate it, both employed the politics of fashion in two ways: by filling up the category fashion with different content—foreign luxuries on the one hand, American products and styles on the other—and by exploiting the logic of social hierarchy. The latter, however, could lead to different conclusions. Since import tariffs did not likely curtail the consumption practices of the wealthy, they functioned almost as a sumptuary regulation, helping to maintain traditional sartorial distinctions of rank. But if buckskin and homespun had been made fashionable, then the American Revolution really had turned the world upside down. What would this mean for social and gender order? Was fashion fine, even salubrious, so long as it could be deemed American or republican in its origin and production? If so, who decided what qualified? Or was fashion legitimate for all who could afford it through the means of their industry, regardless of the styles' origin or appearance? Again, who decided which Americans were, literally, worthy?

Such questions both produced and resulted from a debate about what would best ensure the independence of the new American nation, linking the personal and the political. "Let us examine the dress of a fine gentleman, or even the plainest citizen who walks the streets of Philadelphia," one author directed, and "we will probably find that he pays a much higher yearly tax to Great Britain than to the Congress of the United States." "When we can completely clothe ourselves in the manufactures of America," he concluded, "then, and then only will we be truly independent."[90] Everyone agreed that the nation's political economy and personal economies were intimately connected, but there was little agreement about what economic system would produce the greatest health and wealth for both. All professed to desire American independence, which meant some degree of domestic manufacturing; but would that be large-scale industry or household production? Not everyone embraced Hamilton's plans, and the politics of fashion informed the competing visions of political economy that emerged in the early 1790s, as well as the partisan politics that issued from them.

EPILOGUE

Political Habits and Citizenship's Corset

THE 1790S AND BEYOND

In the 1790s, the corset reentered the world of fashion. This is not to say that the midsections of women's bodies had gone unsupported in the decades, even centuries, before. Stays, or "jumps," and stomachers stiffened by whalebone shaped the forms of many women in the early modern period. But the word "corset," from the Latin for "body" and dating to the late medieval period in reference to an outer garment, one also worn by men, had been out of use for some time. It reappeared in common usage in 1795 as a "closely fitting inner bodice . . . worn chiefly by women to give shape and support to the figure."[1] Following this definition, the corset is an undergarment largely identified with mid-nineteenth-century women's fashionable dress, the site of contests over women's health, dress reform, and, for some, an emblem of women's social, economic, and political subjection. So its emergence at a moment when the supposedly "natural," short-waisted Grecian gown's fashion star was on the rise in Europe and the United States is curious.[2] The style (what we now refer to as "empire") was sometimes touted and other times critiqued for its unrestraining, body-skimming contours. Yet it was underpinned by a newly artificial shaping of certain female bodies into a more "natural" form at a time when Americans were defining the republican body politic in ways that increasingly relied on ideas of "natural" difference.

The Grecian gown is an interesting case in another, related respect: it was undeniably *la mode*, but in referencing the classical republics and the Age of Revolutions, the fashion was political in the state-oriented sense of the term. It thus expressly combined fashion's cultural politics and republican political culture, focusing the intersection of bodies and the body politic.[3] The paradox is that as expressly "political" modes of dress became a visual and material form of participation and inclusion in the realm of the state, fashion itself, and the traits it supposedly symbolized and signified,

Dress, French, ca. 1804, cotton, length: 127 cm (50 in.). This evening dress is a classic example of the neoclassical Grecian gown. The Metropolitan Museum of Art, Purchase, Mrs. Annie C. Kane Bequest, 1926 (26.260.93). Image © Metropolitan Museum of Art, New York, N.Y., U.S.A.

was increasingly, discursively placed outside the bounds of the requirements of formal political participation.[4] As a vehicle through which Americans negotiated who deserved and could handle what kinds of power, fashion served as citizenship's corset, giving particular shape to the body politic in the early republic.

When Mary Wollstonecraft wrote her 1792 *Vindication of the Rights of Woman*, she confronted and addressed the long-standing association of fashion and the feminine using the metaphor of enslavement.[5] Taking on Dr. Gregory's *Legacy to His Daughters*, in which he advised them to "cultivate a fondness for dress because a fondness for dress . . . is natural to them," she countered, curtly, "It is not natural." Rather, the attention to ornament that she acknowledged was indeed "conspicuous in women" resulted from a deficient education and the absence of mental cultivation, which from a girl's infancy society deemed "subordinate to the acquirement of some corporeal accomplishment." Denied the development of reason and kept in an ignorant and deplorable state in which the mind had little to do but "roam around in its gilt cage," women were "slaves to their bodies."[6]

Embracing mind/body dualism, Wollstonecraft also employed the four-stage theory of human history to explain in racialized terms why certain bodies were drawn to fashion. "A strong inclination for external ornaments ever appears in barbarous states," she observed, "only the men not the women adorn themselves." Enlightened societies had moved beyond this for the most part, but like "savages" who displayed an immoderate fondness for dress, Englishwomen inhabited an undeveloped stage of civilization, she posited, linking all women and men of "barbarous states." When people claimed or lived under such irrational, arbitrary forms of power and government, whether fashion's sway or hereditary rule, they behaved as either "abject slaves or capricious tyrants." Yet so natural was an interest in external ornament, not to women necessarily but to uncultivated, uneducated humankind, that "even the hellish yoke of slavery cannot stifle the savage desire of admiration which the black heroes inherit from both their parents," she asserted, for slaves frequently spent their meager earnings on "a little tawdry finery."[7] For Wollstonecraft, appetite for display was both a form of slavery and its inevitable consequence, one that resulted from dependence and subjection and perpetuated those hierarchies; such embodiment equaled enslavement and vice versa. Thus was fashion the mark of a gendered and racialized body.

Wollstonecraft may have succeeded in decoupling the tautological association of fashion and women's nature, but she did so at the expense of securing the connection between fashion and the conceptually, symbolically feminine. Changing readers' closely held ideas about women did not mean improving fashion's reputation. In rescuing women from fashion, Wollstonecraft remained wholly contemptuous of the latter, which was perhaps unfortunate at a time when fashion in dress was being highlighted in state politics. After the homespun campaigns and mourning wear proscriptions of the 1760s, the political, military, and sartorial struggles of the 1770s, and the heated debates over the nation's political economy that featured fashion in the mid-1780s, the century's final years saw a series of intersections between republican politics and *la mode*. Attempts to reconcile the two held out the material possibility of political inclusion, but fashion's discursive qualities functioned as a check.

First, certain Anglo-American women discursively claimed and rehabilitated fashion as their purview, although they did less to dissociate women from it. Although she opined in rhyme that men robbed women of the "power to improve, then declare we only trifles love," Judith Sargent Murray held up changes in dress as evidence of women's creativity and inventiveness in her "On the Equality of the Sexes."[8] Priscilla Mason, in her valedictory address delivered to the Young Ladies Academy of Philadelphia in 1791, with a wink proposed the creation of a senate of women for the "truly important business of regulating dress and fashions," following the example of Emperor Heliogabalus, who had made his grandmother a senator of Rome. Echoing revolutionary rhetoric, Mason acknowledged that the United States "could not be independent while we receive our fashions from other countries." She argued that an elected body composed of women who possessed "wisdom, leaning and taste" and "established at the seat of our federal government" would give "uniformity and even authority to our fashions."[9] In Mason's rendering, it was not fashion per se that was the problem but rather that particular styles from abroad were un-American. She was not the first to suggest the need for sumptuary laws in the new republic, although such notions, generally more rhetorical than genuine, had been passed over in favor of protective tariffs. Following the prevalent strain of thought that made a society's "ladies" the key to its character, and thus blamed them for a nation's shortcomings, Mason turned the dubious yet recognized form of women's knowledge and power, that over fashion, into political control that would legitimate the nation to itself and in the eyes of the world. In drolly suggesting the formation of a congress of dress, she distanced herself from fashion while at the same time suggesting that it might indeed be serious business, the stuff of governance.

In her insistence on national fashions, Mason may have been responding to foreign observers who found Anglo-American women too showy and European in their modes, according to several travel accounts published beginning in the 1780s. But in thinking about fashion as a site of power, she was likely influenced not only by eighteenth-century cultural politics but by the political culture of Philadelphia in the early 1790s. There, fashion assumed a starring role in national politics. Although the previous capital of New York had a similar lively quality, the so-called republican court of heterosocial salons and assemblies that reigned in the Federalist capital cemented the union of the political and social elite, putting them on display to one another and to visiting dignitaries. Such pomp relied on particular displays of fashion. For his weekly levees President George Washington donned "court dress," according to one observer, and expected foreign visitors to do the same. Another described him wearing "black velvet; his hair in full dress, powdered and gathered behind in a silk bag; holding a cocked hat with a cockade in it, the edges adorned with a black feather," marrying Roman austerity to European elegance in an expression of the masculine understatement that was, by the 1790s, *la mode*.[10]

If the Federalist political realm was fashionable in conventional ways, the fashionable world, or beau monde, was, in turn, deeply political. Anne Willing Bingham and her husband, William, who returned to the states after several years abroad, presided over the social scene. Nancy, as she was known, developed an appreciation for French fashions and the political influence of elite Frenchwomen, analogizing the power they claimed and wielded on behalf of "the sex" to the struggles of American revolutionaries.[11] She hosted glittering balls, dinners, and salons in imitation of what she had experienced and admired in Paris—a "Republican Court" that drew the ire of critics. At such events, women of the political class shone in bright and sumptuous array. A letter from Abigail Franks Hamilton to her friend Sarah Franklin Bache, who was abroad in England, described the appearance of Lucy Flucker Knox, Secretary of War Henry Knox's wife and a close friend of Nancy Bingham's, as "worth going to see," even if its author professed to dislike assemblies and seemed almost amused at the woman's attire, if also showing some appreciation for its luxury and Eastern exoticism: "Figure to yourself a fancey dress, purple body, long white sleeves gold muslin train," worn with a purple satin turban festooned with beads and "you have the Goddess of War, in status quo, how do you like her?" There were "many other figures" in attendance, "but no one equal to her!" the writer exclaimed. "Tell me would she not do in England?" she concluded.[12] The power and position that "Madame Knox" asserted through her glittering display was acknowledged and legitimated, perhaps even envied, but also cut down to size as unrepublican.

Such a critique was a form of behind-the-back social censure but could also serve as a political attack at a time of growing division in the Washington administration, polarizing around the figures of Thomas Jefferson and Alexander Hamilton. Henry Knox was a known Hamiltonian; thus the dress of his wife might signify the high-handedness, Anglophilia, and industrial vision of the Treasury secretary and his supporters. As the first party system emerged, fashion became a political football in ways that echoed the revolutionary conflict. Fashion figured prominently in debates about the nation's political economy that pitted commerce against agriculture. James Madison famously argued that fashion, because "she" was ever changing, "void of feeling and deaf to argument," proved the undoing of England's buckle makers due to a sudden preference for shoestrings. This he presented as evidence that related forms of dependence—of consumers on despotic fashion, and of tradespeople on the whims and "caprices of fancy" of a few elites that set the *ton*—stood in contrast to the "independent situation and manly sentiments" of self-sufficient American citizens who lived on their own soil. Connecting the personal with the political, domestic social relations with international ones, and warming to his ultimate target—Hamilton and his ideas—Madison concluded, "The dependence in the case of nations is even greater than among individuals of the same nation; for besides the *mutability of fashion* which is the same in both, the *mutability of policy* is another source of danger in the former."[13]

Fashion in dress served as a partisan cudgel within political culture in another way as well, as Federalists and Democratic Republicans alike tarred one another with the brush of fashion.[14] The bodies and habits of Federalist men came under review by Democratic Republicans as part of attacks on the republican court. Deeming Federalist men "aristocrats" was a powerful imaginary that conjured visions of a brocade-clad, languid male figure, embodying Federalists as monarchical, elitist, and corrupt. George Washington's move from domestic broadcloth, worn at his inauguration in 1789, to imported velvet at a time when his administration championed American manufactures did not help.[15] Federalists, in turn, denounced Jacobinism as an imported fashion, casting Democratic Republicans as too foreign, too French, and even foppish. In the words of historian David Waldstreicher, "Thanks to the Republican antiaristocratic politics of style and the Federalist repression of 'Jacobinism,' partisan causes had been equated with everything, including dress, manners, and religion."[16] Writer Catherine Sedgwick recalled of her girlhood that she and her friends wore gold eagle broaches to church to show their loyalty to Federalism.[17] As Federalists mobilized elite women in public demonstrations of support, Democratic Republicans relied on women's voices to transmit their fashion critiques. A letter to the editor of the *National Gazette* penned by Cornelia reasoned that since "the great influence that fashion has may justly be termed tyranny, and that we direct fashion is incontrovertible," if certain habits were unrepublican, favoring "distinction and inequality," who better than women to point that out?[18] The letter cemented the connection between women and fashion while legitimating certain forms of masculine sartorial expression and disdaining others as "fashion," with all its associations.

Finally, competing versions of republicanism that animated the "style wars" of the 1790s mapped onto positions concerning the French Revolution and the conflict between France and England. The explicit politicization of dress that resulted expanded popular, partisan politics across ranks. We know that French revolutionaries were obsessed with dress as a symbolic political practice, whether reverencing sans-culottes and liberty caps or contemplating a national costume. Such gestures brought sartorial distinction under the purview of government, ostensibly free from fashion's more arbitrary revolutions—perhaps what Priscilla Mason hoped to achieve. As of July 1792, the French legislative assembly required all men to wear the tricolor cockade, which replaced the white of the ancien régime. Men and women in the United States soon adopted the knotted ribbons as a show of solidarity; such sartorial displays were an important form of political participation for women of various ranks. When divisions of sentiment began to emerge in 1793 surrounding the revolution's radical turn and the controversy over Citizen Genet, the black or traditionally English cockade rivaled the tricolor to demonstrate loyalty to Federalists.[19] Of course, neither Federalism nor Democratic Republicanism ensured stylistic unity, particularly as regional differences became more apparent within a national framework. Sartorial divisions within an ostensibly coherent group were vexing, leaving its members open to attack on the very grounds from which they launched partisan shots.

But even as (or perhaps precisely because) certain elements of dress became explicitly and formally "political" in the Age of Revolutions, expressing a person's relationship to and participation in the state, fashion's cultural politics placed it and its followers beyond the bounds of citizenship.

American newspapers and magazines of the late 1780s and 1790s presented two prevailing discourses to an elite and middling readership. First, they prescribed an independency of dress for the nation, often charging Anglo-American women with its creation. Writers insisted on a national mode that would be simple and ornament-free—appropriately republican and a symbol of "true taste," which also served as a social prescription for women.[20] Second, they continued to cast fashion as feminine, capricious, and unreasonable, tyrannical and enslaving. Some writers, in contrast to Wollstonecraft, continued to associate women with fashion, asserting that dress was "one of the principal objects of female pursuit," that women were more naturally inclined toward it than men, and that the cultivation of appearance was a weapon provided "by nature to compensate for the weakness of her sex."[21] But as common was the characterization of fashion as form of slavery that men as well as women might labor under. "A slave to fashion is a most passive animal," the *Massachusetts Magazine* proclaimed, while the *Weekly Magazine* declared men and women of fashion to be the "veriest slaves in society." The *New York Magazine* argued that "no chains are so cumbrous and galling as those which we are pleased to wear by grace and ornament." Putting a fine point on it, the author continued, "Vain is the possibility of political liberty if there exists a tyrant of our own creation," linking the independence and political legitimacy of the free, rights-bearing individual with that of the nation.[22]

Because in these renderings "fashion" was a vague signifier not attached to any particular style, anything that might be deemed fashion bespoke an irrational and inconstant mind and a dependent, servile body. The inextricability of the two made the figure beneath unsuitable for participation in governance, since it clearly could not govern itself. Therefore, the neoclassical Grecian gown that appeared to be in such harmony with prescriptions of republican simplicity and even with calls for a national dress could never secure access to political rights because it was an imported style that made legible the female body and reinforced the association between fashion and women. The style may have visually married republicanism to *la mode*, but discursively the two would not be reconciled. Women who donned Grecian gowns embraced their union of European luxury and Roman simplicity as an expression of status and social power that indicated their identities as women "of sense" rather than "of fashion"—the taste and education that was code for wealth.[23] This did not keep the gown from being the object of debate and even satire, as women's fashions had long been. Some railed against its immodesty, while others found it healthful as well as becoming. As a site of feminine social power, fashion remained secure; as a form of politics it was limited.

As for men, fashion's cultural politics helped effect the revolution of 1800, in which country bested court. Men's fashionable dress grew ever more understated, and leaders such as Jefferson deliberately dressed down rather than up as more non-elite white men became involved in formal politics.[24] Such antifashion was itself a fashion and an important mode of social and political distinction, but one that could be coded as mere "dress." The figure of the fop or dandy remained as feminine, laughable, and suspect as he had since stepping foot on the Restoration stage more than a hundred years earlier. These brainless and servile men of fashion received their fair share of censure in the periodical literature, contrasted with men of sense who could afford to dress finely because "there is something, still more eminent than dress, to attract the imagination."[25] That "something more" was ostensibly their independent and cultivated minds, but as was the case with women, "man of sense" was code for a particular, exalted social position. Fops and dandies were men without sense and thus not part of the natural aristocracy, the key to political legitimacy in the 1790s.

Fashion as a form of individual distinction and social currency continued to run headlong into its associations with women and embodiment, emulation and pretense, dependence and enslavement. By the early nineteenth century, the figure of the dandy had become racialized as an uppity, socially clueless African American man, as free black communities expanded in the port cities.[26] As ideologies of racial and gender difference hardened into the nineteenth century, certain forms of fashionability made the bodies of all women and men of color legible in ways that placed them outside the bounds of the electoral body politic. In contrast, claims of masculine rationality and independence provided the basis for political participation; there was no reliance on women for that kind of status, and, at least in theory, no need for fashion to assert masculine power. For men, the fashion of sartorial understatement, of antifashion, had triumphed. Ostensibly separated from those who governed, fashion could be pursued by other Americans without threatening the nation; in fact, the very consumption and display that eventually fueled the national economy indicated an inability to share in its governance. Fashion was citizenship's corset: a hidden but foundational device that underpinned the figurative garb of democracy and equality.

NOTES

ABBREVIATIONS

AAS	American Antiquarian Society, Worcester, Mass.
APS	American Philosophical Society, Philadelphia, Pa.
CRBMC	Rare Book and Manuscript Collection, Columbia University Library, New York, N.Y.
DL	David Library of the American Revolution, Washington Crossing, Pa.
HSP	Historical Society of Pennsylvania, Philadelphia, Pa.
LC	Library of Congress, Washington, D.C.
LCP	Library Company of Philadelphia, Philadelphia, Pa.
MMA	Metropolitan Museum of Art, New York, N.Y.
NYBGS	New York Biographical and Genealogical Society
NYHS	New-York Historical Society
PMA	Philadelphia Museum of Art
PMHB	*Pennsylvania Magazine of History and Biography*
SCHS	South Carolina Historical Society, Charleston
WML	Winterthur Museum and Library, Winterthur, Del.
WMQ	*William and Mary Quarterly*

INTRODUCTION

1 Bernard Mandeville, *The Fable of the Bees and Other Writings*, ed. E. J. Hundert (Indianapolis, Ind., 1997), 28, 33.
2 Erin Mackie, *Market à la Mode: Fashion, Commodity, and Gender in "The Tatler" and "The Spectator"* (Baltimore, 1997), 14–20. Mackie focuses on fashion as antithetical to an emerging bourgeois public sphere of rational debate.
3 Mandeville, *Fable of the Bees*, 138.
4 Samuel Adams to James Warren, October 20, 1778, in Paul H. Smith, Gerard W. Gawalt, Rosemary Fry Plakas, Eugene R. Sheridan, and Ronald M. Gephard, eds., *Letters of Delegates to Congress, 1774–1789*, CD ROM (Summerfield, Fla., 1998).
5 James Eli Adams writes that the dandy, the fop's equally fashionable and effeminate nineteenth-century counterpart, came into focus during periods of masculine identity under stress or revision. See Adams, *Dandies and Desert Saints: Styles of Victorian Masculinity* (Ithaca, N.Y., 1995), 55.
6 Objects are an element of my study, but its focus is not a consideration of material culture. Rather than beginning with and proceeding from an analysis of artifacts, I approach fashion first as a discursive practice, which illuminates material culture as a site of power struggles and contested meanings. Studies of early America that

employ a material culture approach include Laurel Thatcher Ulrich, *The Age of Homespun: Objects and Stories in the Creation of an American Myth* (New York, 2001); and Ann Smart Martin, *Buying into the World of Goods: Early Consumers in Backcountry Virginia* (Baltimore, 2008). On dress, see Linda Baumgarten, *What Clothes Reveal: The Language of Clothing in Colonial and Federal America* (Williamsburg, Va., 2002). On England, see John Styles, *The Dress of the People: Everyday Fashion in England* (New Haven, Conn., 2008); and Ann Buck, *Dress in Eighteenth-Century England* (New York, 1979). A collection that considers material culture in transatlantic perspective is John Styles and Amanda Vickery, eds., *Gender, Taste, and Material Culture in Britain and North America, 1700–1830* (New Haven, Conn., 2006); and on England and France, see Aileen Ribeiro, *The Art of Dress: Fashion in England and France, 1750–1820* (New Haven, Conn., 1995).

7 William H. Sewell Jr., "The Concept(s) of Culture," in Victoria E. Bonnell and Lynn Hunt, eds., *Beyond the Cultural Turn: New Directions in the Study of Society and Culture* (Berkeley, Calif., 1999), 49–50. Borrowing from cultural anthropology's concern with the meaning of things, literature's close attention to language, and sociological theory, I interpret a range of sources, including printed texts, letters and diaries, images, artifacts, and merchant accounts and correspondence in order to connect ideas and experiences, and to illuminate the relationship among different forms of power in early America—social, economic, political, and cultural.

8 Dress can be considered a form of performance in everyday life. See Richard Schechner, *Performance Theory* (New York, 1977). Dress's messages do not rely on the spoken or the gestural but can be confirmed or invalidated by such acts. On "orature" such as song, dance, gesture, storytelling, and rituals as performance, see Joseph Roach, *Cities of the Dead: Circum-Atlantic Performance* (New York, 1996), 11.

9 On attempts to perform gentility, and dancing masters in particular as suspect purveyors of status, see Serena R. Zabin, *Dangerous Economies: Status and Commerce in Imperial New York* (Philadelphia, 2009), 81–105.

10 For a comparative discussion of the northern port cities, see Gary B. Nash, *The Urban Crucible: Social Change, Political Consciousness, and the Origins of the American Revolution* (Cambridge, Mass., 1979); and on the five major British North American cities, Boston, New York, Newport, Charleston, and Philadelphia, in the revolutionary era, see Benjamin L. Carp, *Rebels Rising: Cities and the American Revolution* (New York, 2007).

11 Phyllis Whitman Hunter, *Purchasing Identity in the Atlantic World: Massachusetts Merchants, 1670–1780* (Ithaca, N.Y., 2001), 1–32; Mark A. Peterson, "Life on the Margins: Boston's Anxieties of Influence in the Atlantic World," in Wim Klooster and Alfred Padula, eds., *The Atlantic World: Essays on Slavery, Migration and Immigration* (Upper Saddle River, N.J., 2005), 45–59.

12 Gary B. Nash, *First City: Philadelphia and the Forging of Historical Memory* (Philadelphia, 2002), 63–78. On the culture of Philadelphia, see also Peter Thompson, *Rum Punch and Revolution: Tavern-going and Public Life in Eighteenth-Century Philadelphia* (Philadelphia, 1999); and on African American communities and culture in particular, see Gary B. Nash, *Forging Freedom: The Formation of Philadelphia's Black*

Community, 1720–1840 (Cambridge, Mass., 1988). On Quakers, see Gary B. Nash, *Quakers and Politics: Pennsylvania, 1681–1726* (Boston, 1991); Frederick Barnes Tolles, *Meeting House and Counting House: The Quaker Merchants of Philadelphia, 1682–1763* (Chapel Hill, N.C., 1948); and John Smolenski, *Friends and Strangers: The Making of a Creole Culture in Colonial Pennsylvania* (Philadelphia, 2010).

13 See Zabin, *Dangerous Economies*. On New York politics, see Patricia U. Bonomi, *A Factious People: Society and Politics in Colonial New York* (New York, 1971). On immigration, see Joyce Goodfriend, *Before the Melting Pot: Society and Culture in Colonial New York* (Princeton, N.J., 1991).

14 Nash, *Urban Crucible*, 26–53, 76–101.

15 On Charleston's growth and economic role as a center of commerce, see R. C. Nash, "Urbanization in the Colonial South: Charleston, South Carolina as Case Study," *Journal of Urban History* 19:3 (1992): 3–29. On the city's black population, see Philip D. Morgan, "Black Life in Eighteenth-Century Charleston," *Perspectives in American History* 1 (1984): 188. On the planter class, see Edward Pearson, "'Planters Full of Money': The Self-Fashioning of the Eighteenth-Century South Carolina Elite," in Jack P. Greene, Rosemary Brana-Shute, and Randy J. Sparks, eds., *Money, Trade, and Power: The Evolution of South Carolina's Planter Society* (Columbia, S.C., 2001), 299–321; and on exchanges and power struggles involving slave women in the marketplace, see Robert Olwell, "'Loose, Idle and Disorderly': Slave Women in the Eighteenth-Century Charleston Marketplace," in David Barry Gaspar and Darlene Clark Hine, eds., *More than Chattel: Black Women and Slavery in the Americas* (Bloomington, Ind., 1996), 111–25.

16 A seminal foray into the causes and effects of expanding consumption in eighteenth-century England, informed by a trickle-down theory of consumption driven by social emulation was John H. Plumb, Neil McKendrick, and John Brewer, eds., *The Birth of a Consumer Society: The Commercialization of Eighteenth-Century England* (Bloomington, Ind., 1982). Over a decade later, essays in John Brewer and Roy Porter, eds., *Consumption and the World of Goods* (New York, 1993), employed approaches that recognized the multidirectional movements of goods and styles to assess the meanings that underlay consumption. Social and material studies such as Lorna Weatherhill's *Consumer Behaviour and Material Culture in Britain, 1660–1760* (New York, 1988) and Carole Shammas's *The Pre-industrial Consumer in England and America* (New York, 1990) have thoroughly documented the numerical evidence establishing the expanding consumption of goods. The topic of consumption and its role in the spread of gentility in early America is explored in Richard L. Bushman, *The Refinement of America: Persons, Houses, Cities* (New York, 1992); and Cary Carson, Ronald Hoffman, and Peter J. Albert, eds., *Of Consuming Interests: The Style of Life in the Eighteenth Century* (Charlottesville, Va., 1994), a collection of essays that includes Karin Calvert's "The Function of Fashion in Eighteenth-Century America," 253–83. For consumption and gentility as keys to imperial identity, see the first half of T. H. Breen's *The Marketplace of Revolution: How Consumer Politics Shaped American Independence* (New York, 2004). For an examination of Native American consumption of European goods, a topic this book does not explore, see James Axtell, "The First Consumer Revolution," in *Beyond*

1492 (New York, 1992), 125–51; and Timothy J. Shannon, "Dressing for Success on the Mohawk Frontier: Hendrick, William Johnson and the Indian Fashion," *WMQ*, 3rd ser., 53 (1996): 13–42. On men's attire as a vehicle for exploring the emergence of capitalism and democracy in nineteenth-century America, see Michael Zakim, *Ready-Made Democracy: A History of Men's Dress in the American Republic, 1760–1860* (Chicago, 2003).

17 Gilles Lipovetsky, *The Empire of Fashion: Dressing Modern Democracy* (Princeton, N.J., 1994), 31. Lipovetsky argues that the origins of fashion can be traced to the late Middle Ages, when new desires for personal identity and freedom emerged, as well as a new position of the individual in relationship to the community.

18 This book is informed by sociologist Pierre Bourdieu's work on the practices of social distinction. See Bourdieu, *Distinction: A Social Critique of the Judgment of Taste* (Cambridge, Mass., 1984).

19 Cary Carson, "The Consumer Revolution in Colonial America: Why Demand?," in Carson, Hoffman, and Albert, *Of Consuming Interests*, quote on 682–83.

20 Joanne Entwistle, *The Fashioned Body: Fashion, Dress and Modern Social Theory* (Cambridge, 2000), 52. On the performance and thus creation of gender through appearance and behavior, see Judith Butler, *Gender Trouble: Feminism and the Subversion of Identity* (New York, 1990).

21 On the emergence of a dichotomous sex model, see Thomas Laqueur, *Making Sex: Body and Gender from the Greeks to Freud* (Cambridge, Mass., 1990), 3–8. On the relationship between status and gender, see Michael McKeon, "Historicizing Patriarchy: The Emergence of Gender Difference in England, 1660–1760," *Eighteenth-Century Studies* 28 (1995): 303, 307. On the feminization of consumption, see Amanda Vickery, "Women and the World of Goods: A Lancashire Consumer and Her Possessions, 1751–1781," in Brewer and Porter, *Consumption and the World of Goods*, 274–301; and Shawn Lisa Mauer, *Proposing Men: Dialectics of Gender and Class in the Eighteenth-Century English Periodical* (Stanford, Calif., 1998). The anthology *The Sex of Things: Gender and Consumption in Historical Perspective*, edited by Victoria de Grazia and Ellen Furlough (Berkeley, Calif., 1996), explores the gendered nature of consumer culture in Europe. On the feminization of fashion in England, see Mackie, *Market à la Mode*; and David Kuchta, *The Three-Piece Suit and Modern Masculinity: England, 1550–1850* (Berkeley, Calif., 2002); and for women's fashionable display as expressions of empire—indeed, women's consuming bodies as scapegoats for imperial projects—see Laura Brown, *Ends of Empire: Women and Ideology in Early Eighteenth-Century English Literature* (Ithaca, N.Y., 1993).

22 On the gender and class dimensions of sexual practices and changing ideas about them in the revolutionary era, see Clare A. Lyons, *Sex among the Rabble: An Intimate History of Gender and Power in the Age of Revolution, Philadelphia, 1730–1830* (Chapel Hill, N.C., 2006). Works on early America that make arguments about gender while also using it to illuminate other social, economic, political, and cultural transformations include Kathleen M. Brown, *Good Wives, Nasty Wenches, and Anxious Patriarchs: Gender, Race, and Power in Colonial Virginia* (Chapel Hill, N.C., 1996); Cornelia Hughes Dayton, *Women before the Bar: Gender, Law, and Society in Connecticut, 1639–1789* (Chapel Hill, N.C., 1995); Mary Beth Norton, *Founding Mothers and*

Fathers: Gendered Power and the Forming of American Society (New York, 1996); and, on a later period, Catherine E. Kelly, *In the New England Fashion: Reshaping Women's Lives in the Nineteenth Century* (Ithaca, N.Y., 1999).

23 In her study of the English, American, and French revolutions, Leora Auslander argues that "each moment of political turmoil . . . brought with it a moment of rethinking of the relation between culture and politics." The place of culture in the making of political change helped give cultural forms the importance they have in the modern nation-state. See Auslander, *Cultural Revolutions: Everyday Life and Politics in Britain, North America, and France* (Berkeley, Calif., 2009), quote on 3, 7. For studies of revolutionary-era contests in British North America conducted through cultural forms and their meanings, see Simon Newman, *Parades and the Politics of the Street: Festive Culture in the Early American Republic* (Philadelphia, 1997); David Waldstreicher, *In the Midst of Perpetual Fetes: The Making of American Nationalism, 1776–1820* (Chapel Hill, N.C., 1997); Robert Blair St. George, *Conversing by Signs: Poetics of Implication in Colonial New England Culture* (Chapel Hill, N.C., 1998); Nicole E. Eustace, *Passion Is the Gale: Emotion, Power, and the Coming of the American Revolution* (Chapel Hill, N.C., 2008); and Sarah Knott, *Sensibility and the American Revolution* (Chapel Hill, N.C., 2009). Two essays exploring dress in the context of early national political culture are David Waldstreicher, "Why Thomas Jefferson and African Americans Wore Their Politics on Their Sleeves: Dress and Mobilization between American Revolutions," in Jeffrey L. Pasley, Andrew W. Robertson, and David Waldstreicher, eds., *Beyond the Founders: New Approaches to the Political History of the Early American Republic* (Chapel Hill, N.C., 2004), 79–103; and Linzy Brekke, "'To Make a Figure': Clothing and the Politics of Male Identity in Eighteenth-Century America," in Styles and Vickery, *Gender, Taste, and Material Culture*, 225–46.

24 On the role of gender and racial difference in defining the white, masculine identity of the new American citizen, see Carroll Smith-Rosenberg, "Dis-covering the Subject of the 'Great Constitutional Discussion,' 1786–1789," *Journal of American History* 79 (1992): 841–73.

CHAPTER 1

1 Mary Alexander, Fabric order, 1726, in Alexander Papers, Box 68, Folder 2, NYHS. Crape was "light and transparent" and made of raw silk or sometimes worsted mixed with silk. Camlet (here camblet) was mixed silk or linen with wool, used for men's and women's clothing as well as upholstery. See Florence M. Montgomery, *Textiles in America, 1650–1870* (New York, 2007), 207, 188. A "ps," or piece, equaled roughly twelve to fourteen yards of fabric, as shown by a 1754 Boston broadside reprinted in Florence M. Montgomery, *Printed Textiles: English and American Cottons and Linens, 1700–1850* (New York, 1970), 17–18.

2 On the use of the language of fashion as a selling point and marketing strategy, see Richard L. Bushman, "Shopping and Advertising in Colonial America," in Cary Carson, Ronald Hoffman, and Peter J. Albert, eds., *Of Consuming Interests: The Style of Life in the Eighteenth Century* (Charlottesville, Va., 1994), 236–37. In a period

in which forms of dress changed slowly, fabric served as a primary indicator of fashion. See Beverly Lemire, *Fashion's Favourite: The Cotton Trade and the Consumer in Britain, 1660–1800* (New York, 1991), 7, 168. For visual documentation of this point, see Natalie Rothstein, ed., *Barbara Johnson's Album of Fashions and Fabrics* (London, 1987). On cloth as the "material lingua franca of Atlantic commerce," see Kathleen M. Brown, *Foul Bodies: Cleanliness in Early America* (New Haven, Conn., 2008), 99.

3   Works on consumption and consumer culture in British North America that are informed by the concept of emulation include Richard L. Bushman, *The Refinement of America: Persons, Houses, Cities* (New York, 1992); and the essays in Carson, Hoffman, Albert, *Of Consuming Interests*, which includes Karin Calvert's piece, "The Function of Fashion in Eighteenth-Century America," 253–83.

4   Carl F. Bridenbaugh, ed., *Gentleman's Progress: The Itinerarium of Dr. Alexander Hamilton, 1744* (Chapel Hill, N.C., 1948). For a recent biography of Hamilton, see Elaine G. Breslaw, *Dr. Alexander Hamilton and Provincial America: Expanding the Orbit of Scottish Culture* (Baton Rouge, La., 2008). On forums of sociability and display, including tea tables, coffeehouses, taverns, clubs, and assemblies, see David S. Shields, *Civil Tongues and Polite Letters in British America* (Chapel Hill, N.C., 1997).

5   Bridenbaugh, *Gentleman's Progress*, 23–24, 26; Ann Smart Martin, "Fashionable Sugar Dishes, Latest Fashion Ware: The Creamware Revolution in the Eighteenth-Century Chesapeake," in Paul A. Shackel and Barbara J. Little, eds., *Historical Archaeology of the Chesapeake* (Washington, D.C., 1994), 172; Shields, *Civil Tongues and Polite Letters*, 104–20.

6   Bridenbaugh, *Gentleman's Progress*, 22–23, 146, 29, 109; William Smith Jr., *The History of the Province of New York . . . to the Year 1732* (London, 1757), ed. Michael G. Kammen, 2 vols. (Cambridge, Mass., 1972), 1:226; Shields, *Civil Tongues and Polite Letters*, 141–58. On Boston's outdoor venues, see Phyllis Whitman Hunter, *Purchasing Identity in the Atlantic World: Massachusetts Merchants, 1670–1780* (Ithaca, N.Y., 2001), 87. On churches as spaces of social performance, see Rhys Isaac, *The Transformation of Virginia, 1740–1790* (Chapel Hill, N.C., 1982), 58–70.

7   Bridenbaugh, *Gentleman's Progress*, 44, 193.

8   Gary B. Nash, *The Urban Crucible: Social Change, Political Consciousness, and the Origins of the American Revolution* (Cambridge, Mass., 1979), 102–28; Benjamin L. Carp, *Rebels Rising: Cities and the American Revolution* (New York, 2007), 6–7, 156. On the growth of Philadelphia's black population beginning in the 1720s and attempts to restrict the activities of enslaved men and women, see Gary B. Nash, *Forging Freedom: The Formation of Philadelphia's Black Community, 1720–1840* (Cambridge, Mass., 1988), 9–10. On Boston as thriving and diverse port city, see Hunter, *Purchasing Identity in the Atlantic World*, 1–70. On Charleston's population, see Philip D. Morgan, "Black Life in Eighteenth-Century Charleston," *Perspectives in American History* 1 (1984): 188. Itinerant evangelist George Whitfield remarked on the gay dress of his Charleston audiences. See Kathleen Staples, "'Useful, Ornamental or Necessary in This Province': The Textile Inventory of John Dart, 1754," *Journal of Early Southern Decorative Arts* 29:2 (2003): 58.

9 Cary Carson's essay "The Consumer Revolution in Colonial British America: Why Demand?," in Carson, Hoffman, and Albert, *Of Consuming Interests*, 483–697, convincingly demonstrates that demand for goods preceded supply in the colonies, posits some explanations, and suggests possible avenues of inquiry toward resolving the question of demand.

10 For the explosion of consumer goods documented by advertisements in the 1750s, see Breen, *Marketplace of Revolution*, 55–56.

11 *Pennsylvania Gazette*, January 13, 1730, and July 17, 1732; *New York Gazette*, January 28, 1735. Advertisements provide some of the clearest indications of appetites for items of fashion in British America. Analyzing them as carefully constructed tools of marketing that employed deliberate linguistic structures, rather than as laundry-style lists of items, allows for an understanding of what appealed to urban colonial consumers—what cultivated desire, attracted attention, and drew customers.

12 Bushman, *Refinement of America*, 64–68. Even working women tended to wear stays for support, but enslaved women who labored in the fields did not. See Linda Baumgarten, *What Clothes Reveal: The Language of Clothing in Colonial and Federal America* (Williamsburg, Va., 2002), 121–22, 134.

13 Lemire, *Fashion's Favourite*, 7, 168. See also Ann Buck, *Dress in Eighteenth-Century England* (New York, 1979), 18.

14 Bushman, "Shopping and Advertising in Colonial America," 236–37. Bushman notes the importance of the term "fashionable" in promoting goods.

15 *New York Gazette*, May 31, 1736; *Pennsylvania Gazette*, January 27, 1737.

16 See James Walvin, *Fruits of Empire: Exotic Produce and British Taste, 1660–1800* (New York, 1997); and Maxine Berg, *Luxury and Pleasure in Eighteenth-Century Britain* (New York, 2005).

17 Willing advertisement, *Pennsylvania Gazette*, August 19, 1742; Wallace advertisement, *Pennsylvania Gazette*, June 21, 1750. For language regarding number and assortment, see *Pennsylvania Gazette*, January 27, 1737; December 8, 1737; and October 8, 1741, among many others.

18 On Mary Alexander's life, see Jean Jordan, "Women Merchants in Colonial New York," *New York History* 58 (1977): 416–18; and Serena R. Zabin, *Dangerous Economies: Status and Commerce in Imperial New York* (Philadelphia, 2009), 39–41.

19 Mary Alexander, Fabric order, 1726, in Alexander Papers, Box 68, Folder 2, NYHS.

20 Ibid.

21 "Invoice of goods requested by James Alexander of Messrs. Collinsons to come in the fall of 1737," June 7, 1737, typescript of Alexanders' Orders, in Alexander Papers, Box 68, NYHS. James Alexander's name on the invoice might lead to the incorrect assumption that he handled the fabric orders, but most of the correspondence is addressed to Mary or in her hand.

22 "Invoice of goods requested by Ja. Alexander of Messrs Collinsons," March 12, 1740, in ibid. Shalloon, "one of the materials most commonly imported into America," was a twilled worsted (lightweight wool cloth) used for lining clothes. Rushell (also spelled "russel") was worsted damask sometimes hot-pressed to give it the appearance of satin and used for men's banyans and women's shoes. See Montgomery, *Textiles in America*, 346, 336.

23. On the Junto, see Edmund Morgan, ed., *The Autobiography of Benjamin Franklin*, 2nd ed. (New York, 2003), 116–18.
24. Bridenbaugh, *Gentleman's Progress*, 38, 80–82. Hamilton regularly noted attire he considered remarkable, whether in fineness, coarseness, or singularity, and observed the myriad ways in which fashion in dress affected social intercourse.
25. On Quaker visual and material culture, see Emma Jones Lapsansky and Anne Verplanck, eds., *Quaker Aesthetics: Reflections on a Quaker Ethic in American Design and Consumption* (Philadelphia, 2003). On Quaker economic successes and social hegemony, see Frederick Barnes Tolles, *Meeting House and Counting House: The Quaker Merchants of Colonial Philadelphia, 1682–1763* (Chapel Hill, N.C., 1948).
26. Quoted in Tolles, *Meeting House and Counting House*, 126.
27. Adolph B. Benson, ed., *Peter Kalm's Travels in North America: The English Version of 1770* (Mineola, N.Y., 1987), 651. On Quaker plainness but fineness, see also Amelia Mott Gunmere, *The Quaker: A Study in Costume* (New York, 1968), 10–24.
28. Image of Benjamin Lay, Print and Photograph Department, LCP.
29. I take this phrase from Beverly Lemire's discussion of the trade in secondhand clothing in England in *Fashion's Favourite*, 61.
30. For the underground economy of theft, pawning, and trade of secondhand goods in New York City, see Zabin, *Dangerous Economies*, 65–75, and for the larceny statistic, 68.
31. Bridenbaugh, *Gentleman's Progress*, 29.
32. *Pennsylvania Gazette*, January 7, 1762; February 4, 1752.
33. Serena Zabin notes the number of cases in New York in which stolen clothing had "little or no practical use" in terms of providing protection from the elements. Buying or stealing silk stockings suggests more than a need to cover one's legs. See Zabin, *Dangerous Economies*, 68.
34. *Pennsylvania Gazette*, September 25, 1734.
35. Ibid., July 27, 1749.
36. Robert Olwell, "'Loose, Idle, and Disorderly': Slave Women in the Eighteenth-Century Charleston Marketplace," in David Barry Gaspar and Darlene Clark Hine, eds., *More than Chattel: Black Women and Slavery in the Americas* (Bloomington, Ind., 1996), 97–110. On enslaved women's economic activities and self-fashioning in Charleston, see also Ellen Hartigan-O'Connor, *The Ties that Buy: Women and Commerce in Revolutionary America* (Philadelphia, 2009), 53–55, 148, 174.
37. Philip D. Morgan, *Slave Counterpoint: Black Culture in the Eighteenth-Century Chesapeake and Low Country* (Chapel Hill, N.C., 1998), quote on 601; material on cast-off clothing on 131–32. On slaves purchasing clothing, see Staples, "'Useful, Ornamental or Necessary in This Province,'" 59, 61.
38. Robert Olwell, *Masters, Slaves, and Subjects: The Culture of Power in the South Carolina Low Country, 1740–1790* (Ithaca, N.Y., 1998), 63. Prescribed fabrics for slaves included "negro cloth, duffels, coarse kearsies, osnabrugs, blue linen, checked linen, coarse garlix or calicoes, checked cottons or scotch plaids." For this list, see Staples, "'Useful, Ornamental or Necessary in This Province,'" 59.
39. Quoted in Morgan, *Slave Counterpoint*, 601. See also Staples, "'Useful, Ornamental or Necessary in This Province,'" 63.

40 *Pennsylvania Gazette*, March 4, 1735.
41 Ibid.
42 On self-emancipated slaves' attempts to manipulate their linguistic skills, trades, and attire, see David Waldstreicher, "Reading the Runaways: Self-Fashioning, Print Culture, and Confidence in Slavery in the Eighteenth-Century Mid-Atlantic," *WMQ*, 3rd ser., 56 (1999): 243–72. On the importance of clothing and its description in "runaway ads," see Jonathan Prude, "To Look Upon the 'Lower Sort': Runaway Ads and the Appearance of Unfree Laborers in America, 1750–1800," *Journal of American History* 78:1 (1991): 143–59.
43 Prude, "To Look Upon the 'Lower Sort,'" 148.
44 *Pennsylvania Gazette*, November 2, 1738; October 26, 1752. Dodd also stole "money, tea, sugar and sundry other things too tedious to mention" (*New York Gazette*, November 20, 1732). "Negro man's" is a curious designation, for why would the notice include to whom the item had originally belonged? It may refer to the jacket's construction of osnabrug or "negro cloth." See Montgomery, *Textiles in America*, 312.
45 Waldstreicher, "Reading the Runaways," 252–53.
46 *Pennsylvania Gazette*, November 2, 1738. On holland, originally named for its place of origin, see Montgomery, *Textiles in America*, 258.
47 *Pennsylvania Gazette*, September 17, 1730; September 12, 1734.
48 Shane White and Graham White, *Stylin': African American Expressive Culture from Its Beginnings to the Zoot Suit* (Ithaca, N.Y., 1998), 10–19. On distinctive African-influenced styles and clothing as an expression of identity among "runaways," see Prude, "To Look Upon the 'Lower Sort'," 156–57.
49 *American Weekly Mercury*, May 24, 1722; *Boston News-Letter*, March 1, 1740; April 21, 1737. On black women's head wear, see Helen Bradley Foster, *New Raiments of Self: African American Clothing in the Antebellum South* (Oxford, 1997), 272–315; and Morgan, *Slave Counterpoint*, 600.
50 Such notices deployed what T. H. Breen calls a "language of goods" in his essay "The Meanings of Things: Interpreting the Consumer Economy in the Eighteenth Century," in John Brewer and Roy Porter, eds., *Consumption and the World of Goods* (New York, 1993), 249–60.
51 See Waldstreicher, "Reading the Runaways."
52 *Pennsylvania Gazette*, April 23, 1730; September 12, 1734; November 2, 1738; November 18, 1738; October 26, 1752.
53 Jacqueline Jones, "Race, Sex, and Self-Evident Truths: The Status of Slave Women during the Era of the American Revolution," in Ronald Hoffman and Peter J. Albert, eds., *Women in the Age of the American Revolution* (Charlottesville, Va., 1989), 321, 327. According to newspaper advertisements, women comprised 10 percent of self-emancipated slaves during the colonial period, but the portion may have been as high as one-third during the American War of Independence.
54 Prude, "To Look Upon the 'Lower Sort,'" 151.
55 Lemire, *Fashion's Favourite*, 3–42. On the trade in calico, see also Audrey W. Douglas, "Cotton Textiles in England: the East India Company's Attempt to Exploit Developments in Fashion," *Journal of British Studies* 8:2 (1969): 28–43; and Erin

Mackie, *Market à la Mode: Fashion, Commodity, and Gender in "The Tatler" and "The Spectator"* (Baltimore, 1997), 45–46.

56 On the origins and history of calico see Lemire, *Fashion's Favourite*, 3–42; Jeremy Adamson, *Calico and Chintz* (Washington, D.C., 1997), 13–39 (Defoe quote on p. 20); and John Irwin and Katherine B. Brett, *Origins of Chintz* (London, 1970), 1–5. Van Varick's inventory appears in Montgomery, *Textiles in America*, 185; and Adamson, *Calico and Chintz*, 14. The terms "calico" and "chintz" were often used interchangeably in the eighteenth century.

57 Lemire, *Fashion's Favourite*, 15.

58 Ibid., 12–28.

59 Ibid., 34–41; Florence M. Montgomery, *Printed Textiles: English and American Cottons and Linens, 1700–1850* (New York, 1970), 17. The law permitted printers to produce cottons for export; however, the merchants who sold the cloth, looking to profit from the popularity of India cottons, did not bother to distinguish domestic fabrics. It remains uncertain whether Mary Alexander ordered and received English or India calico. On the gender and class dimensions of calico and its proscription in England, see Chloe Wigston-Smith, "'Calico Madams': Servants, Consumption, and the Calico Crisis," *Eighteenth-Century Life* 31:2 (2007): 29–55.

60 Lemire, *Fashion's Favourite*, 16; 35–37; Wigston-Smith, "'Calico Madams,'" 29–30, 24; Robert Shoemaker, "The London 'Mob' in the Early Eighteenth Century," *Journal of British Studies* 25 (1987): 292–97.

61 *American Weekly Mercury*, April 11, 1722.

62 For a few examples of advertisements listing calicos, see *Pennsylvania Gazette*, September 23, 1731; December 9, 1736; June 25, 1741; November 1746; December 18, 1750. On Boston and Salem merchants' involvement in the calico trade, see Hunter, *Purchasing Identity in the Atlantic World*, 96–101.

63 *New York Gazette*, November 20, 1732; December 19, 1737; *Pennsylvania Gazette*, November 18, 1736.

64 Breen, *Marketplace of Revolution*, 167–70; Bushman, "Shopping and Advertising in Colonial America," 233–51.

65 *New York Gazette*, May 31, 1736; *Pennsylvania Gazette*, January 6, 1737; December 18, 1740; July 22, 1742. The mercantilist system meant that all foreign goods, no matter their origin, came to the colonies via England. The Navigation Acts, a series of bills passed from the mid- to late seventeenth century, required that certain American products could be sold only in England or to other English colonies, and dictated that all foreign goods were to be conveyed to the colonies by way of England, and subject to English import duties. Smuggling, however, persisted in most port towns, where American merchants could sell items and procure foreign goods on which duties had not been assessed. See Lawrence Harper, *The English Navigation Laws: A Seventeenth-Century Experiment in Social Engineering* (New York, 1939), 50–62, 151–227.

66 *New York Gazette*, May 17, 1736.

67 For the existence of a mixed print/manuscript, written/oral culture in colonial America that fostered commercial, imperial knowledge and sentiments, see

David S. Shields, *Oracles of Empire: Poetry, Politics, and Commerce in British America, 1690–1750* (Chicago, 1990).

68 Buck, *Dress in Eighteenth-Century England*, 35. England was at war with France for much of the century. Linda Colley's *Britons: Forging the Nation, 1707–1837* (New Haven, Conn., 1992) uncovers the construction of a French "other" in the production of a British national identity, whereas Gerald Newman's *The Rise of English Nationalism: A Cultural History, 1740–1830* (New York, 1987) complicates the notion of a unified national identity by contending that an increasingly cosmopolitan English aristocracy identified with their corresponding social equals in France in a class alliance.

69 "Account and ceremony of the Prince and Princesses Marriage," *New York Gazette*, June 21, 1736; *New York Gazette*, March 27, 1739; Linda Baumgarten, *Eighteenth-Century Clothing at Williamsburg* (Williamsburg, Va., 1986), 23.

70 *New York Gazette*, March 27, 1739.

71 Will Downright, "French Fashions Exploded," *American Magazine and Historical Chronicle*, May 1746, 204.

72 Zabin, *Dangerous Economies*, 87–100.

73 *Pennsylvania Gazette*, November 1, 1733.

74 Shields, *Civil Tongues and Polite Letters*, 148.

75 See *The Spectator*, No. 64 in *The Spectator*, 8 vols. (London, 1747), 1:393–98. On monarchical consumer culture in British America, see Brendan McConville, *The King's Three Faces: The Rise and Fall of Royal America, 1688–1776* (Chapel Hill, N.C., 2006), 121–27; and Richard L. Bushman, *King and People in Provincial Massachusetts* (Chapel Hill, N.C., 1985).

76 Roderigo Pacheco, London, to Mary Alexander, New York, January 16, 1737, in Alexander Papers, Box 6, NYHS.

77 John Van der Kiste, *King George II and Queen Caroline* (Gloucester, 1997), 160–65. The king's grief was extreme and her death regarded as a "national calamity."

78 Roderigo Pacheco, London, to Mary Alexander, New York, January 16, 1737, in Alexander Papers, Box 6, NYHS.

79 On October 17, 1726, Roderigo Pacheco placed a notice in the *New York Gazette* that all debts with him should be settled as soon as possible. He made no mention of leaving, but I have extrapolated the information from Jacob Franks's similar notice a few years later (in which he intended to settle accounts before going abroad) and from Pacheco's own letters from London. Historian Cathy Matson lists Pacheco among the most prominent merchants as of 1713 and identifies him as one of the city's top personal and real property holders of 1728. See Matson, *Merchants and Empire: Trading in Colonial New York* (Baltimore, 1998), 135, 373 n. 29.

80 Roderigo Pacheco, London, to Mary Alexander, New York, January 16, 1737, in Alexander Papers, Box 6, NYHS.

81 *Pennsylvania Gazette*, February 21, 1737; *New York Gazette*, February 21, 1737. "Undress" meant attire in which women would be seen at home, or informally, rather than at a social event.

82 Buck, *Dress in Eighteenth-Century England*, 22–23.

83 "Invoice of goods requested by James Alexander of Messrs. Collinsons to come in the fall of 1737," June 7, 1737, in typescript of Alexanders' Orders, Alexander Papers, Box 68, NYHS.
84 *Pennsylvania Gazette*, November 16, 1738.
85 Roderigo Pacheco, London, to James Alexander, New York, June 1, 1738, in Alexander Papers, Box 6, NYHS. On the commercial success of New York's merchant community through transatlantic trade, see Matson, *Merchants and Empire*, 121–69; and on Massachusetts merchants as purveyors of culture as well as men of commerce, see Hunter, *Purchasing Identity in the Atlantic World*.
86 Roderigo Pacheco, London, to James Alexander, New York, February 11, 1737, in Alexander Papers, Box 6, NYHS.
87 David Barclay and Sons, London, to Mary Alexander, New York, October 14, 1757, in Alexander Papers, Box 8, Collection of invoices for merchandise ordered from David Barclay and Sons of London, consigned to Mary Alexander, New York, 1756–58, NYHS.
88 David Barclay and Sons, London, to Mary Alexander, New York, May 31, 1758, in ibid.
89 Philip L. White, ed., *The Beekman Mercantile Papers, 1746–1799*, vol. 2 (New York, 1956), 542–45. James Beekman hailed from a wealthy and prominent family, which helped him establish connections with businesses in London. He expected special consideration and often received it. See Philip L. White, *The Beekmans of New York in Politics and Commerce, 1647–1877* (New York, 1956), 348.
90 "Invoice of goods Desired of Peter and James Collinsons to come in the fall of 1735" and "Invoice of goods requested by James Alexander of Messrs. Collinsons to come in the fall of 1737," June 7, 1737, in typescript of Alexanders' Orders, Alexander Papers, Box 68, NYHS. Lustring was a "light, crisp plain silk with a high luster" and grazette a "silk and worsted dress material"; see Montgomery, *Textiles in America*, 185, 283, 248, 375.
91 Mary Alexander, Fabric order, 1726, Alexander Papers, Box 68, NYHS.
92 Walter B. Edgar, ed., *The Letterbook of Robert Pringle*, vol. 1 (Columbia, S.C., 1972), 31, 224, 317, 568.
93 White, *Beekman Mercantile Papers*, 542–45.
94 Ibid., 630.
95 Edgar, *Letterbook of Robert Pringle*, 56, 55.
96 William Pollard to Jonathan Hammerton, August 28, 1764, William Pollard Letterbook, 14–15, CRBMC; *Pennsylvania Gazette*, October 25, 1764. Pollard had already met with some misfortune in 1764. On April 10, he placed a notice in the *Pennsylvania Gazette* for a lost "Pocket Book," which contained not only a small amount of money but also bills of exchange amounting to £1001 sterling, payable from the accounts of several London merchants. He offered three pounds reward for their safe return and cautioned readers against attempting to cash them. Since his letterbook does not begin until June of 1764, it is difficult to know for what he was paid.
97 "Invoice of goods requested by James Alexander of Messrs. Collinsons to come in the fall of 1737," June 7, 1737, typescript of Alexanders' Orders, Alexander Papers, Box 68, NYHS.

98 Edgar, *Letterbook of Robert Pringle*, 440. Charleston was apparently glutted with goods in 1742, as several of Pringle's letters complain of dry goods in general being a "drugg" and "unsaleable" (ibid., 317, 321, 392, 524). This meant that items had to be especially desirable and of high quality in order to sell.

99 William Pollard to Jonathan Woolmer, December 13, 1764, William Pollard Letterbook, 38, CRBMC.

100 Knight quoted in Shields, *Civil Tongues and Polite Letters*, 118.

101 For the time lag that characterized adoption of new fashions in provincial England in the eighteenth century, see Lemire, *Fashion's Favourite*, 167.

102 William Smith, *History of the Province of New York*, 1:226.

CHAPTER 2

1 Carl Bridenbaugh, ed., *Gentleman's Progress: The Itinerarium of Dr. Alexander Hamilton, 1744* (Chapel Hill, N.C., 1948), 39.

2 Ibid., 74, 29, 89, 146, 110, 134. Dishabille referred to casual dress or "undress," in the eighteenth century but also indicated a disordered state of mind. See *Oxford English Dictionary Online*, s.v. "dishabille."

3 On fashion and gender, see Joanne Entwistle, *The Fashioned Body: Fashion, Dress, and Modern Social Theory* (Cambridge, 2000), 140. On gender as performed through appearances and behavior, see also Judith Butler, *Gender Trouble: Feminism and the Subversion of Identity* (New York, 1990).

4 On the gendering of empire, see Laura Brown, *Ends of Empire: Women and Ideology in Early Eighteenth-Century English Literature* (Ithaca, N.Y., 1993); and Kathleen Wilson, *Island Race: Englishness, Empire, and Gender in the Eighteenth Century* (New York, 2003).

5 Erin Mackie, *Market à la Mode: Fashion, Commodity, and Gender in "The Tatler" and "The Spectator"* (Baltimore, 1997). Colonial newspapers occasionally excerpted the *Spectator*, but I found no "fashion" pieces from it in either the *New York* or *Pennsylvania Gazettes* prior to 1739. However, some colonists may have had access to copies of the periodicals earlier. For example, according to a notice in the *Pennsylvania Gazette* of July 14, 1737, "Charles Read, Esq. now deceased" kept them in his lending library—and his estate wanted them promptly returned. The *Tatler* was first advertised for sale by auction in 1745, and the *Spectator* "imported and sold by B. Franklin" in 1747, shortly after its publication in bound volumes. See *Pennsylvania Gazette*, March 5, 1745; June 18, 1747. A young Benjamin Franklin apparently honed his own writing style through reading and emulating the *Spectator*. See Ned C. Landsman, *From Colonials to Provincials: American Thought and Culture, 1680–1760* (Ithaca, N.Y., 2000), 22. Discussing colonial reading and reception of the *Spectator*, Landsmen convincingly argues that the periodical allowed colonists to "spectate" on and adjudicate metropolitan tastes and manners.

6 Thomas Laqueur, *Making Sex: Body and Gender from the Greeks to Freud* (Cambridge, Mass., 1990), 3–8.

7 Scholars have rightly questioned the utility of "separate spheres" for understanding gender relations in the eighteenth century. See Lawrence E. Klein, "Gender

and the Public/Private Distinction in the Eighteenth Century: Some Questions about Evidence and Analytic Procedure," *Eighteenth-Century Studies* 29 (1995): 97–109. Yet the ideology of distinct male and female roles, although not adhered to in practice or spatially, was more or less in place by the early decades of the eighteenth century.

8   Mackie, *Market à la Mode*, xiii; Shawn Lisa Mauer, *Proposing Men: Dialectics of Gender and Class in the Eighteenth-Century English Periodical* (Stanford, Calif., 1998), 135–36.

9   Michael McKeon, "Historicizing Patriarchy: The Emergence of Gender Difference in England, 1660–1760," *Eighteenth-Century Studies* 28 (1995): 303, 307. McKeon argues that the potential elision of social distinctions resulting from the markers of status being "for sale" necessitated a firmer establishment of gender difference, but I show how expressions of social status itself became gendered.

10 On the feminization of consumption, see Amanda Vickery, "Women and the World of Goods: A Lancashire Consumer and Her Possessions, 1751–1781," in John Brewer and Roy Porter, eds., *Consumption and the World of Goods* (New York, 1993), 274–301. See also Mackie, *Market à la Mode*; and, for quote, Mauer, *Proposing Men*, 136.

11 *New York Gazette*, August 7, 1732. On callimanco, see Florence M. Montgomery, *Textiles in America, 1650–1870* (New York, 1984), 185.

12 *New York Gazette*, April 9, 1739.

13 See Vickery, "Women and the World of Goods."

14 Quoted in Beverly Lemire, *Fashion's Favourite: The Cotton Trade and the Consumer in Britain, 1600–1800* (New York, 1991), 20.

15 As G. J. Barker-Benfield notes in *The Culture of Sensibility: Sex and Society in Eighteenth-Century Britain* (Chicago, 1992), "The evident fact of women's appetite for consumer pleasures had always gone hand in hand with attempts to control it" (205).

16 "The Busy Body, No. 19," *American Weekly Mercury*, June 26, 1729.

17 This is a variation on Laura Brown's theme in *Ends of Empire* that English writers used women's supposed appetites for exotic goods as the rationale for imperial projects. See also Kathleen M. Brown, *Good Wives, Nasty Wenches, and Anxious Patriarchs: Gender, Race, and Power in Colonial Virginia* (Chapel Hill, N.C., 1996), 292–93.

18 For a discussion of public debates over the hoop in England, see Kimberly Chrisman, "'Unhoop the Fair Sex': The Campaign against the Hoop Petticoat in Eighteenth-Century England," *Eighteenth-Century Studies* 30 (1996): 5–23. See also Mackie, *Market à la Mode*, 104–43.

19 Massachusetts passed a sumptuary law in 1651, but it proscribed neither hoops nor wigs and was repealed later in the century. See ⟨http://www.constitution.org/primarysources/sumptuary.html⟩.

20 Butler, *Gender Trouble*.

21 Chrisman, "'Unhoop the Fair Sex,'" 5–10.

22 Ibid. On female fashions commanding the gaze, see also David S. Shields, *Civil Tongues and Polite Letters in British America* (Chapel Hill, N.C., 1997), 108.

23 Chrisman, "'Unhoop the Fair Sex,'" 12–15, 19–20.
24 *The Review*, 68x2.7, Collection 463, Joseph Downs Manuscript Collection, WML.
25 Ibid.
26 Ibid.
27 Ibid.
28 *Origin of the Whale Bone Petticoat, A Satyr* (Boston, 1714), 1.
29 Ibid., 2.
30 Ibid.
31 Ibid., 3–4; quote on 7.
32 On North American climates as distinct from England, and the potential effect of this difference on apparel and on culture generally, see Linda Baumgarten, *What Clothes Reveal: The Language of Clothing in Colonial and Federal America* (Williamsburg, Va., 2002), 54.
33 *Origin of the Whale Bone Petticoat*, 3–4.
34 Ibid., 6–7.
35 On British Francophobia, see Linda Colley, *Britons: Forging the Nation, 1707–1837* (New Haven, Conn., 1992). Three decades after the appearance of the *Satyr*, a piece in a short-lived colonial magazine also pinned the hoop's invention on the "sprightly Gauls." See *American Magazine and Historical Chronicle*, November 1746, 497.
36 *Origin of the Whale Bone Petticoat*, 8.
37 On "wearing the breeches" as a phrase for the practice of women playing men onstage dating from the late seventeenth century, see Elizabeth Reitz Mullinex, *Wearing the Breeches: Gender on the Antebellum Stage* (New York, 2000), 1–19. For the phrase as expressive of gender contest, see also Anna Clark, *The Struggle for the Breeches: Gender and the Making of the British Working Class* (Berkeley, Calif., 1995).
38 Richard Godbeer, "Perversions of Anatomy, Anatomies of Perversion: The Periwig Controversy in Colonial Massachusetts," *Proceedings of the Massachusetts Historical Society* 109 (1997): 2–3. On wigs and shifting notions of identity, see also Lynn Festa, "Personal Effects: Wigs and Possessive Individualism in the Long Eighteenth Century," *Eighteenth-Century Life* 29:2 (2005): 47–90. Festa writes, "Whereas seventeenth-century Puritan polemics rail against the gender-eroding and soul-corrupting potential of outer layers, eighteenth-century writers on wigs are principally concerned with distinctions of rank, nation, gender, and occupation" (ibid., 49). On continued ambivalence about consumption among Massachusetts's elites in the eighteenth century, see Phyllis Whitman Hunter, *Purchasing Identity in the Atlantic World: Massachusetts Merchants, 1670–1780* (Ithaca, N.Y., 2001), 92–96.
39 Godbeer, "Perversions of Anatomy," 1–23.
40 Solomon Stoddard, *An Answer to Cases of Conscience Respecting the Country* (Boston, 1722), 4–7.
41 Ibid., 15. The typeface on the pamphlet's final page is visually arresting. The word "hooped" appears not only in all capital letters but in a size and calligraphic font much larger than the rest of the text. Upon turning the last page it draws the eye, much as hoops did.

42 Jacob Taylor, *A Compleat Ephemeris for the Year of Christ, 1726* (Philadelphia, 1725). Here the term "man" is universal. For a discussion of the relationship among masculine identity, character, and sexual performance, see Thomas A. Foster, "Deficient Husbands: Manhood, Sexual Incapacity and Male Marital Sexuality in Seventeenth-Century New England," *WMQ*, 3rd ser., 56 (1999): 723–44.

43 *Hoop-Petticoats Arraigned and Condemned by the Light of Nature and the Law of GOD* (Boston, 1722), 1–8. The publication lists no author, but Evans Early American Imprints suggests Benjamin Franklin as the probable creator, given the pamphlet's style, tone, and the fact that it was printed by his brother James.

44 Ibid., 7.

45 Baumgarten, *What Clothes Reveal*, 222–30. On the hoops of the 1770s, see Chapter 4.

46 William Hogarth, "The Five Orders of Perriwigs," Winterthur Object File 1959.98.19, WML. Hogarth identifies some of the faces as particular men in public life, and the women's heads at the bottom as Queen Charlotte and her ladies of the bedchamber. See William Hogarth, *Anecdotes of William Hogarth, written by himself* (London, 1833), 256–58. The back view of the "Lexonic" order looks suspiciously like a sheep's hindquarters. In early modern usage "queer" meant strange, odd, peculiar, or eccentric in dress or character; or of questionable character; suspicious. See *Oxford English Dictionary Online*, s.v. "queer." On wigs producing gendered social identity, see Festa, "Personal Effects," 68–71.

47 William DeWitt, Day Book, 1739–52, Manuscript Division, NYHS. On bob wigs, see Ann Buck, *Dress in Eighteenth-Century England* (New York, 1979), 30.

48 Walter B. Edgar, ed., *The Letterbook of Robert Pringle*, vol. 1 (Columbia, S.C., 1972), 76, 834; John Fanning Watson, extra-illustrated autograph manuscript of "Annals of Philadelphia" (Philadelphia, 1823), 51, LCP. On ramelie wigs, see Elisabeth McClellan, *Historic Dress in America, 1607–1870*, vol. 1 (New York, 1977), 299, 391.

49 Bridenbaugh, *Gentleman's Progress*, 134.

50 *Poor Richard's Almanack and Ephemeris for the Year of Our Lord 1746* (Philadelphia, 1745). "How unattractive was the man who was 'out of mode,'" Esther Singleton writes in *Social New York under the Georges, 1714–1776* (New York, 1902), 171.

51 Baumgarten, *What Clothes Reveal*, 226.

52 Pocketbook, 1744, Stenton (Logan family country house), Philadelphia, Pa.

53 John Fanning Watson, extra-illustrated autograph manuscript of "Annals of Philadelphia" (Philadelphia, 1823), 51, 66–67, LCP. See also Linda Baumgarten, *Eighteenth-Century Clothing at Williamsburg* (Williamsburg, Va., 1986), 54. For an analysis of what costume historians refer to as the "great masculine renunciation" in dress in Western culture that dates the trend to the late seventeenth century, see David Kuchta, *The Three-Piece Suit and Modern Masculinity: England, 1550–1850* (Berkeley, Calif., 2002). In the second half and especially the final third of the eighteenth century the silhouette of men's suits gradually grew slimmer, coats shorter, colors more subdued, and wigs less common. The cultural and political uses of these changes are discussed in subsequent chapters.

54 John J. McCusker and Russell R. Menard, *The Economy of British America, 1607–1789* (Chapel Hill, N.C., 1985), 277–81. Imports increased steadily between 1720 and 1750, and exponentially between 1750 and 1770. See also T. H. Breen, *The Market-*

place of Revolution: How Consumer Politics Shaped American Independence (New York, 2004), 33–192; and Cary Carson, "The Consumer Revolution in Colonial America: Why Demand?," in Cary Carson, Ronald Hoffman, and Peter J. Albert, eds., *Of Consuming Interests: The Style of Life in the Eighteenth Century* (Charlottesville, Va., 1994), 483–697.

55 Most fashion tradespeople probably hailed from Ireland or elsewhere, such as the "parcel of likely men and women" that included tailors, wig makers, and stay makers. See *Pennsylvania Gazette*, August 8, 1751.

56 Ibid., December 8, 1748; *New York Mercury*, January 3, 1757; May 19, 1755. For other examples of advertisements by men and women in the fashion trades, see *Pennsylvania Gazette*, March 11, 1735; November 10, 1748; May 24, 1750.

57 Philip L. White, ed., *The Beekman Mercantile Papers, 1746–1799*, vol. 2 (New York, 1956), 96.

58 Edgar, *Letterbook of Robert Pringle*, 63, 188.

59 Ibid.

60 Richard Saunders, *Poor Richard's Almanack and Ephemeris for the Year of Our Lord 1756* (Philadelphia, 1755).

61 Benjamin Franklin, Cash Book, in Benjamin Franklin Account Books, 1714–87, DL.

62 Quoted in Harriott Horry Ravenel, *Eliza Pinckney* (New York, 1896), 58. Lutestring was a "light, crisp plain silk with a high luster" (Montgomery, *Textiles in America*, 283).

63 Elise Pinckney, ed., *The Letterbook of Eliza Lucas Pinckney, 1739–1762* (Columbia, S.C., 1997), 155. Pinckney also reversed the transatlantic flow somewhat when she brought silk she had cultivated in South Carolina to England in 1753 to be woven into fabric and made up into three gowns. She gave one to the queen and one to Lord Chesterfield and kept the third, which was inherited by her daughter. See text accompanying Harriott Horry gown, Collection of the National Society of Colonial Dames of America in the State of South Carolina, Exchange Building, Charleston, S.C.

64 Henry Livingston, London, to Robert Livingston Jr., New York, March 5, 1743, in Livingston Papers, reel 7, Gilder Lehrman Collection, Pierpont Morgan Library, New York. My thanks to Serena Zabin for this reference.

65 William Vincent Byars, ed., *B. and M. Gratz: Merchants in Philadelphia, 1754–1798* (Jefferson City, Mo., 1916), 9, 37–38.

66 Benjamin Franklin, London, to Deborah Franklin, Philadelphia, November 22, 1757; February 19, 1758; June 10, 1758, Papers of Benjamin Franklin Database, APS. Although Britain was engaged in a war for empire with France in 1758, English and colonial consumers happily consumed the French pieces of glass that rivaled more precious gems, as well as other French fashions.

67 William Franklin, London, to Elizabeth Graeme, Philadelphia, October 24, 1758, in Simon Gratz, "Some Material for a Biography of Mrs. Elizabeth Fergusson née Graeme," *PMHB* 39 (1915): 260, 266–67. A tippet was a neck covering made of gauze or fur, and muffs were usually made of fur. Although worn in part for warmth, the items were mostly ornamental. See McClellan, *Historic Dress*, 393.

On "Billy" Franklin, see Sheila L. Skemp, *Benjamin and William Franklin: Father and Son, Patriot and Loyalist* (Boston, 1994). On the failed Franklin-Graeme courtship, see Nicole E. Eustace, *Passion Is the Gale: Emotion, Power, and the Coming of the American Revolution* (Chapel Hill, N.C., 2008), 108, 144–45; and on women's fleeting power in courtship, see 145–46.

68 Quoted in Gratz, "Some Material for a Biography of Mrs. Elizabeth Fergusson," 259.

69 Sarah Sandwith Drinker, Commonplace Book, 1775, HSP. On the sexual connotations of ribbons in particular as tokens of affection and seduction, see Ann Smart Martin, *Buying into the World of Goods: Early Consumers in Backcountry Virginia* (Baltimore, 2008), 168–72.

70 On the importance of "good matches" in English bourgeois society, see Margaret R. Hunt, *The Middling Sort: Commerce, Gender, and the Family in England, 1680–1780* (Berkeley, Calif., 1996), 147–70.

71 "To the Reformer of Manners, The Petition of Several of the Young Tradesmen and Artificers of the City of New York," *New York Gazette*, June 7, 1731.

72 *New York Gazette*, June 21, 1731.

73 Esther Singleton (*Social New York under the Georges*, 171) calls the fop "universal" in eighteenth-century New York. In nineteenth-century England, critiques of the dandy, the fop's successor, expressed anxieties about the status of gentleman being attained through appearance and behavior, rather than inherited. See James Eli Adams, *Dandies and Desert Saints: Styles of Victorian Masculinity* (Ithaca, N.Y., 1995), 53.

74 *Oxford English Dictionary Online*, s.v. "fop."

75 "A Short View of Some of the World's Contents," *New York Gazette*, March 22, 1737.

76 *Poor Richard's Almanack and Ephemeris for the Year of Our Lord 1750* (Philadelphia, 1749).

77 On the charge of "effeminacy" in the eighteenth century, see Barker-Benfield, *Culture of Sensibility*, 141–49.

78 *New York Gazette*, April 9, 1739.

79 "The Lady's Lap Dog," *New York Gazette*, April 3, 1738.

80 Philip Carter, "Men about Town: Representations of Foppery and Masculinity in Early Eighteenth-Century Urban Society," in Hannah Barker and Elaine Chalus, eds., *Gender in Eighteenth-Century England: Roles, Representations, and Responsibilities* (New York, 1997), 40. For the fine line between enlightened gallantry, or masculine politeness, and foppery, see Barbara Taylor, "Feminists and Gallants: Manners and Morals in Enlightenment Britain," in Sarah Knott and Barbara Taylor, eds., *Women, Gender, and Enlightenment* (New York, 2005), 30–52.

81 *A Dictionary of Love* (Philadelphia, 1798), 53–55. The term "fribble" appears far earlier (for example, in a notice for a production of *The Fair Penitent* appearing in the *Pennsylvania Gazette*, April 11, 1754), but the *Dictionary of Love*, although published in 1798, provides a concise definition. Esther Singleton notes the presence of the word in 1749 in *Social New York under the Georges*, 181. For a discussion of unfixed and permeable gender boundaries made manifest in the toilette and adornment practices of the French aristocracy, see Melissa Hyde, "Confound-

ing Conventions: Gender Ambiguity and Francois Boucher's Painted Pastorals," *Eighteenth-Century Studies* 30 (1996): 25–26.
82 John Fanning Watson, extra-illustrated autograph manuscript of "Annals of Philadelphia" (Philadelphia, 1823), 51, LCP.
83 Laqueur, *Making Sex*.
84 *Oxford English Dictionary Online*, s.v. "fop."
85 Bridenbaugh, *Gentleman's Progress*, 186.
86 *New York Gazette*, April 9, 1739.
87 "The Lady's Lap Dog," *New York Gazette*, April 3, 1738.
88 *Hutchin's Improved, Being an Almanack and Ephemeris . . . for the Year of Our Lord 1760* (New York, 1759), March.
89 Other scholars somewhat anachronistically regard fops as eighteenth-century homosexuals—"sodomites," "pretty fellows," or "mollies." For a discussion of this debate, see Clare A. Lyons, "Mapping an Atlantic Sexual Culture: Homoeroticism in Eighteenth-Century Philadelphia," *WMQ*, 3rd ser., 60 (2003): 119–54. On the non-normative sexuality of fops, see Thomas A. Foster, *Sex and the Eighteenth-Century Man* (Boston, 2006), 109–14. See also Mackie, *Market à la Mode*, 189–202, and Mauer, *Proposing Men*, 32. For the argument that "social rather than sexual criteria" defined the fop, one that critiques the contention that fops were "mollies," see Carter, "Men about Town," 31–57, quote on 34. On men as seducers of women, see Barker-Benfield, *Culture of Sensibility*, 331–36; and on the development of a "third gender" in late-seventeenth-century England, see Randolph Trumbach, *Sex and the Gender Revolution* (Chicago, 1998).
90 *Dictionary of Love*, 49.
91 "The Power of Beauty, and the Influence the Fair Sex Might Have in Reforming," *American Magazine and Historical Chronicle*, September 1745, 401.
92 *New York Mercury* January 31, 1757.
93 "To a Lady Who Ask'd, What Is Love?," *American Magazine and Historical Chronicle*, February 1744, 257; *Pennsylvania Gazette*, February 28, 1749; "A Caution to a Young Gentleman," *American Magazine and Historical Chronicle*, November 1743, 112.
94 Bridenbaugh, *Gentleman's Progress*, 129.

CHAPTER 3

1 Robert R. Livingston, "A Letter on the Ladies Wearing Homespun at the Time of the Stamp Act," n.d., Livingston Papers, NYHS. On homespun and its meanings, see Laurel Thatcher Ulrich, *The Age of Homespun: Objects and Stories in the Creation of an American Myth* (New York, 2001), in particular chapter 4 on midcentury pastoral motifs and chapter 5 on the homespun campaigns of the 1760s.
2 The most important recent study documenting the increasing volume of goods and access to them in the 1750s is T. H. Breen, *The Marketplace of Revolution: How Consumer Politics Shaped American Independence* (New York, 2004), chaps. 2–7 comprising "Part One: An Empire of Goods." This chapter builds on Breen's valuable connection of the discourses and practices of the 1750s to the movements of the 1760s. Yet it differs in its emphasis on the ways in which nonconsumption utilized

and magnified social and gendered hierarchy through combining long-standing ideas about emulation with a newer set of gender ideals.

3. On sensibility, see G. J. Barker-Benfield, *The Culture of Sensibility: Sex and Society in Eighteenth-Century Britain* (Chicago, 1992); and for its operation in a revolutionary context, see Sarah Knott, *Sensibility and the American Revolution* (Chapel Hill, N.C., 2009). On the characterological tenets of the Scottish Enlightenment, see Rosemarie Zagarri, "Morals, Manners, and the Republican Mother," *American Quarterly* 44 (June 1992): 194–203. On the ways in which literary sentimentalism created a feminine version of virtue, see Ruth H. Bloch, "The Gendered Meanings of Virtue in Revolutionary America," *Signs* 13 (1987): 51–53.

4. Catherine A. Haulman, "The Empire's New Clothes: The Politics of Fashion in Eighteenth-Century America" (Ph.D. diss., Cornell University, 2002), chap. 3.

5. Ibid. On the ways in which consumption connected colonists within an empire of goods, making nonimportation and nonconsumption feasible and unifying political strategies in the making of a popular movement, see Breen, *Marketplace of Revolution*, especially chaps. 6 and 7. For the argument that nonimportation was viable due to class conflicts and contests over the meanings of goods, see Barbara Clark Smith, "Social Visions of the American Resistance Movement," in Ronald Hoffman and Peter J. Albert, eds., *The Transforming Hand of Revolution: Reconsidering the American Revolution as a Social Movement* (Charlottesville, Va., 1996), 27–58.

6. From introductory notes by George Vaux to Diary of Hannah Callender, 1758–88, APS. See also the excellent introduction to Susan E. Klepp and Karin Wulf, eds., *The Diary of Hannah Callender Sansom: Sense and Sensibility in the Age of the American Revolution* (Ithaca, N.Y., 2010). The editors see a shift from sociability to sensibility over the course of the diary, and note the tensions between the world of sensibility in which women's presence and opinions mattered and their traditional roles and duties. Callender was smart, opinionated, and even outspoken, yet she "labored to conform" (Klepp and Wulf, *Diary of Hannah Callender Sansom*, 2–3, 13).

7. Hannah Callender was a voracious reader and her favorite novel was Samuel Richardson's *Clarissa*. See Klepp and Wulf, *Diary of Hannah Callender Sansom*, 162. On the prescriptions of sentimental fiction, see Bloch, "Gendered Meanings of Virtue," 51–53. On sentimental fiction as a device for consolidating readers along lines of class, race, and nation in an imperial context, see Lynn Festa, *Sentimental Figures of Empire in Eighteenth-Century Britain and France* (Baltimore, 2006); and on sentimental reading in the colonies, see Knott, *Sensibility and the American Revolution*, 27–68.

8. Eve Tavor Bannet, "The Marriage Act of 1753: 'A Most Cruel Law for the Fair Sex,'" *Eighteenth-Century Studies* 30 (1997): 233–54. See also Lawrence Stone, *Uncertain Unions and Broken Lives: Marriage and Divorce in England, 1660–1857* (New York, 1995), 33. Stone claims that barristers grew tired of suits over clandestine "marriages" that were actually seductions and impregnations, but Bannet argues that the real impetus behind the act was the regulation of women's sexual practices and increasing the "legitimate" and productive population of the nation. The penalty

under the act for clergy who performed marriages without the proper documentation was fourteen years transportation to America.

9 For descriptions of the status of a *feme covert*, or "covered woman," and the unity of personhood within marriage that coverture fixed, see Cornelia Hughes Dayton, *Women before the Bar: Gender, Law, and Society in Connecticut, 1639–1789* (Chapel Hill, N.C., 1995), 19–20; Mary Beth Norton, *Liberty's Daughters: The Revolutionary Experience of American Women, 1750–1800* (Boston, 1980), 45–50; and Linda K. Kerber, *Women of the Republic: Intellect and Ideology in Revolutionary America* (Chapel Hill, N.C., 1980), 119–20.

10 Bannet, "Marriage Act of 1753," 233.

11 See Karin A. Wulf, *Not All Wives: Women of Colonial Philadelphia* (Ithaca, N.Y., 2000), 2, 93. Wulf finds that between 1750 and 1770 urban men were more likely than rural men to will their estates to wives. Consequently, the number of independent, female-headed households in Philadelphia grew. For the claim that men were "afraid to enter upon matrimony . . . lest Bankruptcy should be the consequence from the present extravagance of the fair sex," see *New York Gazette*, January 28, 1765.

12 Martha C. Slotten, "Elizabeth Graeme Ferguson: A Poet in 'The Athens of North America,'" *PMHB* 108 (1984): 259–65. On Graeme's hesitancy to wed, see Nicole E. Eustace, *Passion Is the Gale: Emotion, Power, and the Coming of the American Revolution* (Chapel Hill, N.C., 2008), 121.

13 Diary of Hannah Callender, September 24, 1758, APS. This was not Elizabeth Brooke who married Charles Carroll of Annapolis in 1757 after a long-standing courtship but probably a member of the same Brooke family. See Ronald Hoffman, in collaboration with Sally D. Mason, *Princes of Ireland, Planters of Maryland: A Carroll Saga, 1500–1782* (Chapel Hill, N.C., 2000), 131–39. Cambletee was a stuff of mixed wool and goat's hair, thread, or cotton, slighter, thinner, and coarser than camblet. See Florence M. Montgomery, *Textiles in America, 1650–1870* (New York, 2007), 189.

14 Diary of Hannah Callender, October 19, 1758, APS.

15 Ann MacVicar Grant, *Memoirs of an American Lady with Sketches of Manners and Scenery in America as They Existed Prior to the Revolution* (New York, 1809), 198. Grant also waxed nostalgic for the "early" colonial settlements, where dress was "very plain and not subject to the caprice of fashion . . . yet no person appeared uncouth or ill bred" (ibid., 18–19). On the collapse of rural virtue into genteel domesticity in the nineteenth century, see Catherine E. Kelly, *In the New England Fashion: Reshaping Women's Lives in the Nineteenth Century* (Ithaca, N.Y., 1999), 3.

16 *Poor Richard's Almanack and Ephemeris for the Year of Our Lord 1747* (Philadelphia, 1746).

17 This claim is based upon a systematic survey of Pennsylvania almanacs between the years 1720 and 1780. See also Cornelia Hughes Dayton, "Satire and Sensationalism: The Emergence of Misogyny in Mid-Eighteenth Century New England Newspapers and Almanacs," unpublished paper presented at the New England Seminar at the American Antiquarian Society, November 15, 1991.

18 Margaret R. Hunt, *The Middling Sort: Commerce, Gender, and the Family in England, 1680–1780* (Berkeley, Calif., 1996), 2–3.
19 *Poor Richard's Almanack and Ephemeris for the Year of Our Lord 1749* (Philadelphia, 1748).
20 Diary of Hannah Callender, October 18, 1758, APS.
21 See Samuel Richardson, *Clarissa; or, The History of a Young Lady* (London, 1748). For the importance of female chastity in the eighteenth century, see Hunt, *Middling Sort*, 98, 202. Hunt notes that, by the 1740s in England, "moral high-mindedness" had itself come into fashion. On the role of dress in *Pamela; or, Virtue Rewarded*, see Anne Buck, *Dress in Eighteenth-Century England* (New York, 1979), 118.
22 Diary of Hannah Callendar, October 19, 1758, APS.
23 Hunt, *Middling Sort*, 162.
24 Diary of Hannah Callender, July 26, 1758, APS.
25 Ned C. Landsman, *From Colonials to Provincials: American Thought and Culture, 1680–1760* (Ithaca, N.Y., 2000), 126. See also Zagarri, "Morals, Manners, and the Republican Mother."
26 Letter to "Mrs. H," n.d., in Elise Pinckney, ed., *The Letterbook of Eliza Lucas Pinckney, 1739–1762* (Columbia, S.C., 1997), 48.
27 "Extract from the Universal Spectator," *Pennsylvania Gazette*, August 29, 1751.
28 *Poor Richard's Almanack and Ephemeris for the Year of Our Lord 1761* (Philadelphia, 1760).
29 Carol F. Karlsen and Laurie Crumpacker, eds., *The Journal of Esther Edwards Burr, 1754–1757* (New Haven, Conn., 1986), 38, 257. Edwards and close friend Sarah Prince engaged in an ongoing correspondence in which they "devoted a great deal of intellectual energy to evaluating what was written about courtship and marriage" (ibid., 39).
30 "Extract from the Universal Spectator," *Pennsylvania Gazette*, August 29, 1751.
31 Quoted in David S. Shields, *Civil Tongues and Polite Letters in British America* (Chapel Hill, N.C., 1997), 150–51.
32 "Advice to the Ladies" and "On Female Education by a Woman of Quality," *Poor Richard's Almanack* (1760).
33 Diary of Hannah Callender, April 5, 1758, APS.
34 Hannah Callender's own marriage to Samuel Sansom in 1762 was a good match by contemporary standards, uniting two affluent Quaker families and generating a stable household economy, but it was not a "love match." She followed the guidance of her father to marry Sansom, perhaps to her detriment. See Klepp and Wulf, *Diary of Hannah Callender Sansom*, 163–67.
35 Harriot Pinckney to Dorothy (Dolly) Golightly, July 20, 1763, Harriot Horry Letterbooks, 1763–67, SCHS.
36 *Pennsylvania Gazette*, April 11, 1765.
37 Deborah Morris Account Book, 1763–1777, HSP.
38 Hunt, *Middling Sort*, 12.
39 On the importance of "traditional" women's work in urban, commercial economies, see Ellen Hartigan-O'Connor, *The Ties that Buy: Women and Commerce in Revolutionary America* (Philadelphia, 2009).

40 "A Young Lady's Advice to One Lately Married," *Poor Richard's Almanack and Ephemeris for the Year of Our Lord 1760* (Philadelphia, 1759). For more on the "small circle of domestic concerns," see Norton, *Liberty's Daughters*, chap. 1.

41 Andrew Burnaby, *Travels Through the Middle Settlements in North America in the Years 1759 and 1760* (London, 1775), 36–37.

42 On the embrace of commerce, see Breen, *Marketplace of Revolution*, 72–101, and on advertising, 53–59.

43 *Poor Richard's Almanack and Ephemeris for the Year of Our Lord 1748* (Philadelphia, 1747).

44 *Industry and Frugality Proposed as the Surest Means to Make Us a Rich and Flourishing People and the Linen Manufacture Recommended as Tending to Promote These among Us* . . . (Boston, 1753). On poor women spinning and wealthy women embroidering pastoral scenes as trends that located women's work in the household, regardless of class position, see Laurel Thatcher Ulrich, "Sheep in the Parlor, Wheels on the Common: Pastoralism and Poverty in Eighteenth-Century Boston," in Carla Gardina Pestana and Sharon V. Salinger, eds., *Inequality in Early America* (Hanover, N.H., 1999), 182–200; quote on 193.

45 See Gary B. Nash, "The Failure of Female Factor Labor in Colonial Boston," *Labor History* 20 (1979): 179. The manufactory ultimately failed because its linen was consistently undersold by imported cloth.

46 *Industry and Frugality Proposed*, 7, 11.

47 *Hutchins's Almanack, or Ephemeris for the Year of Christian Account, 1758* (New York, 1757).

48 *Poor Richard's Almanack and Ephemeris for the Year of Our Lord 1756* (Philadelphia, 1755).

49 *Poor Richard's Almanack and Ephemeris for the Year of Our Lord 1758* (Philadelphia, 1757).

50 On the class dimensions of sensibility, see Knott, *Sensibility and the American Revolution*, 17–18.

51 *Industry and Frugality Proposed*, 7. As T. H. Breen aptly puts it, "Colonial women had the great misfortunate to become ensnared in one of the major controversies of the eighteenth century, the so-called luxury debate" (Breen, *Marketplace of Revolution*, 172–82; quote on 173).

52 *Industry and Frugality Proposed*, 13. As Catherine E. Kelly argues for the early nineteenth century, women's virtue was not abstract but "took shape in the particular standards and practices of the household economy" (Kelly, *In the New England Fashion*, 128).

53 *Boston Gazette*, April 3, 1750.

54 Landsman, *From Colonials to Provincials*, 166–71.

55 For example, the pastoralism that characterized middling and elite colonial women's embroidery connected them and their families to the English gentry yet signified "private property, companionate marriage, and female industry—the pursuit of happiness, American style," according to Ulrich, "Sheep in the Parlor," 193, 196. The colonies' association with nature added to this dual resonance. On the rise of the country look and its modification for town wear, see Buck, *Dress in Eighteenth-Century England*, 52–56.

56 On self-fashioning and the importance of attire in portraiture, see T. H. Breen, "The Meaning of 'Likeness': Portrait Painting in an Eighteenth-Century Consumer Society," in Ellen G. Miles, ed., *The Portrait in Eighteenth-Century America* (Newark, Del., 1993), 37–60.

57 For the relative "newness" of colonial elites and their differences from English gentry, see Stephanie Grauman Wolf, "Rarer than Riches: Gentility in Eighteenth-Century America," in Miles, *Portrait in Eighteenth-Century America*, 92–93. On the self-fashioning of Massachusetts merchants and their families as a "polite and commercial people," see Phyllis Whitman Hunter, *Purchasing Identity in the Atlantic World: Massachusetts Merchants, 1670–1780* (Ithaca, N.Y., 2001).

58 Robert Feke, *Isaac Winslow*, 1748, MFA.

59 Joseph Blackburn, *Isaac Winslow and His Family*, 1755, MFA. See also Richard Saunders and Ellen G. Miles, *American Colonial Portraits, 1700–1776* (Washington, D.C., 1987), 194–95.

60 Joseph Blackburn, *Isaac Winslow and His Family*, 1755, MFA.

61 On the association of women with the natural world, and this as a site of elite women's power in eighteenth-century British America, see Susan Scott Parrish, "Women's Nature: Curiosity, Pastoral and the New Science in British America," *Early American Literature* 37:2 (2004): 195–238.

62 Joseph Blackburn, *Mary Sylvester*, 1754, MMA; John Singleton Copley, *Ann Tyng*, 1756, MFA.

63 Benjamin West, *Jane Galloway*, 1757, HSP. See Saunders and Miles, *American Colonial Portraits*, 196–97, 212.

64 Elizabeth Galloway Commonplace Book, n.d. (1757?), HSP.

65 Quoted in Saunders and Miles, *American Colonial Portraits*, 196.

66 John Singleton Copley, *Rebecca Boylston*, 1767, MFA.

67 John Singleton Copley, *Nicholas Boylston*, 1767, MFA.

68 Margaretta M. Lovell, *Art in a Season of Revolution: Painters, Artisans, and Patrons in Early America* (Philadelphia, 2005), 99–104.

69 John Swick to John Tabor Kempe, June 8, 1764, Kempe Papers, Box 1, NYHS. Many thanks to Serena Zabin for this reference. On frock coats as more informal than earlier styles but increasingly acceptable as formal wear after midcentury, see Buck, *Dress in Eighteenth-Century England*, 32–33.

70 Grant, *Memoirs of an American Lady*, 199–200; John Fanning Watson, extra-illustrated autograph manuscript of "Annals of Philadelphia" (Philadelphia, 1823), 51, LCP. On the new fashion for natural hair among men in the 1760s, see Buck, *Dress in Eighteenth-Century England*, 30; and Lynn Festa, "Personal Effects: Wigs and Possessive Individualism in the Long Eighteenth Century," *Eighteenth-Century Life* 29:2 (2005): 74–75. By the late eighteenth century, the wig had evolved from a sign of masculine autonomy to one of dependence.

71 *Boston Evening Post*, February 18, 1760.

72 Burnaby, *Travels Through the Middle Settlements*, 37. On male fishing companies, see Shields, *Civil Tongues and Polite Letters*, 189–98. On women fishing, see Susan A. Popkin and Roger B. Allen, eds., *Gone Fishing! A History of Fishing in River, Bay, and Sea. An Almanac for the Leisure Time Pleasure of All Who Succumb to the Lure*

of Fishing Accompanied by Illustrations of Objects from the Exhibit (Philadelphia, 1987), 5–7. For more on the embrace of the pastoral by the colonial beau monde, see Shields, *Civil Tongues and Polite Letters*, 126–31.

73 The recollection of gown cutting is recorded in John Fanning Watson, extra-illustrated autograph manuscript of "Annals of Philadelphia" (Philadelphia, 1823), 51, LCP. The episodes recalled the calicos riots of Spitalfields in 1720, in which angry men ripped women's dresses from their bodies, making the women's attire unwearable. See Robert Shoemaker, "The London 'Mob' in the Early Eighteenth Century," *Journal of British Studies* 25 (1987): 292–97. On the contracting postwar economies of the northern port cities, see Gary B. Nash, *The Urban Crucible: Social Change, Political Consciousness, and the Origins of the American Revolution* (Cambridge, Mass., 1979).

74 Grant, *Memoirs of an American Lady*, 291–92, 296.

75 "Extract of a Letter from London, dated March 24," *Pennsylvania Gazette*, June 7, 1764.

76 The Sugar Act, April 5, 1764, in Edmund S. Morgan, ed., *Prologue to Revolution: Sources and Documents on the Stamp Act Crisis, 1764–1766* (Chapel Hill, N.C., 1959), 5. See also Edmund S. Morgan and Helen M. Morgan, *The Stamp Act Crisis: Prologue to Revolution* (New York, 1962), 36–58.

77 Arthur M. Schlesinger, *The Colonial Merchants and the American Revolution* (New York, 1917; reprint, 1968), 53.

78 Landsman, *From Colonials to Provincials*, 165; Breen, *Marketplace of Revolution*, 206.

79 *Pennsylvania Gazette*, August 30, 1764; *New York Gazette*, August 30, 1764. A year earlier, Boston merchants organized the Society for Encouraging Trade and Commerce within the Province of Massachusetts Bay. See Schlesinger, *Colonial Merchants*, 59. On Boston's merchant community, see also John W. Tyler, *Smugglers and Patriots: Boston Merchants and the Advent of the American Revolution* (Boston, 1986).

80 *Pennsylvania Gazette*, August 30, 1764; *Boston Gazette*, September 24, 1764. On the 1764 curtailment of mourning dress, see Ann Fairfax Withington, *Toward a More Perfect Union: Virtue and the Formation of American Republics* (New York, 1991), 96–97.

81 "Petition of the New York Assembly," in Morgan, *Prologue to Revolution*, 12.

82 Quoted in Schlesinger, *Colonial Merchants*, 60. For reactions to mercantile fortunes and their trappings in England, see James Raven, *Judging New Wealth: Popular Publishing and Responses to Commerce in England, 1750–1800* (New York, 1992). For general distrust of merchants and their ensuing attempts to perform candor, see Toby L. Ditz, "Secret Selves, Credible Personas: The Problematics of Trust and Public Display in the Writing of Eighteenth-Century Philadelphia Merchants," in Robert Blair St. George, ed., *Possible Pasts: Becoming Colonial in Early America* (Ithaca, N.Y., 2000), 221–42.

83 John Watts to Moses Franks, June 9, 1764, *Letterbook of John Watts, Merchant and Councillor of New York, January 1, 1762–December 22, 1765. Collections of the New York Historical Society for the Year 1928* (New York, 1928), 261–62.

84. *New York Gazette*, August 30, 1764. According to Gary Nash, the Philadelphia linen manufactory "had no greater success than in New York or Boston, although it employed about 200 poor women for several winters" (Nash, *Urban Crucible*, 255).
85. *New York Gazette*, November 12, 1764; *Boston News-Letter*, November 30, 1764; *New York Gazette*, October 15, 1764. On homespun as a political ideology and means of revolutionary resistance, see Michael Zakim, *Ready-Made Democracy: A History of Men's Dress in the American Republic, 1760–1860* (Chicago, 2003), 1–22. Zakim regards homespun's badge of civic membership as a "consciously leveling moment" (21).
86. William Lux to Samuel Bowne, July 29, 1765, in William Lux Letterbook, 1765–66, NYHS.
87. Pomeroy and Hodgkin, London, to John Keteltas, New York, February 7, 1764, in Business Papers of John Keteltas, Folder 4, NYHS.
88. As Woody Holton notes in his discussion of nonconsumption and the Virginia gentry, fashion was the primary concern in selecting goods. See Holton, *Forced Founders: Slaves, Debtors, and the Making of the American Revolution in Virginia* (Chapel Hill, N.C., 1999), 77.
89. Samuel Deall Account Book, volume A, nos. 13–15, NYBGS.
90. *Pennsylvania Gazette*, May 24, 1764; September 22, 1768.
91. On the Stamp Act and responses, see Breen, *Marketplace of Revolution*, 218–34.
92. *New York Mercury*, February 11, 1765; *Pennsylvania Gazette*, March 28, 1765. Bengal could refer to any India fabric, and broglio was a "silk and wool textile woven in small geometric patterns." See Montgomery, *Textiles in America*, 163, 181. The definition of lillepusia is unknown—there is no entry in the *Oxford English Dictionary*. But the term might refer to some sort of India cloth (perhaps small-figured print) due to its reference to the fictional island nation of Lilliput from Jonathan Swift's *Gulliver's Travels*.
93. Sophia Thrifty, "To the Society for the Promotion of Arts, Agriculture, and Oeconomy from a Lady," *New York Gazette*, December 24, 1764.
94. *New York Gazette*, November 12, 1764.
95. *New York Post Boy*, May 29, 1765.
96. *Pennsylvania Gazette*, May 23, 1765.
97. Andrew Elliot to brother, November 10, 1766, Andrew Elliot Letters, 1747–77, Folder 39, NYHS.
98. *Pennsylvania Gazette*, September 26, 1765; October 3, 1765.
99. Ibid., November 7, 1765.
100. Thomas M. Doerflinger, *A Vigorous Spirit of Enterprise: Merchants and Economic Development in Revolutionary Philadelphia* (Chapel Hill, N.C., 1986), 175, 180. Doerflinger argues that although Philadelphia's merchants weathered periodic economic downturns, financial woes did not propel them toward revolution.
101. For the class positions of Philadelphia merchants who signed the first nonimportation agreement, see Robert F. Oaks, "Philadelphia Merchants and the Origins of American Independence," *Proceedings of the American Philosophical Society* 121 (1977): 409–11.
102. Raven, *Judging New Wealth*, 82. Raven writes, "Three interlocking and negative reactions—against luxury and fashion, against vulgarity and against sudden elevation

103   Leonard W. Labaree, ed., *The Papers of Benjamin Franklin*, vol. 13, *January 1 through December 31, 1766* (New Haven, Conn., 1969), 135.
104   Ibid., 140.
105   Ibid., 143.
106   Ibid., 159.
107   Evert Bancker, New York, to unknown, January 7, 1766, in New Netherlands, Oldest New York and the Colonial Government Historical Letters and Manuscripts, NYHS; William Pollard, Philadelphia, to Jonathan Woolmer, Halifax, April 25, 1766, William Pollard Letterbook, 205, CRBMC; Benjamin Franklin, "Homespun: Second Reply Vindex Patriae," January 2, 1766, Papers of Benjamin Franklin Database, APS.
108   "Journal of Lord Adam Gordon," in Newton D. Mereness, ed., *Travels in the American Colonies* (New York, 1916), 412.
109   William Lux, Baltimore, to William Molleson, January 13, 1766, William Lux Letterbook, 1765–68, NYHS.
110   Kerber, *Women of the Republic*, 73–113; Norton, *Liberty's Daughters*, 155–94.
111   *Pennsylvania Gazette*, April 3, 1766.
112   Sophia Thrifty, "To the Society for the Promotion of Arts, Agriculture, and Oeconomy from a Lady," *New York Gazette*, December 24, 1764.
113   Robert R. Livingston, "A Letter on the Ladies Wearing of Homespun at the Time of the Stamp Act," n.d., Livingston Papers, NYHS.
114   John Jay to Robert R. Livingston Jr., March 4, 1766, Livingston Papers, reel 1, NYHS.
115   *New York Gazette*, January 28, 1765.
116   Robert R. Livingston, "A Letter on the Ladies Wearing Homespun at the Time of the Stamp Act," n.d., Livingston Papers, NYHS.
117   Lux to Molleson, April 7, 1766, in William Lux Letterbook, 1765–66, NYHS.
118   *Pennsylvania Gazette*, May 22, 1766.
119   Samuel Deall Account Book, volume A, nos. 104–5, NYBGS.

CHAPTER 4

1   Eva Eve Jones, ed., "Extracts from the Journal of Miss Sarah Eve," *PMHB* 5 (1881): 19–36 and 191–205.
2   Reminiscent of Elizabeth Graeme's satirical verse on Scarborough composed in 1764, in which the town women of fashion shop endlessly but make no purchases, their activity productive of nothing. See David S. Shields, *Civil Tongues and Polite Letters in British America* (Chapel Hill, N.C., 1996), 122–24.
3   Jones, "Journal of Miss Sarah Eve," 202.
4   Whereas the schemes of confidence men and the sartorial practices of "lower sorts" had complicated the association among appearance, character, and social position, elite Philadelphians such as Eve sought to reclaim and redefine the connection by making an excess of fineness the mark of one who was distinctly

inferior. See previous chapters and Steven C. Bullock, "A Mumper among the Gentle: Tom Bell, Colonial Confidence Man," *WMQ*, 3rd ser., 55 (1998): 231–58; and David Waldstreicher, "Reading the Runaways: Self-Fashioning, Print Culture, and Confidence in Slavery in the Eighteenth-Century Mid-Atlantic," *WMQ*, 3rd ser., 56 (1999): 243–72.

5 Historians have demonstrated the importance of consumer behavior—women's in particular—to the boycotts of the 1760s and 1770s but have not considered the ways in which the cultural politics of fashion shaped the imperial crisis. See Linda K. Kerber, *Women of the Republic: Intellect and Ideology in Revolutionary America* (Chapel Hill, N.C., 1980), 37–45; Mary Beth Norton, *Liberty's Daughters: The Revolutionary Experience of American Women, 1750–1800* (Boston, 1980), 157–63; T. H. Breen, *The Marketplace of Revolution: How Consumer Politics Shaped American Independence* (New York, 2004), 230–34, 279–89; and Barbara Clark Smith, "Social Visions of the American Resistance Movement," in Ronald Hoffman and Peter J. Albert, eds., *The Transforming Hand of Revolution: Reconsidering the American Revolution as a Social Movement* (Charlottesville, Va., 1999), 52–55.

6 On the social and economic climate of Philadelphia in the 1760s and 1770s, see Gary B. Nash, *The Urban Crucible: Social Change, Political Consciousness, and the Origins of the American Revolution* (Cambridge, Mass., 1979), 264–384; and Benjamin L. Carp, *Rebels Rising: Cities and the American Revolution* (New York, 2007), 172–212. On Philadelphia as a cosmopolitan cultural center, see Gary B. Nash, *First City: Philadelphia and the Forging of Historical Memory* (Philadelphia, 2002), 63–78.

7 See Barbara Clark Smith, "Social Visions of the American Resistance Movement," 49.

8 Robert J. Chaffin, "The Townshend Acts of 1767," *WMQ*, 3rd ser., 27 (1970): 94–97.

9 Thomas M. Doerflinger, *A Vigorous Spirit of Enterprise: Merchants and Economic Development in Revolutionary Philadelphia* (Chapel Hill, N.C., 1986), 168–90; Robert F. Oaks, "Philadelphia Merchants and the Origins of American Independence," *Proceedings of the American Philosophical Society* 121 (1977): 414–17. Doerflinger and Oaks differ in their assessment of merchants' centrality in the break from England, Doerflinger calling them "reluctant revolutionaries," Oaks arguing that they dictated the direction of politics. Doerflinger convincingly demonstrates that most Philadelphia merchants were not experiencing unprecedented or dramatic economic difficulties during the period in question.

10 Edward Countryman, *The American Revolution* (New York, 1985), 66.

11 John Dickinson, "Letter from a Farmer in Pennsylvania to the Inhabitants of the British Colonies," in Samuel Eliot Morrison, ed., *Sources and Documents Illustrating the American Revolution, 1764–1788, and the Formation of the Federal Constitution* (New York, 1979), 34. On Quaker wealth and its trappings, see Frederick Barnes Tolles, *Meeting House and Counting House: The Quaker Merchants of Colonial Philadelphia, 1682–1763* (Chapel Hill, N.C., 1948), 109, 126–42.

12 Arthur Schlesinger, *The Colonial Merchants and the American Revolution* (New York, 1917; reprint, 1968), 117–18.

13 *Pennsylvania Gazette*, March 31, 1768. For the public rituals of American national identity and their roots in English popular culture, see David Waldstreicher, *In the*

Midst of Perpetual Fetes: The Making of American Nationalism, 1776–1820 (Chapel Hill, N.C., 1996), 17–52.

14 *Pennsylvania Gazette*, May 12, 1768.

15 "The Bullfinch and Sparrow, A Fable by the King of Prussia," *Hutchins Improved . . . for the Year 1768* (New York, 1767). On the trope of enslavement in revolutionary rhetoric, see Bernard Bailyn, *The Ideological Origins of the American Revolution* (Cambridge, Mass., 1969), 232–46; and Francois Furstenberg, *In the Name of the Father: Washington's Legacy, Slavery, and the Making of a Nation* (New York, 2006), 193–99. On the transition from language about specific English "liberties" that were particular to individual identity to a more general concept of "liberty" in which all might (theoretically) share, see Edward Countryman, "'To Secure the Blessings of Liberty': Language, the Revolution and American Capitalism," in Alfred F. Young, ed., *Beyond the American Revolution: Explorations in the History of American Radicalism* (DeKalb, Ill., 1993), 123–48. A piece in the *South Carolina Gazette* claimed that women would eventually obey their husbands on the issue of nonconsumption or risk being regarded as "slaves to dress." See Carp, *Rebels Rising*, 157.

16 "The Bullfinch and Sparrow."

17 *Pennsylvania Gazette*, November 12, 1767; December 31, 1767.

18 For a discussion of spinning groups as "ideological showcases" with more symbolic than actual value, see Norton, *Liberty's Daughters*, 168. For the performative nature of these events, see Laurel Thatcher Ulrich, "'Daughters of Liberty': Religious Women in Revolutionary New England," in Ronald Hoffman and Peter J. Albert, eds., *Women in the Age of the American Revolution* (Charlottesvillle, Va., 1989), 218.

19 *New York Gazette*, February 29, 1768; *Pennsylvania Gazette*, January 14, 1768; March 23, 1769.

20 *Pennsylvania Gazette*, November 12, 1767; December 10, 1767.

21 Ibid., December 24, 1767.

22 Ibid., May 25, 1769.

23 Ibid., January 14, 1768. On the rhetoric of emotion during the revolutionary crisis and for the claim that colonists regarded "emotional capabilities as the linchpin of liberty," see Nicole E. Eustace, *Passion Is the Gale: Emotion, Power, and the Coming of the American Revolution* (Chapel Hill, N.C., 2008), 385. For responses to the Townshend Acts, see Eustace, *Passion Is the Gale*, 418–27.

24 *Pennsylvania Gazette*, May 12, 1768.

25 Ibid., December 22, 1768. This tale presented yet another inversion. Anglicans had taken the lead in educating and "christianizing" enslaved and free blacks in Philadelphia, but in this account, it is the slave who provides the example and instruction to would-be proselytizers gone "worldly." See Gary B. Nash, *Forging Freedom: The Formation of Philadelphia's Black Community, 1720–1840* (Cambridge, Mass., 1988), 17, 23.

26 *Pennsylvania Gazette*, June 2, 1768.

27 For this argument, see Breen, *Marketplace of Revolution*, 269–79.

28 Douglas Adair and John A. Schutz, eds., *Peter Oliver's Origin and Progress of the American Rebellion: A Tory View* (San Mateo, Calif., 1961), 61.

29 Schlesinger, *Colonial Merchants*, 126–27; Doerflinger, *Vigorous Spirit of Enterprise*, 189.
30 Schlesinger, *Colonial Merchants*, 128.
31 Oaks, "Philadelphia Merchants," 416–17.
32 John Reynell to his brother, February 2, 1769, Reynell Letterbook, HSP.
33 Doerflinger, *Vigorous Spirit of Enterprise*, 191.
34 Editors of the *PMHB*, "Effects of the 'Non-Importation Agreement' in Philadelphia," *PMHB* 14 (1890): 41. The "poll" was hotly contested. T. H. Breen writes, "Leaders of a more radical persuasion in New York found themselves confronted with a quandary that has haunted democratic theorists since ancient Greece. How does a minority respond when it is certain that a majority has made a mistake?" (Breen, *Marketplace of Revolution*, 276).
35 Carp, *Rebels Rising*, 157. In South Carolina, white women did not take up spinning, but newspapers did feature the "blame game" between men and women over the issue of consumption. See ibid., 158–59.
36 John C. Fitzpatrick, *The Diaries of George Washington, 1748–1799* (Boston, 1925), 273. Fitzpatrick notes that "these letters and invoices were to Washington's factors in London, Robert Cary and Co., and to certain London tradesmen," June 18–19, 1768.
37 March 16, 1769, in James A. Bear Jr. and Lucia C. Stanton, eds., *Jefferson's Memorandum Books: Accounts, with Legal Records and Miscellany*, 2 vols. (Princeton, N.J., 1997), 1:16.
38 Robert F. Oaks, "Big Wheels in Philadelphia: Du Simitiere's List of Carriage Owners," *PMHB* 95 (1971): 354–56.
39 Cadwalader Tailoring Receipts, 1768–75, Cadwalader Papers, HSP.
40 Adair and Schutz, *Peter Oliver's Origin and Progress of the American Rebellion*, 62. On political "funerals," see Eustace, *Passion Is the Gale*, 411–12.
41 For Richardson quote, see G. J. Barker-Benfield, *The Culture of Sensibility: Sex and Society in Eighteenth-Century England* (Chicago, 1992), 34.
42 Adair and Schutz, *Peter Oliver's Origin and Progress of the American Rebellion*, 62–63.
43 On Lady Mary Wortley Montagu's description of Islamic veils as liberatory because they afforded freedom of female expression, see David S. Shields and Fredrika J. Teute, "The Meschianza: Sum of all Fetes; or, The Meschianza's Meaning: 'How will it sparkle—page the future?,'" 7, Paper presented at the Organization of American Historians Annual Meeting, Chicago, Illinois, March 28, 1996.
44 *Pennsylvania Chronicle*, January 29, 1770.
45 For use of the term "quiet period," see Kenneth Silverman, *A Cultural History of the American Revolution: Painting, Music, Literature, and the Theatre in the Colonies and the United States from the Treaty of Paris to the Inauguration of George Washington, 1763–1789* (New York, 1976), 162; and Robert A. Gross, *The Minutemen and Their World* (New York, 1976), 31.
46 On the growing rift between merchants and artisans in early 1770s Philadelphia, see Nash, *Urban Crucible*, 233–47. On shifting nonimportation coalitions and agreements among the city's merchants, see Doerflinger, *Vigorous Spirit of Enterprise*, 167–92; and Oaks, "Philadelphia Merchants," 407–36.

47 Nash, *First City*, 65–68.
48 Cadwalader Tailoring Receipts, 1768–75; and Cadwalader Receipts, Folder S, Cadwalader Papers, HSP.
49 Charles Willson Peale, *Portrait of John and Elizabeth Lloyd Cadwalader and Their Daughter Anne*, 1772, The Cadwalader Collection, PMA.
50 William Pollard, Philadelphia, to Thomas Earle, Liverpool, June 19, 1772, in William Pollard Letterbook, HSP; William Bradford Reed, *Life of Esther De Berdt, Afterwards Esther Reed, of Philadelphia* (New York, 1953), 157, 177. For data on imported dry goods in the early 1770s, see Doerflinger, *Vigorous Spirit of Enterprise*, 176–77.
51 J. Thomas Scharf and Thompson Westcott, *A History of Philadelphia, 1609–1844*, vol. 2 (Philadelphia, 1884), 889. Several runaway slaves and servants stole umbrellas, along with other luxury items, probably to pawn. See *Pennsylvania Gazette*, May 10, 1775; August 23, 1775; July 31, 1776. On umbrellas, see also T. S. Crawford, *A History of the Umbrella* (Devon, 1970), 113–33. Crawford quotes one French marquis as saying that carrying an umbrella was a sure sign that one did not possess a carriage.
52 *Pennsylvania Gazette*, August 8, 1771.
53 "Minutes of the Transactions of the Taylors Company of Philadelphia Instituted and Begun the 20th Day of August 1771," 1771–76, unpaginated, NYHS. On August 20, 1771, sixty-eight tailors signed their names to a document that professed the "necessity of uniting and coming under proper regulations respecting our business." The Taylors Company aimed to secure certain wages and suppress competition, yet it also served as a social organization and marked an upwardly mobile class of men.
54 *The Miraculous Power of Clothes and Dignity of the Taylors, Being an Essay on the Words Clothes Make Men, Translated from the German* (Philadelphia, 1772).
55 Ibid.
56 Nash, *Urban Crucible*, 204. On credit, see also Serena R. Zabin, *Dangerous Economies: Status and Commerce in Imperial New York* (Philadelphia, 2009), 10–31.
57 *Miraculous Power of Clothes*. By "grand assemblies," the author was likely referring to the Philadelphia Assembly. See Thomas Willing Balch, *The Philadelphia Assemblies* (Philadelphia, 1916).
58 "Minutes of the Transactions of the Taylors Company of Philadelphia Instituted and Begun the 20th Day of August 1771," 1771–76, unpaginated, NYHS.
59 Ibid.
60 Nash, *Urban Crucible*, 237.
61 *Pennsylvania Gazette*, July 28, 1773.
62 Aileen Ribeiro, *Dress in Eighteenth-Century Europe, 1715–1789* (New York, 1984), 142. See also Aileen Ribeiro, *Dress and Morality* (London, 1986), 111, for the macaroni style as the "last fling of frivolity" in male dress; and Valerie Steele, "The Social and Political Significance of Macaroni Fashion," *Costume: The Journal of the Costume Society* 19 (1985): 94–109. In 1773, English playwright Richard Hitchcock wrote a comedy titled *The Macaroni*, which was sold the following year in Philadelphia by William Woodhouse. See the advertisement in *Pennsylvania Gazette*, May 18, 1774. On macaronis, see also Aileen Ribeiro, "The Macaronis," *History Today* 28 (1978): 463–68; and for an excellent discussion of the ways in which the Darlys's macaroni

prints focused the relationship among class, character, gender, and individuality, see Shearer West, "The Darly Macaroni Prints and the Politics of 'Private Man,'" *Eighteenth-Century Life* 25 (2001): 170–82. For a similar argument, see Amelia Rauser, "Hair, Authenticity and the Self-Made Macaroni," *Eighteenth-Century Studies* 38 (2004): 101–17.

63   M. D. George, *British Museum Department of Prints and Drawings Catalogue of Personal and Political Satires*, vol. 5, *1771–1783* (London, 1942), 38, 236. The Darlys issued six sets of twenty-four caricatures each between 1771 and 1773, earning the business its nickname "The Macaroni Printshop."

64   Peter M. Briggs, "English Satire and Connecticut Wit," *American Quarterly* 37 (1985): 21.

65   John Trumbull, *The Progress of Dulness, part second; or, An Essay on the Life and Character of Dick Hairbrain* (New Haven, Conn., 1773), 16.

66   Ibid., 14–15.

67   Ibid. On men of fashion as counterfeit gentlemen, see James Eli Adams, *Dandies and Desert Saints: Styles of Victorian Masculinity* (Ithaca, N.Y., 1995), 53.

68   Jones, "Journal of Miss Sarah Eve," 23.

69   *Universal Almanack for the Year of Our Lord 1773* (Philadelphia, 1772). On the gender ambiguity of men of fashion, see Chapter 2. On the conflation of sex and gender, and the increasingly rigid understanding of gender as binary and fixed in the early modern era, see Thomas Laqueur, *Making Sex: Body and Gender from the Greeks to Freud* (Cambridge, Mass., 1990). Scholars have disagreed on the sexual proclivities of men of fashion in the early modern period. Was their effeminacy an attempt to court women, or did it signal the desire to be like women sexually—to be subordinate and penetrated? See Clare A. Lyons, "Mapping an Atlantic Sexual Culture: Homoeroticism in Eighteenth-Century Philadelphia," *WMQ*, 3rd ser., 60 (2003): 119–54, in particular note 15. On the non-normative sexuality of unmarried men of fashion in New England, see Thomas A. Foster, *Sex and the Eighteenth-Century Man* (Boston, 2006), 109–27.

70   Steele, "Macaroni Fashion," 102. So similar were the large wigs and the status pretensions that London periodicals noted the existence of "female macaronis" or "macaronesses." In 2004, *Eighteenth-Century Studies* devoted an entire issue to the topic of "Big Hair." In her introduction to the volume Angela Rosenthal writes, "The peculiar urgency of hair in eighteenth-century culture is . . . related to fundamental notions of sexual, national, and racial difference within a rapidly expanding global economy. Not only could hair, by virtue of its fashioning, mark (or dangerously blur) the seemingly natural differences between the sexes, but it was also perceived as registering ethnic divides" (Rosenthal, "Raising Hair," *Eighteenth-Century Studies* 38 [2004], 2). In the same issue, see also Margaret K. Powell and Joseph Roach, "Big Hair," 79–99.

71   Quoted in Scharf and Westcott, *History of Philadelphia*, 889.

72   For examples of the many advertisements that used this marketing strategy, see any issue of the *Pennsylvania Gazette* between 1771 and 1774. For a discussion of fashion as a means by which elite women commanded "the gaze" and exerted social power, see Shields, *Civil Tongues and Polite Letters*, 108.

73 Kate Haulman, "A Short History of the High Roll: Big Hair, Eighteenth-Century Style," ⟨www.common-place.org/vol-02/no-01⟩ (2001).

74 *Pennsylvania Gazette*, August 1, 1771; December 15, 1773.

75 Thompson Westcott, *A History of Philadelphia, from the Time of the First Settlements on the Delaware to the Consolidation of the City and Districts in 1854*, vol. 2 (Philadelphia, 1886), 402.

76 Charles Willson Peale, *Portrait of John and Elizabeth Lloyd Cadwalader and Their Daughter Anne*, 1772, The Cadwalader Collection, PMA.

77 Jones, "Journal of Miss Sarah Eve," 26.

78 Alice Morse Earle, ed., *The Diary of Anna Green Winslow: A Boston School Girl of 1771* (Cambridge, Mass., 1894), 71.

79 *Advertisement* broadside, n.d. (1770?), AAS.

80 Don Herzog, *Poisoning the Minds of the Lower Orders* (Princeton, N.J., 1998), 468.

81 Jones, "Journal of Miss Sarah Eve," 28.

82 *Advertisement* broadside, n.d. (1770?), AAS.

83 Jones, "Journal of Miss Sarah Eve," 26–27.

84 Hannah Griffits, "The Female Patriots Address'd to the Daughters of Liberty in America by the Same, 1768," in Karin A. Wulf and Catherine LaCourreye Blecki, eds., *Milcah Martha Moore's Book: A Commonplace Book from Revolutionary America* (University Park, Pa., 1997), 172–73.

85 Earle, *Diary of Anna Green Winslow*, 72.

86 *Lady's Magazine*, August 1770 preface; *Lady's Magazine*, November 1770, 179.

87 Four out of five poems in *Poor Richard's* for 1772 and 1773—an increase from none in 1770 and one in 1771—dealt with women's appearance and behavior.

88 "To the Ladies, on the Present Fashions," *Father Abraham's Almanack for the Year of Our Lord 1770* (Philadelphia, 1769).

89 "Real Beauty," *Poor Richard's Improved, Being an Almanack and Ephemeris for the Year of Our Lord 1773* (Philadelphia, 1772); "The Country Lass," *Poor Richard's Almanack and Ephemeris for the Year of Our Lord 1772* (Philadelphia, 1771).

90 "The Way to Get Him, Addressed to the Fair," *Poor Richard's Almanack* (1771).

91 "Rules for the Choice of a Wife," ibid.

92 "The Fox and the Goose," *Father Abraham's Almanac for the Year of Our Lord 1772* (Philadelphia, 1771).

93 "The Reason Why Miss Jenny Tinderbox, Miss Squeeze, Miss Betty Tempest, and Sagacious Sophronia Are Not Married," ibid.

94 "Reflections on Gallantry, and on the Education of Women," *Pennsylvania Gazette*, November 11, 1772; "On Fashion," *The Universal Almanack for the Year of Our Lord 1773* (Philadelphia, 1772).

95 See Erin Mackie, *Market à la Mode: Fashion, Commodity, and Gender in "The Tatler" and "The Spectator"* (Baltimore, 1997); and Chapter 2.

96 Jones, "Journal of Miss Sarah Eve," 23.

97 Richard Cumberland, *The Fashionable Lover; a Comedy as It Is Acted at the Theater-Royal in Drury Lane* (London, 1772). Excerpts from the *Fashionable Lover* were printed in the *Lady's Magazine*, January 1772.

98 Cumberland, *Fashionable Lover*, epilogue.

99   Ibid.
100 Jones, "Journal of Miss Sarah Eve," 20.
101 Ibid., 203.
102 Ibid., 20.
103 Ibid., 192.
104 *Pennsylvania Packet*, December 12, 1774, quoted in Jones, "Journal of Miss Sarah Eve," 20–21.

CHAPTER 5

1   See Kate Haulman, "Fashion and the Culture Wars of Revolutionary Philadelphia," *WMQ*, 3rd ser., 62 (2005): 625–62. I define "culture war" as a struggle between competing visions of society, shaped by the ways in which certain hot-button topics, such as religion, morality, education, gender, sexuality, the family, and the arts, intersect with the institutions of the nation-state. This chapter heeds anthropologist Sherry B. Ortner's call to "situate cultural analysis within . . . analyses of social and political events and processes" (introduction to Ortner, ed., *The Fate of "Culture": Geertz and Beyond* [Berkeley, Calif., 1999], 9). For studies of revolutionary-era contests conducted through cultural forms and their meanings, see, for example, Simon Newman, *Parades and the Politics of the Street: Festive Culture in the Early American Republic* (Philadelphia, 1997); David Waldstreicher, *In the Midst of Perpetual Fetes: The Making of American Nationalism, 1776–1820* (Chapel Hill, N.C., 1997); Robert Blair St. George, *Conversing by Signs: Poetics of Implication in Colonial New England Culture* (Chapel Hill, N.C., 1998); Nicole E. Eustace, *Passion is the Gale: Emotion, Power, and the Coming of the American Revolution* (Chapel Hill, N.C., 2008); and Sarah Knott, *Sensibility and the American Revolution* (Chapel Hill, N.C., 2009). On the social and economic climate of eighteenth-century Philadelphia, see Gary B. Nash, *The Urban Crucible: Social Change, Political Consciousness, and the Origins of the American Revolution* (Cambridge, Mass., 1979); and Benjamin L. Carp, *Rebels Rising: Cities and the American Revolution* (New York, 2007), 172–212. On Philadelphia as cosmopolitan cultural center, see Gary B. Nash, *First City: Philadelphia and the Forging of Historical Memory* (Philadelphia, 2002), 63–78.

2   Gilles Lipovetsky, *The Empire of Fashion: Dressing Modern Democracy* (Princeton, N.J., 1994), 31. On the aesthetic paradox that plagued the early American republic, see Richard L. Bushman, *The Refinement of America: Persons, Houses, Cities* (New York, 1992), 181–203.

3   "The Association, 20 October 1774," in Samuel Eliot Morrison, ed., *Sources and Documents Illustrating the American Revolution, 1764–1788, and the Formation of the Federal Constitution* (New York, 1979), 123. On the Continental Association and its proscriptions, see Ann Withington Fairfax, *Toward a More Perfect Union: Virtue and the Formation of American Republics* (New York, 1991), 13. On male homosocial pastimes in colonial Virginia, see Rhys Isaac, *The Transformation of Virginia, 1740–1790* (Chapel Hill, N.C., 1982), 94–104.

4   Memoranda of the Committee appointed to inspect and observe importations to Philadelphia, in Manuscripts relating to Nonimportation resolutions, 1766–75, APS.

5 Cadwalader Receipts, Folder S, Cadwalader Papers, HSP.
6 *Pennsylvania Gazette*, August 16, 1775.
7 Mary and Matthew Darly, *Bunker's Hill; or, America's Head Dress*, n.d., and *Miss Carolina Sullivan, One of the Obstinate Daughters of America*, 1776, Print Department, NYHS; Mary and Matthew Darly, *Oh Heigh Oh; or, A View of the Back Settlements*, 1776, British Cartoon Prints Collection, Prints and Photographs Division, LC.
8 See Judith Van Buskirk, "They Didn't Join the Band: Disaffected Women in Revolutionary Philadelphia," *Pennsylvania History* 62 (1995): 306–29. On revolutionary-era political and social divisions in Pennsylvania, see Anne Ousterhout, *A State Divided: Opposition in Pennsylvania to the American Revolution* (Westport, Conn., 1987); and Richard Ryerson, *The Revolution Is Now Begun: The Radical Committees of Philadelphia, 1765–1776* (Philadelphia, 1978).
9 *Pennsylvania Gazette*, August 7, 1776; *Pennsylvania Evening Post*, June 15, 1775.
10 John Adams to William Tudor, July 6, 1775, Philadelphia, in Paul H. Smith, Gerard W. Gawalt, Rosemary Fry Plakas, Eugene R. Sheridan, and Ronald M. Gephard, eds. *Letters of Delegates to Congress: 1774–1789*, CD ROM (Summerfield, Fla., 1998). All correspondence is from Philadelphia, unless otherwise indicated. William Bradford Reed, *The Life of Esther De Berdt, Afterwards Esther Reed, of Philadelphia* (Philadelphia, 1853), 217; Eliza Farmer Letterbook, 1774–77, June 28, 1775, HSP.
11 John Adams to William Tudor, July 6, 1775, in Smith et al., *Letters of Delegates*.
12 John E. Ferling, "'Oh That I Was a Soldier': John Adams and the Anguish of War," *American Quarterly* 36 (1984): 266.
13 Fred Anderson, *A People's Army: Massachusetts Soldiers and Society in the Seven Years' War* (Chapel Hill, N.C., 1984), 111–13.
14 Charles Royster, *A Revolutionary People at War: The Continental Army and American Character, 1775–1783* (Chapel Hill, N.C., 1979), 10.
15 J. Thomas Scharf and Thompson Westcott, *History of Philadelphia: 1609–1884*, vol. 2 (Philadelphia, 1884), 721. On the militia, see Steven Rosswurm, *Arms, Country, and Class: The Philadelphia Militia and the "Lower Sort" during the American Revolution, 1775–1783* (New Brunswick, N.J., 1987).
16 On hunting shirts and other revolutionary uniforms, see Fritz Kredel and Fredrick P. Todd, *Soldiers of the American Army, 1775–1954* (Chicago, 1941); and Charles M. Lefferts, *Uniforms of the American, French, and German Armies in the War of the American Revolution, 1775–1783* (New York, 1926). See also Linda Baumgarten, *What Clothes Reveal: The Language of Clothing in Colonial and Federal America* (Williamsburg, Va., 2002), 71–74.
17 Reed, *Life of Esther De Berdt*, 217. On the "Indian fashion," an amalgam of Native and Anglo-American styles, as frontier power dressing, see Timothy J. Shannon, "Dressing for Success on the Mohawk Frontier: Hendrick, William Johnson and the Indian Fashion," *WMQ*, 3rd ser., 53 (1996): 13–42. On the appropriation of Indian modes and identities in American culture, see Philip J. Deloria, *Playing Indian* (New Haven, Conn., 1998).
18 John Adams to Abigail Adams, August 14, 1776, in Smith et al., *Letters of Delegates*. The medal was designed by Pierre DuSimitiere. Adams's remark seems illustrative

of the ways in which American leaders attempted to balance distinctively North American cultural modes with European inheritances.

19 Abbé Robin, *New Travels Through North America*, trans. Philip Freneau (Philadelphia, 1783), 35.
20 *To the Associators of the City of Philadelphia* (Philadelphia, 1775).
21 Samuel Adams to William Health, October 20, 1775, in Smith et al., *Letters of Delegates*.
22 Cadwalader Receipts, Folder W, Cadwalader Papers, HSP.
23 William Paca to Maryland Council, May 24, 1777, in Smith et al., *Letters of Delegates*; Committee at Headquarters to George Washington, July 20, 1780, Preakness, in ibid.
24 Royster, *Revolutionary People at War*, quote on 236.
25 Ibid., 236–38.
26 *The Army Correspondence of Colonel John Laurens in the Years 1777–8* (New York, 1969), 119.
27 Eva Eve Jones, ed., "Extracts from the Journal of Miss Sarah Eve," *PMHB* 5 (1881): 26–27.
28 Henry Laurens to John Laurens, March 3, 1778, in Smith et al., *Letters of Delegates*. Laurens's *friseur* was no mere tradesman but an artist.
29 Quoted in Kenneth Silverman, *A Cultural History of the American Revolution: Painting, Music, Literature, and the Theatre in the Colonies and the United States from the Treaty of Paris to the Inauguration of George Washington, 1763–1789* (New York, 1976), 286. General John Burgoyne, known as "Gentleman Johnny," was widely regarded as a fop and was referred to as such by members of Congress in an attempt to minimize his prowess. See Henry Laurens to Solomon Legare, August 27, 1777; and Laurens to Lachlan McIntosh, September 1, 1777, in Smith et al., *Letters of Delegates*.
30 Royster, *Revolutionary People at War*, 30.
31 *Pennsylvania Gazette*, July 16, 1777.
32 John Adams to James Warren, October 19 and 20, 1775, in Smith et al., *Letters of Delegates*.
33 John Adams to Abigail Adams, April 14, 1776, in ibid.
34 Durand Echeverria, trans. and ed., "The American Character: A Frenchman Views the New Republic from Philadelphia," *WMQ*, 3rd ser., 16 (1959): 409.
35 Ibid.
36 Robin, *New Travels Through North America*, 14.
37 Echeverria, "American Character," 391. Josiah Quincy of Boston noted the persistence of extravagant funerals in Charleston. See Fairfax, *Toward a More Perfect Union*, 185.
38 Jay Fleigelman has termed Chesterfield's *Letters* such in *Prodigals and Pilgrims: The American Revolution against Patriarchal Authority, 1750–1800* (New York, 1982), 39.
39 *The Life of the Late Earl of Chesterfield; or, The Man of the World* (Philadelphia, 1775), 238, 241.
40 *Principles of Politeness, and of Knowing the World: By the Late Lord Chesterfield* (Philadelphia, 1778), 247; *Life of the Late Earl of Chesterfield*, 192.
41 *Life of the Late Earl of Chesterfield*, 239.

42 Ibid., 191.
43 "A Comparative View of the Virtues and Abilities of Men and Women; or, A Modest Defence of the Female Sex," *Lady's Magazine*, May 1781, 254–55.
44 Edmund M. Hayes, "Mercy Warren versus Lord Chesterfield, 1779," *WMQ*, 3rd ser., 40 (1983): 619. Warren made good use of men of fashion characters, making them signify actual Tories, in her politically charged revolutionary-era plays. *The Group* contains Beau Trumps and Scriblerus Fribble; *The Blockheads*, Lord Dapper. See *The Plays and Poems of Mercy Otis Warren* (New York, 1980). As early as 1730, Elizabeth Magawly was taking indignant exception to the notion that all women were impressed by coxcombs. See Lawrence Klein, "Gender and the Public/Private Distinction in the Eighteenth Century," *Eighteenth-Century Studies* 29 (1996): 100.
45 On the economic crisis in Philadelphia, where by 1779 prices rose to seven times those of 1777, see Eric Foner, *Tom Paine and Revolutionary America* (New York, 1976), 161–62.
46 Kathryn Zabelle Derounian, "'A dear, dear friend': Six Letters from Deborah Norris to Sarah Wister, 1778–1779," *PMHB* 108 (1984): 488.
47 Albert Cook Myers, ed., *Sally Wister's Journal* (New York, 1969), 71–72.
48 Ibid., 76, 87, 95–96, 162. Wister was dismayed because a short gown was an informal work dress, certainly not the height of beauty and fashion by Anglo-American standards. See Claudia Kidwell, "Short Gowns," *Dress* 4 (1978): 30–65.
49 Myers, *Sally Wister's Journal*, 174–75.
50 Ibid., 162–63.
51 Derounian, "'Dear, dear friend,'" 506–7.
52 *The Wishing Females*, Caricatures: Eighteenth Century Folder, Print Department, NYHS.
53 David S. Shields and Fredrika J. Teute, "The Meschianza: Sum of all Fetes; or The Meschianza's Meaning: 'How Will It Sparkle—Page the Future?,'" paper presented at the Organization of American Historians Annual Meeting, Chicago, Illinois, March 28, 1996. Also on the Meschianza and its aftermath, see Susan Klepp, "Rough Music on Independence Day: Philadelphia," in Matthew Dennis, Simon P. Newman, and William Pencak, eds., *Riot and Revelry in Early America* (University Park, Pa., 2002).
54 John Fanning Watson, extra-illustrated autograph manuscript of "Annals of Philadelphia" (Philadelphia, 1823), 242, LCP.
55 Pierre DuSimitiere Sketches and Watercolors and Typescript of Diary, Print Department, LCP. The woman's face is barely sketched, whereas the headdress is rendered in much greater detail.
56 Shields and Teute, "Meschianza," 14.
57 Josiah Bartlett to Mary Bartlett, August 24, 1778, in Smith et al., *Letters of Delegates*.
58 Quoted in Scharf and Westcott, *History of Philadelphia*, 900.
59 Josiah Bartlett to Mary Bartlett, August 24, 1778, in Smith et al., *Letters of Delegates*. According to Ann Fairfax Withington (*Toward a More Perfect Union*, 235), Whigs sometimes ridiculed and humiliated Tory men by dressing them up as "men of fashion."
60 Quoted in Shields and Teute, "Meschianza," 18–19.

61 Samuel Holton's Diary July 4, 1778; and Richard Henry Lee to Francis Lightfoot Lee, July 5, 1778, in Smith et al., *Letters of Delegates*.

62 Richard Henry Lee to Francis Lightfoot Lee, July 5, 1778; and Josiah Bartlett to Mary Bartlett, August 24, 1778, in ibid.

63 Quoted in Scharf and Westcott, *History of Philadelphia*, 900. Franks was one of the Meschianza belles and a celebrated wit. At the fete, she reportedly jeered at her knight, "How the ass glories in the lion's skin," and when General Henry Clinton ordered the band to play "Britons Strike Home" during a ball given for the ladies of New York, she called out, "The Commander in Chief has made a mistake, he meant to say, Britons go home." For these anecdotes, see typescript accompanying letter from Rebecca Franks to Mrs. Andrew Hamilton (Abigail Franks Hamilton), 1781, Society Collection, HSP. When in 1779 Franks disdainfully observed that American general Charles Lee wore green breeches patched with leather, he retorted that they were, in fact, "legitimate sherryvalies, such as his Majesty of Poland Wears (who, let me tell you, has made more fashions than all your knights of the Meschianza put together)." For the exchange between Franks and Lee, see Scharf and Westcott, *History of Philadelphia*, 718.

64 Robin, *New Travels Through North America*, 44.

65 Quoted in Scharf and Westcott, *History of Philadelphia*, 900.

66 On national celebrations and the need to make long-standing English practices appropriately American and republican, see Waldstreicher, *In the Midst of Perpetual Fetes*, 17–52.

67 Samuel Adams to James Warren, October 20, 1778, in Smith et al., *Letters of Delegates*.

68 Marquis de Chastellux, *Travels in North America in the Years 1780–81–82* (London, 1787), 187–88.

69 Shields and Teute, "Meschianza," 23.

70 Quoted in Scharf and Westcott, *History of Philadelphia*, 899.

71 Sarah Franklin Bache, Philadelphia, to Benjamin Franklin, London, Benjamin Franklin Papers Database, APS.

72 *Pennsylvania Gazette*, August 29, 1778.

73 On the nature of eighteenth-century print culture, informed by the work of Jurgen Habermas on the public sphere, see Erin Mackie, *Market à la Mode: Fashion, Commodity, and Gender in "The Tatler" and "The Spectator"* (Baltimore, 1997); and Michael Warner, *Letters of the Republic: Publication and the Public Sphere in Eighteenth-Century America* (Cambridge, Mass., 1990).

74 "A Defence of the Female HeadDress at Present in Fashion," *U.S. Magazine*, June 1779, 268–71.

75 "The Retaliation, Occasioned by the Defence of the Ladies Head-dress in the Last Magazine," *U.S. Magazine*, July 1779, 308–11. The "Notes to Correspondents" that appeared in the fall continued the satire, indicating that the matter was both silly and serious by recommending a legal regulation on headdresses so that vigilante justice (likely a reference to the previous year's events) might be avoided. See "Notes to Correspondents," *U.S. Magazine*, September 1779, 368–70.

76 John Fell to Robert Morris, March 5, 1780, in Smith et al., *Letters of Delegates*.

77 Chastellux, *Travels in North America*, 197–98.
78 "The Sentiments of an American Woman," *Pennsylvania Gazette*, June 21, 1780. The subscription widened the rift among Philadelphia's elites; see Teute and Shields, "Meschianza," 26–29. For a full explanation of subscription service and the Ladies Association, see Mary Beth Norton, *Liberty's Daughters: The Revolutionary Experience of American Women, 1750–1800* (Boston, 1980), 177–88. Reed wanted to donate the funds collected directly to the troops, but George Washington insisted that they be spent on linen for shirts to be produced by the women themselves rather than seamstresses, which worked to further inscribe a domestic, productive feminine ideal.
79 Robin, *New Travels Through North America*, 24.
80 Hugh Williamson to James Iredell, December 2, 1782, in Smith et al., *Letters of Delegates*.
81 John Fell to Robert Morris, March 5, 1780; and Arthur Lee to James Warren, March 12, 1783, in Congress, in Smith et al., *Letters of Delegates*. Lee revised the city's recent past because, as this and the previous chapter show, the preceding decade had seen an upsurge in extravagance in what he regarded as a plain and simple Quaker town. On the wealth and spending patterns of Quaker "grandees," see Frederick Barnes Tolles, *Meeting House and Counting House: The Quaker Merchants of Colonial Philadelphia, 1682–1763* (Chapel Hill, N.C., 1948). On the assumed but complicated association of Quakerism with plainness, see the essays in Emma Jones Lapsansky and Anne A. Verplanck, eds., *Quaker Aesthetics: Reflections on a Quaker Ethic in American Design and Consumption* (Philadelphia, 2003).
82 Samuel Adams to Elbridge Gerry, November 27, 1780; and Samuel Huntington to John Lawrence, January 18, 1780, in Smith et al., *Letters of Delegates*.
83 Chastellux, *Travels in North America*, 148.
84 Hugh Williamson to James Iredell, December 2, 1782, in Smith et al., *Letters of Delegates*.
85 Benjamin Rush, "The French Fete in Philadelphia in Honor of the Dauphin's Birthday, 1892," *PMHB* 21 (1897): 260.
86 Shields, *Civil Tongues and Polite Letters*, 6–10. Seven hundred attended, leaving some ten thousand, Rush speculated, to watch, aided by the replacement of an opaque fence that blocked the ball's setting with a transparent one. Whereas no nonmembers had observed the intricate social machinery of the Philadelphia Assembly in the past, now the many were invited—not to participate, but to watch the few.
87 Hannah Pemberton described the fine dress of refugee "first families" from the Carolinas. See Hannah Pemberton to John and Sarah Cox and Sarah Pemberton, August 1781, piece 178, Folder 18, volume 35, Pemberton Papers, HSP.
88 Elizabeth Wister, Journal of a Trip to Bristol, 1783, 4–5, Eastwick Collection, APS; Anna Rawle to Rebecca Shoemaker, November 5, 1780; and January 9, 1781, in *The Shoemaker Papers: Diaries and Letters of a Loyalist Family of Philadelphia Written between the Years 1780 and 1786*, vol. 1, 1780–82, HSP; Rebecca Franks to Mrs. Andrew Hamilton (Abigail Franks Hamilton), n.d., 1781 Society Collection, HSP.

89 Memoranda of the committee appointed to inspect and observe importations to Philadelphia, in Manuscripts Relating to Nonimportation Resolutions, 1766–75, APS.
90 Arthur Lee to James Warren, March 12, 1783, in Smith et al., *Letters of Delegates*.

CHAPTER 6

1 On the role of culture, specifically objects, in crafting the United States' identity, see Leora Auslander, *Cultural Revolutions: Everyday Life and Politics in Britain, North America, and France* (Berkeley, Calif., 2009), 95–111; and Kariann Yokota, "Postcolonialism and Material Culture in the Early United States," *WMQ*, 3rd ser., 64 (2007): 263–74.
2 See Chapter 5. On the importance of cultural practices to the formation of nascent nationalism, see Simon Newman, *Parades and the Politics of the Street: Festive Culture in the Early American Republic* (Philadelphia, 1997); and David Waldstreicher, *In the Midst of Perpetual Fetes: The Making of American Nationalism, 1776–1820* (Chapel Hill, N.C., 1997).
3 On the anxieties and practices of the political class within the "theater of national politics," see Joanne Freeman, *Affairs of Honor: National Politics in the New Republic* (New Haven, Conn., 2001). Quote is taken from the title of chapter 2.
4 David Howell to William Greene, Annapolis, December 24, 1783, in Paul H. Smith, Gerard W. Gawalt, Rosemary Fry Plakas, Eugene R. Sheridan, and Ronald M. Gephard, eds., *Letters of Delegates to Congress: 1774–1789*, CD ROM (Summerfield, Fla., 1998). On the death and mourning of Washington, see Francois Furstenberg, *In the Name of the Father: Washington's Legacy, Slavery, and the Making of a Nation* (New York, 2006), 25–30.
5 David Howell to William Greene, Annapolis, December 24, 1783; John Beatty to Reading Beatty, Annapolis, March 5, 1784; and Charles DeWitt to Gerret DeWitt, Annapolis, May 21, 1784, in Smith et al., *Letters of Delegates*; Abbé Robin, *New Travels Through North America*, trans. Philip Freneau (Philadelphia, 1783), 51.
6 Charles DeWitt to Gerret DeWitt, Annapolis, May 21, 1784, in Smith et al., *Letters of Delegates*.
7 Charles DeWitt (1727–87), *Biographical Directory of the United States Congress*, ⟨http://bioguide.congress.gov/scripts/biodisplay.pl?index=D000283⟩.
8 On the fraught relationship between men and dress in the early republic, see Linzy Brekke, "'To Make a Figure': Clothing and the Politics of Male Identity in Eighteenth-Century America," in John Styles and Amanda Vickery, eds., *Gender, Taste, and Material Culture in Britain and North America, 1700–1830* (New Haven, Conn., 2006), 225–46.
9 Richard Henry Lee to Thomas Lee Shippen, New York City, January 17, 1785, and January 20, 1785, in Smith et al., *Letters of Delegates*. The use of "beau" as a synonym for "fop" dates from the late seventeenth century, and the term came to refer to a suitor in the eighteenth. See *Oxford English Dictionary Online*, s.v. "beau."
10 Linda Baumgarten, *What Clothes Reveal: The Language of Clothing in Colonial and Federal America* (Williamsburg, Va., 2002), 56.

11 Examples of these waistcoats appear in the costume collections of various repositories in the United States. I have examined the waistcoats at the Winterthur Museum and Library and viewed the Lee Simonsen Waistcoat Collection at the Metropolitan Museum of Art Costume Department.
12 Kristen Wetzel, "Masculine Elegance: Waistcoats at the Winterthur Museum," Textile Connoisseurship unpublished paper, March 12, 2002, Object File 60.79, WML. Quote on page 5.
13 *Independent Journal* (or *General Advertiser*), September 22, 1787.
14 Baumgarten, *What Clothes Reveal*, 224–32; Wetzel, "Masculine Elegance."
15 Richard Saunders, "On Dress," *Poor Richard Improved: Being an Almanack and Ephemeris for the Year of Our Lord 1783* (Philadelphia, 1782).
16 Erin Mackie, *Market à la Mode: Fashion, Commodity, and Gender in "The Tatler" and "The Spectator"* (Baltimore, 1997).
17 Linda Colley, *Britons: Forging the Nation, 1707–1837* (New Haven, Conn., 1992). See also Chapters 1 and 2 of this book.
18 Robin, *New Travels Through North America*, 45.
19 George Fox to William Temple Franklin, St. Florentine, October 12, 1780, in William Temple Franklin Papers, 1775–82, APS. On the ancien sartorial régime in France, see Daniel Roche, *The Culture of Clothing: Dress and Fashion in the Ancien Régime* (Cambridge, 1994); and Jennifer M. Jones, *Sexing la Mode: Gender, Fashion, and Commercial Culture in Old Regime France* (New York, 2004).
20 Mary Norris to Mary Dickinson, Philadelphia, May 17, 1786, Maria Dickinson Logan Collection, HSP.
21 See Caroline Weber, *Queen of Fashion: What Marie Antoinette Wore to the Revolution* (New York, 2006).
22 Howard C. Rice, *The Adams Family in Auteuil, 1784–1785, as Told in the Letters of Abigail Adams* (Boston, 1892), 11–12.
23 Ibid., 22.
24 For the relationship among status, gender, sexual practices, and ideas about sexuality in the eighteenth century, see Clare A. Lyons, *Sex among the Rabble: An Intimate History of Gender and Power in the Age of Revolution, Philadelphia, 1730–1830* (Chapel Hill, N.C., 2006).
25 Paine Wingate to Hannah Wingate, New York, July 21, 1788, in Smith et al., *Letters of Delegates*.
26 *Pennsylvania Gazette*, December 8, 1784; *New York Daily Advertiser*, February 17, 1786; *New York Gazette*, June 24, 1785.
27 See Chapter 2, as well as Kimberly Chrisman, "'Unhoop the Fair Sex': The Campaign against the Hoop Petticoat in Eighteenth-Century England," *Eighteenth-Century Studies* 30 (1996): 5–23; and Mackie, *Market à la Mode*, 104–43.
28 Baumgarten, *What Clothes Reveal*, 230.
29 A Female Antiquarian, "Cursory Remarks on the Female Dress of Antiquity," *Lady's Magazine*, August 1782, 415; "Fashionable Dresses for May and June by a Lady of Fashion," *Lady's Magazine*, June 1784, 304.
30 *Independent Journal* (or *General Advertiser*), February 8, 1786.
31 *New-York Packet*, January 2, 1786.

32 Paine Wingate to Sarah Wingate, New York, February 23, 1788, in Smith et al., *Letters of Delegates*. A calash was a large bonnet made of fabric overlaying a series of hoop-shaped wires that could be pulled forward or back, accordion style, to show off or obscure the face. See Elisabeth McClellan, *Historic Dress in America, 1607–1870: Volume One, 1607–1800* (New York, reprint, 1977), 222, 225, 227, 233.
33 Paine Wingate to Mary Wingate Wiggin, New York, February 16, 1788, in Smith et al., *Letters of Delegates*.
34 Paine Wingate to Sarah Wingate, March 30, 1788, in ibid.
35 "On the Modesty-piece or Neck-attire of the Ladies," *Universal Asylum*, March 1790, 154–55.
36 Paine Wingate to Sarah Wingate, New York, May 21, 1788, in Smith et al., *Letters of the Delegates*.
37 Ibid., February 23 and March 30, 1788.
38 Ibid., March 30 and May 21, 1788.
39 Ibid., May 21, 1788.
40 Jean Pierre Brissot de Warville, *New Travels in the United States of America, Performed in 1788* (Dublin, 1792), 95–96, 156–57, 319, 380–81.
41 Ann Head Warder Papers, Collection 2175, Finding Aid, HSP.
42 Journals of Ann Head Warder, vol. 2, May 31 and June 25, 1786; vol. 3, July 3 and August 20, 1786, HSP. On short gowns, see Chapter 1 and Claudia Kidwell, "Short Gowns," *Dress* 4 (1978): 30–65.
43 Journals of Ann Head Warder, vol. 2, May 31, June 22, and June 25, 1786; vol. 3, July 21, 1786; vol. 6, November 9, 1786; vol. 7, December 23, 1786, HSP.
44 Ibid., vol. 4, August 1, 1786; vol. 6, December 2, 1786.
45 Ibid., vol. 3, July 6, 1786.
46 Ibid., vol. 3, July 2, 1786; vol. 5, September 23, September 30, and October 8, 1786; vol. 14, December 16, 1786.
47 William Dillwyn to Susanna Dillwyn, London, April 28, 1783, and June 23, 1783, in William and Susanna Dillwyn Correspondence, 1778–93, Manuscripts, LCP; Sarah Dillwyn to Susanna Dillwyn, Wapping, July 8, 1784, in ibid.; William Dillwyn to Susanna Dillwyn, Clapton, April 17, 1785, in ibid.
48 Susanna Dillwyn to William Dillwyn, Burlington, October 17, 1788, in ibid.
49 Samuel Shoemaker, *The Shoemaker Papers: Diary of Samuel Shoemaker of Philadelphia, from November 7, 1783 to October 5, 1785, Copied from the Original in the Possession of the Historical Society of Pennsylvania* (Philadelphia, 1892), 23–27.
50 Ibid., 47, 76, 80, 96, 130, 176.
51 Advertisements in the *Pennsylvania Gazette*, February 25, April 14, June 9, October 20, 1784; May 18, 1785; May 4, 1785.
52 Philip L. White, ed., *The Beekman Mercantile Papers, 1746–1799*, vol. 3 (New York, 1956), 1115–17.
53 On the postwar economy, see John J. McCusker and Russell R. Menard, *The Economy of British America, 1607–1789* (Chapel Hill, N.C., 1991), 351–77. On the role of consumption in debates over political economy, see Linzy A. Brekke, "'The Scourge of Fashion': Political Economy and the Politics of Consumption in the Early Republic," *Early American Studies* 3:1 (Spring 2005): 111–38. On luxury,

dependence, and American national identity, see Auslander, *Cultural Revolutions*, 99–101.
54 *Pennsylvania Gazette*, February 25, 1784.
55 Ibid., June 30, 1784; July 21, 1784; July 6, 1785; September 14, 1785; December 21, 1785.
56 Ibid., June 13, 1787; October 11, 1786; August 9, 1786. On the ways in which the Federalist press depicted Shaysite farmers in particular as indebted, luxurious, and effeminate as they complained of economic hardship, see Carroll Smith-Rosenberg, "Dis-covering the Subject of the 'Great Constitutional Discussion,' 1786–1789," *Journal of American History* 79 (1992): 854–57.
57 *Pennsylvania Gazette*, June 21, 1786; August 8, 1786.
58 "Primitive Whig No. 1," *Pennsylvania Gazette*, January 9, 1786; "Primitive Whig No. 2," ibid., January 25, 1786. On the blaming of middle-class, consuming women for social and economic disorder, see also Smith-Rosenberg, "Dis-covering the Subject," 859–61.
59 *Pennsylvania Gazette*, June 30, 1784.
60 Ibid., August 2, 1786; April 9, 1788. On the resurgence of the homespun ideal in the 1780s, see Michael Zakim, *Ready-Made Democracy: A History of Men's Dress in the American Republic, 1760–1860* (Chicago, 2003), 22.
61 *Pennsylvania Gazette*, May 17, 1786; "Political Fragments, supposed either to be written by Dr. Franklin," ibid., November 17, 1784.
62 J. Login, "On Luxury, Idleness, and Industry," *The Columbian Almanac for the Year of Our Lord, 1795* (Philadelphia, 1794). See also Brekke, "'Scourge of Fashion,'" 111, for another treatment of this anecdote.
63 *Pennsylvania Gazette*, July 11, 1787.
64 "An Essay on the Means of Promoting Federal Sentiments in the United States, by a Foreign Spectator," *Pennsylvania Gazette*, August 8, 1787.
65 "An Essay on the Means of Promoting Federal Sentiments in the United States, by a Foreign Spectator, *Pennsylvania Gazette*, August 29, 1787; "Winter Clothes," *The American Museum*, October 1787, 359; "Letter from Chemung to a Gentleman in Baltimore," *Pennsylvania Gazette*, August 29, 1787.
66 "An Essay on the Means of Promoting Federal Sentiments, by a Foreign Spectator," *Pennsylvania Gazette*, August 29, 1787.
67 Ibid.
68 Ibid.
69 "An Essay on the Means of Promoting Federal Sentiments, by a Foreign Spectator," *Pennsylvania Gazette*, September 5, 1787.
70 Ibid.
71 Middle-class women, whose consumption both signified men's wealth and undermined it, were "both sign and scapegoat" (Smith-Rosenberg, "Dis-covering the Subject," 861).
72 *The Contrast, a Comedy in Five Acts: Written by a Citizen of the United States* (Philadelphia, 1790), list of subscribers at front. Also on *The Contrast*, see John Evelev, "*The Contrast*: The Problem of Theatricality and Political and Social Crisis in Postrevolutionary America," *Early American Literature* 31 (1996): 74–97; and Richard S.

Pressman, "Class Positioning and Shays' Rebellion: The Contradictions of *The Contrast*," *Early American Literature* 21 (1986): 87–102.

73 *The Contrast*, 5.
74 The conduct book figures prominently in *The Contrast*. That Tyler included four references to it in the short play indicates the popularity of and familiarity with the text. The satirical nature of those references indicates the ways in which Tyler hoped to discredit and ridicule Chesterfield and his adherents.
75 *The Contrast*, 37, 27.
76 Ibid.
77 Ibid., 21.
78 Symbolically, a Dimple–Van Rough union would have "prostituted the wealth of the American mercantilist class to Britain." See Pressman, "Class Positioning and Shays' Rebellion," 99.
79 For a fine account of this tale, see Edith B. Gelles, "Gossip: An Eighteenth-Century Case," *Journal of Social History* 22 (1989): 667–83.
80 Extract from a letter from New York, *Pennsylvania Gazette*, June 25, 1788. On the ratification debates, see Saul Cornell, *The Other Founders: Anti-Federalism and the Dissenting Tradition in America, 1788–1828* (Chapel Hill, N.C., 1999), 19–50.
81 For a full account of the procession, see *Pennsylvania Gazette*, July 9, 1788. See also Waldstreicher, *In the Midst of Perpetual Fetes*, 90–107. On the featuring of domestic cloth, see Zakim, *Ready-Made Democracy*, 25.
82 On Hewson, see Florence M. Montgomery, *Printed Textiles: English and American Cotton Linens, 1750–1850* (New York, 1970), 92–98.
83 *Pennsylvania Gazette*, July 9, 1788.
84 "To the Working People of Maryland," extracted from the *Maryland Journal*, *Pennsylvania Gazette*, April 2, 1788.
85 *New-York Packet*, May 22, 1786.
86 *Pennsylvania Gazette*, April 15, 1789.
87 Ibid., May 7, 1789; May 13, 1789.
88 Stanley Elkins and Eric McKitrick, *The Age of Federalism: The Early American Republic, 1788–1800* (New York, 1993), 65–75.
89 "The Observer No. XII," *Pennsylvania Gazette*, January 20, 1790; "To the Friends of American Manufactures," *Pennsylvania Gazette*, October 29, 1788.
90 *Pennsylvania Gazette*, August 24, 1791.

EPILOGUE

1 *Oxford English Dictionary Online*, s.v. "corset."
2 On the Grecian gown, see Caroline Winterer, *The Mirror of Antiquity: American Women and the Classical Tradition* (Ithaca, N.Y., 2007), 117–25.
3 David Waldstreicher takes a similar approach in his essay "Why Thomas Jefferson and African Americans Wore Their Politics on Their Sleeves: Dress and Mobilization between American Revolutions," in Jeffrey L. Pasley, Andrew W. Robertson, and David Waldstreicher, eds., *Beyond the Founders: New Approaches to the Political History of the Early American Republic* (Chapel Hill, N.C., 2004), 79–103, arguing

that political leaders such as Jefferson and the disenfranchised alike used clothing in ways that "served to broaden politics beyond its structural limitations in the early American republic" (81).

4 I attempt to heed Rosemarie Zagarri's caution that we not lose sight of institutions of formal governance as we broaden the definition of the political to include all forms of power and power relations. Attention to the discursive practices of fashion may help us understand the processes behind what she terms the "revolutionary backlash." See Zagarri, "Women and Party Politics," in Pasley, Robertson, and Waldstreicher, *Beyond the Founders*, 108; and Zagarri, *Revolutionary Backlash: Women and Politics in the Early American Republic* (Philadelphia, 2007).

5 Erin Mackie, *Market à la Mode: Fashion, Commodity, and Gender in "The Tatler" and "The Spectator"* (Baltimore, 1997).

6 Mary Wollstonecraft, *A Vindication of the Rights of Woman; with Strictures on Moral and Political Subjects*, 3rd ed. (London, 1796), 41, 53, 85–90.

7 Ibid. On the four-stage theory of human progress, see Rosemarie Zagarri, "Morals, Manners and the Republican Mother," *American Quarterly* 44 (June 1992): 197–203. On the tropes of body and appetite in Wollstonecraft's text, see Ewa Badowska, "The Anorexic Body of Liberal Feminism: Mary Wollstonecraft's *A Vindication of the Rights of Woman*," *Tulsa Studies in Women's Literature* 17 (Autumn 1998): 283–303.

8 Judith Sargent Murray, "On the Equality of the Sexes," in Sharon M. Harris, ed., *Selected Writings of Judith Sargent Murray* (New York, 1995), 4–5. On Murray's investment in social rank and as representative of the ways in which elite women claimed political identity and participation in the 1790s, see Jeanne Boydston, "Making Gender in the Early Republic: Judith Sargent Murray and the Revolution of 1800," in James Horn, Jan Ellen Lewis, and Peter S. Onuf, eds., *The Revolution of 1800: Democracy, Race, and the New Republic* (Charlottesville, Va., 2002), 240–66.

9 "The Salutatory Oration of Miss Mason," in *The Rise and Progress of the Young Ladies Academy* (Philadelphia, 1794), 94.

10 Stanley Elkins and Eric McKitrick, *The Age of Federalism; The Early American Republic, 1788–1800* (New York, 1993), 49. On salon culture in the 1790s, see Susan Branson, *These Fiery Frenchified Dames: Women and Political Culture in Early National Philadelphia* (Philadelphia, 2001), 125–42.

11 Margaret L. Brown, "Mr. and Mrs. William Bingham of Philadelphia: Rulers of the Republican Court," *PMHB* 61 (July 1937): 286–324. On Bingham, see also Branson, *These Fiery Frenchified Dames*, 125–42. On the republican court, see David Waldstreicher, "Federalism, the Styles of Politics, and the Politics of Style," in Doron Ben-Atar and Barbara B. Oberg, eds., *Federalism Reconsidered* (Charlottesville, Va., 1998), 104. On Parisian salons as a site of women's power in the ancien régime, see Dena Goodman, *The Republic of Letters: A Cultural History of the French Enlightenment* (Ithaca, N.Y., 1994), chaps. 3 and 6.

12 A.[bigail?] Hamilton to Sarah Franklin Bache, Philadelphia, November 25, 1792, Miscellaneous Manuscripts, APS. The marriage of Lucy Flucker to Henry Knox was a perfect union of old money and social position and new political clout. She was the daughter of wealthy Crown appointee Thomas Flucker, who founded Charles-

town, Massachusetts, and owned large pieces of property in Maine. Her family objected to her marriage to Knox in 1774 and fled with the loyalists the following year, while she followed her husband. Yet years later she would inherit the Maine property on which the Knoxes built their estate, Montpelier. See Diana Forbes-Robertson, "'Lady' Knox," *American Heritage Magazine* 17 (April 1966): 46–47, 74–79.

13 "Fashion," *National Gazette*, March 22, 1792. On fashion and political economy, see also Linzy A. Brekke, "'The Scourge of Fashion': Political Economy and the Politics of Consumption in the Early Republic," *Early American Studies* 3:1 (Spring 2005): 111–38.

14 Waldstreicher, "Federalism, the Styles of Politics, and the Politics of Style," 106–8.

15 *Pennsylvania Gazette*, May 7, 1789; May 13, 1789.

16 David Waldstreicher, *In the Midst of Perpetual Fetes: The Making of American Nationalism, 1776–1820* (Chapel Hill, N.C., 1997), 203. See also page 178 for a quote by Abraham Bishop about "well dressed" and "levee reveling" Federalists. According to Federalists, supporters of Democratic Republicans were part of an un-American, radical, Jacobin fringe. See Seth Cotlar, "The Federalists' Transatlantic Cultural Offensive of 1798 and the Moderation of American Democratic Discourse," in Pasley, Robertson, and Waldstreicher, *Beyond the Founders*, 274–99.

17 Catherine Sedgwick, *Tales and Sketches* (Philadelphia, 1835), 23–24. The pins were carried by the town horse, Clover, who, festooned with notes and banners from both parties, became an equine billboard, a "walking gazette."

18 *National Gazette*, December 26, 1792. On Federalists and women, see Waldstreicher, "Federalism, the Styles of Politics, and the Politics of Style," 114–15. On the role of discourses of fashion in juxtaposing republican and patrician culture, see Catherine E. Kelly, *In the New England Fashion: Reshaping Women's Lives in the Nineteenth Century* (Ithaca, N.Y., 1999), 219.

19 Lynn Hunt, *Politics, Culture, and Class in the French Revolution* (Berkeley, Calif., 1984), 52–86; Branson, *These Fiery Frenchified Dames*, 68–75, 80–87. Considering mind/body dualism, it is interesting that men wore cockades on their heads (hats) and women on their breasts.

20 "Thoughts on the Dress of American Ladies," *Columbian Magazine*, September 1787, 638–39; "On Dress, a Conversation Piece," *Lady's Magazine*, March/April 1793, 223, 225.

21 "General Observations on Fashion in Dress, with Particular Remarks on Certain Female Ornaments," *Universal Asylum*, April 1790, 217; "Letters to a Young Lady: Letter X, On Dress," *American Museum*, March 1792, 93; "Thought on the Dress of American Ladies," *Columbian Magazine*, September 1787, 638.

22 "Essay on Fashion," *Massachusetts Magazine*, September 1791, 551–52; "On Dress and Fashion," *Weekly Magazine*, February 3, 1798; "Fashion a Vision, in a Letter to a Young Lady," *New York Magazine*, November 1797, 578–79.

23 Winterer, *Mirror of Antiquity*, 117–25.

24 Waldstreicher, "Why Thomas Jefferson and African Americans Wore Their Politics on Their Sleeves," 84; Cotlar, "Federalists' Transatlantic Cultural Offensive," 293.

On the democratizing effects of the election of 1800, see Jeffrey L. Pasley, "1800 as a Revolution in Political Culture: Newspapers, Celebrations, Voting, and Democratization in the Early Republic," in Horn, Lewis, and Onuf, *Revolution of 1800*, 121–52.
25 "Remarks on Dress," *American Museum*, June 1789, 586.
26 Waldstreicher, "Why Thomas Jefferson and African Americans Wore Their Politics on Their Sleeves," 90. See also Shane White and Graham White, *Stylin': African American Expressive Culture from its Beginnings to the Zoot Suit* (Ithaca, N.Y., 1998), 85–124, and images in the University of Michigan's William L. Clement Library's exhibit *Reframing the Color Line: Race and Visual Culture of the Atlantic World*, ⟨http://www.clements.umich.edu/Exhibits/colorline/colorline.html⟩.

INDEX

Italicized page numbers indicate illustrations.

Adams, Abigail, 187–88, 211–12
Adams, John, 157, 161, 165–66, 211–12, 214, 261 (n. 18)
Adams, Nabby, 211–12
Adams, Samuel, 1–2, 162, 175, 178
Addison, Joseph, 49–51, 239 (n. 5)
African Americans, 4, 17, 25, 54, 219, 225. *See also* Enslaved men; Enslaved women; Self-emancipated slaves
Alexander, Mary (née Mary Spratt), 11, *12, 13*, 19–20, 33, 39–43, 45, 238 (n. 90)
American Revolutionary War, 5, 153–80. *See also* Colonial resistance; Culture wars/political loyalty; Political transformation post–American Revolution; Sacrifice ethic
Amusements/theater, 51, 126, 128, 145, 156, 166, 183, 209–10, 263 (n. 44)
Anne (queen), 17, 38, 52, 56
Antifashion for men, 225
Anti-luxury discourse, 82–83, 84, 93–94, 110–12, 249 (n. 51). *See also* Imported fabrics versus domestic cloth production
Arenas/settings for display, 14, 34–35, 46; balls/assemblies as, 38, 170, 172, 174, 178–79, 264 (n. 63), 265 (n. 86); churches as, 14–16, 51, 166, 192, 223; country houses and, 104–5; individual expressions of fashion and, 14–17

Balloon petticoats, 189–91, *190*
Balls/assemblies, 38–39, 170, 172, 174, 178–79, 264 (n. 63), 265 (n. 86)
Beekman, James, 42, 43–44, 45, 68, 238 (n. 89)

Bickerstaff, Isaac (pseud. for Richard Steele), 53, 54–56, 60
Binary gender system (dichotomous model), 50, 51, 239 (n. 7)
Blackburn, Joseph, 96, 97, *99*, 99–100
Body/body politic, 1–2, 5; adornment of, 60; antifashion for men and, 225; corsets and, 217, 219, 225; Democratic Republicanism and, 222–23; enslavement metaphor and, 219, 224; Federalism and, 220–23; feminization of fashion and, 219–20, 223–24; France/French and, 223; Grecian gowns paradox and, 217, 219, 224–25; imported fabrics versus domestic cloth production and, 221–23; independency of dress and, 223–24; masculine sensibility versus consumer society and, 225; mind/body dualism and, 219; nationhood and, 223–24; racialized, 219, 225; republicanism/fashion intersection and, 217, 220, 221–22, 224–25, 271 (n. 12); "review" of bodies of women and, 53–54; social power of women and, 217, 220–25, 271 (n. 12); symbolic significance of fashion and, 217, 219, 223; women and, 18, 51, 53–54, 89, 150
Boston, 3–4
Boycotts, 126, 127–28, 130, 151, 254 (n. 5), 256 (n. 34)
Boylston, Nicholas, 102
Boylston, Rebecca, 102, *103*
Bradford, Thomas, 64, 67, 76, 104
Britain/British, 3, 5; calico fashion and, 32–34; colonial connections with, 34–36, 38–41, 42, 74, 161–62, 261 (n. 18); con-

sumer society and, 1; court culture and, 75, 104, 106, 142, 188; crisis of colonial resistance and, 5, 7, 8, 82; economic stimulus of fashion and, 3; English Civil War of 1640s, 58; French and Indian War, 104, 243 (n. 66); French/Parisian fashion and, 36, 38, 42, 237 (n. 68); hairstyles and, 157, 191; Marriage Act of 1753, 85–86, 246 (n. 8); mercantilist system and, 35, 236 (n. 65); Meschianza and, 170, 172, *173*, 174, 264 (n. 63); military styles for British army/redcoats and, 154, 169, 170; plainness/sacrifice as fashionable for women and, 124–25; prostitution and, 148; Queen Anne's War, 17, 38, 56; Revenue Act, 105–7, 116, 128; robe à la anglaise and, 36; Stamp Act, 106–12, 115–16, 118–22, 126–27; Sugar Act, 105, 110, 116, 120; Townshend Acts, 118, 120–23, 128, 130, 150–51

British army/redcoats, 154, 169, 170, *171*, 172, 174, 264 (n. 63). *See also* Britain/British

Cadwalader, Anne, 131, *132*
Cadwalader, Elizabeth Lloyd, 128, 130–31, *132*, 139–40, 156
Cadwalader, John, 128, 130–31, *132*, 162
Callender, Hannah, 83–91, 116, 147, 246 (nn. 6–7), 248 (n. 34)
Caroline (queen), 35–36, 39–40, 42
Carson, Cary, 233 (n. 9)
Charleston, 3, 4
Chastellux, Marquis de, 175–76, 177, 178
Chesterfield, Earl of, 167–68, 210, 243 (n. 63), 262 (n. 38), 270 (n. 74)
Churches, and fashion displays, 14–16, 51, 166, 192, 223
Clarissa; or, The History of a Young Lady (Richardson), 88, 129, 246 (n. 7)
Cloth. *See* Fabric
Cockades, 9, *155*, 221, 223, 272 (n. 19)
Colonial elites, 4–5; balls/assemblies and, 38; counteridentification and, 20–21, 234 (n. 24); men's pursuit of fashion and, 67; personal identity of women and, 96, 100; personal identity through country styles and, 104–5; portraiture/art and, 100. *See also* Country fashion for colonial elites

Colonial resistance, 5; domestic economy and, 7, 105, 106, 107, 251 (n. 79), 252 (nn. 84–85); gender roles and, 7; gender/social propriety and, 118; homespun and, 8, 107, 109, 114–15, 252 (n. 85); imported fabrics versus domestic cloth production and, 110–12; masculine performances/identity and, 110, 252 (n. 100); masculine sensibility and, 5, 81–82; political power of men and, 110, 252 (n. 100); Quakerism and, 120; sacrifice ethic and, 118, 254 (n. 5), 254 (n. 9); social power of women and, 108–9; social status and, 7; tradespeople and, 110, 252 (n. 102). *See also* Country fashion, and colonial resistance; Sacrifice ethic

Conspicuous consumption, 130, 143–44; gender relations and, 142–43; hairdressers and, 138, 139, 142–43, 144, 147; high roll hairstyle and, 139, 142–43; lower class and, 131, 133, 142–43; marriage/fashion relationship and, 147; meritocracy and, 132–34; social status of men and, 133–35, 137–38, 257 (n. 53); social status of women and, 142–43; tailors and, 119, 128, 133–36, 138, 144, 147, 257 (n. 53); umbrellas and, 131, 133, 144, 257 (n. 51); Whigs and, 130–31. *See also* Macaroni style; Sacrifice ethic

Consumer society, 4, 5–6, 9; Britain/British and, 1; economic stimulus of consumption and, 1–2, 3, 5–6, 51, 53, 114–15, 208–9, 269 (n. 71); masculine sensibility versus, 225; meritocracy and, 84, 94, 114; political economy of fashion and, 7–8. *See also* Men's appetite for/control of fashion; Women's appetite for/control of fashion

Continental army, 154, 161, 163, 168–69, 170, 175, 184, 213; military styles and, 169–70, 174–75
Continental Association, 5, 156, 180

Continental Congress, 156, 162, 184
Contrast, The (Tyler), 209–12, 270 (n. 74), 270 (n. 78)
Control of fashion. *See* Men's appetite for/control of fashion; Women's appetite for/control of fashion
Copley, John Singleton, 96, 100, 101, 102, *103*
Coquettes, 47–48, 73, 74, 78, 109, 194–95
Corsets, 217, 219, 225
Counteridentification: individual expressions of fashion and, 20–22, 234 (n. 24); Quakerism and, 20–22, 121, 127, 186, 194–95, 234 (n. 24). *See also* Group identification
Country fashion, 8, 81–83, 115–16, 245 (n. 2); anti-luxury discourse and, 82–83, 84, 93–94, 249 (n. 51); domestic economy and, 82–83, 84, 93–94, 249 (n. 51); gender roles/social hierarchy and, 109; gender/social propriety and, 82; hairstyles of men and, 104; imported fabrics versus domestic cloth production and, 92–94, 249 (n. 45), 249 (n. 51); masculine sensibility and, 85, 89–90, 94; men's hairstyles and, 104; meritocracy and, 84, 87–88, 94, 114; military styles and, 96, 102, 104, 106; nationhood versus consumption of imported fabrics and, 92; pastoralism/poverty and, 92; political power of men and, 96, 99, 102, 104; power of fashion and, 116; Scottish Enlightenment and, 82, 89; social status and, 105, 109–10, 114–15, 251 (n. 73); social tension and, 105, 251 (n. 73); virtuous masculinity and, 90–91; women as scapegoat and, 114–15. *See also* Country fashion, and colonial resistance; Country fashion for colonial elites; Country fashion for women
Country fashion, and colonial resistance: domestic cloth production and, 112–13; domestic economy and, 105, 106, 107, 251 (n. 79), 252 (nn. 84–85); gender distinction/feminization of fashion and, 211; gender/social propriety and, 118; homespun consumption and, 107, 109, 114–15, 252 (n. 85); imported fabrics versus domestic cloth production, 110–12; legislation to raise funds through consumption of imported fabrics and, 105–12, 115–16, 251 (n. 79); masculine performances/identity and, 110, 252 (n. 100); men's appetite for/control of fashion and, 107–8, 109–10, 115; men's reform of women's appetite for fashion and, 113–14; political power of men and, 110, 252 (n. 100); social power of women and, 108–9, 113–14; tradespeople and, 110, 252 (n. 102); virtuous masculinity and, 110; women's appetite for/control of fashion and, 108–9, 113–14; women's reform of men's appetite for fashion and, 108–9, 113. *See also* Colonial resistance; Country fashion; Country fashion for colonial elites; Country fashion for women
Country fashion for colonial elites, 96, 104–5, 249 (n. 55); domestic discourse and, 99–100, 102, 104–5; gentility and, 96–97; homespun consumption and, 107, 109, 114–15, 252 (n. 85); marriage/women's country fashion relationship and, 100; men's appetite for/control of fashion and, 107–8, 109–10, 115; men's country fashion and, 96, 97, *98, 99*, 99–100; men's portraiture and, 96–97, *98, 99*, 99–100; pastoralism and, 96–97, 99, 99–100, *101*, 102, *103*, 105, 249 (n. 55); social status and, 106–7; women's appetite for/control of fashion and, 108–9; women's portraiture and, 96–97, 99, 99–100, *101*, 102, *103*. *See also* Colonial elites; Country fashion; Country fashion, and colonial resistance; Country fashion for women
Country fashion for women: class-specific female ideal and, 83–85, 246 (nn. 6–7); coquettish behavior and, 89; domestic discourse and, 84, 85, 91–93, 94, *95*, 96, 249 (n. 52); domestic labors of women and, 92–93, 94; economic power of

INDEX   277

women and, 85–86, 91, 247 (n. 11); education and, 84–85, 86, 89–92, 246 (n. 7), 248 (n. 29); gender roles/social status intersection and, 83–84; genteel femininity and, 83–85, 88–89, 246 (nn. 6–7); marriage relationship with, 85–88, 90–92, 94, 247 (n. 11), 248 (n. 34); sensibility and, 83–84, 246 (n. 6); social power of/blame placement paradox and, 114–15; social power of women and, 84–86, 91, 247 (n. 11); social status and, 92–93, 114–15; virtuous femininity and, 84, 86–88, 92–93, 94, 247 (n. 15), 249 (n. 52). *See also* Country fashion; Country fashion, and colonial resistance; Country fashion for colonial elites; Women

Culture wars/political loyalty, 8, 153–54, 179–80, 260 (n. 1); balls/assemblies and, 178–79, 265 (n. 86); domestic labors of women and, 265 (n. 78); foreign relations/social status and, 178, 180, 186–88; French military assistance/fashion influence and, 175–78; gender relations and, 163–65; hairstyles and, 157; imported fabrics versus homespun, 156–57; men's appetite for/control of fashion and, 165–66, 179–80, 263 (n. 44); Meschianza/balls and, 170, 172, 174, 264 (n. 63); military styles and, 157, 161–65, *164*, 176–77, 261 (n. 18); nationhood and, 175–80, 186–88, 264 (n. 75), 265 (n. 78), 265 (n. 86); republicanism and, 156–57, 161–64, 166–70, 172, 174–77, 261 (n. 18), 262 (n. 37), 263 (n. 44); social power of women and, 167–68, 172, 263 (n. 44); symbolic significance of fashion and, 206; Tories/loyalists and, 153–54, 165–66, 172, 174–75, 263 (n. 44), 263 (n. 59), 272 (n. 12); virtuous femininity and, 172; Whigs and, 153–54; women's appetite for/control of fashion and, 156–57, 166–67, 175–78, 262 (n. 37), 264 (n. 75), 265 (n. 78); women's loyalties and, 168–70, 172, 174–75; women's modest dress/lower-class confusion and, 166

Dandy. *See* Fops/foppery
Darlys prints, 135, 157, *157*, *160*, 258 (n. 63)
David Barclay and Sons, 42, 45
Democratic Republicanism, 8–9, 222–23, 272 (nn. 16–17)
DeWitt, Charles, 183–84, 186
Dichotomous model (binary gender system), 50, 51, 239 (n. 7)
Discursive practices of fashion, 3–4, 219–20, 227 (n. 6), 271 (n. 4)
Domestic cloth production. *See* Homespun; Imported fabrics versus domestic cloth production
Domestic discourse: country fashion for colonial elites and, 99–100, 102, 104–5; country fashion for women and, 84, 85, 91–93, 94, *95*, 96, 249 (n. 52); female sensibility and, 83–84; plainness/sacrifice as fashionable and, 123. *See also* Marriage
Domestic economy: anti-luxury discourse and, 82–83, 84, 93–94, 110–12, 249 (n. 51); colonial resistance and, 7, 105, 106, 107, 251 (n. 79), 252 (nn. 84–85); country fashion and, 82–83, 84, 93–94, 105, 106, 107, 249 (n. 51), 251 (n. 79), 252 (nn. 84–85); economic stimulus of fashion and, 1, 5–6; economic success and, 147–50; fashion and, 200–204; hairdressers and, 144; imported fabrics versus domestic cloth production, 82–83, 84, 93–94, 110–12, 249 (n. 51); linen manufactory and, 92, 107, 177, 249 (n. 45), 252 (n. 84), 265 (n. 78); meritocracy and, 84, 94, 147–50; nationhood and, 82–83, 84, 93–94, 212–16, 214–15, 216, 249 (n. 51); plainness/sacrifice as fashionable and, 120, 254 (n. 9); sacrifice ethic and, 147–50; smuggling and, 105, 236 (n. 65); social status of women and, 147–50; tailors and, 110, 144; women and, 94, 249 (n. 51). *See also* Homespun; Imported fabrics versus domestic cloth production

Domestic labors of women, 92–93, 94, 112–13, 123–24, 127, 204, 265 (n. 78)
Drinker, Sarah, 72–73

Economic power of women: country fashion for women and, 85–86, 91, 247 (n. 11); feminization of fashion and, 49, 51–52, 240 (n. 17); gender roles/social status intersection and, 51–52, 240 (n. 17); hoop petticoats and, 52, 53; women and, 4, 49, 51–53, 240 (n. 17); women's appetite for/control of fashion and, 51–52. *See also* Women
Economic stimulus of consumption, 1–2, 3, 5–6, 51, 53, 114–15, 208–9, 269 (n. 71)
Education for women, 84–86, 89–92, 193, 219, 246 (n. 7), 248 (n. 29)
Egalitarianism/democratic movement, 122, 126, 162, 207, 220, 223, 225
Empire gowns (Grecian gowns), 217, *218*, 219, 224–25
England/English. *See* Britain/British
Enslaved men: bodies of women under "review" by, 54; calico fabric and, 34; fashion of, 17, 34, 51; Meschianza and, 172; populations of, 4, 17; Slave Act of 1735, 25; slave fabric/"negro cloth" and, 25, 234 (n. 38), 235 (n. 44); sumptuary laws and, 25, 153; as virtuous, 126, 255 (n. 25). *See also* Men; Self-emancipated slaves
Enslaved women: enslavement metaphor, 219, 224; as fashionable, 25; fashion of, 34, 51; marketing of goods and, 24–25; personal/identity and, 24–25, 233 (n. 12); social status and, 24–25; stays in fashion and, 233 (n. 12); sumptuary laws and, 25, 153. *See also* Self-emancipated slaves; Women
Entwistle, Joanne, 6
Eve, Sarah, 117–18, 138, 139, 143, 147–50, 163

Fabric, 18–19; arenas/settings for display and, 35; British/colonial connections and, 36, 42; counteridentification and, 20–21; country fashion and, 96–97, *98*, *99*, 99–100, *101*, 102, *103*, 116; domestic cloth production and, 112–13; fashionability of, 18–19, 25, 232 (n. 2); French/Parisian fashion and, 36, *37*, 42; gender roles/social status intersection and, 18–19, 47, 65–66, 67–68, 70; legislation and, 106, 107; linen cloth and, 92, 107, 177, 249 (n. 45), 252 (n. 84), 265 (n. 78); literacy of fashion and, 27; men's portraiture and, 96–97, *98*, *99*, 99–100; mourning performance and, 39–41; plainness and, 21–22; political transformation post–American Revolution and, 182, 185, 187, 192, 199–200, 206–7; quality of, 21–22, 24; republicanism and, 182; sacrifice ethic and, 124, 128, 139; for slaves, 25, 234 (n. 38), 235 (n. 44); swatches for orders of, 11, *12*, *13*, 19–20, 27, 43, 231 (nn. 1–2), 233 (n. 22), 235 (n. 46); theft of, 24; transmittal of goods from colonies to Britain and, 243 (n. 63); underground economy of consumer goods and, 31; women's portraiture and, 96–97, *99*, 99–100, *101*, 102, *103*. *See also* Homespun; Hoop petticoats; Imported fabrics versus domestic cloth production; India/Indian fabric
Farmer ideal, 120–22
Fashionable Lover, The (Cumberland), 148, 150, 259 (n. 97)
Fashion paradox, 1–2, 4, 9, 65, 71–73, 227 (n. 2)
Federalism, 8–9; body/body politic and, 220–23, 272 (nn. 16–17); on Democratic Republicanism, 272 (n. 16); domestic cloth production and, 212–13; men's appetite for/control of fashion and, 222–23, 272 (n. 16); nationhood and, 212; political debates and, 205, 222; political reforms and, 204–9, 214; social power of women and, 220
Feke, Robert, 96, 97, *98*, 99
Feminization of fashion, 1, 2, 3, 6, 49–52; economic power of women and, 49,

51–52, 240 (n. 17); education of women and, 219; enslavement metaphor and, 219, 224; meritocracy and, 84; mourning performance and, 106; social power of women and, 2, 3, 51–52; symbolic significance of fashion and, 30, 49, 220; umbrellas and, 76, 131, 133. *See also* Feminization of men

Feminization of men, 73; fops/foppery and, 50; France/French and, 50, 93, 175; nonnormative sexuality and, 76–77, 138–39, 245 (n. 89), 258 (n. 69); paradox of fashion and, 1–2, 6; political reforms and, 50, 75, 175; pursuit of women and, 73, 74–76; self-emancipated slaves and, 30; sexual conquests and, 73–74; social status and, 73, 74, 133; tradespeople and, 122. *See also* Feminization of fashion

Fichu, 166, 192

Fops/foppery: conspicuous consumption and, 133, 135, 137–38; Democratic Republicanism and, 222; description of, 48, 75, 76, 77, 244 (n. 73), 245 (n. 89); feminization of men and, 50, 75, 175, 225; gender relations and, 76–77; imported fabrics versus domestic cloth production, 201; literacy of fashion and, 48, 74–75; masculine performances/identity and, 2, 75, 227 (n. 5); military styles and, 154, 162–65, *164*, 262 (n. 29); military styles compared with, 106; nationhood threats and, 1–2; negative influence of fashion on gender relations and, 74–75, 76–77; nonnormative sexuality and, 76–77, 245 (n. 89); paradox of fashion and, 1–2, 4; political reforms and, 206, 209, 222, 225, 262 (n. 29), 266 (n. 9); pursuit of women, and sexual appetite of, 75, 77, 78, 90, 168; republicanism and, 178; social power of/blame on women and, 77–78; social status and, 73, 76, 77, 78, 203; tradespeople and, 119; virtuous femininity compared with, 88–89

Foreign relations, and social status, 178, 180, 186–88, 194–95

France/French: body/body politic and, 223; court culture and, 57–58; fashion and, 36, *37*, 38, 42, 237 (n. 68); feminization of men and, 50, 93, 175, 222; foolish fashion/characteristics and, 50, 60, 188; French and Indian War, 104, 243 (n. 66); French army/alliance and, 104, 175–76, 178–79; gender/social propriety and, 191; hairstyles/hairdressers and, 187, 191; high roll hairstyle and, 178; hoop petticoats critiques and, 57–58; men's ambivalence about fashion and, 186–88; military styles of men's fashion and, 104; mourning performance and, 187–88; prostitution and, 58; Queen Anne's War, 17, 38, 56; robe à la française and, 36, *37*, *37*; servants' fashion and, 188; women's fashion and, 166, 177–78, 181, 243 (n. 66)

Franklin, Benjamin (pseud. Poor Richard): on counteridentification, 20, 186; on domestic economy, 106, 110–11; on fashion, 71; on fops/foppery, 75; on hoop petticoats' benefits, 60, 62, 242 (n. 43); on imported fabrics versus domestic cloth production, 110–12; on men's ambivalence in fashion choices, 185–86; men's attraction to women based on fashion and, 71, 243 (n. 66); men's pursuit of fashion and, 69; on "plainness" in Quaker fashion, 186; *Poor Richard's Almanack*, 65, 69, 87, 89–93, 107, 145, 185–86, 259 (n. 87); socioeconomic consequences of consumer society and, 82–83, 84, 93–94

Franklin, Benjamin "Billy," 71–72, 243 (n. 67)

Franks, Rebecca, 174, 179, 264 (n. 63)

French and Indian War (Seven Years' War), 5, 8, 83, 96, 104–6, 161, 243 (n. 66)

French/France. *See* France/French

Freneau, Philip, 163–64

"Fribble," 75–77, 244 (n. 81)

Frontier-style fashion, 8, 28, 96, 161, 165

Galloway, Jane, 100, 102
Gender bending, 52, 58, 59, 138–39, 258 (nn. 69–70)
Gendered performance: domestic labors of women and, 112–13; "fribble" described, 75–77, 244 (n. 81); gender bending and, 52, 58, 59, 138–39, 258 (nn. 69–70); nationhood/political order and, 2; social influence and, 2, 46. *See also* Gender relations; Gender roles; Gender roles/social status intersection; Gender/social propriety
Gender relations, 3; balls/assemblies and, 38–39; gender roles/social status intersection and, 6, 48–49, 76; hoop petticoats and, 59, 64; negative influence of fashion on, 72–78; social status and, 78–79; wigs/periwigs and, 59, 64. *See also* Gendered performance; Gender roles; Gender roles/social status intersection; Gender/social propriety
Gender roles, 2–3, 4, 6; binary gender system and, 50, 51, 239 (n. 7); calico fashion and, 33–34; economic conflicts and, 3; feminization of fashion and, 50–51, 240 (n. 17); political conflicts and, 3, 4, 5; social conflicts and, 3, 4; social fluidity and, 50. *See also* Gendered performance; Gender relations; Gender roles/social status intersection; Gender/social propriety
Gender roles/social status intersection, 7, 47–49, 52, 73–74, 78–79; binary gender system and, 50, 239 (n. 7); consumer appetites of women and, 51–52; coquettes and, 47–48, 73, 74, 78; country fashion for women and, 83–84; economic power of women and, 51–52, 240 (n. 17); feminization of fashion and, 49–52; foppery and, 74–77; gendered social taxonomy and, 47–48; gender relations and, 48–49, 59, 64, 73, 78–79; gender/social propriety and, 52; hoop petticoats and, 47, 52–60, 62, 64; literacy of fashion and, 47–48; sexuality and, 49; social power of women and, 51–52, 77–78, 240 (n. 17); wigs/periwigs and, 58–60, 62, 63, 64–65; women as scapegoat and, 51; women's appetite for/control of fashion and, 240 (n. 15), 243 (n. 17). *See also* Fops/foppery; Gendered performance; Gender relations; Gender roles; Gender/social propriety
Gender/social propriety: colonial resistance and, 118; country fashion and, 82, 118; feminine/fashionability contradictions and, 144–47, 259 (n. 87); France/French and, 191; gender roles/social status intersection and, 52; high roll hairstyle and, 176; macaroni style and, 176, 180; nationhood and, 186–88, 195; political transformation post–American Revolution and, 186–88, 191, 195. *See also* Gendered performance; Gender relations; Gender roles; Gender roles/social status intersection
Godbeer, Richard, 58–59
Graeme, Elizabeth, 71–72, 243 (n. 67)
Grecian gowns (empire gowns), 217, 218, 219, 224–25
Group identification, 17–18, 20–22, 234 (n. 24). *See also* Counteridentification

Hairstyles/hairdressers: conspicuous consumption and, 138, 139, 142–43, 144, 147; domestic economy and, 144; fashionability and, 119, 147; French fashion and, 187, 191, 194; social status and, 142–43, 194. *See also* High roll hairstyle; Macaroni style; Wigs/periwigs
Hamilton, Alexander, federal politics/commerce debates and, 222; Tariff of 1789 and, 214–15, 216
Hamilton, Alexander, Dr.: on coquettes, 78; on cost of fashion, 22; on counteridentification, 20–21, 234 (n. 24); on fashion dos and don'ts, 47; on fops/foppery, 76, 77; literacy of fashion and, 48; on power of fashion, 64–65; on settings for display, 15–16

INDEX 281

High roll hairstyle: conspicuous consumption and, 139, 142–43; culture wars/political loyalty and, 156–57, 170, 172, 174, 176–78, 264 (n. 75); gender/social propriety and, 176; lower-class women and, 174; nationhood and, 176–78, 264 (n. 75); sacrifice ethic and, 139, 142–43; social status and, 174; symbolic significance of fashion and, 144; Tories/loyalists and, 172, 174; Whigs on, 172, 174. *See also* Hairstyles/hairdressers

Hogarth, William, 62, *63*, 242 (n. 46)

Homespun: colonial resistance and, 8, 107, 109, 114–15, 252 (n. 85); country fashion and, 107, 109, 252 (n. 85); as fashion, 107, 109, 114–15, 252 (n. 85); imported fabrics versus, 19, 34, 107, 115–16, 156–57; men's consumption of, 107, 109, 252 (n. 85); robe à la polonaise style and, 189–91, *190*; women's consumption of, 109, 114–15

Hoop petticoats, 52–53, 62, 64, 240 (n. 19); attraction/repulsion dynamic and, 52, 53–54; bodies of women under review and, 53–54, *55*; Boston and, 56; Britain and, 54–56; critiques, 56–58, 59, 60, *61*, 241 (n. 41); economic power of women and, 52, 53; as economic stimulus, 53; France/French mode and, 58, 59–60, 241 (n. 35); gender bending and, 58; gender relations and, 59, 60, 64; male fears and, 52; men's sexual appetite and, 59–60; military metaphors in defense of, 56; prostitution and, 58, 62; regulations of fashion and, 54–56; satire on critiques, 60, 62, 242 (n. 43); sexuality and, 52, 53, 58; social power of women and, 52, 53, 58; social status of women and, 58; trial lampoon of, 53–56, *55*

Identity. *See* Individual expressions of fashion

Imperial court. *See* Britain/British

Imported fabrics versus domestic cloth production: anti-luxury discourse and, 82–83, 84, 93–94, 110–12, 249 (n. 51); body/body politic and, 221–23; colonial resistance and, 110–12; country fashion and, 92–94, 110–12, 249 (n. 45), 249 (n. 51); domestic economy, 82–83, 84, 93–94, 110–12, 249 (n. 51); nationhood, 82–83, 84, 92, 93–94, 249 (n. 51); plainness/sacrifice as fashionable and, 123–24, 127; political transformation post–American Revolution and, 200–202, *201–2*, *203*, *204*; trade cards and, *215*

Independency of dress, 223–24

India/Indian fabrics: calico, 19, 31–33, 236 (n. 56), 236 (n. 59); country fashion and, 93, 105, 252 (n. 92); culture wars/political loyalty and, 156; hoop petticoats and, 53; individual expressions of fashion and, 42; thefts of goods and, 25–26

Individual expressions of fashion, 7, 11, 13–14, 46; balls/assemblies and, 38–39; British/colonial connections and, 34–36, 38–41, 42; calico fashion and, 31–34, 236 (n. 56); counteridentification and, 20–22, 234 (n. 24); demand/supply for goods and, 17, 233 (n. 9); enslaved women and, 24–25, 233 (n. 12); fabric as fashion and, 18–19, 25; fabric/fabric swatches and patterns demands and, 11, *12*, *13*, 19–20, 27, 43, 231 (nn. 1–2), 233 (n. 22), 235 (n. 46); fabric for slaves and, 25, 234 (n. 38); female fashion for self-emancipated slaves and, 30–31, 235 (n. 53); feminization of fashion and, 50–51; feminized self-emancipated males and, 30; French/Parisian fashion and, 36, *37*, 38, 42, 237 (n. 68); gender intersection/men and, 21–22, 25–27, 33, 39–40, 235 (n. 44); gender intersection/women and, 24–26, 30–31; group identification and, 17–18, 20–22, 234 (n. 24); imported fabrics versus homespun, 19, 34; income from theft of goods and, 25–26, 27; literacy of fashion and, 27–30, 34; mercantilist system and, 35, 236 (n. 65); mourning performance and, 39–41; personal identity and, 11, 13,

282 INDEX

17–18, 28–29; physical characteristics/ appearances of self-emancipated slaves and, 27–30, 235 (n. 46); populations of color and, 17; self-emancipated slaves and, 26, 28–31, 235 (n. 46), 235 (n. 53); settings for display and, 14–17; smuggling and, 236 (n. 65); social fluidity and, 4, 17, 34; social status and, 11, 13, 17–31; status from reversal of fashion for self-emancipated slaves and, 29–30; status from theft of goods for self-emancipated slaves and, 26, 28; stays/stay makers and, 18, 233 (n. 12); style preferences of colonials and, 41–46, 238 (nn. 89–90); theft of goods and, 22–24, 25–26, 28, 234 (n. 3); transatlantic perspectives and, 45; underground economy of consumer goods and, 22–27, 234 (n. 3). *See also* Culture wars/political loyalty

Jefferson, Thomas, 128, 187–88, 222, 225, 271 (n. 3)
Junto/Leather Apron Club, 20, 234 (n. 23)

Kalm, Peter, 22
Knox, Henry, 221–22, 271 (n. 12)
Knox, Lucy Flucker, 221–22, 271 (n. 12)

Language of fashion, 6, 11, 29–30, 35, 235 (n. 50)
Lay, Benjamin, 22, 23
Lee, Richard Henry, 174, 184–85
Legislation: Marriage Act of 1753, 85–86, 246 (n. 8); Revenue Act, 105–7, 116, 128; Slave Act of 1735, 25; Stamp Act, 106–12, 115–16, 118–22, 126–27; Sugar Act, 105, 110, 116, 120; Townshend Acts, 118, 120–23, 128, 130, 150–51
Linen manufactory, 92, 107, 177, 249 (n. 45), 252 (n. 84), 265 (n. 78)
Lipovetsky, Gilles, 6
Literacy of fashion, 27–30, 34, 47–48, 74–75, 78
Livingston, Henry, 70
Livingston, Philip, 45

Livingston, Robert R., 81, 82–83, 113–15
Lower-class women: conspicuous consumption and, 131, 257 (n. 51); Continental army compared with, 174–75; culture wars/political loyalty and, 166; high roll hairstyle and, 174; modest dress confusion with, 166; plainness/sacrifice as fashionable and, 124; social power of/ blame placement paradox and, 114–15; social status and, 1, 2, 30–31, 51, 58, 62, 92–93, 114, 148; virtuous femininity of, 124. *See also* Enslaved women; Prostitutes/prostitution; Self-emancipated slaves; Women
Loyalists/Tories, 153–54, 165–66, 172, 174–75, 263 (n. 44), 263 (n. 59), 272 (n. 12)
Lucas, Eliza, 69–70, 243 (n. 63)

Macaroni style: gender bending and, 138–39, 258 (nn. 69–70), 258 (n. 70); gender/social propriety and, 176, 180; "macaronesses" women's hairstyle and, 138–39, 157, *158*, 258 (n. 70); men's conspicuous consumption and, 135, *136*, 137–39, 258 (nn. 69–70); military styles and, 162–63; nonnormative sexuality and, 138–39, 258 (n. 69); satires/folly and, 135, *136*, 157, *158*, *159*, *160*, 257 (n. 62), 258 (n. 70); social status and, 137–38; symbolic significance of fashion and, 138; tarring and feathering/"macaroni making" and, 153–54, *155*; women's conspicuous consumption and, 138–39, 157, *158*, 258 (n. 70)
Madison, James, 205, 222
Mandeville, Bernard, 1, 2, 51
Marriage: as allegory for nationhood, 209–12, 270 (n. 78); country fashion and, 85–86, 87–88, 90–91, 100, 247 (n. 11), 248 (n. 34); domestic labors of women and, 90, 92, 94; education of women and, 90, 92; female sensibility and, 193–94, 195; gender roles/social status intersection and, 73, 74; social status/

INDEX 283

politics and, 221–22, 271 (n. 12). *See also* Domestic discourse

Marriage Act of 1753, 85–86, 246 (n. 8)

Martial styles. *See* Military styles

Masculine performances/identity: colonial resistance and, 110, 252 (n. 100); conspicuous consumption and, 133; country fashion and, 110, 252 (n. 100); farmer ideal and, 120–22; fops/foppery and, 2, 75, 227 (n. 5); men's pursuit of fashion and, 65; meritocracy and, 84; military styles and, 75, 96, 102, 106; personal identity and, 6, 9; plainness/sacrifice as fashionable and, 120–22; politics and, 9; wigs/periwigs/perukes and, 59. *See also* Masculine sensibility; Men; Men's appetite for/control of fashion; Men's pursuit of fashion

Masculine sensibility, 4, 82; body/body politic and, 225; colonial resistance and, 5, 81–82; country fashion and, 85, 89–90, 94; language of fashion and, 6; plainness/sacrifice as fashionable and, 120, 122; political transformation post–American Revolution and, 208–9. *See also* Men

Men: ambivalence about French fashion and, 186–88; ambivalence in fashion choices post-Revolution and, 182–86; antifashion and, 225; appetites for/control of fashion and, 109–10, 113, 115, 165–66; attraction to women based on fashion and, 71, 243 (n. 66); body/body politic and, 185; cross-class sexual indiscretions and, 33; hairstyles of, 104; homespun consumption and, 107, 109, 252 (n. 85); portraiture in country fashion and, 96–97, 98, 99, 99–100; productive role for, 50, 51, 239 (n. 7); public space and, 50, 51, 239 (n. 7); sexual appetite of, 33, 59–60, 73–78, 90, 168; virtuous masculinity and, 90–91, 110, 124; women's sexual appetite, and pursuit of, 73, 74, 78. *See also* Domestic discourse; Enslaved men; Feminization of men; Gender roles; Gender roles/social status intersection; Macaroni style; Marriage; Masculine sensibility; Masculine performances/identity; Men's appetite for/control of fashion; Men's pursuit of fashion; Political power of men; Self-emancipated slaves; Wigs/periwigs

Men's appetite for/control of fashion: country fashion for colonial elites and, 107–8, 109–10, 115; culture wars/political loyalty and, 165–66, 179–80, 263 (n. 44); Federalism and, 222–23, 272 (n. 16); women's reform of, 108–9, 113, 123, 124. *See also* Macaroni style; Masculine sensibility; Men; Men's pursuit of fashion; Wigs/periwigs

Men's pursuit of fashion, 3, 64, 73; appetite for/control of fashion and, 113; British/colonial connections and, 67–69, 243 (n. 55); calico fashion and, 33; counteridentification and, 21–22; country fashion and, 102, 104, 106; description of fashions and, 65–67, 242 (nn. 53–54); "fribble" described, 75–77, 244 (n. 81); gender ambiguity and, 75–77; gender relations and, 67, 70, 71–73, 243 (n. 67); hairstyles of, 104; imported fabrics and, 67, 242 (n. 54); income generation from theft of goods and, 25–26; masculine performances/identity and, 65; men's advice and, 69–71; military styles and, 102, 104, 106; mourning performance and, 39–40; power and importance of fashion and, 64–65, 242 (n. 50); shape of male figure and, 65; social power of women and, 70; social relations and, 64–65, 67; social status and, 25–26, 65; tailors and, 67–68; tradespeople and, 64, 67–68, 243 (n. 55); transmittal of goods from Britain for women and, 69–70; wigs/periwigs and, 65, 67, 76. *See also* Macaroni style; Masculine sensibility; Men; Men's appetite for/control of fashion; Wigs/periwigs

Meritocracy: consumer society and, 84, 94, 114; country fashion and, 84, 87–88, 94, 114; domestic economy and, 84, 94,

147–50; economic success and, 147–50; masculine performances/identity and, 84; virtuous femininity and, 84, 94, 249 (n. 51)

Meschianza, 170, 172, *173*, 174, 178–79, 264 (n. 63), 265 (n. 86)

Military styles: for British army/redcoats, 154, 169, 170, *171*; Continental army and, 169–70, 174–75; country fashion and, 96, 102, 104, 106; fops/foppery compared with, 106; hairstyles for men and, 104, 162–63; lower class and, 174–75, 264 (n. 63); macaroni style and, 162–63; masculine performances/identity and, 75, 96, 102, 106; men's pursuit of fashion and, 102, 104, 106; paradox of fashion and, 1–2; republicanism and, 157, 161–65, *164*, 261 (n. 18)

Mind/body dualism, 219

Morality of men. *See* Virtuous masculinity

Morality of women. *See* Virtuous femininity

Mourning performance, 39–41, 106, 166–67, 187–88, 262 (n. 29)

Nationhood: anti-luxury discourse and, 82–83, 84, 93–94, 249 (n. 51); balls/assemblies and, 178–79, 265 (n. 86); body/body politic and, 223–24; British fashion and, 198; country fashion and, 92; culture wars/political loyalty and, 175–80, 186–88, 264 (n. 75), 265 (n. 78), 265 (n. 86); domestic economy and, 82–83, 84, 93–94, 212–16, 214–15, 216, 249 (n. 51); domestic labors of women and, 265 (n. 78); foreign relations and, 186–88, 194–95; foreign relations/social status and, 178, 180, 186–88, 194–95; French military assistance/fashion influence and, 175–78; gender/social propriety and, 186–88, 195; imported fabrics versus domestic cloth production, 92; independency of dress and, 223–24; Marriage Act of 1753, 246 (n. 8); marriage as allegory for, 209–12, 270 (n. 78); men's appetite for/control of fashion and, 179–80; military styles and, 176–77; paradox of fashion and, 1–2; republicanism/political loyalties balances with, 175–77; social influence and, 2; social power of women and, 223–24; social status and, 186–88, 194–95; women's appetite for/control of fashion and, 175–78, 264 (n. 75), 265 (n. 78)

"Negro cloth" (fabric for slaves), 25, 234 (n. 38), 235 (n. 44)

New York, 3, 4

Nonconsumption: country fashion and, 83, 109, 113–16, 245 (n. 2), 252 (n. 88); culture wars/political loyalty and, 156, 180; political transformation post–American Revolution and, 201; sacrifice ethic and, 118–20, 121, 123–30, 150–51, 255 (n. 15). *See also* Imported fabrics versus domestic cloth production; Men's appetite for/control of fashion; Women's appetite for/control of fashion

Nonimportation, 112, 113, 118–21, 126–28, 134, 150–51, 156, 246 (n. 4)

Nonnormative sexuality, 76–77, 138–39, 245 (n. 89), 258 (n. 69)

Norris, Debby, 168–70

Pacheco, Roderigo, 39–42

Pamela; or, Virtue Rewarded (Richardson), 88, 248 (n. 21)

Parke, Daniel, II, 66, 67

Pastoralism: balloon petticoats and, 189–91, *190*; country fashion and, 92; country fashion for colonial elites and, 96–97, 99, 99–100, *101*, 102, *103*, 105, 249 (n. 55)

Perukes (wigs/periwigs). *See* Wigs/periwigs

Philadelphia, 3, 4

Pickney, Eliza Lucas, 69–70, 84, 89, 90–91, 243 (n. 63)

Plainness/sacrifice as fashionable, 8, 119–20, 129–30; amusements and, 125–26; colonial elite's appetite for/control of fashion and, 128; domestic discourse and, 123; domestic economy and, 120, 254 (n. 9); domestic labors of women and,

INDEX 285

123–24, 127; egalitarianism and, 126; enslaved men and, 126, 255 (n. 25); farmer ideal and, 120–22; female sensibility and, 123; homespun and, 124, 127; imported fabrics versus domestic cloth production and, 123–24, 127; masculine performances/identity and, 120–22; masculine sensibility and, 120, 122; men's reform of women's appetite for/control of fashion and, 255 (n. 15); mourning performance and, 128–29; social power of women and, 123; social status and, 123–24, 126, 127, 128–29; tradespeople and, 120–21, 122, 126–27, 254 (n. 9); virtuous femininity and, 124; virtuous masculinity and, 124; women's appetite for/control of fashion and, 122–25, 255 (n. 15); women's reform of men's appetite for fashion and, 123, 124. *See also* Sacrifice ethic

Political loyalty. *See* Culture wars/political loyalty; Political transformation post–American Revolution

Political power of men, 3, 9, 227 (n. 6); colonial resistance and, 110, 252 (n. 100); country fashion and, 96, 99, 102, 104, 106; military styles and, 96, 102, 106; nationhood and, 2; social influence and, 2. *See also* Culture wars/political loyalty; Politics

Political reforms: Federalism and, 204–9, 214; feminization of men and, 50, 75, 175; fops/foppery and, 206, 209, 222, 225, 262 (n. 29), 266 (n. 9); political transformation post–American Revolution and, 204–9. *See also* Politics

Political transformation post–American Revolution, 8, 181–82, 216; balloon petticoats/pastoralism and, 189–91, *190*; British fashion and, 198; British women's fashion and hairstyles and, 187; consumption and, 200–209; domestic economy and, 212–16; domestic economy/fashion intersection and, 200–204; domestic labors of women and, 204; education of women and, 193; Federalism and, 204–9, 212–14; female sensibility and, 193–94, 195; foreign relations and, 186–88, 194–95; French fashion and, 186–88; gender/social propriety and, 186–88, 190, 195; hairstyles and, 191; imported fabrics versus domestic cloth production and, 200–202, 203, 204; individual expressions of fashion and, 204–7; marriage and, 193–94, 195; marriage as allegory for, 209–12, 270 (n. 78); marriage/fashion relationship and, 193–94, 195; marriage/social status conflicts and, 207; masculine sensibility and, 208–9; men's ambivalence about fashion and, 182–88; men's reform of women's appetite for/control of fashion and, 203–4; meritocracy and, 202–3; mourning dress and, 201–2; nationhood and, 186–88, 194–95, 198, 209–12, 270 (n. 78); political reforms and, 204–9; robe à la polonaise and, 189–91, *190*; social fluidity and, 202–3; social power of women and, 206; social status and, 186–88, 194–95, 202–3, 207; trade card for imported fabrics and, *215*; virtuous femininity and, 193–94, 195, 203–4; women and, 182–91, *190*, 192–99, 208–9, 268 (n. 32), 269 (n. 71); women as scapegoat and, 208–9, 269 (n. 71); women's ambivalence about fashion and, 188–90, 192–99, 208–9, 268 (n. 32); women's fashion choices and, 182–86, 192–93. *See also* Politics

Politics, 2, 3, 5, 8–9; Democratic Republicanism and, 8–9, 222–23, 272 (nn. 16–17); gender roles and, 9. *See also* Body/body politic; Culture wars/political loyalty; Federalism; Political power of men; Political reforms; Political transformation post–American Revolution; Republicanism

Pollard, William, 44, 45, 109, 112, 131, 139, 238 (n. 96)

Poor Richard's Almanack (Franklin), 65, 69, 87, 89–93, 107, 145, 185–86, 259 (n. 87)

Portraiture, and country fashion, 96–97, *98*, *99*, 99–100, *101*, 102, *103*
Pringle, Robert, 43–45, 64, 68–69, 239 (n. 98)
Propriety. *See* Gender/social propriety
Prostitutes/prostitution: Britain/British and, 148; Continental army compared with, 174–75; France/French and, 58; high roll hairstyle and, 174; hoop petticoats and, 58, 62; social status and, 1, 2, 58, 62, 148, 174. *See also* Morality of women
Public space, 50, 51, 239 (n. 7). *See also* Domestic discourse
Puritans, 3, 58–59, 60, 241 (n. 38)

Quakerism, 4; colonial resistance and, 120; coquettes and, 194–95; counteridentification and, 20–22, 121, 127, 186, 194–95, 234 (n. 24); republicanism and, 157
Queen Anne's War, 17, 38, 56

Racialized fashion, 219, 225
Redcoats/British army, 154, 169, 170, *171*, 172, 174, 264 (n. 63)
Reed, Esther De Berdt, 131, 157, 161–62, 177, 265 (n. 78)
Republicanism, 5, 8–9; culture wars/political loyalty and, 156–57, 161–65, 166–70, 172, 174–75, 261 (n. 18), 262 (n. 37), 263 (n. 44); fashion intersection with, 217, 220, 221–22, 224–25, 271 (n. 12); gender relations control and, 163–65; Grecian gowns paradox and, 217, *218*, 219, 224–25; hairstyles and, 157, 172; high roll hairstyle as sign of Tories/loyalists and, 172, 174; imported fabrics versus homespun and, 156–57; military styles and, 157, 161–65, *164*, 261 (n. 18); social power of women and, 167–68, 172, 263 (n. 44); virtuous femininity and, 172; Whigs and, 157, 163–64; women and, 166, 168–70, *171*, 172, 174–75; women's appetite for/control of fashion and, 156–57, *158*–60, 166–67, 262 (n. 37). *See also* Whigs

Revenue Act, 105–7, 116, 128
Robe à la anglaise, 36
Robe à la française, 36, *37*
Robe à la polonaise, 189–91, *190*
Robin, Abbé, 162, 166, 177–78, 183, 186
Rush, Benjamin, 150, 178–79, 208, 265 (n. 86)

Sacrifice ethic, 8, 117–19, 130, 143–44, 150–51, 253 (nn. 2, 4), 254 (n. 5); boycotts and, 126, 127–28, 130, 151, 254 (n. 5), 256 (n. 34); colonial resistance and, 118, 254 (n. 5), 254 (n. 9); domestic economy and, 147–50; feminine propriety/fashionability contradictions and, 144–47, 259 (n. 87); gender relations and, 142–43; hairdressers and, 138, *139*, 142–43, 144, 147; legislation to raise funds through consumption of imported fabrics and, 118, 120–23, 128, 130, 150–51; lower class and, 131, 133, 142–43; macaroni style and, 135, 137–39, 143–44, 145, 147, 151, 257 (n. 62), 258 (n. 63), 258 (nn. 69–70); marriage/fashion relationship and, 147; meritocracy and, 132–34, 147–50; social status for men and, 133–35, 137–38, 257 (n. 53); social status of women and, 142–43, 147–50; tailors and, 119, 128, 133–36, 138, 144, 147, 257 (n. 53); umbrellas and, 131, 133, 144, 257 (n. 51); Whigs and, 130–31. *See also* Colonial resistance; Conspicuous consumption
Scottish Enlightenment, 82, 89
Self-emancipated slaves, 4; fashion of, 11, 17, 26, 34; female fashion and, 235 (n. 53); feminization of men and, 30; income generation from theft of goods and, 26–27, 257 (n. 51); language of fashion and, 29, 235 (n. 50); literacy of fashion and, 27–30; personal identity of, 28–29; physical characteristics/appearances of, 27–30, 235 (n. 46); reversal of fashion and, 29–30; social status and, 26–30; status from theft of goods and, 26–27, 28; women's fashion and, 30–31, 34

INDEX 287

Servants, 17, 34, 51, 54, 166, 187–88, 257 (n. 51)

Settings/arenas for display. *See* Arenas/settings for display

Seven Years' War (French and Indian War), 5, 8, 83, 96, 104–6, 161, 243 (n. 66)

Sexuality: fops' sexual appetite and, 75, 77, 78, 90, 168; gender roles/social status intersection and, 49; hoop petticoats and, 52, 53, 58; men's sexual appetite, 33, 59–60, 73–78, 90, 168; nonnormative and, 76–77, 138–39, 245 (n. 89), 258 (n. 69); women's sexual appetite and, 73, 74, 78

Shields, David S., 15

Shoemaker, Samuel, 199

Short gown, 27, 166, 169, 195–96, 198, 263 (n. 48), 268 (n. 42)

Slave fabric ("negro cloth"), 25, 234 (n. 38), 235 (n. 44)

Smith, Adam, 118

Smith, William, Jr., 15, 45–46

Smith, Willy, 172, 174

Smuggling, 105, 236 (n. 65)

Social fluidity, 4, 17, 34, 48, 50, 203

Social/gender propriety. *See* Gender/social propriety

Social hierarchy. *See* Social status

Social influence, 2, 46

Social order. *See* Social status

Social power of women, 2; body/body politic and, 217, 220–25, 271 (n. 12); colonial resistance and, 108–9, 113–14; country fashion and, 108–9, 113–14; country fashion for women and, 84–86, 91, 247 (n. 11); culture wars/political loyalty and, 167–68, 172, 263 (n. 44); Federalism and, 220; hoop petticoats and, 52, 53, 58; meritocracy versus, 84, 114; nationhood and, 223–24; plainness/sacrifice as fashionable and, 123; political transformation post–American Revolution and, 206; republicanism and, 167–68, 172, 263 (n. 44); social influence and, 46; women as scapegoat and, 51, 114–15, 208–9, 269 (n. 71)

Social status, 1, 2, 3, 4, 5, 9, 17, 31; British/colonial connections and, 38; calico fashion and, 33–34; conspicuous consumption and, 133; coquettes and, 73, 74, 78; counteridentification and, 20–22, 234 (n. 24); country fashion and, 105, 109–10, 114–15, 251 (n. 73); domestic labors of women and, 92–93, 112–13, 123–24, 127; economic links with, 7; enslaved women and, 24–25; fabric as fashion and, 18–19; feminization of fashion and, 6; foreign relations and, 178, 180, 186–88, 194–95; gender roles intersection with, 6; high roll hairstyle and, 174; hoop petticoats and, 58; literacy of fashion and, 27–30, 34; marketing of goods by enslaved women/bondswomen and, 24–25; men's appetite for/control of fashion and, 109–10, 115; men's pursuit of fashion and, 65; meritocracy versus, 84, 116; mourning performance and, 128–29; paradox of fashion and, 1–2, 5–6; reversal of fashion and, 29–30; self-emancipated slaves and, 26–30; social fluidity and, 4, 17, 34, 48, 203; social tension and, 105, 251 (n. 73); stays for erect stance and, 18, 47, 233 (n. 12); tailors and, 133–35, 257 (n. 53); theft of goods to alter, 25–28; women as scapegoat and, 114–15. *See also* Enslaved men; Enslaved women; Fops/foppery; Gender roles; Gender roles/social status intersection; Individual expressions of fashion; Lower-class women; Macaroni style

Social status of women: conspicuous consumption and, 142–43; domestic economy and, 147–50; sacrifice ethic and, 142–43, 147–50

Spectator, The (periodical), 49–51, 239 (n. 5)

Spratt, Mary (Mary Alexander), 33, 39–43, 45, 238 (n. 90)

Stamp Act, 106–12, 115–16, 118–22, 126–27

Stays/stay makers, 18, 47, 196, 217, 233 (n. 12)
Steele, Richard (pseud. Isaac Bickerstaff), 50, 53, 54–56, 60, 239 (n. 5)
Stoddard, Solomon, 59, 60, *61*, 241 (n. 41)
Sugar Act, 105, 110, 116, 120
Sumptuary laws, 25, 33, 153, 206, 207, 214–16, 240 (n. 19)
Symbolic significance of fashion, 3, 6, 7, 228 (n. 7); body/body politic and, 217, 219, 223; cockades and, 9, *155*, 221, 223, 272, 272 (n. 19); culture wars/political loyalty and, 206; eagle and, 206, *215*, 223, 272 (n. 17); feminization of fashion and, 30, 49, 220; hairstyles and, 138, 144; plainness/sacrifice as fashionable and, 130

Tailors: domestic economy and, 110, 144; fashionability and, 65, 76, 104, 108, 119, 128, 133, 138, 147; social status and, 67–69, 76, 133–36, 243 (n. 55), 257 (n. 53). *See also* Tradespeople
Tariff of 1789, 214–15, 216
Tarring and feathering/"macaroni making," 153–54, *155*
Tatler, The (periodical), 50, 53, 54–56, 60, 239 (n. 5)
Taylor, Jacob, 59–60
Theater/amusements, 51, 126, 128, 145, 156, 166, 183, 209–10, 263 (n. 44)
Theft of goods, 25–28, 257 (n. 51)
Tories/loyalists, 153–54, 165–66, 172, 174–75, 263 (n. 4), 263 (n. 59), 272 (n. 12); high roll hairstyle and, 172, 174
Townshend Acts, 118, 120–23, 128, 130, 150–51
Tradespeople: cards for, *215*; colonial resistance and, 110, 252 (n. 102); feminization of men and, 122; men's pursuit of fashion and, 64, 67–68, 243 (n. 55); political power of men and, 110; social status and, 122; style preferences of colonials and, 43–45, 239 (n. 98); wig makers and, 65, 76, 139, 243 (n. 55). *See also* Hairstyles/hairdressers; Tailors

Tyler, Royall: *The Contrast*, 209–12, 270 (n. 74), 270 (n. 78)
Tyng, Ann (Mrs. Thomas Smelt), 100, *101*

Umbrellas, 131, 133, 144, 257 (n. 51)
Underground economy of consumer goods, 22–27, 105, 234 (n. 3), 236 (n. 65)

Virtuous femininity, 1–2, 84, 94, 112–13, 249 (n. 51). *See also* Prostitutes/prostitution
Virtuous masculinity, 90–91, 110, 124

Waistcoat, as element of men's fashion, 67, 68, 69, 97, 128, 131, 185, 196
Warder, Ann Head, 195–98
Warren, Mercy Otis, 168, 263 (n. 44)
Washington, George, 128, 162, 177, 182–83, 209, 213–14, 221, 222, 265 (n. 78)
Whigs: boycotts and, 127; conspicuous consumption and, 130–31, 151; fashion as political and, 172, 173, 174–75, 263 (n. 59); gender relations and, 163–65, 170, 172; "macaroni making"/tarring and feathering and, 153–54, *155*; plainness/sacrifice as fashionable and, 8, 131; republicanism and, 157, 163–65; women's appetite for/control of fashion and, 5, 172, 174, 175–76, 177. *See also* Republicanism
Wigs/periwigs (perukes), 58–59, 62, 64, 104, 240 (n. 19), 241 (n. 38); critiques, 58–59, 60, 62; gender bending and, 52, 59; gender relations and, 59, 60, 64; masculine performances/identity threats and, 59; men's sexual appetite and, 59–60; personal identity and, 59, 62; wig makers and, 65, 76, 139, 243 (n. 55)
Wingate, Paine, 188, 191, 192–95, 268 (n. 32)
Winslow, Isaac, 97, *98*, *99*, 99–100
Winslow family portrait, 97, *99*, 99–100
Wister, Sally, 168–70
Wollstonecraft, Mary, 219–20
Women, 3; ambivalence about fashion post-Revolution and, 188–89, 191–99,

208–9, 268 (n. 32); anti-luxury discourse and, 94, 249 (n. 51); balloon petticoats and, 189–91; body/body politic and, 18, 51, 53–54, 89, 150, 217; calico fashion and, 33; conspicuous consumption in hairstyles and, 138–39, 157, 258 (n. 70); as coquettes, 47–48, 73, 74, 78, 109, 194–95; culture wars/political loyalty and, 168–70, 172, 174–75; domestic economy and, 94, 249 (n. 51); domestic labors of, 92–93, 94, 112–13, 265 (n. 78); domestic space for, 50, 51, 239 (n. 7); economic power of, 4, 49, 51–53, 240 (n. 17); education for, 84–86, 89–92, 193, 219, 246 (n. 7), 248 (n. 29); fashion choices post-Revolution and, 183–86, 192–93; fashion/hairstyles of British and, 187; feminization of fashion, and economic power of, 49, 51–52, 240 (n. 17); fichu and, 166, 192; French fashion and, 243 (n. 66); gender bending and, 58; gender intersection and, 24–26, 30–31; homespun consumption by, 109, 114–15; income generation from theft of goods and, 25–26, 27; independency of dress and, 223–24; "macaronesses" hairstyle and, 157, *158*, 258 (n. 70); men's attraction to, 71, 243 (n. 66); men's sexual appetite, and pursuit of, 33, 59–60, 73, 74–78, 77, 90, 168; men's transmittal of goods from Britain for, 69–70; meritocracy and, 84, 94, 249 (n. 51); mourning performance and, 39–40, 237 (n. 81); personal identity of, 24–25, 96, 100, 233 (n. 12); plainness/sacrifice as fashionable and, 123–25; political transformation post–American Revolution and, 182–89, 191–99, 208–9, 268 (n. 32), 269 (n. 71); portraiture in country fashion and, 96–97, 99, 99–100, *101*, 102, *103*; reform of men's appetite for fashion and, 108–9, 113, 123, 124; republicanism and, 166, 168–70, 172, 174–75; "review" of bodies of, 53–54; as scapegoat, 51, 114–15, 208–9, 269 (n. 71); self-emancipated, 30–31, 34; sensibility of, 83–84, 123–25, 193–94, 195; sexual appetite of, 73, 74, 78; social influence and, 46; social tension and cutting clothing of, 105, 251 (n. 73); status from theft of goods and, 25; stays/stay makers and, 18, 47, 196, 217, 233 (n. 12); subjection of, 217; transmittal of goods from colonies to Britain by, 243 (n. 63); undress style and, 40, 170, 237 (n. 81); virtuous femininity and, 1–2, 84, 94, 112–13, 249 (n. 51).
See also Country fashion for women; Domestic discourse; Economic power of women; Enslaved women; Feminization of fashion; Feminization of men; Gender roles; Gender roles/social status intersection; Hairstyles/hairdressers; High roll hairstyle; Hoop petticoats; Lower-class women; Marriage; Self-emancipated slaves

Women's appetite for/control of fashion: country fashion for colonial elites and, 108–9; culture wars/political loyalty and, 156–57, 166–67, 175–78, 262 (n. 37), 264 (n. 75), 265 (n. 78); economic power of women and, 51–52; gender roles/social status intersection and, 243 (n. 15), 243 (n. 17); men's reform of, 113–14, 203–4, 255 (n. 15); nationhood and, 175–78, 264 (n. 75), 265 (n. 78); plainness/sacrifice as fashionable and, 122–25, 255 (n. 15); republicanism and, 156–57, 166–67, 262 (n. 37); Tories/loyalists and, 175–76; Whigs and, 5, 172, 174, 175–76, 177